1001 DAYS OUT
Historic Houses, Gardens & Places to Visit

1001 DAYS OUT

Historic Houses, Gardens &
■ ■ ■ ■ ■ ■ ■ ■ ■ ■ ■ *Places to Visit*

p

This is a Parragon Book
First Published in 2004

Parragon
Queen Street House
4 Queen Street
Bath BA1 1HE, UK

ISBN 1-40542-897-X

Designed by designsection
Printed in the UK

Frontispiece
Garden gate with roses, Penshurst Place, Kent
Right
Stonehenge, Wiltshire

Contents

Introduction

BRITAIN IS ONE of the most popular holiday destinations in the world. It's easy to see why. Major cities like London, Glasgow and York with their world-famous museums, palaces and stately architecture attract visitors all the year round. There are also areas of outstanding natural beauty like the Lake District and the Peak District, the Brecon Beacons and the Gower Peninsular in Wales and the Highlands in Scotland – all with their own natural history and wildlife. There are mountains and moors, industrial landscapes, castles, gardens ... and all surrounded by at least 3,000 miles of coastline. But with so many things to choose from, it's hard to know where to begin.

1001 Days Out will help you do just that. The book is packed with ideas to form the basis of a day out in Britain where you will discover the natural beauty, rich heritage and cultural attractions that England, Scotland and Wales have to offer. This practical guide offers a broad selection of attractions ranging from world famous castles, stately homes and gardens to carefully restored windmills, ancient ruins and rediscovered gardens. But also included are many small and more unusual places to visit. With 1001 entries, all tastes are catered for.

Of course, at any one time, many attractions are closed for renovation or refurbishment. For this reason, we have not included the Museum of the Moving Image on London's South Bank, or the Maritime Museum in Swansea for example. As this book is published annually, these attractions will be considered for inclusion next year.

About this Guide

This guide covers England, Scotland (including the Northern and Western Islands) and Wales and is arranged in regions, shown on the national map on page 8. The counties within each region, the towns within each county and the attractions within each town are all, where possible, arranged alphabetically. Each attraction also has a reference number and this is used on the regional maps at the beginning of each section.

Understanding the Entries

Coloured bands at top of each page indicate regions; the numbers in the top corners next to the regional name refer to the numbered range of attractions on the page. The nearest major town or village to the attraction is indicated above the name of the attraction.

Quick reference icons

⟐ an all-weather attraction

☀ an attraction for sunny days only

⧗ the expected duration of your visit
1 hr +

🔓 when the attraction is open
Apr–Oct

Description

Each entry has a brief description of the attraction and a flavour of what visitors may expect to find. Additional features are also highlighted beneath the description.

Facilities

WC toilet facilities available

🛆 space available for you to eat your own food

🍴 restaurant, café or kiosk facilities available

♿ good access for wheelchairs   ♿ᴿ restricted access

🐕 dogs allowed, but they may have to be kept on a lead

Disabled Visitors

Visitors with mobility difficulties should look for the wheelchair symbol showing where all or most of the attraction is accessible to wheelchair bound visitors. We strongly recommend that visitors telephone in advance of a visit to check exact details, including access to toilets and refreshment facilities. Assistance dogs are usually accepted unless stated otherwise. For the hard of hearing, please check that hearing induction loops are available by contacting the attraction itself.

Location

These are simple directions, usually for motorists (although directions are given for those using the Underground in London) and have been provided by the attraction itself.

Opening Times

These times are inclusive, e.g. Apr–Oct indicates that the attraction will be open from the beginning of April to the end of October. Where an attraction has varied opening times, these are indicated; and if it is open 7 days a week, this is simply referred to as 'Daily'. Bank Holiday opening is indicated where provided by the attraction. If you are travelling a long way please check with the attraction itself to ensure any unexpected circumstances are not going to prevent your entry.

Admission

Wherever possible the charges quoted are for the 2004–5 season, but please note that prices are subject to change and are only correct at the time of going to print. If no price is quoted, it does not mean that a charge will not be made. Many places that do not charge admission may ask for a voluntary donation. In some instances discounts maybe available to families, groups, local residents or members of certain organisations such as English Heritage and the National Trust.

Contact Details

We have given details of the administrative address and telephone number for each attraction, while this is usually the details of the attraction itself, some properties are administered by an area office, in which case these details are given (several English Heritage properties fall into this category).

Telephone numbers, email and website addresses are also included wherever possible.

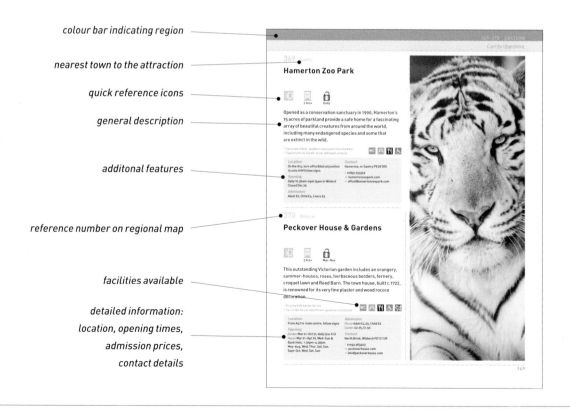

colour bar indicating region

nearest town to the attraction

quick reference icons

general description

additonal features

reference number on regional map

facilities available

detailed information: location, opening times, admission prices, contact details

Regional colour key

- South East
- South West
- Eastern
- East Midlands
- West Midlands
- Wales
- Yorkshire
- North West
- North East
- Scotland

HIGHLANDS & ISLANDS

GRAMPIAN

CENTRAL SCOTLAND

SOUTHERN SCOTLAND

NORTHUMBERLAND

TYNE & WEAR

DURHAM

CUMBRIA

NORTH YORKSHIRE

EAST RIDING OF YORKSHIRE

LANCASHIRE

W. YORKSHIRE

MANCHESTER

SOUTH YORKSHIRE

MERSEY-SIDE

CHESHIRE

DERBYSHIRE

LINCOLNSHIRE

NORTH WALES

NOTTING-HAMSHIRE

STAFFORD-SHIRE

LEICESTER-SHIRE

RUT-LAND

NORFOLK

SHROPSHIRE

WEST MIDLANDS

CENTRAL WALES

WORCESTER-SHIRE

WARWICK-SHIRE

NORTHAMPTON-SHIRE

CAMBRIDGESHIRE

SUFFOLK

HEREFORD-SHIRE

BEDFORD-SHIRE

GLOUCESTER-SHIRE

BUCKING-HAMSHIRE

HERTFORD-SHIRE

ESSEX

SOUTH WALES

OXFORDSHIRE

LONDON

WILTSHIRE

BERKSHIRE

SURREY

KENT

SOMERSET

HAMPSHIRE

WEST SUSSEX

E. SUSSEX

DEVON

DORSET

ISLE OF WIGHT

CORNWALL

The White Cliffs, Dover, Kent

South East

Berkshire Buckinghamshire East Sussex
Greater London Hampshire and Isle of Wight Kent
Oxfordshire Surrey West Sussex

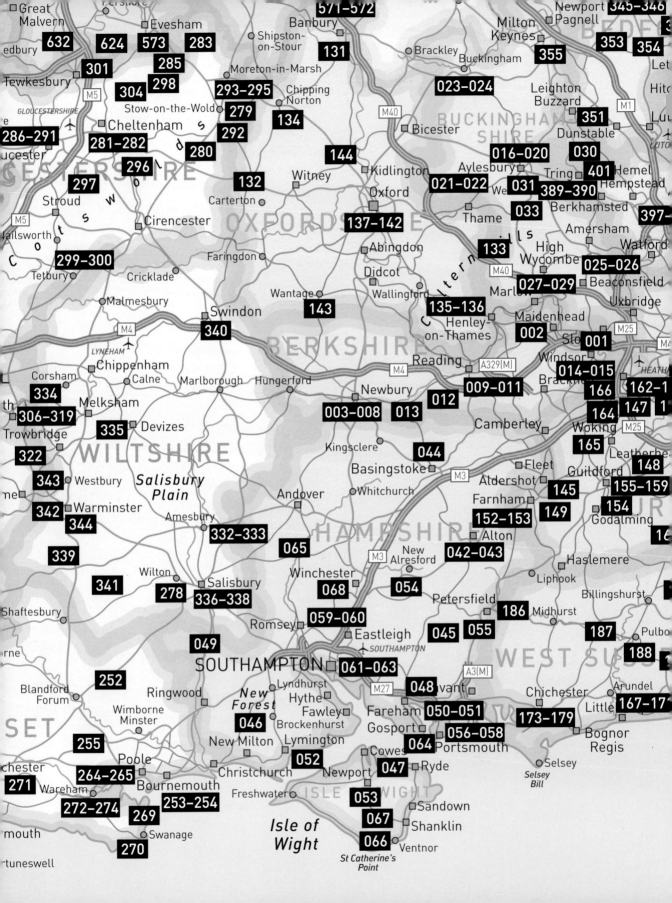

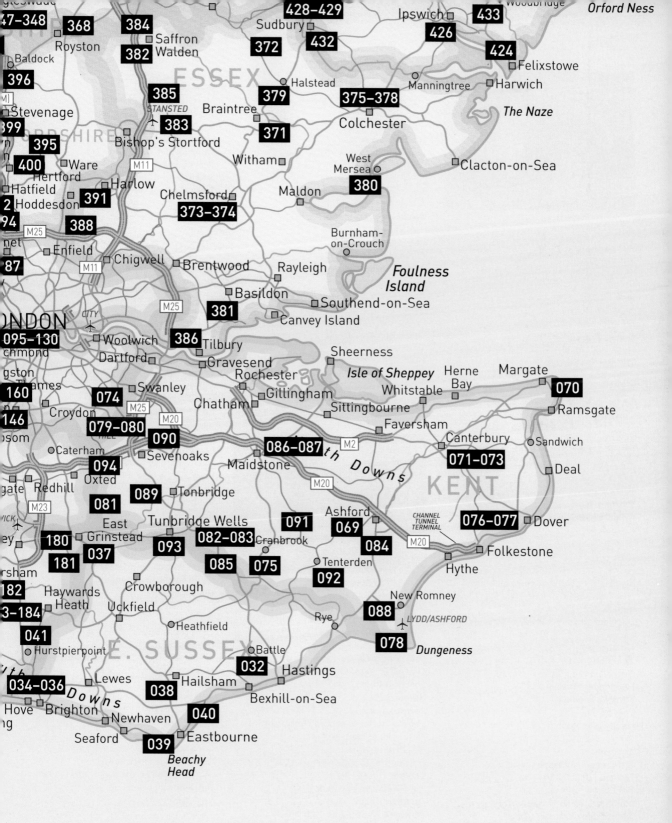

001   Eton

Museum of Eton Life

1 hr   Apr–Oct

The museum tells the story of the foundation of Eton College in 1440 and provides a glimpse into the world of the Eton schoolboy, past and present. Find out about work, games, punishment, and some of the colourful customs of the past.

* Discover well-known Old Etonians, from poets to PMs
* Explore the College buildings

Location
Eton High Street

Opening
Apr–Oct 10.30am–4.30pm school hols
2.30pm–4.30pm term time

Admission
Adult £3.70, Child & Concs £2.50
Tours £4.70, £3.50, £3.50

Contact
Visits Manager, Eton College, Eton, Windsor SL4 6DW

t 01753 671177
w etoncollege.com
e r.hunkin@etoncollege.org.uk

002   Maidenhead

Cliveden

3 hrs   Mar–Oct

This spectacular estate overlooking the River Thames has a series of gardens, each with its own character, featuring topiary, statuary, water gardens, a formal parterre, informal vistas, woodland and riverside walks. It was once the home of Nancy, Lady Astor.

* Magnificent Italianate palace
* Winter parks and gardens

Location
2 miles N of Taplow, A404 to Marlow & follow brown signs

Opening
Estate & Garden Daily Mar–Oct
11am–6pm, Nov–Dec 11am–4pm
House Apr–Oct Thurs & Sat
3pm–5.30pm

Admission
Adult £6.50, Concs £3.20

Contact
Taplow, nr Maidenhead SL6 0JA

t 01628 605069
w nationaltrust.org.uk
e cliveden@nationaltrust.org.uk

003   Newbury

Ashdown House

1 hr   Apr–Oct

An extraordinary Dutch-style C17 house, famous for its association with Elizabeth of Bohemia, Charles I's sister, to whom the house was consecrated. The interior has a great staircase rising from hall to attic, and important paintings contemporary with the house.

* Spectacular views from the roof over the gardens
* Beautiful walks in neighbouring Ashdown Woods

Location
2 miles S of Ashbury, 3 miles N of Lambourn, on W side of B4000

Opening
House & Garden Apr–Oct Wed–Sat
2pm–5pm
Woodland open all year ex Fri

Admission
House & Garden Adult £2.10

Contact
Lambourn, Newbury RG16 7RE

t 01488 72584
w nationaltrust.org.uk
e ashdownhouse@nationaltrust.org.uk

004   Newbury

Desmoulin

½ hr+   All year

Desmoulin is housed in the granary on the wharf, in one of Newbury's finest old buildings. This contemporary gallery exhibits an ever-changing collection of quality art and artifacts – paintings, photographs, furniture, jewellery in silver and gold, glassware and ceramics.

* Café supplies light lunches, caters for vegetarians

Location
Town centre next to tourist information

Opening
Mon–Sat 10am–5pm
Sun by appointment

Admission
Free

Contact
The Granary, The Wharf, Newbury RG14 5AS

t 01635 35001
w desmoulin.co.uk
e snail@desmoulin.co.uk

005 Newbury

Highclere Castle

3 hrs   Jul–Sep

Highclere is probably the finest Victorian house in existence. The three men who made Highclere what it is today were the 3rd Earl of Carnarvon who built the new house, Sir Charles Barry who designed it and the 4th Earl of Carnarvon who finished the interiors.

* Georgian pleasure grounds laid out by Robert Herbert
* 5th Earl of Carnarvon found the tomb of Tutankhamun

Location
Off A34, 4½ miles S of Newbury

Opening
Jul 6–Sep 5 Tues–Fri & Sun 11am–5pm
All Bank Hols (ex Mons)
last entry 1 hr before close

Admission
Adults £7, Child £3.50, Concs £5.50

Contact
Highclere, Newbury RG20 9RN
t 01635 253210
w highclerecastle.co.uk
e theoffice@highclerecastle.co.uk

006 Newbury

Donnington Castle

½ hr+   All year

Constructed during the late C14, the striking twin-towered gatehouse of this castle survives amid some impressive earthworks. Originally built as a fortified residence, it was seized by Royalists at the beginning of the English Civil War.

* External viewing only

Location
1 mile N of Newbury off B4494

Opening
Dawn to dusk

Admission
Free

Contact
Newbury RG14 8LT
t 0845 3010008
w english–heritage.org.uk

007   Newbury

Greenham & Crookham Common

2 hrs+   All year

After many years as a military site, the common has been restored and reopened to the public. Paths and marked walk routes allow you to explore the heathland and visit old bombsites, taxi ways and the cruise missile silo enclosure.

* The area is a Site of Special Scientific Interest (SSSI)
* Rare plant communities

Location
Car Park at Bury's Bank Road, Greenham

Opening
Daily

Admission
Free

Contact
West Berkshire Council, Countryside & Environment, Council Offices, Faraday Road, Newbury RG14 5AS

t 01635 519808
w westberks.gov.uk
e tourism@westberks.gov.uk

008   Newbury

The Living Rainforest

1 hr+   All year

Explore the rainforest and discover its wonders for yourself. This living rainforest aims to promote a sustainable future by providing education on the world's rainforests. The site features a tropical rainforest-inspired ecological garden with free-roaming animals.

* Endangered Goeldi's monkeys leap among branches
* Birds, butterflies, lizards roam freely as you explore

Location
Clearly signposted from junction 13 of the M4

Opening
Daily 10am–5.15pm (last admission 4.30pm) closed Dec 25/26

Admission
Phone for details or check website

Contact
Hampstead, Norreys RG18 0TN

t 01635 202444
w livingrainforest.org
e enquiries@livingrainforest.org

009   Reading

Beale Park

4 hrs   Easter–Oct

This unique RBST-approved charity, is home to an amazing collection of birds including swans, owls, parrots and pheasants. It also boasts a narrow gauge railway. There are boat trips in summer, acres of lawns and gardens for picnics, sculpture, ponds and fountains.

* The Trust breeds and rears endangered species
* National collection of model boats

Location
6 miles from Reading on the A329 between Pangbourne and Streatley

Opening
Easter–Oct daily 10am–6pm

Admission
Adult £5.50, Child £4, Concs £4.50

Contact
Lower Basildon, Reading RG8 9NH

t 0118 9845172
w bealepark.co.uk
e administration@bealepark.co.uk

010 Reading

Basildon Park

1 hr+   Mar–Nov

Fascinating and beautiful, this C18 Palladian mansion has an extraordinary history. It was used as a hospital during the First World War, and as a base for American sevicemen during the Second World War when it was left a near ruin. It has been lovingly restored by Lord and Lady Iliffe.

* Studies for the tapestry 'Christ in Glory' on show
* pleasure gardens and trails through woodland

Location
A329 between Pangbourne & Streatley

Opening
Mar–Nov Wed–Sun & Bank Hols
House 1pm–5.30pm
Grounds noon–5.30pm

Admission
Adult £4.70, Child £2.35

Contact
Lower Basildon, Reading RG8 9NR

t 0118 9843040
w nationaltrust.org.uk
e basildonpark@nationaltrust.org.uk

011 Reading

Museum of English Rural Life

1 hr   All year

Founded by the University of Reading in 1951, the museum reflects the changing face of farming and the countryside. It houses collections of national importance, including objects, archives, photographs, film and books.

* A programme of free fun family days
* Part of the University's Museum & Collections Service

Location
On the Whiteknights' campus of the University, 2 miles SE of Reading

Opening
Tue–Sat 10am–1pm & 2pm–4.30pm
Closed Christmas, New Year & Easter

Admission
Adult £1, Child & Concs free

Contact
University of Reading, PO Box 229, Whiteknights, Reading RG6 6AG

t 0118 378 8660
w ruralhistory.org
e merl@reading.ac.uk

012 Sulhamstead

Thames Valley Police Museum

2 hrs   By appointment

The museum includes displays on the history of Thames Valley Police. Collections include items from the Great Train Robbery of 1963, uniforms, equipment, medals, photographs, scenes of crime evidence, and occurrence and charge books.

* A Triumph Saint motorbike
* History of the force covering Berks, Bucks and Oxon

Location
3 miles W of junction 12 off M4

Opening
By appointment, phone for details

Admission
Adult £3, Child free

Contact
Thames Valley Police Training Centre, Sulhamstead, Reading RG7 4DX

t 0118 9325748
w thamesvalley.police.uk
e ken.wells@thamesvalley.pnn.police.uk

013 Thatcham

Thatcham Nature Discovery Centre

2 hrs+   All year

An exciting place to learn about local wildlife. The wide range of hand-on exhibits in Discovery Hall are set against a dramatic backdrop of giant insect models, colourful banners and wildlife quilts. Visitors can enjoy a walk around the lake and visit the reed-bed bird hide.

* Gallery with changing exhibitions
* Bird hide

Location
Between Thatcham & Newbury signposted from A4

Opening
Nov–Feb Tues–Sun 1pm–4pm
Mar–Oct Tues–Sun 11am–5pm

Admission
Free, donations appreciated

Contact
Muddy Lane, Lower Way, Thatcham RG19 3FU

t 01635 874381
w westberks.gov.uk
e naturecentre@westberks.gov.uk

The Household Cavalry Museum

1 hr+   All year

The museum collection relates to the Life Guards (1st and 2nd), Royal Horse Guards (Blues), 1st Royal Dragoons (Royals) and the Blues and Royals, covering over 300 years of the history of the Sovereign's mounted bodyguard.

* Uniforms, weapons, standards and guidons
* Horse furniture, campaign and gallantry medals

Location
Combermere Barracks, on the B3022

Opening
Mon–Fri 10am–4pm
Closed Sat & Sun, Bank Hols & public hols

Admission
Free, donations appreciated

Contact
Combermere, Windsor SL4 3DN

t 01753 755112
w householdcavalry.co.uk
e museum@householdcavalry.co.uk

Windsor Castle

2 hrs+   All year

This is an official residence of the Queen and the largest occupied castle in the world. A fortress for over 900 years, the castle remains a working palace today. Visit the state apartments, extensive suites of rooms at the heart of the working palace.

* The magnificent and beautiful St George's Chapel
* Apr–Jun, the Changing of the Guard at 11am (not Sun)

Location
Follow brown signs to central Windsor

Opening
Mar–Oct 9.45am–5.15pm
Nov–Feb 9.45am–4.15pm
Closed Dec 25/26

Admission
Prices vary, phone for details

Contact
Ticket Sales and Information Office,
The Official Residences of The Queen,
London SW1A 1AA

t 0207 766 7304
w royal.gov.uk
e information@royalcollection.org.uk

Buckinghamshire

016 Aylesbury

Buckinghamshire County Museum & Roald Dahl Gallery

1 hr+   Daily

This award-winning museum is housed in beautifully restored buildings, some dating from the C15. It is a showcase for the county's heritage and runs a varied programme of exhibitions as well as interactive fun in the Roald Dahl Children's Gallery.

* Regular Roald Dahl activities and events
* Collections of British studio pottery, costume and lace

Location
Aylesbury town centre

Opening
Museum **Mon–Sat, 10am–5pm**
Sun 2pm–5pm
Roald Dahl Gallery **Mon–Fri 3–5pm**
(term time) 10am–5pm (hols)
Sat 10am–5pm, Sun 2pm–5pm

Admission
Museum **Free**
Roald Dahl Gallery **Adult £3.50, Child £2.75**

Contact
Church Street, Aylesbury HP20 2QP

t 01296 331441
w buckscc.gov.uk/museum

017 Aylesbury

Buckinghamshire Railway Centre

2 hrs+   Apr–Oct

This is a working steam museum where you can experience the sights, sounds and smells of the golden age of steam. Ride behind a full-sized steam engine or the miniature railway. The centre has a large collection of steam locomotives, carriages and wagons.

* The Royal Train of 1901
* Santa Steaming the four weekends before Christmas

Location
Signposted from A41 near Waddesdon & A413 at Whitchurch

Opening
Apr–Oct Wed–Sun 10.30am–4.30pm

Admission
Adult £6, Child £4, Concs £2

Contact
Quainton Road Station, Quainton Aylesbury HP22 4BY

t 01296 655720
w bucksrailcentre.org.uk
e abaker@bucksrailcentre.btopenworld.com

018 Aylesbury

The King's Head

½ hr+   All year

The King's Head is thought to be one of the oldest surviving courtyard inns in the country. The cobblestone courtyard protects two older, hidden layers below. Enclosed by the public area and the stable block, it provided services for the many horse-drawn carriages.

* Excavation proved activity from the Bronze Age
* Large mullioned window contains pieces of C15 glass

Location
At the NW corner of Market Square in Aylesbury

Opening
Normal licensing hours

Admission
Adult £2, Child free

Contact
King's Head Passage, Market Square, Aylesbury HP20 2RW

t 01296 381501
w nationaltrust.org.uk
e kingshead@ntrust.org.uk

Buckinghamshire

019   Aylesbury

Tiggywinkles, The Wildlife Hospital Trust

1½ hrs+   All year

Since opening its doors the Wildlife Hospital Trust has treated over 100,000 patients. Watch and learn about a remarkable number of patients including hedgehogs, badgers, rabbits, deer, wild birds, snakes, in fact virtually all species of British wildlife.

* New hedgehog museum and baby mammal viewing
* Some permanent disabled residents roam the garden

Location
Signposted off the A418 from Aylesbury

Opening
Easter–Sep Mon–Sun 10am–4pm
Oct–Easter Mon–Fri 10am–4pm

Admission
Adult £3.80, Concs £2.80

Contact
Aston Road, Haddenham,
Aylesbury HP17 8AF

t 01844 292292
w sttiggywinkles.org.uk
e mail@sttiggywinkles.org.uk

020   Aylesbury

Waddesdon Manor

2 hrs+   Mar–Dec

Created by Baron Ferdinand de Rothschild, this Renaissance-style chateau was built in the 1870s for his house parties. The house contains a unique collection of French C18 objects. The landscape gardens are famous for their spectacular views.

* Meissen exhibition
* Good example of C19 needlework window dressings

Location
Via Waddesdon village, 6 miles NW of Aylesbury on A41

Opening
Grounds Mar 3–Dec 23 Wed–Sun 10am–5pm
House Mar 31–Oct 31 Wed–Sun & Bank Hols Mon 11am–4pm

Admission
Grounds Adult £4, Child £2
House Adult £7, Child £6

Contact
Waddesdon, Aylesbury HP18 0JH

t 01296 653211/01296 653226
w waddesdon.org.uk

021   Brill

Brill Windmill

½ hr+   Apr–Sep

Brill Windmill is a fine example of a postmill, dating from the 1680s. It is not in working condition but much of the machinery is intact and can be viewed from two floors within the mill. The mill stands amidst the abandoned clay diggings of Brill Common.

* Superb view of the Vale of Oxford and the Cotswolds

Location
On the NW edge of the village. Brill lies N of B4011 Thame to Bicester road, 6 miles NW of Thame

Opening
Apr–Sep Sun 2pm–5pm

Admission
Adult 50p, Child 30p

Contact
Mrs Sue Horton, The Old Forge,
Windmill Street, Brill HP18 9TG

t 01844 238662

Brill

Boarstall Tower

1 hr   Mar–Oct

Visit the C14 gatehouse and gardens of Boarstall House (demolished 1778). Built by John de Haudlo in 1312, and updated in 1615 for use as a banqueting pavilion or hunting lodge, it retained its medieval belfry, crossloops and crenellations, so keeping its fortified look.

* Many rooms remain virtually unchanged since 1615
* Handsome oriel windows

Location
Midway between Bicester and Thame,
2 miles W of Brill

Opening
Mar 27–Oct 30 Wed 2pm–6pm
Bank Hols Mon & Sat by appointment

Admission
Adult £2.10, Child £1.05

Contact
Boarstall, Aylesbury HP18 9UX

t 01844 239339
w nationaltrust.org.uk
e rob.dixon@boarstall.com

Buckingham

The Old Gaol

½ hr+   All Year

The Old Gaol is the landmark building in Buckingham town centre. Restored by the Buckingham Heritage Trust, it contains a fascinating museum reflecting the building's history through an audio-visual display, and exhibits of Buckingham's past and its military history.

* Regular themed exhibitions
* The ancient cells with their double doors still remain.

Location
Buckingham town centre

Opening
All year Mon–Sat 10am–4pm

Admission
Adult £1.50, Child & Concs £1

Contact
Market Hill, Buckingham MK18 1JX

t 01280 823020
w mkheritage.co.uk
e old.gaol@lineone.net

©Rob Dixon

024 Buckingham

Stowe Landscape Gardens

2 hrs+   All year

This is one of the finest Georgian landscape gardens, made up of valleys and vistas, narrow lakes and rivers and more than 30 temples and monuments designed by many of the leading architects of the C18. At the centre is Stowe House, now Stowe School, surrounded by Stowe Park.

* Audio–visual display about the evolution of Stowe
* Allow plenty of time as gardens are extensive

Location
3 miles NW of Buckingham via Stowe Avenue, off A422

Opening
Jan–Oct Wed–Sun 10am–5.30pm
Nov–Dec Wed–Sun 10am–4pm

Admission
Adult £5, Child £2.50

Contact
Buckingham MK18 5EH

t 01280 822850
w nationaltrust.org.uk
e stowegarden@nationaltrust.org.uk

026 Chalfont St Giles

Chiltern Open Air Museum

2 hrs+   Apr–Oct

This unusual museum contains over 30 historic buildings, including a 1940s, fully furnished prefab, a working Victorian farm and forge. Set in beautiful open parkland with a nature walk and seat-sculpture trail, the museum is a wonderful place for all ages to visit .

* Explore more than 30 rescued historic buildings
* Visit Skippings Barn, home to the Hawk and Owl Trust

Location
Signposted from A413 at Chalfont St Giles and Chalfont St Peter

Opening
Apr–Oct daily 10am–5pm

Admission
Adult £6, Child £3.50, Concs £5

Contact
Newland Park, Gorelands Lane, Chalfont St Giles HP8 4AB

t 01494 871117
w coam.org.uk
e coamuseum@netscape.net

025 Chalfont St Giles

John Milton's Cottage

1 hr+   Mar–Oct

This picturesque late C16 Grade I-listed cottage, set in an attractive garden, is the only surviving building in which the famous writer and parliamentarian lived. It was bought by public subscription in 1887 to celebrate Queen Victoria's jubilee and to preserve it for visitors.

* Milton came here in 1665 to escape the Plague
* He completed *Paradise Lost* here

Location
On A40 to Chalfont St Giles, cottage in the centre of village

Opening
Mar 1–Oct 31 10am–1pm & 2pm–6pm (closed Mon, ex Bank Hol Mons)

Admission
Adult £3, Child £1

Contact
Chalfont St Giles HP8 4JH

t 01494 872313
w miltonscottage.org
e info@miltonscottage.org

027 High Wycombe

Hellfire Caves

1 hr+   Mar–Oct

These caves were originally excavated in the 1750s by Sir Francis Dashwood on the site of an ancient quarry. It is thought that his inspiration for the design of the caves came from his grand tour of Europe and the Ottoman Empire.

* Sir Francis Dashwood founded the Hellfire Club
* The caves are haunted by Sir Paul Whitehead.

Location
Approx 3 miles from High Wycombe on the A40 towards Oxford

Opening
Mar–Oct daily 11am–5.30pm

Admission
Prices vary, phone for details

Contact
High Wycombe HP14 3AJ

t 01494 533739
w hellfirecaves.co.uk

028 High Wycombe

Hughenden Manor

2 hrs+   Mar–Oct

The home of Victorian prime minister and statesman Benjamin Disraeli from 1848 until his death in 1881. Most of his furniture, books and pictures remain here – his private retreat from parliamentary life in London. There are beautiful walks through surrounding park.

* Certain rooms have low electric light – avoid dull days
* Events throughout the house and park

Location
1 mile N of High Wycombe W of the Great Missenden road (A4128)

Opening
House Mar Sat & Sun 1pm–5pm
Apr 1–Oct 31 Wed–Sun, 12noon–5pm
Garden Mar 1–Oct 31 Sat & Sun
Apr 1–Oct 31 Wed–Sun

Admission
House & Garden Adult £4.70, Child £2.30, *Garden only* £1.70, 80p

Contact
High Wycombe HP14 4LA

t 01497 755565/01494 755573
w nationaltrust.org.uk
e hughenden@nationaltrust.org.uk

029 High Wycombe

Wycombe Museum

1 hr+   All year

Trails and special activities combine with imaginative displays to make this a lively museum for visitors. Permanent exhibits, videos and sound recordings tell the story of High Wycombe and the local district.

* Superb collection of Windsor chairs
* Gardens include a Norman 'castle' mound

Location
Off A404 towards Amersham

Opening
Mon–Sat 10am–5pm, Sun 2pm–5pm
Closed Bank Hols

Admission
Free, donations appreciated

Contact
Priory Avenue,
High Wycombe HP13 6PX

t 01494 421895
w wycombe.gov.uk/museum
e enquiries@wycombemuseum.
demon.co.uk

030 Ivinghoe

Pitstone Windmill

½ hr   Jun–Aug

This post mill is believed to be one of the oldest windmills in Britain, dating back to at least 1627. The mill was given to the National Trust in 1937. Restoration was started in 1963 and that work is now regarded as one of the forerunners of voluntary restoration work in the UK.

Location
Located S of Ivinghoe on B488 to Tring

Opening
Jun–Aug Sun 2.30pm–6pm

Admission
Adult £1, Child 30p

Contact
Holland Cottage, Whipsnade,
Dunstable, Bedfordshire LU6 2LG

t 01582 872303
w nationaltrust.org.uk

Buckinghamshire

East Sussex

031 Stoke Mandeville

Obsidian Art

  ½ hr+ All year

This large art gallery houses over 300 original paintings, drawings, sculpture and limited edition prints. The gallery exhibits a range of British art, from traditional to modern abstract.

* Regularly changing exhibitions and local artists
* Opportunity to purchase original artwork and gifts

Location
On A4010 S of Stoke Mandeville, follow signposts for Goat Centre

Opening
Tue–Sun 10am–5pm
Closed Dec 24–Jan 1

Admission
Free

Contact
The Bucks Goat Centre,
Old Risborough Road,
Stoke Mandeville HP22 5XJ

t 01296 612150
w obsidianart.co.uk
e info@obsidianart.co.uk

033 Wendover

The Chiltern Brewery

  1 hr All year

Opened in 1980, this family-run establishment is now Buckinghamshire's oldest working brewery. The site offers tours and tastings and also includes England's first breweriana museum – featuring brewing artefacts and traditions from the local area.

* Five bespoke, award-winning beers are produced here
* Tours on Sat only, booking necessary

Location
On the B4009, which joins the A413 about one mile from Wendover

Opening
Mon–Sat 9am–5pm

Admission
Free
Tours £3.50

Contact
Nash Lee Road, Terrick,
Aylesbury HP17 0TQ

t 01296 613647
w chilternbrewery.co.uk
e enquiries@chilternbrewery.co.uk

032 Battle

Battle Abbey & Battlefield

  1 hr+ All year

There is almost as much myth surrounding the Battle of Hastings as known fact. The two armies did not even fight at Hastings, but at a place south of the town now named Battle. Visit the ruins of the abbey that William the Conqueror built to commemorate his victory.

* Interactive audio tour recreates the sounds of battle
* Stand on the spot where defeated King Harold fell

Location
In Battle, at S end of High Street. Battle is reached by turning off A21 onto A2100 10 mins from Battle Station

Opening
Apr 1–Sep 31 daily 10am–6pm
Oct 1–Oct 31 daily 10am–5pm
Nov 1–Mar 31 daily 10am–4pm

Admission
Adult £5, Child £2.50, Concs £3.80

Contact
High St, Battle TN3 30AD

t 01424 773792
w english–heritage.org.uk

034 Brighton

Brighton Museum & Art Gallery

2 hrs+   All year

The museum has a famous collection of Arts & Crafts, Art Nouveau and Art Deco; Salvador Dali's sofa in the shape of Mae West's lips and stunning gowns from Schiaparelli to Zandra Rhodes. Exhibits include intricate sculptures, decorated masks and beautiful textiles.

* Paintings by Duncan Grant and Edward Lear
* Regularly changing exhibits

Location
Brighton town centre

Opening
Tue 10am–7pm, Wed–Sat 10am–5pm, Sun 2pm–5pm, Mon and Christmas closed

Admission
Free

Contact
Royal Pavilion Gardens, Brighton BN1 1EE

t 01273 290900
w virtualmuseum.info
e museums@brighton-hove.gov.uk

035 Brighton

The Royal Pavilion

2 hrs+   All year

This former seaside residence of King George IV with its exotic Indian-style exterior boasts a myriad of domes and minarets. Admire magnificent decorations and furnishings in the Chinese style and gardens replanted to the original Regency scheme. Complete with a superb shop.

* Tactile/Sennheiser tours for partially sighted/hearing
* Wonderful Regency furniture and antiques

Location
Brighton town centre, 15 mins walk from Brighton station

Opening
Oct– Mar daily 10am–5.15pm
Apr–Sep daily 9.30am–5.45pm

Admission
Prices vary, phone for details

Contact
Brighton BN1 1EE

t 01273 603005
w royalpavilion.org.uk
e virtualmuseum.info

East Sussex

036 Brighton

University of Brighton Gallery & Theatre

1 hr   All year

The presence of some of the country's most innovative artists and students make this one of the most appealing gallery spaces in the south. A modern gallery presents exhibitions covering many aspects of the arts.

* A frequently changing exhibition programme
* Theatre has lectures and musical performances

Location
Grand Parade university campus, Central Brighton

Opening
Gallery Mon–Sat 10am–5pm
Theatre Many evenings, phone for details

Admission
Gallery Free
Theatre Prices vary, phone for details

Contact
Grand Parade, Brighton BN2 0JY

t 01273 643012
w brighton.ac.uk/gallery–theatre/
e c.l.matthews@bton.ac.uk

037 East Grinstead

Ashdown Forest Llama Park

2 hrs   All year

See over a hundred llamas and alpacas! Watch them in the fields or get close to them in the barns. Enjoy farm walks, a museum, a picnic area, a coffee shop, an adventure play area and a lovely shop selling alpaca knit wear and South American crafts.

* 100+ llamas and alpacas
* Angora & cashmere goats

Location
Located beside A22, 300 yards south of junction with A275

Opening
Daily 10am–5pm

Admission
Adult £3.50, Child & Concs £3

Contact
Wychross Forest Row RH18 5JN

t 01825 712040
w llamapark.co.uk
e info@llamapark.co.uk

038 Hailsham

Herstmonceux Castle

2–4 hrs   Easter–Oct

Herstmonceux is renowned for its magnificent moated castle, beautiful parkland and Elizabethan gardens. Built originally as a country home in the mid-C15, the castle embodies the history of medieval England and the romance of Renaissance Europe.

* Castle is only open to guided tour parties
* Tours last for approximately 1 hr

Location
Off A27 on the A22 toward Hailsham

Opening
Gardens Easter–Sep daily 10am–6pm
Sep–Oct daily 10am–5pm
Castle Only with guided tour, Easter–Oct Sun–Fri

Admission
Gardens Adult £4.50, Child £3, Concs £3.50 *Castle* £2.50, £1, £2.50

Contact
Hailsham BN27 1RN

t 01323 833816
w herstmonceux–castle.com
e c_dennett@isc.queensu.ac.uk

039 Eastbourne

Towner Art Gallery and History Museum

½ hr+   All year

Elegant C18 building with C19 and C20 British art. Includes a south east arts collection of contemporary art and a gallery of work by Eric Ravilious, Eastbourne's most acclaimed C20 artist. Eastbourne past and present is explored in the local history exhibition.

* Strong temporary exhibition of international contemporary art

Location	Contact
Off the A259 or the A27	High Street, Old Town, Eastbourne BN20 8BB
Opening	t 01323 411688 / 417961
Apr 1–Oct 30 Tue–Sat noon–5pm, Sun 2pm–5pm, Nov 1–Apr 1 Tue–Sat 12noon–4pm, Sun noon–5pm	w eastbournemuseums.co.uk
	e townergallery@eastbourne.gov.uk
Admission	
Free (except special exhibitions)	

040 Pevensey

Pevensey Castle

1 hr   All year

The ruins of this medieval castle stand in one corner of a Roman fort, on what was once a peninsula surrounded by the sea and salt marshes. The Roman fort, named Anderida, was built in about AD 290. It is one of the largest surviving examples in Britain.

* 491 AD, Britons massacred here by Anglo-Saxons
* 1066, William the Conqueror landed his army here

Location	Contact
In Pevensey off A259	High Street, Pevensey BN24 5LE
Opening	t 01323 762604
Apr 1–Sep 30 daily 10am–6pm	w english-heritage.org.uk
Oct daily 10am–5pm	
Nov 1–Mar 31 Wed–Sun 10am–4pm	
Admission	
Adult £3, Child £1.50, Concs £2.30	

041 Sheffield Park

Bluebell Railway

1 hr+   All year

This is the UK's first preserved standard gauge railway, which runs along the Lewes to East Grinstead line of the old London Brighton and South Coast Railway. It serves to preserve this country branch line, its steam locomotives, coaches and signalling systems.

* Famous Terrier class engines, Stepney & Fenchurch
* Featured in the film *The Railway Children*

Location	Contact
Sheffield Park Station	Sheffield Park Station TN22 3QL
Opening	t 01825 720800
May–Sep daily 11am–4pm	w bluebell-railway.co.uk
Oct–Apr Sat & Sun 11am–4pm	e info@bluebell-railway.co.uk
Admission	
Adult £8.50, Child £4.20 (subject to change)	

Hampshire

042   Alton

The Allen Gallery

2 hrs+   All year

The gallery is housed in a group of C16 and C18 buildings and named after local artist William Herbert Allen. Its collection of decorative arts with ceramics, dating from 1250 to the present day, is considered to be one of the best in the south of England.

* Displays of W.H.Allen's watercolours and oil paintings
* Walled garden with outdoor sculptures

Location
Located in Church Street just off Alton High Street

Opening
Tue–Sat 10am–5pm
Closed Dec 21–Jan 2 & Good Friday

Admission
Free

Contact
Church Street,
Alton GU34 2BW

t 01420 82802
w hants.gov.uk/musuem/allen

---

044   Basingstoke

The Manor House at Upton Grey

1.5 hrs   Apr–Sep

This garden designed by Gertrude Jekyll in 1908 was unknown to the public until 18 years ago. Jekyll was commissioned by Charles Holme, an established figure in the Arts & Crafts movement, to design the garden for his house at Upton Grey in Hampshire.

* Formal garden within a framework of yew hedges
* Jekyll's only surviving and restored wild garden

Location
Upton Grey, beside the church

Opening
Weekdays, by appointment only

Admission
Adult £4.50

Contact
Upton Grey RG25 2RD

t 01256 862827
w gertrudejekyllgarden.co.uk
e uptongrey.garden@lineone.net

043   Alton

Jane Austen's House

1 hr+   All year

Jane Austen's house is a pleasant C17 house in the pretty village of Chawton, not far from her birthplace of Steventon. The museum houses an attractive collection of items connected with Jane and her family including the table at which she wrote her novels.

* Pretty garden with varieties of C18 plants and herbs
* Examples of Austen's jewellery and needlework skill

Location
Situated in the village of Chawton,
2 miles SW of Alton

Opening
Mar 1–Nov 30 11am–4pm
Dec–Feb Sat & Sun only

Admission
Adult £4.50, Child £1, Concs £3.50

Contact
Chawton, Alton GU34 1SD

t 01420 83262
w janeaustenmuseum.org.uk
e janeaustenshouse@museum.org.uk

045 Bishop's Waltham

Bishop's Waltham Palace

1 hr   Apr–Oct

The last Bishop of Winchester to live at Bishop's Waltham left in a dung cart, disguised as a farm labourer! He was escaping from Oliver Cromwell's troops after unsuccessfully defending his palace. Much of what can be seen today dates from the C12 and C14.

* Exhibition on the powerful bishops of Winchester
* Decorative and furnished Victorian farmhouse

Location
5 miles from junction 8 of M27

Opening
Apr 1–Sep 30 daily 10am–6pm
Oct 1–31 daily 10am–5pm

Admission
Adult £2.50, Child £1.30, Concs £1.90

Contact
Winchester Road,
Bishop's Waltham SO32 1DH

t 01489 892460

046 Brockenhurst

Beaulieu Abbey and National Motor Museum

3 hrs+   All year

Visit the C13 Beaulieu Abbey, Palace House and grounds, and the National Motor Museum. Few car museums in the world can match the unique collection of the world-renowned National Motor Museum at Beaulieu, with legendary world record breakers like Bluebird and Golden Arrow.

* Exhibition of James Bond vehicles and props
* In 2004 the abbey celebrates its 800 year anniversary

Location
Going W on M27 take A326.
Signposted Beaulieu or National Motor Museum

Opening
May–Sep 10am– 6pm, Oct–April
10am–5pm Closed Dec 25

Admission
Adult £13.50, Child £7.50, Concs £12.50

Contact
Brockenhurst SO42 7ZN

t 01590 612345
w beaulieu.co.uk
e info@beaulieu.co.uk

047 East Cowes

Osborne House

4 hrs+   Apr–Sep

Queen Victoria's favourite country home captures the spirit of a world unchanged since the country's longest-reigning monarch died here 100 years ago. Queen Victoria and Prince Albert rebuilt the original Osborne House in 1845 as a 'modest country home'.

* Indian Durbar Room, Queen Victoria's gifts from India
* Glorious gardens and Swiss cottage

Location
1 mile SE of East Cowes

Opening
Apr–Sep, 10am–5pm

Admission
Prices vary, phone for details

Contact
East Cowes PO32 6JY

t 01983 200022
w english–heritage.org.uk

048 Fareham

Titchfield Abbey

0.5 hr   All year

An abbey was first founded at Titchfield in the C13 by the Bishop of Winchester. Its history was uneventful until the Dissolution when drastic alterations were made to convert the abbey into a mansion known as Place House. Now a ruin, the remains are magnificent.

* Residents were the Earls of Southampton
* The 3rd Earl was closely connected to Shakespeare

Location
½ mile N of Titchfield off A27

Opening
Apr–Sep 10am–6pm Oct, 10am–5pm
Nov 1–Mar 31 10am–4pm

Admission
Free

Contact
Mill Lane, Titchfield,
Fareham PO15 5RA

t 01329 842133
w english–heritage.org.uk

049 Fordingbridge

Braemore House & Museum

2½ hrs   Apr–Sep

This is a large Elizabethan house, set in beautiful parkland, with a Saxon church nearby. Former kitchen gardens house a major countryside museum, village workshops and a reconstructed cottage. Pleasant walks lead to an ancient maze on the downs.

* Fine collection of pictures and C17 furniture
* Visitors go back to when a village was self sufficient

Location
3 miles north of Fordingbridge,
off the A338

Opening
House Apr–Sep, 2pm–5.30pm
Museum 1pm–5.30pm
Closed Mon & Fri (last tour 4.30pm)

Admission
Adult £6, Child £4, Concs £5

Contact
Nr Fordingbridge SP6 2DF

t 01725 512233
w braemorehouse.com
e braemore@ukonline.co.uk

050 Gosport

Fort Brockhurst

1 hr   Apr–Oct

Designed in the C19, this fort was built to protect Portsmouth with formidable fire power. Largely unaltered, the parade ground, gun ramps and moated keep can all be viewed.

* See nesting birds
* Look out for ghostly activity in Prisoner Cell No 3

       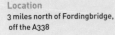

Location
Off A32 in Gunners Way, Elson is on
N side of Gosport

Opening
Apr 1–Sep 30, Sun & Bank Hols only
10am–6pm Oct Sun only 10am–5pm

Admission
Adult £2.20, Child £1.70

Contact
Gunners Way, Elson, Gosport
PO12 4DS

t 02392 581059
w english–heritage.org.uk

051 Gosport

Explosion! The Museum of Naval Firepower

1½ hrs+   All year

An award-winning visitor experience on the shores of Portsmouth Harbour, Explosion! tells the story of naval warfare from the day of gunpowder to the Exocet with a hands-on, interactive museum set in historic buildings of the Navy's former armaments depot in Gosport.

* 2004 exhibit The Blunt End, D-Day at Priddy's Hard
* Dramatic audio-visual effects and scene-setting

Location
M27 to junction 11. Follow A32 to Gosport and brown tourist signs

Opening
Apr–Oct daily 10am–5.30pm
Nov–Mar Thu, Sat & Sun
10am–4.30pm

Admission
Prices vary, phone for details

Contact
Priddy's Hard, Gosport PO12 4LE

t 023 9250 5600
w explosion.org.uk
e info@explosion.org.uk

052 Lymington

Hurst Castle

3 hrs+   Apr–Oct

Hurst Castle was built by Henry VIII as one of a chain of coastal fortresses and it was completed in 1544. The location was perfect to defend the western approach to the Solent. Charles I was imprisoned here in 1648 before being taken to London for his trial and execution.

* Modernised during the Napoleonic wars
* Two huge 38-ton guns can be viewed

Location
By ferry from Keyhaven or on foot from Milford-on-Sea

Opening
Apr–Sep 10am–5.30pm
Oct 10am–4pm

Admission
Adult £2.80, Child £1.60, Concs £2.50

Contact
Hurst Spit, Keyhaven,
Lymington SO41 0QU

t 01590 642500
w hurst-castle.co.uk
e info@hurst-castle.co.uk

053 Newport

Carisbrooke Castle

1 hrs +   All year

Built over 1,000 years ago, this castle has had a rich and varied history. Since time immemorial, whoever controlled Carisbrooke controlled the Isle of Wight. The castle has been a feature of the island since its foundation as a Saxon camp during the C18.

* Remnants of a Saxon wall and a Norman keep remain
* Interactive museum displays the history of the castle

Location
1 mile SW of Newport on B3323

Opening
Apr–Sep 10am–6pm, Oct 10am–5pm
Nov–Mar 10am–4pm
Closed Dec 24–26 & Jan 1

Admission
Prices vary phone for details

Contact
Carisbrooke, Newport, Isle of Wight

t 01983 522107
w english-heritage.org.uk

054 New Alresford

Northington Grange

½ hr+   All year

The magnificent Northington Grange and its landscaped park were designed by William Wilkins in 1809 and is now regarded as one of the earliest Greek Revival country houses in Europe. Opera evenings are regularly held here throughout the summer.

* *Onegin* (1999) with Ralph Fiennes was filmed here
* Opera festival in summer months

Location	Contact
4 miles N of New Alresford off B3046 – 450 metres along a farm track	New Alresford
	t 02392 581059
Opening	w english–heritage.org.uk
Apr 1–Sep 30 10am–6pm	
Oct 10–5pm Nov 1–Mar 31 10am–4pm	
Admission	
Free	

055 Petersfield

Queen Elizabeth Country Park

3 hrs+   All year

This park forms a part of the landscape of the South Downs and falls within the East Hampshire Area of Outstanding Natural Beauty. There are 1,400 acres of open access woodland and downland. The site features trackways, barrows, lynchets and the site of a Roman farmstead.

* Visitor centre
* National nature reserve

Location	Contact
Located in SE Hampshire, 4 miles S of Petersfield	Hampshire County Council
	t 02392 595040
Opening	w hants.gov.uk/countryside
Daily	e info.centres@hants.gov.uk
Admission	
Car parking £1 per day Mon–Sat	
£1.50 per day Sun & Bank Hols	

056 Portsmouth

Portsmouth Historic Dockyard

2 hrs+   All year

This is the home of the Tudor warship *Mary Rose*, Admiral Lord Nelson's flagship HMS *Victory*, the mighty iron-hulled HMS *Warrior* (1860), the Royal Naval Museum and a new attraction Action Stations. together they make Portsmouth Historic Dockyard an essential stopping place.

* Frigates, destroyers, mine warefare ships and more
* Harbour boat tour

Location	Contact
Follow Historic Waterfront & Historic Dockyard signs from junction 12 of M27	Porter's Lodge, College Road, HM Naval Base. Portsmouth PO1 3LJ
	t 02392 861533
Opening	w historicdockyard.co.uk
Apr–Oct 10am–5.30pm, Nov–March	e mail@historicdockyard.co.uk
10am–5pm last entry 4.30pm	
Admission	
Adult £14.85, Child £11.90, Concs £11.90	
Single attraction: £9.50, £8, £8	

057 Portsmouth

Royal Garrison Church

0.5 hrs+   Apr–Sep

This church was constructed around 1212 as a hostel for pilgrims. It was also used as a store for weapons and ammunition before becoming a garrison church in the 1560s. The church was badly damaged in 1941 and modern windows tell the story of the building.

* Charles II married Catherine of Braganza here in 1662
* Once known as Cathedral Church of the British Army

Location
On Grand Parade S of Portsmouth High Street

Opening
Apr 1–Sep 30 11am–4pm Mon–Sat

Admission
Free

Contact
Grand Parade, Old Portsmouth

t 02392 823973/02392 735521
w english–heritage.org.uk

058 Portsmouth

Charles Dickens' Birthplace Museum

3 hrs+   Apr–Sep

The famous writer, Charles Dickens, was born in this modest house in Portsmouth in 1812. The house has survived and is now preserved as a museum furnished in the style of 1809, the year John and Elizabeth Dickens began their married life together.

* Regency-style furniture and household objects
* Charles Dickens and Portsmouth exhibition

Location
Just off the A3 heading S towards the city centre

Opening
Daily Apr–Sep 10am–5.30pm

Admission
Adult £2.50, Child £1.50, Concs £1.80

Contact
393 Old Commercial Road, Portsmouth PO1 4QL

t 02392 827261
w charlesdickensbirthplace.co.uk
e info@charlesdickensbirthplace.co.uk

059 Romsey

Sir Harold Hillier Gardens

3 hrs+   All year

These gardens, which were formerly known as the Hillier Arboretum, hold the greatest collection of hardy trees and shrubs in the world. Started by the late Sir Harold Hillier in 1953, the gardens now extend to 180 acres.

*Gurkha memorial garden
* Largest winter garden of its kind in Europe

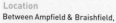   

Location
Between Ampfield & Braishfield, 3 miles NE of Romsey

Opening
Daily 10.30am–6pm

Admission
Adult £5, Child free, Concs £4.50

Contact
Jermyns Lane, Ampfield, Romsey SO51 0QA

t 01794 368787
w hilliergardens.org.uk
e info@hilliergardens.org.uk

060   Romsey

Mottisfont Abbey

1 hr+   Mar–Oct

This C12 Augustinian priory boasts sweeping lawns and magnificent old trees, set amidst glorious countryside. Medieval monastic remains include a *cellarium* and original stonework revealed through cut-away sections of the building.

* Unusual *trompe-l'oeil* painting by Rex Whistler
* National Collection of old-fashioned roses

Location
4½ miles NW of Romsey,
1 mile W of A3057

Opening
Mar–Jun & Sep–Oct 11am–6pm
closed Thu & Fri
Jun–Aug 11am–6pm closed Fri

Admission
Adult £6.50, Child £3,

Contact
Mottisfont, nr Romsey SO51 0LP

t 01794 340757
w nationaltrust.org.uk
e mottisfontabbey@nationaltrust.org.uk

061   Southampton

Maritime Museum

1 hrs+   All year

Originally a warehouse for Southampton's wool trade, this building was used to house hundreds of prisoners of war 200 years ago; more recently it was an aircraft factory. Now the museum tells the history of the port from the building of the first docks to the present day.

* Titanic Voices exhibition

Location
Between town centre & the waterfront

Opening
Tue–Fri 10am–5pm
Sat 10–4pm, Sun 2pm–5pm

Admission
Free

Contact
Wool House, Town Quay,
Southampton SO14 2AR

t 02380 635904
w southampton.gov.uk/heritage
e historic.sites@southampton.gov.uk

062 Southampton

Netley Abbey

  ½ hr+ All year

The first monks entered the Cistercian abbey at Netley in 1239 but little building work took place until after it received the Royal patronage of Henry III a few years later. Few major alterations were made to the monastic buildings, so most of those visible date back to C13.

* Inspiration for Horace Walpole and Jane Austen
* Queen Elizabeth I stayed at the mansion

Location	Contact
In Netley, 4 miles SE of Southampton	Netley, nr Southampton
Opening	t 02392 581059
Any reasonable time	w english–heritage.org.uk
Admission	
Free	

063 Southampton

Southampton City Art Gallery

   3 hrs+ All year

This gallery is internationally renowned for its impressive collection of contemporary works by British artists. A fine selection of works by the Camden Town Group, and paintings by Sir Stanley Spencer, Matthew Smith and Philip Wilson Steer are brought together.

* Studio potters work from between the wars
* Regular exhibitions throughout the year

Location	Contact
Central Southampton	Civic Centre, Commercial Road, Southampton SO14 7LP
Opening	t 02380 832277
Tue–Sat 10am–5pm, Sun 1pm–4pm	w southampton.gov.uk/art
Closed Dec 21–Jan 2 & Good Friday	e art.gallery@southampton.gov.uk
Admission	
Free	

064 Southsea

The D–Day Museum & Overlord Embroidery

  1 hr+ All year

This museum was established in 1984 to tell the story of Operation Overlord from its origins in the dark days of 1940 to victory in Normandy in 1944. The museum's centrepiece is the Overlord embroidery.

* Audio-visual theatre
* Dawn-to-dusk reconstruction of the Allied landings

Location	Contact
On seafront, 2 miles from town centre	Clarence Esplanade, Southsea PO5 3NT
Opening	t 023 9282 7261
Apr–Sep 10–5.30pm	w ddaymuseum.co.uk
Mar–Oct 10–5pm	e enquiries@ddaymuseum.co.uk
Closed Dec 24–26	
Admission	
Adults £5, Child £3, Concs £3.75	

065 Stockbridge

Museum of Army Flying

2 hrs+   All year

Celebrating over 100 years of army aviation, this award-winning museum houses one of the country's finest collect-ions of military kites, gliders, aeroplanes and helicopters. Trace the development of army flying from the Royal Flying Corps to the present day.

* Children's science and education centre
* Viewing gallery overlooking airfield

Location
A343 6 miles from Andover & 12 miles from Salisbury. Accessible from A30, A303 & M3

Opening
Daily 10am–4.30pm.
Closed Dec 24–Jan 1

Admission
Prices vary, phone for details

Contact
Middle Wallop, Stockbridge SO20 8DY

t 01980 674421
w flying-museum.org.uk
e enquiries@flying-museum.org.uk

066 Ventnor

Ventnor Botanic Garden

2 hrs+   All year

This is one of the youngest botanic gardens in Britain. The southern edge of the garden comprises clifftop grassland and cliffs, and the eastern end is backed by a cliff face to the north. Enjoy the large number of British native flowers.

* Japanese plant collection and visitor centre
* New exhibition 'the greenhouse'

Location
The southern tip of the Isle of Wight

Opening
Summer 10am–6pm
Winter Weekends only 10–6pm

Admission
Free

Contact
Undercliff Drive, Ventnor
Isle of Wight PO38 1UL

t 01983 855397
w botanic.co.uk
e simon.goodenough@iow.gov.uk

067 Wroxall

Appuldurcombe House Owl & Falconry Centre

2 hrs+   Feb–Dec

Visit the ruin of Appuldurcombe, designed by Capability Brown and once the grandest house on the Isle of Wight. A display of prints and photographs depicts the house and its history. The former servants' quarters now house the owl and falconry centre.

* Old brew house used for indoor bird flying
* C18 baroque mansion

Location
In Wroxall off the B3327 to Ventnor

Opening
Feb–Apr & Oct–Dec 10am–4pm
May–Sep 10am–5pm

Admission
House Adult £2.50, Child £1.50,
Concs £2.25

House & Falconry Centre
£5.75, £2.75, £5.20

Contact
Wroxall, Isle of Wight PO38 3EW

t 01983 852484
w appuldurcombe.co.uk
e enquiries@appuldurcombe.co.uk

Kent

Winchester Cathedral

1 hr+   All year

Visit this 900-year-old cathedral and see the memorials of Jane Austen and Isaac Walton, a unique collection of chantry chapels and hear the story of the diver, William Walker, who saved the cathedral in 1906. Visit the crypt with its renowned Sound II sculpture.

* The longest medieval cathedral
* The Winchester Bible – finest of the great C12 bibles

Location	Contact
Winchester town centre	Cathedral Office, 1 The Close, Winchester SO23 9LS
Opening	
Mon–Sat 8.30am–6pm	t 01962 857200
Sun 8.30am–5pm	w winchester–cathedral.org.uk
Admission	e cathedral.office@
Donations appreciated Adult £3.50, Concs £2.50	winchester–cathedral.org.uk

Godinton House & Gardens

1 hr+   Mon–Oct

Built in the C14, Godinton House is one of the most fascinating homes in Kent whose history, from its medieval origins to the present day, is revealed through the variety of its style, taste and furnishings. Set in a variety of glorious gardens.

* Collection of porcelain, pictures & furniture
* 3 stunning delphinium borders best in mid Jun–Jul

Location	*House & Gardens* £6. School
Junction 9 off M20, for Maidstone A20.	parties free, phone for details
Opening	**Contact**
Gardens Mar 20–Oct 3 Thu–Mon 2pm–5.30pm. *House* Apr 9–Oct 3 Fri–Sun 2pm–5.30pm (last tour at 4.30pm)	Godinton Lane, Ashford TN23 3BP
	t 01233 620 773
	w godinton–house–gardens.co.uk
Admission	e ghpt@godinton.fsnet.co.uk
Gardens Adults £3, Child free	

Dickens's House Museum

½ hr+   East–Oct

Once the home of Miss Mary Pearson Strong, on whom Charles Dickens based the character of Miss Betsey Trotwood in his novel *David Copperfield*, this building has been adapted as a museum to commemorate the novelist's association with the town of Broadstairs.

* Some of the author's own letters and memorabilia
* Collection of costumes and Victoriana

Location	Contact
On the main seafront at Broadstairs	2 Victoria Parade, Broadstairs CT10 1QS
Opening	
Easter–Oct daily 2pm–5pm	t 01843 861232
	w dickenshouse.co.uk
Admission	e aleeault@aol.com
Adult £2, Child £1	

071 Canterbury

Canterbury Cathedral

1 hr+   All year

Founded in AD 597 by St Augustine, a missionary from Rome, the cathedral has been the home of Christianity in England for 1400 years and has attracted thousands of pilgrims each year since the murder of Archbishop Thomas à Becket in 1170.

* Site of the murder of Archbishop Thomas à Becket
* Stained glass windows from the C12

WC 🍴 ♿

Location
City centre, off the High Street

Opening
Summer 9am–6.30pm, winter 9am–5.30pm. Times vary, phone for details

Admission
Adults £4, Child & Concs £3

Contact
Cathedral House, 11 The Precinct, Canterbury CT1 2EH

t 01227 762862
w canterbury–cathedral.org
e enquiries@canterbury–cathedral.org

073 Canterbury

The Canterbury Tales

1 hr+   All year

This fascinating audio-visual experience, sited in the centre of Canterbury, is one of the town's most popular visitor attractions. Step back in time to experience the sights, sounds and smells of the Middle Ages in this stunning reconstruction of C14 England.

* Uses headsets with earphones
* Recreates the pilgrimages of Chaucerian England

WC ♿

Location
City centre, off the High Street

Opening
Mar–Jun 10am–5pm, Jul to Aug 9.30am–5.30pm, Sep–Oct 10am–5pm, Nov–Jan 10am–4.30pm

Admission
Adults £6.75, Child £5.25, Concs £5.75

Contact
23 St Margaret's Street, Canterbury CT1 2TG

t 01227 479227
w canterburytales.org.uk
e info@canterburytales.org.uk

072 Canterbury

Roman Museum

1 hr   All year

This underground museum of the Roman town is an exciting mix of excavated real objects, authentic reconstructions, and remains of a Roman town house with mosaics. Reconstructions include a Roman market place, with a shoemaker, fruit and vegetable stall.

* Computer reconstruction shows the Roman house
* Touch -screen computer game on Roman technology

WC ♿

Location
Butchery Lane, close to the cathedral

Opening
Mon–Sat 10am–5pm (last admission 4pm). From Jun–Oct 31, also open Sunday 1.30pm–5pm (last admission 4pm).

Admission
Adult £2.70, Child £1.70, Concs £1.70

Contact
Longmarket, Butchery Lane, Canterbury CT1 2JE

t 01227 785575
w canterbury.gov.uk
e museums@canterbury.gov.uk

074 Chislehurst

Chislehurst Caves

1 hr   Wed–Sun

Over 20 miles of dark mysterious passageways form a labyrinth deep beneath Chislehurst. Dug over a period of 8,000 years in search of flint and chalk, these handmade caves include a church, a druid's altar, a haunted pool and much more.

* Lamp-lit tours
* Original Second World War air-raid shelter

Location
Take the A222 between the A20 & A21. At the railway bridge turn into Station Road then right again to Caveside Close

Opening
School hols daily 10am–4pm (except Christmas). Rest of the year Wed–Sun 10am–4pm

Admission
Adults £4, Child & Concs £2

Contact
Old Hill, Chislehurst BR7 5NB

t 020 8467 3264
w chislehurstcaves.co.uk
e enquiries@chislehurstcaves.co.uk

075 Cranbrook

The Union Windmill

1 hr   Apr–Sep

Built in 1814, this is the tallest (72ft/22m) and finest surviving smockmill in the UK. The fixed wooden tower has a brick base and is clad in white weatherboard. Its four sails have patent shutters and the fantail ensures the sails face into the wind at all times.

* Working model of mill-cap
* Wholemeal flour milled and for sale to visitors

Location
Just off the A229 which runs N/S from Maidstone to Hastings

Opening
Sat & Sun in summer hols 2.30pm–5.30pm, Apr–Sep Sat & Bank Hols 2.30pm–5.30pm

Admission
Free, donations appreciated

Contact
Cranbrook Union Mill, The Hill, Cranbrook

t 01580 71256 or 712984 (or 712226)
w users.argonet.co.uk/users/ tonysing/union

076 Dover

Dover Castle

3 hrs+   All year

Commanding the shortest English sea crossing, this site has been the UK's most important defence against invasion since the Iron Age. It was built in the C12 and reinforced by Henry VIII in the 1530s. Underneath the nearby White Cliffs are a series of underground tunnels.

* Reconstruction of Henry VIII's visit in 1539
* Visit the Dunkirk command room

Location
Clearly signposted to the east of the city, on the white cliffs

Opening
Mar–Sep 10am–6pm, Oct 10am–5pm, Nov–Mar 10am–4pm

Admission
Adults £8, Child £4, Concs £6 (includes entry to wartime tunnels)

Contact
Dover CT16 1HU

t 01304 201628
w english-heritage.org.uk

077 Dover

South Foreland Lighthouse

½ hr   Mar–Oct

Built in 1843, this distinctive landmark on the White Cliffs was the first lighthouse to use electricity and the first to display an electrically-powered signal. It was used by Marconi for his first successful international radio transmission.

* Original 3,500-watt lamp on display
* Leaflets on local walks available

Location
2½ miles NE along coast from Dover
2 mile walk from NT car park

Opening
Guided tour only Mar–Oct Thu–Mon 11am–5pm, school hols daily

Admission
Adult £2, Child £1

Contact
The Front, St Margaret's Bay CT15 6HP

t 01304 852463
w nationaltrust.org.uk
e southforeland@nationaltrust.org.uk

078 Eynsford

Dungeness RSPB Nature Reserve

2 hrs   All year

This unique shingle beach abounds with birds, flowers and other wildlife, from nesting gulls and terns to the rare deciminal leach. This site is an important landfall for many migrating birds and is the winter home for hundreds of ducks and geese.

* Guided walks and other events throughout the year
* Binoculars can be hired

Location
Signposted off the Lydd to Dungeness road, 10 miles E of Rye

Opening
Reserve daily 9am–sunset
Visitor Centre 10am–5pm (4pm Nov to Feb)

Admission
Adults £3, Child £1, Concs £2

Contact
Boulderwall Farm, Dungeness Road, Lydd, Romney Marsh TN29 9PN
t 01797 320588
w rspb.org.uk
e dungeness@rspb.org.uk

079 Eynsford

Lullingstone Roman Villa

1 hr+   All year

One of the best preserved Roman villas in England, Lullingstone was built in AD 75 and rediscovered in 1949. It is now housed in a modern two-storey building. Renowned for its mosaics, it also features a frescoe and a bathing complex.

* Free audio tour
* Gift shop

Location
Off M25 at junction 3, just outside Eynsford on A225

Opening
Daily Apr–Sep 10am–6pm, Oct 10am–5pm, Nov–Mar 10am–4pm

Admission
Phone for details

Contact
Lullingstone Lane, Eynsford DA4 0JA
t 01322 863467
w english–heritage.org.uk

080 Eynsford

Eagle Heights Bird of Prey Centre

4 hrs+   All year

With over 100 birds in indoor and outdoor aviaries, the centre gives visitors the opportunity to see birds of prey in action during flying displays, promoting conservation through education. It also provides sanctuary for injured and unwanted animals.

* Five–day falconry courses available
* New reptile house and meercat house

 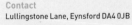

Location
Off M25 at junction 3 onto A20, or M20 at junction 1

Opening
Daily Mar 1–Nov 1 10.30am–5pm, Nov–Feb weekends 11am–4pm

Admission
Adult £6.60, Child £4.60, Concs £5.60

Contact
Lullingstone Lane, Eynsford DA4 0JB
t 01322 866466
w eagleheights.co.uk
e office@eagleheights.co.uk

081 Edenbridge

Hever Castle & Gardens

4 hrs   Mar–Nov

This romantic C13 castle was the childhood home of Anne Boleyn. It is set in magnificent gardens, which include a formal Italian garden, a lake and a Sunday walk. There is a water maze on Sixteen Acre Island and the yew maze challenge.

* Costumed figure exhibition
* Historic instruments of execution and torture

Location
3 miles SE of Edenbridge off B2026 between Sevenoaks & East Grinstead

Opening
Daily Mar 1–Nov 30
Gardens 11am–6pm,
Castle 12noon–6pm (last entry 5pm).
Mar & Nov 11am–4pm.

Admission
Castle & Gardens Adult £8.80,
Child & Concs £4.60,
Gardens £6.70, £5.70, £4.40

Contact
Edenbridge TN8 7NG

t 01732 865224
w hevercastle.co.uk
e ampedley@hevercastle.co.uk

082 Godhurst

Finchcocks Living Museum of Music

3 hrs   Mar–Oct

This Georgian manor house in the Kent countryside houses a huge collection of historical keyboard musical instruments, and contains the world's largest collection of playing instruments. The house is noted for its dramatic brickwork and its beautiful and tranquil garden.

* Annual music festival and special events in Sep
* All openings include a demonstration concert

Location
Take A262, Goudhurst turning, from A21, house is signposted

Opening
Mar–Oct, Sun 2pm–6pm, Mon–Sat by appointment
Aug, Wed Thu and Sun 2pm–6pm
Bank Hols 2pm–6pm

Admission
House & Garden Adult £7.50;
Child £4 *Garden only* £2.50

Contact
Finchcocks, Goudhurst TN17 1HH

t 01580 211702
w finchcocks.co.uk
e Katrina@finchcocks.co.uk

083 Goudhurst

Bedgebury Pinetum

2 hrs   All year

This wooded valley, with the finest collection of conifers in the world, provides enjoyment to visitors who come to appreciate its beauty and tranquillity. This unique attraction nestles quietly among lakes and valleys in the Kentish countryside.

* Special events and tours
* Pinetum Pantry provides light refreshments

Location
On the B2079 from Goudhurst, signposted from A21 before Flimwell

Opening
Daily Apr–Nov 11am–5pm, Nov–Mar 11am–4pm

Admission
Adult £3.50, Child £1.50, Concs £3

Contact
Goudhurst TN17 2SL

t 01580 211044 / 211781
w bedgeburypinetum.org.uk
e bedgebury@forestry.gov.uk

South of England Rare Breeds Centre

3 hrs   All year

Here's a chance to meet and pet all your favourite friendly farm animals as you wander around a farm trail. The centre is also home to many endangered and rare British animals. Set in acres of beautiful woodland there are plenty of places to picnic while the kids play.

* Woodland activity quiz trail
* Piglet racing in season and trailer rides all year

Location
Leave M20 at junction 10, follow signs to Brenzett and Hamstreet. Situated between Hamstreet & Woodchurch

Opening
Apr–Sep daily 10.30am–5.30pm, Oct–Mar Tue–Sun 10.30am–4.30pm

Admission
Adult £5, Child £5, Concs £4

Contact
Woodchurch, Ashford TN26 3RJ

t 01233 861493
w rarebreeds.org.uk
e visit@rarebreeds.org.uk

Bewl Water

1 hr+   All year

This reservoir is the largest area of open water in the south east. Set in an area of outstanding natural beauty, Bewl is home to a huge variety of wildlife. There are many exciting outdoor pursuits here, including windsurfing, fishing, cycling and walking.

* Water-efficient garden
* Interactive exhibition

Location
1 mile S of Lamberhurst, signposted from A21

Opening
Mar–Oct, daily 9.00am–sunset
Winter 9am–4pm

Admission
Apr–Oct cars & motorcycles £4 per

vehicle (weekdays), £5 per vehicle (weekends & Bank Hols), Nov–Mar £2.50 all vehicles

Contact
Bewl Water Reservoir, nr Lamberhurst TN3 8JH

t 01892 890661
w bewl.co.uk

Leeds Castle

3 hrs   All year

This medieval castle, situated on two islands in a lake set in 500 acres of parkland is a popular attraction. Once a Norman stronghold, the castle has since been residence for six of England's medieval queens, a palace for Henry VIII, and a retreat for the powerful.

* Open–air concert programme
* Hot–air balloon rides

Location
Leave M20 at junction 8, castle is 7 miles E of Maidstone

Opening
Apr–Oct daily 10am–5pm
Nov–Mar daily 10am–3pm

Admission
Adult £11, Child £7.50, Concs £9.50

Gardens & attractions £9.50, £6, £8 (reduction during winter months)

Contact
Maidstone ME17 1PL

t 01622 765400
w leeds-castle.com
e enquiries@leeds-castle.co.uk

087 Maidstone

Museum of Kent Life

3 hrs+   Feb–Nov

A unique open-air living museum that celebrates 300 years of Kentish history. Traditional crafts are demonstrated in a working farm. This is one of the only places in England where hops are grown, harvested, dried and packed by hand using time-honoured techniques.

* Calendar of events throughout the year
* Hop-picking festival in September

Location
Off M20 at junction 6, follow road signs

Opening
Feb–Nov 10am–5.30pm daily

Admission
Adult £6, Child £4, Concs £4.50

Contact
Cobtree, Lock Lane, Sandling, Maidstone ME14 3AU

t 01622 763936
w museum–kentlife.co.uk
e enquiries@museum–kentlife.co.uk

089 Penshurst

Penshurst Place & Gardens

1 hrs+   Mar–Nov

This medieval manor house was built in 1341. The great hall, with its 60ft-high, chestnut–beamed roof and trestle tables, is regarded as one of the world's grandest rooms. Much of the house and the gardens remain unchanged since the days when Elizabeth I made her visits here.

* Includes a fabulous toy museum
* 'A Family Home for 450 Years' exhibition

Location
Leave M25 at junction 5 or M20/M26 at junction 2a, follow A21 to Hildenborough, then signposted

Opening
Daily Mar–Nov, *House* 12noon–5pm, *Gardens* 10.30am–6pm

Admission
House & Gardenss Adult £7, Child £5, Concs £6.50 *Gardens* £5.50, £4.50, £5

Contact
Penshurst TN11 8DG

t 01892 870307
w penshurstplace.com
e enquiries@penshurstplace.com

088 New Romney

Romney, Hythe & Dymchurch Railway

3 hrs   All year

This was the world's smallest public railway when it opened in July 1927. It now runs regular passenger services covering a distance of 13½ miles from the picturesque Cinque Port of Hythe, near the channel tunnel, to the fishermen's cottages and lighthouses at Dungeness.

* Thomas the Tank Engine and Santa specials
* Dining-train specials

Location
The stations at New Romney, Dungeness and Hythe are all on or near the A259 trunk road

Opening
Trains run daily Apr–Sep, & weekends Oct–Mar. Please phone or see website for timetable

Admission
Adult £5.80–£9.60, Child half fare Price dependent on journey length

Contact
New Romney TN28 8PL

t 01797 362353
w rhdr.org.uk

090 Sevenoaks

Knole

2 hrs+   Apr–Oct

This great treasure house is set in a magnificent deer park. The original C15 house was enlarged and embellished in 1603 and has remained largely unaltered since then. Thirteen state rooms house a superb collection of furniture, tapestries and paintings.

* Virtual reality tour of state rooms
* Children's period costume events

Location
Sevenoaks town centre, off A225

Opening
Apr–Oct Wed–Sun 11am–4pm

Admission
Adult £6, Child £3

Contact
Sevenoaks TN15 0RP
t 01732 450608
w nationaltrust.org.uk/places/knole
e knole@nationaltrust.org.uk

091 Sissinghurst

Sissinghurst Castle Garden

2 hrs+   Mar–Nov

This is one of the world's most celebrated gardens, created by Vita Sackville-West and her husband, Sir Harold Nicholson, in the ruins of a large Elizabethan house. The library and tower, which are open to the public, include Vita's writing room.

* History of the house and the making of the garden
* Restaurant uses local recipes and produce

Location
1 mile E of Sissinghurst on A262

Opening
Mar 22–Nov 3 Mon, Tue & Fri
11am–6.30pm, Sat & Sun 10am–6.30pm.
Woodland walks open all year

Admission
Phone for details. *Woodland* free

Contact
Sissinghurst, nr Cranbrook TN17 2AB
t 01580 710701
w nationaltrust.org.uk/places/
   sissinghurst
e sissinghurst@nationaltrust.org.uk

092 Tenterden

Tenterden Vineyard

1 hr+   All year

This 15-acre vineyard is at the forefront of the English wine-making industry. Visitors are free to wander around the winery, vineyard, rural museum and plant centre. Guided tours explain the wine-making process in more detail. A free wine tasting follows each tour.

* Café, wine and gift shop
* Guided tours available during the summer months

Location
From Tenterden (A28), turn onto
B2082 to Wittersham & Rye. Vineyard
is 2 miles on the right at Small Hythe

Opening
Open every day 10am–5pm

Admission
Free *Tours* Adult £4, Child £2.50

Contact
Small Hythe, Tenterden TN30 7NG
t 01580 763033
w newwavewines.com
e sales@newwavewines.co.uk

London

093 Tunbridge Wells

Groombridge Place Gardens & The Enchanted Forest

4 hrs+   Apr–Oct

Groombridge Place's history dates back to medieval times. Flanked by a deep moat, and with a classical C17 manor as its backdrop, the formal gardens boast a rich variety of lawns and flower displays. High above the walled gardens and vineyard lies the Enchanted Forest.

* Bird of prey Raptor Centre
* Maze

Location
A26 towards Tunbridge Wells, turn right onto B2176 towards Penshurst. 3 miles past Penshurst village, turn left at T junction with A264. Follow signposts

Opening
Daily Apr–Oct 9.30am–6pm

Admission
Adult £8.30, Child £6.80, Concs £7

Contact
The Estate Office, Groombridge Place, Groombridge, Royal Tunbridge Wells TN3 9QG

t 01892 863999 / 861444
w groombridge.co.uk
e office@groombridge.co.uk

094 Westerham

Chartwell

2 hrs+   Mar–Nov

The home of Winston Churchill, Britain's wartime PM for over 40 years, remains as it was in his day. With many personal possessions and reminders of the man voted greatest Briton of all time, the house enables visitors to capture the mood of some of the key moments in British history.

* Exhibition of sound recordings
* Collection of Churchill's paintings

Location
2 miles S of Westerham, turn off A25 on to B2026, follow signs

Opening
Mar 20–Nov 7 Wed–Sun 11am–4.15pm

Admission
Adult £7, Child £3.50

Contact
Chartwell, Mapleton Road, Westerham TN16 1PS

t 01732 866368
w nationaltrust.org.uk/places/chartwell
e chartwell@nationaltrust.org.uk

095 Aldgate

Ripper Mystery Walks

2 hrs   All year

Take a trip back in time to 1888 when the streets of Whitechapel were not safe for a woman to walk alone at night. Learn how five prostitutes were violently murdered by the most famous serial killer ever.

* Relive the story of Jack the Ripper
* Atmospheric tour of old and hidden London

Location
Meet at Aldgate underground station

Opening
Wed, Fri & Sun 7pm
No booking required, but please phone in advance to check tour is on

Admission
Adult £5, Concs £4
Tour not suitable for under 10s

Contact
t 07957 388280
w tourguides.org.uk
e mysterywalks@hotmail.com

096 Baker Street

Madame Tussaud's

1 hr+   All year

This is the most famous waxworks collection in the world. It includes a whole range of interactive exhibits including Pop Idol, The Hulk, Chamber Live, the World Stage, the Spirit of London and more. The same building also houses the Planetarium.

* Updated and revamped chamber of horrors
* New online ticket booking allows timed ticketing

Location
Underground Baker Street

Opening
Weekdays 9.30am–5.30pm
Weekends 9.00am–6.00pm

Admission
9am–2pm: Adult £19.99, Child £13.99, Concs £14.99.

2pm–5pm: £17.99, £13.49, £14.99,
After 5pm: £12, £7; £10

Contact
Marylebone Road, London NW1 5LR

t 0870 400 3000
w madame-tussauds.com

097 Bloomsbury

The Charles Dickens Museum

1 hr   All year

Charles Dickens lived in this house between 1837–39 and wrote several of his most famous novels during that time. The house is now the world's foremost repository of Dickens-related material and the headquarters of the Dickens Fellowship.

* Regular calendar of special Dickens events
* Collection of letters, first editions and portraits

Location
Underground Russell Square

Opening
Mon–Sat 10am–5pm
Sun 11am–5pm

Admission
Adult £4, Child £2, Concs £3

Contact
48 Doughty Street, London WC1N 2LX

t 020 7405 2127
w dickensmuseum.com
e info@dickensmuseum.com

098 Bloomsbury

The British Museum

1 hr+   All year

The British Museum is home to a collection of art and antiquities from ancient and living cultures. Housed in one of Britain's architectural landmarks, the collection is one of the finest in existence, spanning two million years of human history.

* Spectacular new covered courtyard

Location
Underground Tottenham Court Road

Opening
Daily, Sat–Wed 10am–5.30pm,
Thu–Fri 10am–8.30pm (selected
galleries 5.30pm–8.30pm)

Admission
Free, exhibitions may charge

Contact
Great Russell Street, London
WC1B 3DG

t 020 7323 8299
w thebritishmuseum.ac.uk
e information@
thebritishmuseum.ac.uk

099 Chelsea

Chelsea Physic Garden

1 hr+   Apr–Oct

Founded in 1673 by the Worshipful Society of Apothecaries, this is one of Europe's oldest botanic gardens. Its 3½ acres contain a garden showing the history of medicinal plants, a pharmaceutical garden, botanical order beds, glasshouses and many rare and tender plants.

* Historical walk
* One of the oldest rock gardens in Europe (1773)

Location
Underground Sloane Square

Opening
Apr–Oct, Wed 2pm–5pm
Sun 2pm–6pm

Admission
Adult £5, Child & Concs £3

Contact
66 Royal Hospital Road, Chelsea,
London SW3 4HS

t 020 7352 5646
w chelseaphysicgarden.co.uk

100 City

Monument

  ½ hr All year

Built in memory of the Great Fire of London in 1666 at a cost of £13,700, the monument stands exactly 202 feet (61.5m) from its source in Pudding Lane. This is the tallest free-standing stone column in the world – 311 steps lead to the deck with a great view over London.

* Gain a certificate of achievement for reaching the top
* Superb panoramic views of London from the top

Location
Underground **Monument**

Opening
Daily 10am-6pm

Admission
Adult £2, Child £1

Contact
Monument Street, London EC3R 8AH

t 020 7626 2717

101 City

Museum of London

  2 hrs All year

The Museum of London is the world's largest urban museum and presents a quarter of a million years of history to over seven million modern Londoners. Its collections include over a million items relating to one of the finest cities in the world.

* Covers the history of the city since it began
* Regular calendar of exhibitions and special events

Location
Underground **Barbican, St Paul's**

Opening
Mon-Sat 10am-5.50pm
Sun 12 noon-5.50pm

Admission
Free

Contact
London Wall, London EC2Y 5HN

t 0870 444 3852
w museumoflondon.org.uk
e info@museumoflondon.org.uk

102 City

The Streets of London

2 hrs   All year

The Streets of London invite you to sample the many faces of this great and fascinating city. Journey through 2,000 years of history on walks that will inform, excite and stimulate your curiosity.

* Programme of fascinating walks all over the city
* Each walk lasts approximately 2 hours

Location	Contact
Walks start at different tube stations every day of the week	Please telephone for details
Opening	t 020 8906 8657
Walks start at different times each day	w thestreetsoflondon.co.uk
	e info@thestreetsoflondon.co.uk
Admission	
Adult £5, Child & Concs £4, accompanied under 12s free	

103 County Hall

London Eye

½ hr   All year

This is the most popular tourist attraction in London. The 443 feet (135m)-high big wheel provides the most spectacular views of one of the biggest cities in the world. On a clear day you can see 25 miles in every direction from safe and comfortable capsules.

* Over 15,000 people a day travel on the Eye
* Views are spectacular in all conditions

Location	Contact
On the south bank in County Hall	BA London Eye, Riverside Building,
Underground Waterloo	County Hall, London SE1 7PB
Opening	t 0870 5000 600
Daily 9.30am–8pm	w ba-londoneye.com
times may vary, ring for details	e customer.services@ba-londoneye. com
Admission	
Adult £11, Child £5.50 (must be accompanied by an adult) Concs £10	

104 City

St Paul's Cathedral

1 hr+   All year

The distinctive dome of Sir Christopher Wren's magnificent cathedral is prominent in London's skyline. Its monumental interior, sacred tombs and atmospheric crypt ensure it remains one of London's major tourist attractions.

* Full range of musical performances and events
* Try out the Whispering Gallery

Location	Admission
The top of Ludgate Hill	Free *Guided tours* Adult £6, Child £3,
Underground St Paul's	Concs £5
Opening	Contact
Mon–Sat 8.30am–4pm	The Chapter House, St Paul's
Special services and events may close all or part of the Cathedral	Churchyard, London EC4M 8AD
	w stpauls.co.uk
	e chapter@stpaulscathedral.org.uk

105 County Hall

London Aquarium

1 hr   All year

The London Aquarium is for everyone who appreciates the stunning and unusual natural world. Let your imagination take you on a voyage under the sea, from the beautiful coral reefs and Indian Ocean to the secret depths of the Pacific and Atlantic Oceans.

* Late night opening times in summer
* Themed activity weeks

Location
Inside County Hall on the south bank of the Thames by Westminster Bridge
Underground Westminster

Opening
All year 10am–6pm (7pm on selected summer evenings)

Admission
Prices vary, phone for details

Contact
County Hall, Westminster Bridge Road, London SE1 7PB

t 020 7967 8000
w londonaquarium.co.uk
e info@londonaquarium.co.uk

106 Green Park

Buckingham Palace

1 hr+   Aug–Sep

This is the official London residence of Her Majesty The Queen. The state rooms are used extensively to entertain guests on state, ceremonial and official occasions but are open to the public during August and September when the Queen makes her annual visit to Scotland.

* The State Rooms form the heart of the working palace
* Furnished with treasures from the Royal Collection

Location
Mainline Victoria
Underground Victoria Green Park & Hyde Park Corner

Opening
Aug–Sep daily 9.30am–4.30pm

Admission
Prices vary, phone for details

Contact
Ticket Sales and Information Office, The Official Residences of The Queen, London SW1A 1AA

t 020 7766 7300
w royal.gov.uk
e information@royalcollection.org.uk

 The Royal Collection © 2003 Her Majesty Queen Elizabeth II

107 Greenwich

National Maritime Museum

2 hrs+   All year

This is a World Heritage site comprising the National Maritime Museum, the Royal Observatory and the Queen's House. It houses important items on the history of Britain at sea, including maritime art, ship models and plans, navigational instruments, time-keeping and astronomy.

* Three marvellous museums in close proximity
* Planetarium shows at the Observatory, daily 2.30pm

Location
Main line Greenwich or Maze Hill, *Docklands Light Railway* Cutty Sark station. Boat from Embankment or Westminster

Opening
Summer daily 10am–6pm
Winter daily 10am–5pm

Admission
Free, exhibitions may charge

Contact
Park Row, Greenwich SE10 9NF

t 020 8312 6565
   020 8858 4422
w nmm@ac.uk

108 Greenwich

The *Cutty Sark*

1 hr   All year

Built in 1869 to be the fastest ship in the annual race to bring home the first of the new season's tea from China, the clipper *Cutty Sark* was opened to the public in a specially-built dry dock in 1957. Take a tour of her decks and find out about the urgent need for conservation.

* One of the world's most beautiful ships
* Subject of huge comservation appeal

Location
Docklands Light Railway service south of the Thames.
Underground Canary Wharf
By boat Westminster Pier

Opening
Daily 10am–5pm

Admission
Adult £4.25, Child £2.95, Concs £3.25

Contact
King William Walk, Greenwich, London SE10 9HT

t 020 8858 3445
w cuttysark.org.uk
e info@cuttysark.org.uk

109 Holborn

Sir John Soane Museum

1 hr+   All year

The famous architect Sir John Soane (1753–1837) designed this house to live in, but also to exhibit his antiquities and works of art. Today the house remains as he wanted it – a museum to which amateurs and students should have access.

* Celebrating 250 years of space, light and invention
* For lovers and students of architecture and sculpture

Location
Underground Holborn

Opening
Tue–Sat 10am–5pm

Admission
Free

Contact
13 Lincoln's Inn Fields, London WC2A 3BP

t 020 7005 2107
w soane.org
e jbrock@soane.org.uk

110 Kensington

Science Museum

3 hrs+   All year

This museum presents a record of scientific, technological and medical change since the C18. Originally funded by profits from the Great Exhibition of 1851, the museum was intended to improve scientific and technical education, and has done so for 150 years.

* Huge range of interactive exhibits
* IMAX cinema

Location
Underground South Kensington

Opening
Daily 10am–6pm

Admission
Free, donations welcome, exhibitions may charge

Contact
Exhibition Road, South Kensington, London SW7 2DD

t 0870 870 4868
w sciencemuseum.org.uk
e sciencemuseum@nmsi.ac.uk

111 Kensington

Victoria & Albert Museum

2–6 hrs   All year

The V&A is widely regarded as the world's greatest museum of applied and decorative arts. Home to amazing artefacts from the world's richest cultures, the V&A's unsurpassable collection has inspired and informed for over 150 years.

* A wide choice of special events, exhibitions and activities
* Spend time wandering the 7 miles of corridor

Location
Underground South Kensington

Opening
Daily 10am–5.45, Weds 10am–10pm, last Fri of month 10am–10pm

Admission
Free, exhibitions may charge

Contact
Cromwell Road, South Kensington, London SW7 2RL

t 020 7942 2000
w vam.ac.uk
e vanda@vam.ac.uk

112 London Bridge

London Dungeon

1 hr+   All year

Deep in the heart of London, buried beneath the paving stones of historic Southwark, lies the world's most chillingly famous horror attraction. The London Dungeon brings more than 2,000 years of gruesomely authentic history vividly back to life ... and death.

* Great Plague exhibition & Judgement Day boat ride!
* The terrible truth about Jack the Ripper

Location	Admission
Underground **London Bridge**	Please telephone for prices
Opening	**Contact**
Daily, Apr–Sep 10am–6pm	28–34 Tooley Street, London SE1 2SZ
Some late night summer opening, phone for details	t 020 7403 7221
Oct–Mar 10.30am–5.30pm	w thedungeons.com
	e londondungeon@ merlinentertainments.biz

113 Marylebone

Lord's Tour & MCC Museum

2 hrs   All year

The Lord's tour is an enjoyable and informative visit to the world famous home of cricket. The tour includes the Pavilion, Long Room, dressing room & the MCC museum, which houses cricketing memorabilia including bats, balls, paintings and much more.

* Don Bradman's cricket kit
* Home of the Ashes urn

Location	Admission
Underground **Baker Street**	Adult £7, Child £4.50, Concs £5.50
Opening	**Contact**
Apr–Sep daily tours at 10am, 12 noon & 2pm. No tours on match or preparation days, please phone for details.	Lord's Cricket Ground, St John's Wood, London NW8 8QN
Oct–Mar daily 12 noon & 2pm	t 020 7616 8595 / 8596
	w lords.org
	e tours@mcc.org.uk

114 Regent's Park

London Zoo

4 hrs   All year

Come face to face with some of the hairiest, scariest, tallest and smallest animals on the planet. See our Animals in Action presentation and watch some of our finest flying, leaping and climbing animals showing off their skills. Don't miss a visit to B.U.G.S!

* Regular programme of feeding times & special shows
* Moonlit world of nocturnal animals

Location	Admission
At the NE corner of Regent's Park on the Outer Circle	Adult £13, Child £9.75, Concs £11
Underground **Camden Town**	**Contact**
Opening	Regent's Park, London NW1 4RY
Mar–Oct daily 10am–5.30pm	t 020 7722 3333
Oct–Mar 10am–4pm	w londonzoo.co.uk
	e marketing@zsl.org

115 South

Imperial War Museum

2 hrs+   All year

This is the national museum of C20 conflict. It illustrates and records all aspects of modern war and of the individual's experience of it, whether allied or enemy, service or civilian, military or political. Its role embraces the causes, course and consequences of conflict.

* Special Holocaust exhibition
* Cinema shows museum's collection of film & video

Location
Main line **Waterloo, Elephant and Castle.**
Underground **Lambeth North 5 min walk.**

Opening
Daily 10am–6pm

Admission
Free, exhibitions may charge

Contact
Lambeth Road, London SE1 6HZ

t 020 7416 5320
w iwm.org.uk
e mail@iwn.org.uk

116 South Bank

Clink Prison Museum

1 hr   All year

On the site of the original Clink prison, this fascinating exhibition examines some of London's unsavoury past. From the C12 until its destruction in 1780 its inmates have ranged from priests to prostitutes.

* Possibly the oldest men's prison in London
* Whipping post, torture chair, foot crusher and more

Location
Underground **London Bridge**

Opening
Daily 10am–8pm
Summer & Sat–Sun 10am–9pm

Admission
Adult £4, Child & Concs £3

Contact
1 Clink Street, South Bank, London SE1 9DG

t 020 7378 1558
w clink.co.uk
e museum@clink.co.uk

117 South Bank

Globe Theatre

1–3 hrs   All year

The Globe Theatre is a reconstruction of the open-air playhouse, designed in 1599, where Shakespeare worked and for which he wrote many of his greatest plays. You can see a performance or visit the Globe Exhibition, which provides an introduction to the theatre of Shakespeare's time.

* Annual programme of Shakespeare's plays
* Permanent exhibition and theatre tours

Location
Main line London Bridge, Waterloo
Underground Southwark

Opening
May–Sep, *Theatre* 10am–5pm daily,
Exhibition 9am–5pm (no tours).
Oct–Apr *Exhibition* 10am–5pm
(tours available)

Admission
Exhibition Adult £8, Child £5.50,
Concs £6.50

Contact
21 New Globe Walk, London SE1 9DT
t *Enquiries* 020 7902 1400
  Box office 020 7401 9919
w shakespeares-globe.org
e info@shakespearesglobe.com

118 South Bank

Tate Modern

2 hrs+   All year

This major new gallery of modern and contemporary art is housed in the old Bankside Power Station on the south side of the Thames. This spectacular gallery is one of the world's most popular modern art galleries, featuring a permanent collection alongside temporary exhibits.

* Superb shop at gallery entrance
* Spectacular river views from café on level 7

Location
Opposite St Paul's Cathedral
Underground Southwark, Blackfriars
Boat from Tate Britain to Tate Modern

Opening
Daily Sun–Thu 10am–6pm
Fri & Sat 10am–10pm

Admission
Free, donations welcome, exhibitions
may charge

Contact
Bankside, London SE1 9TG
t 020 7887 8000
w tate.org.uk
e info@1001daysout.com

119 Tower Bridge

Design Museum

2 hrs+   All year

The Design Museum is the world's leading museum of industrial design, fashion and architecture. A programme of critically-acclaimed exhibitions captures the excitement of design's evolution, ingenuity and inspiration through the C20 and C21.

* Permanent collection plus temporary exhibitions
* Full range of talks, courses and kids' activities

Location
Underground Tower Hill, a 10 min walk
over Tower Bridge
Docklands Light Railway to Tower
Gateway

Opening
Daily 10am–5.45pm

Admission
Adult £6, Child/Concs £4

Contact
Shad Thames, London SE1 2YD
t 0870 8339955
w designmuseum.org
e info@designmuseum.org

120 Tower Bridge

HMS *Belfast*

1 hr+   All year

HMS *Belfast* was launched in 1938 and served throughout the Second World War, playing a leading part in the destruction of the German battle cruiser *Scharnhorst* and in the Normandy Landings. In 1971 she was saved as a unique and historic reminder of Britain's naval heritage.

* Experience what life was like for the crew
* Complete tours of this huge and complex warship

Location
Underground London Bridge or Tower
Hill

Opening
Mar–Oct daily 10am–6pm
Nov–Feb daily 10am–5 pm

Admission
Adult £6, Child free, Concs £4.40

Contact
Morgan's Lane, Tooley Street,
London SE1 2JH
t 0207 940 6300
w iwm.org.uk/belfast
e hmsbelfast@iwm.org.uk

121 Tower Hill

Tower of London

3 hrs   All year

Founded by William the Conqueror and modified by successive sovereigns, the Tower of London is one of the world's most famous and spectacular fortresses. Discover its 900-year history as a palace, fortress, prison, mint, arsenal, menagerie and jewel house.

* Ceremony of the keys (please apply in writing)
* Constant calendar of special events

Location
Underground Tower Hill, Fenchurch Street, London Bridge

Opening
Mar–Oct Mon–Sat 9am–5pm
Sun 10am–5pm
Nov–Feb Tue–Sat 9am–4pm
Sun–Mon 10am–4pm

Admission
Adult £13.50, Child £9 Concs £10.50

Contact
Tower Hill, London EC3N 4AB

t 0870 756 6060
w tower-of-london.org.uk

---

123 Trafalgar Square

National Gallery

1 hr+   All year

This gallery houses one of the greatest collections of European painting in the world. The permanent collection spans the period from 1250 to 1900 and includes paintings by artists Leonardo da Vinci, Michelangelo, Rembrandt, J.M.W. Turner and Vincent van Gogh.

* Selection of courses and lectures available
* Weekend and school holiday family events

Location
Trafalgar Square
Underground Leicester Square, Charing Cross

Opening
Daily 10am–6pm (Wed 10am–9pm)

Admission
Free, donations welcome, exhibitions may charge

Contact
Trafalgar Square, London WC2N 5DN

t 020 7747 2885
w nationalgallery.org.uk
e information@ng-london.org.uk

---

122 Tower Bridge

Tower Bridge Exhibition

1 hr   All year

This is one of the world's most famous bridges. Visitors can go inside the Gothic towers to discover its history and see the original Victorian engine rooms. From the high-level walkways you can look out across the modern city skyline and down the river to Canary Wharf.

* New interactive computer displays
* Special ticket rate for Tower Bridge and Monument

Location
Underground Tower Hill and London Bridge *Riverboat* Tower Pier

Opening
Daily 9.30am–6pm

Admission
Adult £4.50, Child & Concs £3

Contact
Tower Bridge, London SE1 2UP

t 020 7403 3761
w towerbridge.org.uk
e enquiries@towe.org.uk

London

124   Trafalgar Square

National Portrait Gallery

2 hrs   Daily

Founded in 1856 to collect the likenesses of famous British men and women, the gallery aimed to be about history not art, and this remains its criterion today. The collection is the most comprehensive of its kind in the world.

* Daytime and evening lectures and events programme
* Roof-top restaurant which boasts stunning views

Location
Underground **Charing Cross, Leicester Square**

Opening
Daily 10am–6pm, Thu & Fri 10am–9pm

Admission
Free, exhibitions may charge

Contact
St Martin's Place, London WC2H OHE

t 020 7306 0055 / 020 7312 2463
w npg.org.uk

125   Twickenham

Museum of Rugby

2 hrs   All year

More than just a collection of interesting artefacts, this museum is an inspirational journey through the history of the ultimate team game. Innovative, interactive exhibits bring to life some of the great moments of the international game.

* Finest and extensive collection of rugby memorabilia
* Action-packed films show footage of matches

Location
Mainline **Twickenham (from Waterloo)**

Opening
Tue–Sat 10am–5pm, Sun 11am–5pm

Admission
Adult £8 Child & Concs £5

Contact
Rugby Road, Twickenham, London TW1 1DZ

t 020 8892 8877
w rfu.com
e museum@rfu.com

126   West End

Wallace Collection

3 hrs   All year

This is both a national museum and the finest private collection of art ever assembled by one family. It is displayed against the opulent backdrop of Hertford House. The collection is best known for its magnificent C18 French paintings, furniture and porcelain.

* Paintings by Titian, Rembrandt and Frans Hals
* Superb new restaurant

Location
Underground **Bond Street**

Opening
Mon–Sat 10am–5pm, Sun 12 noon–5pm

Admission
Free

Contact
Hertford House, Manchester Square, London W1U 3BN

t 020 7563 9500
w wallacecollection.org.uk
e enquiries@wallace-collection.org.uk

127   Westminster

Houses of Parliament

2 hrs   July–Oct

The House of Commons and House of Lords meet in the Palace of Westminster, located next to the River Thames in London. Parliament has met in the Palace of Westminster since around 1550. UK residents and overseas visitors must book tours in advance.

* See and hear debates
* Tours of the clock tower available on request

Location
Underground **Westminster**

Opening
Tours available during summer recess of Jul 18–Oct 13
Please telephone for details

Admission
Please telephone for details

Contact
House of Commons Information Office, Westminster, London SW1A 0AA

t 0870 906 3773
w parliament.uk
e hcinfo@parliament.uk

128 Westminster

Cabinet War Rooms

1 hr   All year

In 1940, as the bombs rained down on London, Winston Churchill, his Cabinet, his War Cabinet and his staff met below ground in a fortified basement in Whitehall known as the Cabinet War Rooms. Today, visitors can see them just as they looked during the war years.

* Newly restored Churchill Suite now open
* New Winston Churchill museum opening in 2005

Location
Underground **Westminster** or
St James's Park
Main line **Charing Cross or Victoria**

Opening
Oct 1–Mar 31 10am–6pm
Apr 1–Sep 30 9.30am–6pm

Admission
Adult £7, Child free, Concs £5.50

Contact
King Charles Street,
London SW1A 2AQ

t 020 7766 0120
w iwm.org.uk/cabinet
e cwr@iwm.org.uk

129 Wimbledon

Wimbledon Lawn Tennis Museum

1 hr+   All year

This museum, on the site of the world's most famous lawn tennis tournament, offers a glimpse of both the centre court and the original trophies. Discover how the original medieval real tennis has become a multi-million pound professional sport.

* Audio/visual presentation of great players in action
* Additional behind the scenes tours are also available

Location
Underground **Southfields**

Opening
Daily 10.30am–5pm

Admission
Adult £6, Child £3.75, Concs £5

Contact
The All England Lawn Tennis Club,
Church Road, Wimbledon, London
SW19 5AE.

t 020 8946 6131
w wimbledon.org/museum
e museum@aeltc.com

130 Westminster

Westminster Abbey

1 hr+   All year

An architectural masterpiece of the C13 to C16, Westminster Abbey presents a unique pageant of British history. It has been the setting for most coronations since 1066 and for numerous royal occasions. Today it is still a church dedicated to regular worship and events.

* The tombs of kings and queens
* Tomb of the Unknown Warrior

Location
Next to Parliament Square, opposite
the Houses of Parliament.
Underground **St James's Park** and
Westminster

Opening
Mon–Fri 9.30am–3.45pm, Wed
9.30am–7pm, Sat 9.30am–1.45pm
Sundays worship only – no visiting

Admission
Adult £6, Concs & Child (over 11) £4,
services free

Contact
20 Dean Yard, London SW1 P3PA

t 020 7654 4900
w wesminster–abbey.org
e info@westminster–abbey.org

131 Banbury

Broughton Castle

1 hr+   May–Sep

In 1300 Sir John de Broughton built this manor house in a sheltered site at the junction of three streams and surrounded it with a substantial moat. William of Wykeham, founder of New College Oxford and Winchester College, was an early owner of Broughton.

* Location for *Shakespeare In Love*
* Medieval manor house enlarged in 1600

Location
2 miles W of Banbury Cross on the B4035 Shipston-on-Stour road

Opening
May 1–Sep 15 Wed & Sun 2pm–5pm
Jul & Aug Thurs 2pm–5pm open all
Bank Hol Mons & Suns

Admission
Adult £5.50, Child £2.50, Concs £4.50

Contact
Broughton, Banbury OX15 5EB

t 01295 722 547/276070
w broughtoncastle.demon.co.uk
e admin@broughtoncastle.demon.co.uk

132 Burford

Cotswold Wildlife Park & Gardens

3 hrs+   All year

The park, which is set in 160 acres of parkland and gardens around a listed Victorian manor house, has been open to the public since 1970. It's home to a collection of mammals, birds, reptiles and invertebrates, from ants to white rhinos and bats to big cats.

* Insect and reptile houses
* Tikki the 7 year old, 19¾ foot long python

Location
On A361, 2 miles S of Burford

Opening
Daily Mar–Sep 10am–4.30pm
Oct–Feb 10am–3.30pm

Admission
Adult £8, Child £5.50, Concs £5.50

Contact
Burford OX18 4JW

t 01993 823006
w cotswoldwildlifepark.co.uk

133 Chinnor

Chinnor & Princes Risborough Railway

1 hr   Mar–Dec

This ex-GWR branch line, originally built in 1870, passes along the foot of the Chiltern Hills parallel to the Icknield Way. The 3½-mile journey affords outstanding views across the vale of Aylesbury with steam and heritage diesel trains.

* Thomas and Santa special events every year
* Cream teas are served on selected afternoon trains

Location
Station Road just off the B4009

Opening
Weekends Mar–Dec 10am–5.30pm, phone for timetable details

Admission
Adult £4–£6, Child £2–£3

Contact
Chinnor Station, Station Road, Chinnor OX39 4ER

t 01844 353535/354117
w cprra.co.uk
e samuel@cprra.co.uk

134 Chipping Norton

The Rollright Stones

1 hr   All year

The Rollright Stones is a ancient site which consists of three main elements. The King's Men stone circle, the King Stone, and the Whispering Knights. The name is believed to derive from 'Hrolla–landriht', the land of Hrolla.

* Discover the folklore of Kings, Witches and Faeries
* 5,000 year old burial chamber of a Neolithic barrow

Location
N of Chipping Norton

Opening
Sunrise to sunset

Admission
Adult 50p, Child 25p

Contact
The Friends of the Rollright Stones
P.O. Box 444, Bicester OX25 4AT

w rollrightstones.co.uk

135 Henley-on-Thames

Greys Court

1 hr+   Apr–Sep

This intriguing Tudor house, is set beside the ruins of C14 fortifications and one surviving tower dating from 1347. The house has an interesting history involving Jacobean court intrigue. The outbuildings include a wheelhouse, a donkey wheel and ice house.

* Wisteria walk and ornamental vegetable garden
* Intimate rooms contain beautiful C18 plasterwork

Location
From Henley take A4130 to Oxford. At Nettlebed roundabout take B481

Opening
Apr–Sep *House* Wed–Fri 2pm–5pm
Garden Tue–Sat 2pm–5pm

Admission
House Adult £5, Child £2.50
Garden £3.40, £1.70

Contact
Rotherfield Greys,
Henley-on-Thames RG9 4PG

t 01491 628529
w nationaltrust.org.uk
e greyscourt@ntrust.org.uk

136 Henley-on-Thames

River and Rowing Museum

2 hrs   All year

The museum has three main galleries devoted to the River Thames, the international sport of rowing and the town of Henley. There are also three special exhibition galleries housed in an astonishing building, raised on columns above water meadows beside the Thames.

* Exhibits from 400 BC to Sydney 2000 Olympic Games
* Architect David Chipperfield designed the building

Location
Signposted from the centre of Henley

Opening
Summer daily 10am–5.30pm
Winter daily 10am–5pm
Closed Dec 24/25/31 & Jan 1

Admission
Prices vary, phone for details

Contact
Mill Meadows, Henley-on-Thames
RG9 1BF

t 01491 415600
w rrm.co.uk
e museum@rrm.co.uk

137 Oxford

The Bate Collection of Musical Instruments

1 hr+   All year

This is a collection of historical woodwind, brass and percussion instruments; over a dozen historical keyboard instruments; a complete bow-maker's (William Retford) workshop and a collection of bows. Complete with a beautiful and well stocked shop.

* A small but interesting archive
* Collection of European woodwind instruments

Location
Situated in the Faculty of Music buildings, next to Christ Church College

Opening
Mon–Fri 2pm–5pm
Sat during term 10am–12 noon

Admission
Free, guided tours at a small cost

Contact
Faculty of Music, St Aldate's,
Oxford OX1 1DB

t 01865 276139
w ashmol.ox.ac.uk
e bate.collection@music.ox.ac.uk

138 Oxford

The Ashmolean Museum of Art & Archaeology

1 hr+   All year

This is a museum of the University of Oxford. Founded in 1683, it is one of the oldest public museums in the world. The collections are divided between five curatorial departments: antiquities, cast gallery, eastern art, heberden coin room and western art.

* Unique collection of early Chinese ceramics
* Sculpture includes an Ideal Head by Antonio Canova

Location
On Beaumont Street, opposite the Randolph Hotel, Oxford

Opening
Tue–Sat 10am–5pm
Sun 2pm–5pm

Admission
Free

Contact
Beaumont Street, Oxford OX1 2PH UK

t 01865 278000
w ashmol.ox.ac.uk

139 Oxford

Inspector Morse Tours of Oxford

2 hrs+   All year

Guided Morse Tours of Oxford take in many of the places made famous by this celebrated fictional detective. Visit his local pub, Blackwell's Bookshop, Oxford Police Station and even Gill's the Ironmongers. The tour routes vary but are always fun.

* Experienced guides entertain with many anecdotes
* Guidebook of Inspector Morse-related sites available

Location
Tours leave from outside Tourist Information Centre, (walking tour)

Opening
every Sat at 1.30pm
Booking essential

Admission
Phone for details

Contact
Tourist Information Centre, Oxford

t 01865 726871
w visitoxford.org.uk/tours
e tic@oxford.gov.uk

140 Oxford

The Oxford University Museum of Natural History

1 hr+   All year

This museum houses Oxford University's extensive, natural history collection in a high-Victorian gothic-building. Exhibits include the remains of the dodo, immortalised in Alice in Wonderland and extinct since 1680, fossil dinosaur materials and many other exhibits.

* The Oxford dinosaurs and other Mesozoic reptiles
* Historic material donated by scientists like Darwin

Location
In Parks Road facing Keble College, signposted

Opening
Daily 12 noon–5pm
Closed Dec 24–26 & Jan 1

Admission
Free, donations appreciated

Contact
Parks Road, Oxford OX1 3PW

t 01865 272950
w oum.ox.ac.uk
e info@oum.ox.ac.uk

141 Oxford

Modern Art Oxford

1 hr   All year

©Stephen White

The gallery has established an international reputation for its pioneering programme of exhibitions and community events. Artists exhibited at the gallery include Joseph Beuys, Yoko Ono, Ed Ruscha, Louise Bourgeois, Carl Andre and Tracey Emin.

* A regular and changing programme of events
* Talks and tours, chidren's events and music evenings

Location
Town centre, 10 mins from train station

Opening
Tue–Sat 10–5pm, Sun 12noon–5pm
Changing exhibitions causes short closed periods, phone for details

Admission
Free

Contact
30 Pembroke Street, Oxford OX1 1BP

t 01865 722733
w modernartoxford.org
e danial.stocks@modernartoxford.org.uk

142 Oxford

University Of Oxford Botanic Garden

1 hr+   All year

This Garden holds a National Collection and has over 8,000 different types of plant, making it the most compact yet diverse collection of plants in the world. There is even more biological diversity here than in tropical rain forests and other biodiversity hotspots.

* Water garden, rock garden and Grade 1 walled garden
* Innovative black border and autumn borders

Location
Opposite Magdalen College in the centre of Oxford

Opening
Mar–Sep daily 9am–5pm
Oct–Feb daily 9am–4.30pm

Admission
Adult £2.50, Child free

Contact
Rose Lane, Oxford OX1 4AZ

t 01 865 286 690
w botanic-garden.ox.ac.uk
e postmaster@botanic-garden.ox.ac.uk

143 Wantage

The Vale & Downland Museum

1 hr+ All year

This museum is housed in a converted C17 cloth-merchant's house – a fine example of local vernacular architecture. The collections held at the museum contain geological, natural history, archeological, social history and contemporary objects.

* The story of Victorian Rural Life in the Vale
* 3D, graphic design and audio-visual presentations

Location
Well signposted from Wantage town centre

Opening
Mon–Sat 10am–4.30pm
Sun 2.30pm–5pm

Admission
Adult £1.50, Child £1

Contact
Church Street, Wantage OX12 8BL

t 01235 771447
w wantage.com/museum
e museum@wantage.com

144 Woodstock

Blenheim Palace

4 hrs Feb–Dec

This beautiful palace was built for John Churchill, 1st Duke of Marlborough, in 1705. Designed by Sir John Vanbrugh, it is one of the largest private houses in the country and contains a superb collection of tapestries, paintings, sculptures and furniture.

* Special exhibitions devoted to Sir Winston Churchill
* Paintings include works by Reynolds and Van Dyck

Location
Approaching Oxford on M40, exit at junction 9 and follow signs to Blenheim Palace

Opening
Palace Feb 14–Dec 12 open daily
10.30am–4.45pm
Nov–Dec closed Mon–Tue
Park All year daily 9am–4.45pm

Admission
Adult £12.50, Child £7, Concs £10, offpeak times vary, phone for details

Contact
Woodstock OX20 1PX

t 01993 811325
w www.blenheimpalace.com
e administrator@blenheimpalace.com

145 Aldershot

Army Medical Services Museum

3 hrs+   Easter–Oct

Archiving the Army's contribution to the development of medicine for both animals and people. Re-opening in February 2004 after a major, lottery funded refit. Medical, veterinary, dental and nursing collections include uniforms, medals, equipment and transport.

* 23 Victoria Crosses on display
* First World War horse drawn ambulance

WC

Location
M3 junction 4 , A331 to Mytchett, follow signs

Opening
Monday – Friday 10am-3.30pm
Closed weekends and public holidays

Admission
Free

Contact
Keogh Barracks, Ash Vale, Aldershot GU12 5RQ

t 01252 868612
e museum@keogh72.freeserve.co.uk

146 Cheam

Whitehall

1 hr+   All year

Whitehall has undergone a major refurbishment to illustrate how the house would have looked throughout its 500-year history. Originally C16, it now shows styles in several periods, all displayed in fully furnished rooms with original architecture.

* Timber framed construction

WC

Location
Off Broadway, centre of Cheam

Opening
Wed–Friday 2.00pm–5.00pm
Sat 10.00am–5.00pm Sun & Bank Hols
Mons 2.00pm–5.00pm
Closed Dec 21–Jan 1

Admission
Adult £1.20, Child 60p

Contact
1 Malden Road, Cheam SM3 8QD

t 020 8643 1236
w sutton.gov.uk
e curators@whitehallcheam.fsnet.co.uk

147 Chertsey

Chertsey Museum

1 hr+   All year

Reopened in 2003 after a major redevelopment. Chertsey is famous as the site of a medieval abbey and has some of the best preserved Georgian architecture in the county. The museum explores the history of the area and includes many items of national interest.

* Hands-on exhibits in Grade II Regency town house
* Nationally famous Olive Matthews costume collection

WC

Location
Chertsey town centre

Opening
Tue–Fri 12.30–4.30pm Sat 11am–4pm
Closed Dec 24–Jan 1

Admission
Free

Contact
The Cedars, 33 Windsor Street
Chertsey KT16 8AT

t 01932 565764
w chertseymuseum.org.uk
e enquiries@chertseymuseum.org.uk

Cobham

Painshill Park

2 hrs+   All year

The Hon. Charles Hamilton created one of the great C18 landscape parks before running out of money in 1773. After years of neglect, the garden won a 'Europa Nostra Award for Exemplary Restoration' with its impressive plant collection being painstakingly reassembled.

* Historic vineyard now replanted for production
* 14 acre lake fed by a spectacular waterwheel

Location	Contact
Off A3 and A245 at Cobham	Portsmouth Road, Cobham KT11 1JE
Opening	t 01932 868 113
Mar–Oct 10.30am–6pm Closed Mon	w painshill.co.uk
Nov–Feb 11.00am–4pm or dusk	e info@painshill.co.uk
Closed Mon & Tue	
Admission	
Adults £6, Child £3.50, Concs £5.25	

Churt

Pride of the Valley Sculpture Park

2 hrs+   All year

Adjoining Frensham Country Park at the foot of Devil's Jumps with the finest views of the county. Some 75 renowned sculptors exhibit works of art in woodland setting. Ten acres of hills, valleys, arboretum and wild fowl inhabited water gardens.

* Frensham Country Park provides extensive walks

Location	Contact
Jumps Road is off A287 S of Farnham	Jumps Road, Churt, nr Farnham GU10 2LE
Opening	t 01428 605453
Tue–Sun 10am–5pm. Closed Mon	w thesculpturepark.com
except Bank Hols	e eddiepowell@thesculpturepark. co.uk
Admission	
Adult £4.50,Child £3, Concs £3	

150 East Molesey

Hampton Court Palace

3 hrs+   All year

With 500 years of royal history, Hampton Court is one of England's finest attractions. It is a magnificent house with diverse rooms such as a Tudor kitchen and the sumptuous State Appartments. The house is complemented by 60 acres of riverside gardens famous all over the world.

* Horse–drawn carriages through gardens in summer
* World–famous maze in which to get lost

Location
From M25, junction 10 to A307 or junction 12 to A308

Opening
Mar–Oct Tue–Sat 9.30am–6pm
Mon 10.15–6pm Nov–Feb shuts at 4.30pm. Closed Dec 24–26

Admission
Adult £11.80, Child £7.50, Concs £8.50

Contact
East Molesey KT8 9AU

t 0870 752 7777
w hampton–court–palace.org.uk

151 Esher

Claremont Landscape Garden

1hr+   All year

Claremont's creation and development involved some of the great names in garden history. Begun c.1715, it became famous throughout Europe. Restoration began in 1975 after years of neglect. The many features include a lake, grotto and great views.

* Design by Capability Brown and Sir John Vanbrugh
* Turf amphitheatre and island with pavilion

Location
1 mile outside Esher on the Cobham road, A307

Opening
Tue–Sun 10am–5pm or dusk
Apr–Oct Mon–Fri 10am–6pm
Sat, Sun & Bank Hols 10am–7pm

Admission
Adult £4, Child £2

Contact
Portsmouth Road, Esher KT10 9JG

t 01372 467806
w nationaltrust.org.uk/claremount
e claremount@nationaltrust.org.uk

152 Farnham

Rural Life Centre

2 hrs+   All year

The Rural Life Centre is a museum of past village life covering the years from 1750 to 1960. It is set in over 10 acres of garden and woodland and housed in purpose-built and reconstructed buildings including a chapel, village hall and cricket pavilion.

* Displays show village crafts and trades
* Arboretum with over 100 species of trees

Location
Off A287, 3 miles S of Farnham

Opening
Mar 21–Oct 5 Wed–Sun & Bank Hol Mons 10am–5pm
Oct–Mar Wed & Sun 11am–4pm

Admission
Adult £5, Child £3, Concs £4

Contact
Old Kiln Museum, Reeds Road Tilford, Farnham GU10 2DL

t 01252 795 571
w rural-life.org.uk
e rural.life@lineone.net

153 Farnham

Farnham Castle Keep

1 hr   Apr–Oct

From the C12 until 1920, Farnham Castle was the seat of the Bishop of Winchester. Kings and Queens were entertained here and hunted in the nearby park. Damage was caused during the English Civil War, though the medieval shell was maintained.

* Inclusive audio tour available
* Motte and bailey castle design

Location
½ mile N of Farnham on A287

Opening
Apr–Sep daily 10am–6pm
Oct 10am–5pm

Admission
Phone for details

Contact
Castle Street, Farnham GU9 0AG

t 01252 713393
w english-heritage.co.uk

154 Godalming

Winkworth Arboretum

2 hrs   All year

A hillside woodland, created in the C20 and now containing over 1,300 different shrubs and trees, many of them rare. Impressive displays of magnolias, bluebells and azeleas in spring and stunning colours in autumn. There are two lakes and wildlife in abundance.

* Trees include Japanese maples and tupelos from US
* Cool, peaceful walks through woodland

Location
2 miles SE of Godalming, off E side of the B2130.

Opening
Daily, dawn-dusk Wed–Sun
Nov 11am–5pm,
Nov 17–Dec 14 weekends only

Admission
Adult £4, Child £2

Contact
Hascombe Road, Godalming GU8 4AD

t 01483 208477
w nationaltrust.org.uk
e winkwortharboretum@ntrust.org.uk

155 Guildford

Clandon Park

2 hrs+   Apr–Oct

Built in 1730, this grand palladian mansion is notable for its magnificent two-storeyed marble hall. The house has a superb collection of C18 furniture and porcelain. The attractive gardens contain a parterre, grotto and a Maori meeting house with a fascinating history.

* Home of Queen's Royal Surrey Regiment museum
* Designed by venetian architect Giacomo Leoni

Location
Off A247 NE of Guildford

Opening
Apr–Nov Tue–Thu & Sun 11am–5pm
Museum 12noon–5pm

Admission
Adult £6, Child £3

Contact
West Clandon, Guildford GU4 7RQ

t 01483 222 482
w nationaltrust.org.uk/clarendon
e clandonpark@nationaltrust.org.uk

156 Guildford

Hatchlands

1 hr+   Apr–Oct

Set in the 430-acre Repton Park, Hatchlands is noted for its nautically themed interiors designed by Robert Adam. It is also home to the Cobbe Collection, the world's largest group of keyboard instruments, many associated with famous composers.

* Paintings by Van Dyck and Gainsborough
* Park offers variety of woodland walks

Location
N of A246 Guildford–Leatherhead road

Opening
Apr–Jun & Sep–Oct Tue–Thu & Sun
2–5.30pm. Aug Tue–Fri & Sun
Open Bank Hol Mons

Admission
Adult £6, Child £3

Contact
East Clandon, Guildford GU4 7RT

t 01483 222 482
w nationaltrust.org.uk
e hatchlands@smtp.ntrust.org.uk

157 Guildford

Loseley Park

2 hrs+   May–Sep

Built in 1562, Loseley House is a fine example of Elizabethan architecture, set in acres of peaceful gardens and parklands. Highlights of its celebrated garden include an award-winning rose garden, a vine walk and an area of native wild flowers. Relax in the serene fountain garden.

* Home of Jersey cows used for eponymous ice-cream
* Herb garden has six areas devoted to specific purposes

Location
A3 SW from Guildford on B3000

Opening
House Jun 1–Aug 25, Wed–Sun
1pm–5pm Bank Hol 11am–5pm
Garden May 5–Sep 28 11am–5pm

Admission
House Adult £6, Child £3, Concs £5
Garden £3, £1.50, £2.50

Contact
Guildford GU3 1HS

t 01483 304440
w loseley-park.com
e enquiries@loseley-park.com

158 Guildford

Guildford House Gallery

½ hr+   All year

Guildford House is a fascinating C17 townhouse that now contains the council's art gallery showing selections from the borough's collection and varied temporary exhibitions. The house has magnificent plaster ceilings, original panelling and period furniture.

* Original craftwork and jewellery in giftshop
* Spectacular carved oak staircase

Location
Guildford High Street

Opening
Tue–Sat 10am–4.45pm
Closed Dec 25–27, 31 & Good Friday

Admission
Free

Contact
155 High Street, Guildford GU1 3AJ
t 01483 444740
w guildfordhouse.co.uk
e guildfordhouse@remote.guildford.gov.uk

159 Guildford

River Wey & Godalming Navigations & Dapdune Wharf

2 hrs+   Mar–Oct

The Wey was one of the first British rivers to be made navigable (1653). This 15-mile waterway linked Guildford to Weybridge on the Thames. The visitor centre at Dapdune Wharf in Guildford tells the story of the people who lived and worked on the waterway.

* Boat trips available
* The entire 19-mile towpath is open to walkers

Location
Wharf Road is behind Surrey County Cricket Ground, off Woodbridge Road

Opening
Mar 27–Oct 31, Mon &Thu–Sun
11am–5pm

Admission
Adult £3, Child £1.50

Contact
Wharf Road, Guildford GU1 4RR
t 01483 561389
w nationaltrust.org.uk
e riverwey@nationaltrust.org.uk

160 Morden

Morden Hall Park

3 hrs+   All year

This oasis in the heart of suburbia covers over 125 acres of parkland with the River Wandle meandering through. The historic mill now used as an environmental centre. The park has a hay meadow and there is an impressive rose garden with over 2,000 roses.

* Planned walks and monthly programme of events
* Variety of bridges across the river

  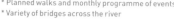

Location
Off Morden Hall Road

Opening
Daily, 8am–6pm (dawn–dusk)
Closed Dec 25/26 & Jan 1

Admission
Free

Contact
Morden Hall Road, Morden SM4 5JD
t 020 8545 6850
w nationaltrust.org.uk/places/mordenhallpark
e mordenhallpark@nationaltrust.org.uk

161 Ockley

The Hannah Peschar Sculpture Garden

2 hrs+   Mar–Oct

A stunning woodland water-garden is the setting for this specialist exhibition of contemporary sculpture. Hannah Peschar and Anthony Paul are in the vanguard of a C21 revolution in garden design that uses predominantly sculpture and water.

Location
A29 to Ockley, near Oakwood Church

Opening
Mar–Oct, Fri–Sat 11am–6pm
Sun & Bank Hol 2pm–5pm
Nov–Apr, Tues & Thu, by appointment

Admission
Adult £8, Child £5, Concs £6

Contact
Black and White Cottage,
Standon Lane, Ockley RH5 5QR
t 01306 627269
w hannahpescharsculpture.com
e hpeschar@easynet.co.uk

162 Richmond

Ham House & Gardens

1 hr+   Apr–Nov

This outstanding Stuart house, built in 1610, is famous for its lavish interiors and spectacular collections of fine furniture, textiles and paintings. The restoration of the C17 formal gardens over the last 30 years has influenced similar projects around the great gardens of Europe.

* C18 dairy
* Reinstated C17 statuary in wilderness garden

Location
Off A307 W of Richmond

Opening
House Apr–Nov, Mon–Wed Sat & Sun, 1–5pm
Gardens All year, Mon–Wed Sat & Sun, 11am–6pm or dusk. Closed Dec 25/26 & Jan 1

Admission
House Adult £7, Child £3.50
Gardens Adult £3, Child £1.50

Contact
Ham Street, Richmond TW10 7RS

t 020 8940 1950
w nationaltrust.org.uk/hamhouse
e hamouse@ntrust.org.uk

163 Richmond

Royal Botanic Gardens Kew

3 hrs+   All year

Established in 1759, Kew has developed into 300 acres of garden containing a collection of over 40,000 varieties of plant. Also see seven spectacular glasshouses and two art galleries, Japanese and rock gardens and regular exhibitions in the restored museum.

* One of England's top 100 attractions
* Inscribed as a World Heritage site in 2003

Location
Off A307 at Kew

Opening
Daily from 09.30–sunset, phone for closing times throughout the year
Closed Dec 25 & Jan 1

Admission
Adult £7.50, Child free, Concs £5.50

Contact
Kew, Richmond TW9 3AB

t 020 8332 5655
w kew.org
e info@kew.org

164 Weybridge

Brooklands Museum

3 hrs+   All year

Constructed in 1907, Brooklands was the first purpose-built motor racing circuit in the world. Not only the birthplace of British motorsport but also of British aviation. The track and many of the original buildings have been restored and a motor museum has been added.

* Extensive programme of motoring events
* Large display of cars, bikes and aircraft

Location
Off B374. A3 to A245, follow signs

Opening
Tue–Sun & Bank Hols
Summer 10am–5pm
Winter 10am–4pm
Closed Dec 24–31 & Good Friday

Admission
Adults £7, Children £5, Concs £6

Contact
Brooklands Rd, Weybridge KT13 0QN

t 01932 857381
w brooklandsmuseum.com
e info@brooklandsmuseum.com

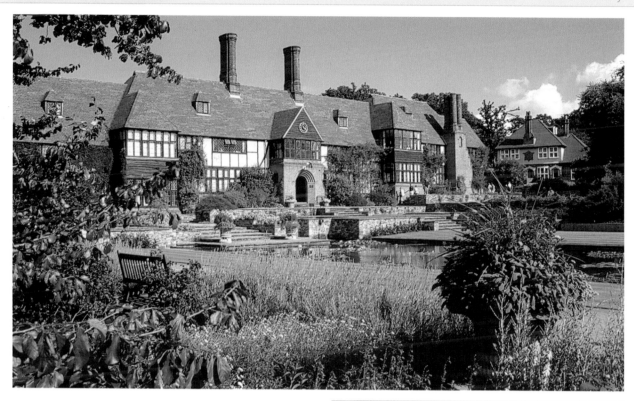

165 Woking

RHS Garden Wisley

3 hrs+   All year

Wisley is Britain's best-loved garden with 240-acres offering a fascinating blend of the beautiful with practical and innovative design and cultivation techniques. It features richly planted borders, luscious rose gardens and the exotica of the glasshouses.

* New plant varieties continuously developed
* Extensive events and educational programmes

Location
Just S of junction 10 of the M25

Opening
Mar–Oct, Mon–Fri, 10am–6pm
Sat & Sun, 9am–6pm
Nov–Feb, Mon–Fri, 10am–4.30pm
Sat & Sun 9am–4.30pm. Closed Dec 25

Admission
Adult £6, Child £2, Concs £5.50

Contact
Woking GU23 6QB
t 01483 224234
w rhs.org.uk
e info@rhs.org.uk

166 Windsor

Runnymede

    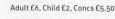

1 hr   All year

These historic meads on the banks of the Thames are the site where the Magna Carta was sealed by King John in June 1215. A network of footpaths links the Magna Carta memorial with two others: one to John F. Kennedy and one to the 20,000 Royal Air Force airmen killed in the Second World War.

* Fairhaven Lodges, designed by Lutyens
* Boat trips along Thames available

Location
6 miles E of Windsor on S side of A308
M25 junction 13

Opening
Daily, phone for details

Admission
Free, charges for parking, fishing and mooring

Contact
North Lodge, Windsor Road,
Old Windsor SL4 2JL
t 01784 432891
w nationaltrust.org.uk/runnymede
e runnymede@nationaltrust.org.uk

167 Arundel

Amberley Working Museum

3 hrs+   Mar–Nov

Amberley is a 36-acre open air museum set in the South Downs. With its historic buildings, working exhibits and demonstrations the museum aims to show how science, technology and industry have affected people's lives.

* Variety of crafts demonstrated daily
* Trips on vintage bus and narrow gauge railway

Location
Off B2139 between Arundel & Storrington

Opening
Mar–Nov Wed–Sun 10am–5.30pm
Open daily in school time & Bank Hols

Admission
Adult £7.50, Child £4.30, Concs £6.50

Contact
Amberley, Arundel,
West Sussex BN18 9LT

t 01798 831370
w amberleymuseum.co.uk
e office@amberleymuseum.co.uk

168 Arundel

Arundel Museum & Heritage Centre

1 hr   Easter–Sep

Arundel Museum and Heritage Centre interprets the rich life and history of Arundel through models, photographs and displays. It is housed in a Grade II listed building, and the museum illustrates Arundel's development as a great south coast port and trading centre.

* 9 display areas
* Themed talks and activities for all age groups

Location
Centre of Arundel

Opening
Easter–Sep
Mon–Sat 10.30am–4.30pm
Sun 10.30am–2.30pm

Admission
Phone for details

Contact
61 High Street, Arundel BN18 9AJ

t 01903 882456/882456
w sussexmuseums.co.uk/arundel

169 Arundel

Denmans Garden

2 hrs+   Mar–Oct

An interesting late C20 garden cultivated to create a 'tamed wilderness'. Great use is made of contrasts in form and foliage, and gravel is widely used as a growing medium to create a very relaxed effect. The herb garden, roses and climbers give inspiration to visiting gardeners.

* Large greenhouse provides shelter to tender plants
* Natural looking lake is home to moorhens

Location
Off the A27 W between Chichester and Arundel, adjacent to Fontwell Racecourse.

Opening
Daily Mar 1–Oct 31 9am–5pm

Admission
Adult £3.50, Child £1.95, Concs £3

Contact
Denmans Garden,
Fontwell, Arundel BN18 0SU

t 01243 542808
w denmans-garden.co.uk
e denmans@denmans-garden.co.uk

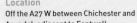

170 Arundel

WWT Arundel

2 hrs+   All year

Surrounded by ancient woodland and overlooked by the town's historic castle, the wetlands at Arundel are home to many rare species of wetland wildlife. Many of the thousands of birds you will see are tame enough to eat from your hand.

* Many rare birds regularly sighted
*Eye of the Wind wildlife art gallery

Location
Close to A27 & A29 follow brown duck signs on approaching Arundel

Opening
Daily 9.30–5.30pm (4–30pm in winter)
Closed Dec 25

Admission
Adult £5.75, Child £3.50, Concs £4.75

Contact
Mill Road, Arundel BN18 9PB
t   01903 883355
w wwt.org.uk/visit/arundel
e   enquiries@wwt.org.uk

171 Arundel

Arundel Castle

1 hr+   Apr–Oct

Originally built in the C11 by the Earl of Arundel, this centre has 1,000 years of fascinating history. there are fabulous displays of furniture, artefacts and paintings by Gainsborough, Reynolds and Van Dyck. The original motte, constructed in 1068, is over 100 feet (30m) high.

* Situated in magnificent grounds overlooking River Arun
* Seat of the Dukes of Norfolk for over 850 years

Location
At Arundel on A27

Opening
Apr–Oct, Sun–Fri 12 noon–5pm
Closed Sat & Good Friday

Admission
Phone for details

Contact
Arundel BN18 9AB
t   01903 883136
w arundelcastle.org
e   info@arundelcastle.org

172 Ashington

Holly Gate Cactus Garden

1 hr+   All year

This fascinating garden houses a world-renowned collection of over 30,000 exotic plants. Rare plants from the more arid areas of the world such as USA, Mexico, South America and Africa are represented, as well as cacti from the Central and South American jungles.

* 10,000² ft of glasshouses
* Many plants in flower throughout the year

Location
Off A24 between Horsham & Worthing

Opening
Daily 9am–5pm (4pm Nov–Jan)

Admission
Adults £2, Concs £1.50, Child £1.50

Contact
Billingshurst Road,
Ashington RH20 3BB
t   01903 892930
w hollygatecactus.co.uk
e   info@hollygatecactus.co.uk

West Sussex

173 Chichester

Chichester Cathedral

½ hr+   All year

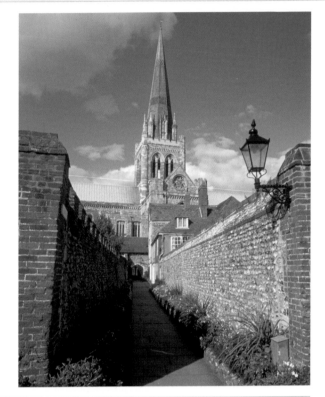

For 900 years Chichester Cathedral has been a landmark from land and sea. Famous for its modern art, it boasts a stunning Chagall window. Its more ancient treasures include the 'Arundel Tomb' which inspired Philip Larkin's poem.

* C12 sculpture depicting Lazarus
* New commisioned icon of St. Richard

Location
City centre

Opening
Daily, subject to services

Admission
Free, donations requested

Contact
The Royal Chantry, Cathedral Cloisters, Chichester PO19 1PX

t 01243 782595
w chichestercathedral.org.uk
e reception@chichestercathedral.org.uk

174 Chichester

Goodwood House

2 hrs   Easter–Oct

Goodwood House is home to one of the most significant private art collections in the country. The state apartments have been richly refurbished to their original Regency elegance and there is an Egyptian state dining room and magnificent ballroom.

* Curator of the collection is author Rosemary Baird
* Fine art collection includes Reynolds, Stubbs and Canaletto

Location
3 miles NE of Chichester of A27

Opening
Mar–Oct, Sun & Mon 1pm–5pm
Aug 3–30, Sun–Thu 1pm–5pm

Admission
Adult £7, Child £3, Concs £6

Contact
Goodwood, Chichester PO18 0PX

t 01243 755 048
w goodwood.co.uk
e housevisiting@goodwood.co.uk

175 Chichester

Fishbourne Roman Palace & Gardens

 2 hrs+   All year

This late C1 palace, discovered in 1960, is the largest Roman residence found to date in Britain. Its treasures include the country's finest collection of Roman mosaic floor, hypocausts etc. *in-situ*. Finds are displayed, while an audio-visual presentation brings the site to life.

* The remains of over 20 mosaics are on display
* Roman garden has been replanted to its original plan

Location
N of A259 off A27 1½ mile W of Chichester

Opening
Feb 1–Dec 15, daily open 10am
Phone for closing times
Dec 16–Jan 31, Sat–Sun only 10–4pm

Admission
Adult £5.20, Child £2.70, Concs £4.50

Contact
Salthill Road, Fishbourne, Chichester PO19 3QR

t 01243 785859
w sussexpast.co.uk
e adminfish@sussexpast.co.uk

176 Chichester

Military Aviation Museum

  (1 hrs+) (Feb–Nov)

Established in 1982, the museum tells the story of military flying from the earliest days, with emphasis on the RAF at Tangmere, and the air war over southern England from 1939–1945. Displays include the world speed record-breaking Meteor and Hunter.

* Opportunity to 'fly' fighter simulator
* Direct bus service from Chichester to museum, no.55

Location
3 miles E of Chichester off A27

Opening
Feb–Nov daily 10am–4.30pm
Mar–Oct daily 10am–5.30pm

Admission
Phone for details

Contact
Military Aviation Museum,
Tangmere, Chichester PO20 6ES

t 01243 775 223
w tangmere-museum.org.uk
e admin@tangmere-museum.org.uk

177 Chichester

Royal Military Police Museum

  (½ hr+) (Feb–Nov)

The museum displays the world-wide activities of military police from Tudor times to the present day, documenting this unique history in a vibrant display. The focus is on artefacts from 1800s Britain to the Gulf and recent Balkan conflicts.

* Armoured reconnaissance vehicle
* Display of weapons used in crimes

Location
Off A286 Chichester–Midhurst Road

Opening
Summer Apr–Sept, Tue–Fri 10am–12.30
/1.30–4.30pm, Sat & Sun 2pm–5pm
Winter Tue–Fri. Closed Dec & Jan

Admission
Free, donations appreciated
Group visits by appointment only

Contact
Broyl Road, Roussillon Barracks
Chichester PO19 6BL

t 01243 534225

178 Chichester

Weald & Downland Open Air Museum

   (3 hrs+) (All Year)

This museum set in 50 acres of beautiful Sussex countryside offfers a chance to wander through a fascinating collection of nearly 50 historic buildings dating from the C13 to the C19. Many with period gardens and farm animals. There are also woodland walks and a picturesque lake.

* The leading museum of historic buildings in England
* See food being prepared in the working Tudor kitchen

Location
Situated 7 miles N of Chichester
on the A286

Opening
Mar–Oct 10.30am to 6pm
Nov– Feb Sat & Sun only
10.30am–4pm

Admission
Adult £7, Child £4, Concs £6.50,
Family £19

Contact
Singleton, Chichester PO18 0EU

t 01243 811363 / 811348
w wealddown.co.uk
e office@wealddown.co.uk

179 Chichester

West Dean Gardens

2 hrs+   Mar–Oct

These Edwardian gardens include 35 acres of ornamental grounds, a 100-yard pergola and herbaceous borders. A 2-mile park walk, walled kitchen and fruit gardens, 16 restored greeenhouses and a 45-acre arboretum are additional features of this restored garden.

* Christie's Garden of the Year 2002
* English Tourism Council 'Quality Assured Attraction'

Location	Contact
6 miles N of Chichester off A286	West Dean, Chichester PO18 0QZ
Opening	t 01243 818210
Mar–Oct 11am–5pm (last entry	w westdean.org.uk
4.30pm), May–Sep 10.30am–5pm	e info@westdean.org.uk
Admission	
Phone for details	

180 East Grinstead

Hammerwood Park

1 hr+   Jun–Sep

An C18 neo-classical house set in a wooded valley. Original designs by Benjamin Latrobe who used ideas developed here when designing the porticos of the White House in Washington. Restoration began in 1982 after years of decay. Dining room left derelict to show work required.

* Private house: refreshments with tours only
* Owned by Led Zepplin in the 1970s

Location	Contact
3½ miles E of East Grinstead off A264	East Grinstead RH19 3QE
Opening	t 01342 850594
Jun 1–Sep end, 2pm–5.30pm	w latrobe@mistral.co.uk
Sat, Wed and Bank Hols	e mistral.co.uk/hammerwood
Admission	
Adult £5, Child £1.50	

181 East Grinstead

Standen

1 hr+   Mar–Nov

Standen shows off pure Victorian style under the influence of the Arts and Crafts movement, and is extensively decorated with William Morris carpets, fabrics and wallpaper. Externally finished in different ways including pebble dash, weatherboards and brick.

* 12-acre garden with fine views over the countryside
* Custom made furniture from Heals and Morris

Location	Contact
2 miles S of East Grinstead off B2110	West Hoathly Road,
	East Grinstead RH19 4NE
House Mar 27–Oct 31, 11am–5pm	t 01342 323029
Garden Mar 27–Oct 31, 11am–6pm, Nov	w nationaltrust.org.uk/standen
5–Dec 19, Fri, Sat & Sun 11am–3pm	e standen@nationaltrust.org.uk
Admission	
Adult £6, Child £3	

182 Handcross

High Beeches – Woodland & Water Garden

1.5 hrs+   Mar–Oct

An exceptionally well-preserved example of a landscaped woodland garden, dating from the early C20. The gardens are listed a Grade II by English Heritage. They cover 20 acres and contain varied and extensive plant collections in a beautiful, natural landscape setting.

* Especially colourful in spring and autumn
* Natural wildflower meadow

Location	Admission
A281 S of Crawley and E of Horsham.	Adult £5, Child free
½ mile E of A23	
Opening	**Contact**
Mar 1–Jun 30 & Sep 1–Oct 31	Handcross RH17 6HQ
1–5pm. Not Wed.	t 01444 400589
Jul–Aug every day except Wed & Sat	w highbeeches.com
	e office@highbeeches.com

183 Haywards Heath

Borde Hill Gardens

1 hrs+   All year

Borde Hill is set in 200 acres of traditional country estate. The garden was established from 1,900 plants gathered from the Himalayas, China, Burma and Tasmania. Today Borde Hill has one of the most comprehensive collections of trees and shrubs in England.

* Magnificent rhododendrons, azaleas and camellias
* Britain's largest private collection of 'champion' trees

Location
1½ miles N of Haywards Heath

Opening
All year, daily 10am–dusk

Admission
Summer Adult £5.50, Child £3.50, Concs £5
Winter £3.50, £3, £3.50

Contact
Balcombe Road,
Haywards Heath RH16 1XP

t 01444 450326
w bordehill.co.uk
e info@bordehill.co.uk

184 Haywards Heath

Nymans Gardens

2 hrs   All year

Nymans is one of the great gardens of the Sussex Weald and is internationally famous for its collection of rare plants. Created by three generations of the Messel family over a period of over a hundred years, Nymans was one of the first gardens to come to the National Trust (1953).

* Huge replanting programme followed 1987 storm
* Garden has individually characterised sections

Location
On B2114 at Handcross, 4½ miles S of Crawley, just off M23/A23

Opening
Garden Feb 18–Oct 31, Wed–Sun 11am–6pm, Nov 6–Feb 20 Sat & Sun, 11am–4pm
House Mar 24–Oct 31, 11am–5pm

Admission
Adults £6.20, Child £3.10

Contact
Nymans Gardens, Handcross, nr Haywards Heath RH17 6EB

t 01444 400321
w nationaltrust.org.uk/nymans
e nymans@nationaltrust.org.uk

185 Horsham

Leonardslee Lakes & Gardens

3 hrs+   Apr–Oct

A woodland garden set in a 240-acre valley with seven lakes. Leonardslee has many features including a rock garden and Alpine House, as well as deer and wallabies roaming in the parkland. It also houses a collection of Victorian motor cars (1889–1900).

* Gold medal winning bonsai & 400 species of alpines
* 'Behind the dollshouse' exhibition ¹/₁₂th scale

Location
On the junction on A281 & B2100 in Lower Beeding

Opening
Apr 1–Oct 31, daily 9.30am–6pm

Admission
Apr, Jun–Oct £6, May Mon–Fri £7, Sat & Sun & Bank Hols £8.
Child £4 at all times

Contact
Lower Beeding, Horsham RH13 6PP

t 01403 891212
w leonardslee.com
e gardens@leonardslee.com

186 Petersfield

Uppark

2 hrs+   Mar–Oct

A late C17 house set high on the South Downs with magnificent sweeping views to the sea. It was rescued from a fire 1989 and the restored Georgian interior houses a famous Grand Tour collection that includes paintings, furniture and ceramics.

* H.G.Wells' mother was a housekeeper
* A C18 dollshouse is a star of the collection

Location
5 miles SE of Petersfield off B2146

Opening
House Mar 28–Oct 28, 1–5pm, Thu–Sun
Grounds 11am–5.30pm

Admission
Adult £5.50, Child £2.75

Contact
South Harting, Petersfield GU31 5QR

t 01730 825415
w nationaltrust.org.uk/uppark
e uppark@nationaltrust.org.uk

187 Petworth

Petworth House & Park

3 hrs+   Easter–Oct

A magnificent late C17 mansion set in a park landscaped by Capability Brown and immortalised in Turner's paintings. The house contains the National Trust's finest and largest collection of pictures, with numerous works by Turner, Van Dyck, Reynolds and Blake.

* Ancient and neo-classical sculpture
* Fine furniture and carvings by Grinling Gibbons

Location
5½ miles E of Midhurst on A272

Opening
Mar 27–Oct 31, Mon–Wed, Sat & Sun 11am–5.30pm. Park open all year

Admission
Adult £7, Child £4

Contact
Petworth GU28 0AE

t 01798 342 207
w nationaltrust.org.uk/petworth
e petworth@nationaltrust.org.uk

188 Pulborough

Parham House & Gardens

2 hrs+   Easter–Oct

In the Middle Ages Parnham House was owned by Westminster Abbey. In 1601 it was sold to Thomas Bysshop and it remained in the family until the C20. Bought in 1922 by Clive Pearson, who purchased many of the paintings, and added his own collections of objets d'art and English furniture.

* Award-winning 4 acre walled garden
* Idyllically sited in heart of an ancient deer park

Location
Off A283 Pulborough–Storrington road

Opening
East Sun–Sep, 12 noon–6pm, Wed, Thu, Sun & Bank Hol Mons (also Tue & Fri in Aug). House 2–6pm

Admission
House & Gardens Adult £6.25,

Child £2.50, Concs £5.50
Gardens only £4.50, £1

Contact
Parham Park,
nr Pulborough RH20 4HS

t 01903 742021
w parhaminsussex.co.uk
e enquiries@parhaminsussex.co.uk

Fisherman's Cove, Cornwall

The South West

Bristol Cornwall Devon Dorset
Gloucestershire Somerset Wiltshire

189 Brislington

Bristol Blue Glass

1 hr   All year

Glassblowing in Bristol was fully established by the mid-C17 when the city was fêted as a centre of excellence for glassmaking and porcelain. See freeblown, handmade glass and watch glassblowing demonstrations from the public viewing gallery.

* Glass available to puchase in giftshop

Location
From M32 junction 3 onto A4, follow signs

Opening
Mon–Sat 9am–5pm
Sun 11am–5pm (closed Sun in Jan)

Admission
Free

Contact
Unit 7, Whitby Road,
Brislington, Bristol BS4 3QF

t 0117 972 0818
w bristol-glass.co.uk
e info@bristol-glass.co.uk

190 City Centre

@Bristol

1 day   All year

This is a unique destination bringing science, nature and art to life. It is a place of discovery and home to three attractions: Wildwalk: a living rainforest in the heart of the city, Explore: a C21 science centre, and a giant IMAX® theatre with digital surround sound.

* Tropical forest with free flying birds & butterflies
* Imaginarium – Bristol's very own planetarium

Location
Off Anchor Road in central Bristol

Opening
Daily 10am–6pm. Closed Dec 25

Admission
Explore
Adult £7.50, Child £4.95, Concs £5.95
Wildwalk & IMAX® £6.50,£4.50,£5.50

Contact
Harbourside, Bristol BS1 5DB

t 0845 345 1235
w at-bristol.org.uk
e information@at-bristol.org.uk

191 City Centre

Bristol Cathedral

1 hr   Daily

This fascinating building is a centre for Bristol's history, civic life and culture. Founded as an abbey in 1140, it became a cathedral in 1542 and developed architecturally through the ages. It is one of the finest examples of a 'hall church' anywhere in the world.

* Fine examples of Saxon stone carvings
* Expressionist window designed by Keith New in 1965

Location
Central Bristol on College Green

Opening
Daily 8am–6pm

Admission
Donation appreciated, £2 per person

Contact
College Green, Bristol BS1 5TJ

t 0117 926 4879
w bristol–cathedral.co.uk
e reception@bristol–cathedral.co.uk

192 City Centre

Bristol Ferry Boat Company

1 hr   Daily

Enjoy the exciting world of Bristol's Historic Harbour – for a round trip tour or just by visiting one of the many attractions. The journey takes in the Pump House, Millennium Square and the SS *Great Britain*.

* River trips and pub ferry can be arranged
* Unique view of Bristol past and present

Location
Catch the ferry in Hotwells or Temple Meads

Opening
Daily, phone for details of timetable

Admission
Multistop Ticket:
Adult £5, Child £2.50, Concs £3

Contact
M V *Tempora*, Welsh Back, Bristol BS1 4SP

t 0117 9273 416
w bristolferryboat.co.uk
e enquiries@bristolferryboat.co.uk

193 City Centre

The British Empire & Commonwealth Museum

2½ hrs+   Daily

This award–winning national museum presents the dramatic 500-year history of the rise and fall of Britain's overseas empire. Located in Isambard Kingdom Brunel's historic old Bristol station at Temple Meads.

* Sixteen permanent and interactive galleries
* Special half-term and holiday activities for families

Location
Located right next to Temple Meads, Bristol's main railway station

Opening
Daily 10am–5pm. Closed Dec 25/26. Phone for dates and times of events

Admission
Adult £5.95, Child £3.95, Concs £4.95

Contact
Station Approach, Temple Meads Bristol BS1 6QH

t 0117 925 4980
w empiremuseum.co.uk
e admin@empiremuseum.co.uk

194 City Centre

City Museum & Art Gallery

2 hrs+   All year

Bristol's major museum and art gallery houses an outstanding and diverse range of objects, from sea dinosaurs to magnificent art. It is one of the few museums to have been awarded Designated status by the government – the mark of an outstanding museum.

* World Wildlife Gallery
* Egyptology gallery

   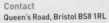

Location
In Clifton, follow brown signs from town centre

Opening
Daily 10am–5pm Closed Dec 25/26

Admission
Free

Contact
Queen's Road, Bristol BS8 1RL

t 0117 922 3571
w bristol–city.gov.uk/museums
e general_museum@
   bristol–city.gov.uk

---

195 City Centre

CREATE Centre

1 hr   All year

The CREATE centre is a showcase of environmental excellence. Bristol's environmental centre provides knowledge and info for environmental initiatives. Visit the Ecohome, a green home of the future, and learn about the challenge of waste in the recycling exhibition.

* A hands-on journey through waste and recycling
* Themed events throughout the year

Location
Cumberland Basin lies at the far end of the docks. CREATE is in a red brick warehouse

Opening
Mon–Fri 9am–5pm Closed Dec 25

Admission
Free

Contact
Smeaton Road, Bristol BS1 6XN

t 0117 925 0505
w createcentre.co.uk
e create@bristol–city.gov.uk

196 City Centre

The Georgian House

1½ hrs   Apr–Oct

This lovely house is an example of Bristol's C18 heritage, illustrating how the city profited from being one of England's premier trading ports. Originally home to John Pinney, a West India merchant, the house is displayed as it might have looked in its heyday.

* Home to the slave Pero
* Displays illustrate life both above and below stairs

Location
Just off Park Street, near the Cabot Tower

Opening
Apr 1– Oct 30, Sat–Wed, 10am–5pm

Admission
Free

Contact
7 Great George Street, Bristol BS1 5RR

t 0117 921 1362
w bristol–city.gov.uk
e general_museum@
    bristol–city.gov.uk

197 City Centre

University Botanic Garden

1½ hrs   All year

This garden cultivates some 4,500 plant species from over 200 plant families within its 5 acre site. This diversity of plants is unique and not found elsewhere in Bristol. Special collections include rare native and threatened plants of the South West.

* Chinese medicinal herb garden
* South African and New Zealand collections

Location
Turning off A369 Bristol to Portishead road, 50 yards from Clifton Suspension Bridge

Opening
Mon–Fri 9am–5pm (closed Bank Hols)

Admission
Free

Contact
Bracken Hill, North Road, Leigh Woods, Bristol, BS8 3PF

t 0117 973 3682
w bris.ac.uk/depts/botanicgardens

198 City Centre

SS *Great Britain*

3 hrs   Daily

The world's first great ocean liner, the SS *Great Britain*, is a unique surviving engineering masterpiece from Victorian times. Docked in the original Great Western Dock, this grand passenger liner has been the forerunner of all modern cruise ships.

* Designed by Isambard Kingdom Brunel
* The largest ship of her day

Location
Follow anchor signs within Bristol Historic Dockyard

Opening
Apr–Oct daily 10–5.30pm, Nov–Mar 10–4.30pm. Closed Dec 24/25

Admission
Adult £6.25, Child £3.75, Concs £5.25

Contact
Great Western Dockyard, Gas Ferry Road, Bristol BS1 6TY

t 0117 926 0680
w ss–great–britain.com
e enquiries@ss–great–britain.com

Bristol

Cornwall

Horseworld

2 hrs+   All year

This is a registered equine welfare charity. Located in beautiful listed Mendip stone farm buildings, dating back to the early C19, meet over 40 of the 300 rescued horses, ponies and donkeys. From Shetland ponies to Shire horses, each has a different story to tell.

* Twice daily presentations
* Museum of the Horse and giftshop

Location
Take A37 from Bristol. Through Whitchurch – Horseworld is on right

Opening
Mar–Sep 10–5pm,Oct–Feb 10–4pm. Closed Mon from 29 Sep–1 Jan

Admission
Adult £4.50, Child £3, Concs £3

Contact
Staunton Manor Farm, Staunton Lane, Whitchurch, Bristol BS14 0QJ

t 01275 540173
w horseworld.org.uk
e visitorcentre@horseworld.org.uk

Lanhydrock House

3 hrs+   Apr–Oct

Largely rebuilt in 1881 after a fire, this fascinating C19 home captures the atmosphere and trappings of a high Victorian country house. 'Below stairs' has a huge kitchen as well as a larder, dairy and bakehouse. The garden , colourful throughout the year, is set in 900 acresof parkland on the River Fowey.

* Great views across the River Fowey
* Magnificent gallery with moulded plaster ceiling

Location
2 miles E of Bodmin, follow signs off either A30 or A38

Opening
Apr–Oct, Tue–Sun & Bank Hols Mon 11am–5.30pm (5pm in Oct)

Admission
House Adult £7.50, Child £3.75

Garden £4.10, £2.10

Contact
Lanhydrock, Bodmin PL30 5AD

t 01208 265950
w nationaltrust.org.uk
e lanhydrock@nationaltrust.org.uk

Military Museum Bodmin

1 hr   Daily

Over 200 years of regimental history is on display at the Duke of Cornwall Light Infantry Museum. The former barracks now houses the regimental museum with uniforms, pictures and medals including one of the country's finest small arms collections.

* General George Washington's bible captured 1777
* Events from the capture of Gibraltar in 1704 to Second World War

Location
Centre of Bodmin

Opening
Mon–Fri, 9am–5pm (+ Sun in Jul–Aug)

Admission
Adult £2.50, Child 50p

Contact
The Keep, Victoria Barracks, Bodmin PL31 1EG

t 01208 72810
w bodmin.gov.uk/things/town.htm
e dclimus@talk21.com

202 Bodmin

Pencarrow

3 hrs   Apr–Oct

Pencarrow houses a superb collection of pictures, furniture, porcelain and antique dolls. The house sits in 50 acres of gardens and woodland with a lake, an ice house and a Victorian rockery. There are marked walks through the woodland and gardens.

* Sir Arthur Sullivan composed the music to *Iolanthe*
* Fine plaster ceiling in music room

Location
Follow signs off A389, 4 miles NW of Bodmin

Opening
House, Restaurant, Shop Apr–Oct
Sun–Thu 11am–5pm
Gardens daily 9am–6pm

Admission
House & Gardens Adult £7, Child £3.50
Gardens Adult £3.50, Child free

Contact
Bodmin PL30 3AG

t 01208 841369
w pencarrow.co.uk
e pencarrow@aol.com

---

203 Bolventor

Colliford Lake Park

3 hrs   Daily

Acres of indoor and outdoor adventure and fun with a 'Beast of Bodmin Moor' theme. Colliford Lake Park is a farm–based attraction with 8 acres of woodland and 30 acres of farm stock with sheep, goats, red deer and other animals.

* Extensive indoor and outdoor play areas
* Nature trails around Colliford Lake

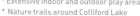   

Location
500 yards off A30 between Launceston & Bodmin

Opening
Easter–End of Oct 10.30am–5pm

Admission
Adult £5, Child £4, Concs £4

Contact
Bolventor, Bodmin Moor P114 6PZ

t 01208 821469
w collifordlakepark.com
e info@collifordlakepark.com

---

204 Camelford

British Cycling Museum

1½ hrs   Daily

Excellent display of cycling history from 1818 to the present day. Over 400 machines on display and large exhibition of cycling memorabilia including the first cycle oil lamps as well as candle lamps. Large display of cycling medals, fobs and badges.

* Extensive library of cycling books
* Gallery of cycling pictures

Location
1 mile N of Camelford on B3266

Opening
Sun–Thu 10am–5pm

Admission
Adult £2.90, Child £1.70

Contact
The Old Station, Camelford PL32 9TZ

t 01840 212811
w chycor.co.uk/britishcycling-museum

205 Falmouth

Falmouth Art Gallery

  ½ hr   All year

Situated above the library on the upper floor of the municipal building, the town's art collection is one of the most important in Cornwall. It features work by several major British artists including: Dame Laura Knight, Sir Alfred Munnings and John William Waterhouse.

Location
Above the library

Opening
Mon–Sat 10am–5pm

Admission
Free

Contact
Municipal Building, The Moor,
Falmouth TR11 2RT

t 01326 313863
w falmouthartgallery.com
e info@falmouthartgallery.com

206 Falmouth

National Maritime Museum Cornwall

  2½ hrs   Daily

A diverse collection of approximately 140 small craft from Britain and overseas. It includes racing craft, working boats, fishing vessels and record breakers. Interactive displays to test your skills at navigation and understanding the weather.

* Cimb to the top of the tower for views over harbour
* Display of Cornish maritime heritage

Location
SE end of harbourside. Or follow signs from A39 for 'Park & Float'

Opening
Daily 10am–5pm Dec25/26,
and last 3 weeks of Jan

Admission
Adult £5.90, Child £3.90, Concs £3.90

Contact
Discovery Quay, Falmouth TR11 3QY

t 01326 313388
w nmmc.co.uk
e enquiries@nmmc.co.uk

207 Falmouth

Pendennis Castle

2 hrs   Daily

A Cornish fortress, ready for military action since C16. Pendennis and its sister, St Mawes Castle, face each other across the mouth of the River Fal. Constructed c. 1540, they are the Cornish end of a chain of castles built by Henry VIII along the south coast.

Location
Pendennis Head, 1 mile SE of Falmouth

Opening
Apr–Sep 10am–6pm
Oct 10am–5pm
Nov–Mar 10am–4pm
Closed Dec 24–26 & Jan 1

Admission
Adult £4.20, Child £2.10, Concs £3.20

Contact
Pendennis Head, Falmouth TR11 4LP

t 01326 316594
w english-heritage.org.uk

208 Goonhilly

Goonhilly Satellite Earth Station

2 hrs+   Daily

One of the most striking attractions in Cornwall, on the Lizard Peninsula. Goonhilly is able to transmit to every corner of the globe and simultaneously handles millions of international phone calls, emails, and TV broadcasts. Explore international communications in the visitor centre.

* Largest satellite station on Earth
* See yourself in space and move a satellite

Location
Follow B3293 Helston to St Keverne road

Opening
Daily opens 10am Closing times vary from 4pm–6pm. Phone for details
Closed Mon in Feb, Mar & Nov

Admission
Summer Adult £5, Child £3.50
Winter see website for prices

Contact
Goonhilly TR12 6LQ

t 0800 679593
w goonhilly.bt.com
e goonhilly.visitorscentre@bt.com

209 Godolphin Cross

Godolphin Estate & House

2 hrs   Daily

This historic landscape includes Godolphin Hill with its wonderful views over west Cornwall. The house has fine C16 and C17 English oak furniture and equine paintings including Wotton's painting of Godolphin Arabian – one of three ancestors to all British bloodstock.

*The estate has over 400 archaeological features
* House dates from C15

Location
Follow signs from B3302 from Sithney Common

Opening
Estate daily
House Apr–Sep

Admission
Estate Free
House Adult £6.00, Child £2.00

Contact
Godolphin Cross TR13 9RE

t 01736 763194
w nationaltrust.org.uk
e godolphin@nationaltrust.org.uk

---

211 Helston

Poldark Mine & Heritage Complex

3½ hrs   Easter–Nov

This Cornish tin mine has several underground routes with tunnels and stairs. Believed to be Europe's most complete mine workings that are open to the public. Also some machines and waterpumping engines are on display around the garden.

* Entry to the site itself is free
* Family entertainment attractions in addition to mine

Location
2 miles from Helston on B3297

Opening
Easter–Nov 1 10am–6pm
Closed Sat May–Jun & Sep–Nov

Admission
Underground tour Adult £5.95,
Child £3.75

Contact
Wendron, Helston TR13 0ER

t 01326 573173
w poldark-mine.co.uk
e info@poldark-mine.co.uk

---

210 Mawnan Smith

Trebah Gardens

3 hrs   Daily

This lovely wild sub–tropical ravine paradise winds through huge plantations of 100-year-old giant tree ferns, rhododendrons, magnolias, camellias, palms and 2 acres of massed hydrangeas to a private beach on the Helford River.

* Part of the 'Eden Trail'
* Unique collection of rare plants and trees

Location
Follow signs from junction of f A39 & A394

Opening
Daily 10.30am–5pm

Admission
Mar–Oct Adult £5, Child £3, Concs £4.50

Nov–Feb £2.50, £1.50, £2.25

Contact
Mawnan Smith TR11 5JZ

t 01326 250448
w trebah-garden.co.uk
e mail@trebah-garden.co.uk

212 Isles of Scilly

Isles of Scilly Museum

  1½ hrs Daily

Established following severe gales in the winter of 1962 which yielded up some remarkable Romano-British finds. The museum now houses an extremely diverse collection including material from wrecks, wild flowers (during summer) as well as the original Romano-British artefacts.

WC

Location
10 mins walk from Hugh Town harbour

Opening
Easter–Sep, 10am–4.30pm
Oct 1–Easter, 10am–12 noon

Admission
Adults £2, Child 50p, Concs £1

Contact
Church Street, St Mary's, Isles of Scilly TR21 0JT

t 01720 422337
w iosmuseum.org
e info@iosmuseum.org

213 Launceston

Launceston Castle

   1 hr Daily

Set on the high motte of a stronghold built soon after the Norman Conquest, this strategically important building controlled the river crossing in and out of Cornwall. As the venue for the county assizes and jail, the castle witnessed many trials and hangings.

* Built first as earthwork after Norman Conquest
* Administrative centre for the Earls of Cornwall

Location
Centre of Launceston

Opening
Apr–Oct, 10am–6pm, Oct till 5pm
Nov–Mar, Fri–Sun 10am–4pm

Admission
Adult £2.10, Child £1.10, Concs £1.60

Contact
Launceston PL15 7DR

t 01566 772365
w english-heritage.org.uk
e launceston.castle@english-heritage.org.uk

214 Marazion

St Michael's Mount

 Fine 2 hrs   Daily

This former Benedictine priory and castle is one of Britain's most visited properties. Linked to the mainland when the tide is out by a 500-yard causeway. Beautiful gardens contain many rare plants that are not often found growing out of doors in Britain.

* Once an important harbour and home to 300 people
* Castle is full of history including garrison and armoury

WC

Location
Off coast of Marazion on A394

Opening
Apr–Oct, Mon–Fri 10.30am–5.30pm & most weekends in season
Shops open all year

Admission
Adult £4.80, Child £2.40

Contact
Marazion TR17 0HT

t 01736 710507
w stmichaelsmount.co.uk
e godolphin@manor-office.co.uk

215 Newlyn

Newlyn Art Gallery

   1 hr   Daily

Initially established to exhibit the work of the Newlyn School, the gallery has developed into one of the South West's leading contemporary art organisations with a national and international reputation for its innovative exhibitions.

* The gallery has an active educational programme
* Newlyn Art Society still exhibits three times a year

WC

Location
1 mile out of Penzance

Opening
Mon–Sat, 10am–5pm

Admission
Free

Contact
New Road, Newlyn, Penzance TR18 5PZ

t 01736 363715
w newlynartgallery.co.uk
e mail@newlyngallery.co.uk

216   Padstow

Prideaux Place

2 hrs   May–Oct

Explore 40 acres of landscaped grounds with terraced walks, formal garden, temple, Roman antiquities and the C9 Cornish Cross. An ancient deer park overlooks the estuary of the River Camel. Also see the Elizabethan plastered ceiling in the Great Chamber.

* Treasures include the Prideaux porcelain collection
* Guided tours of house available

Location
Off B326, Padstow to Newquay road

Opening
Easter & Spring Bank Hols
May–Oct, Sun–Thurs 12.30–5pm

Admission
Adult £6, Child £2
Grounds: £2, £1

Contact
Padstow PL28 8RP

t 01841 532411
e office@prideauxplace.fsnet.co.uk

217   Penzance

Geevor Tin Mine

2 hrs   Daily

The last working mine in West Penwith and now a mining museum and the largest preserved mining site in the UK extending a mile inland. Some areas of the mine are 200 years old. A museum provides insight into the history of this traditional Cornish industry.

* Expert guides conduct underground tours
* Display of original mining machinery

Location
On B3306, St Ives to Lands End road

Opening
Apr–Oct, 10am–5pm
Nov–Mar, 10am–4pm (closed Sat)

Admission
Adult £6.50, Child £4, Concs £6

Contact
Pendeen, Penzance TR19 7EW

t 01736 788662
w geevor.com
e pch@geevor.com

218   Porthcurno

Minack Theatre

2 hrs+   Daily

This has to be one of world's most spectacular theatres – an open-air auditorium carved into the cliffs high above Porthcurno's sandy cove. Founded and largely built by Rowena Cade in the 1930s, its remarkable story is now told in the visitor centre.

* Full programme of performances through summer
* Fantastic views from visitor centre

Location
3 miles from Lands End off A30

Opening
Apr–Sep, 9.30am–5.30
Oct–Mar, 10am–4pm

Admission
Adult £2.50, Child £1, Concs £1.80

Contact
Porthcurno, Penzance TR19 6JU

t 01736 810181
w minack.com
e info@minack.com

219   Porthcurno

Porthcurno Telegraph Museum

2 hrs   Jan–Nov

This award-winning industrial heritage museum explains the development of international telegraphy at the site of the first underground cables that linked Britain to the rest of the world (1870). It is housed in an underground station built for protection during the Second World War.

* Staff on hand to show how instruments work
* Adjacent to stunning Minack Theatre (see p??)

Location
3 miles from Lands End off A30

Opening
Jan–Mar, Sun–Mon, 10am–5pm
Apr–Jun, Sep–Nov, Sun–Fri
10am–5pm
Nov–Mar, 10am–5pm (Jul–Aug daily)

Admission
Adult £4, Child £2.50, Concs £3.50

Contact
Porthcurno, Penzance TR19 6JX

t 01736 810966
w porthcurno.org.uk
e mary.godwin@cw.com

220 St Austell

The Eden Project

Fine 4 hrs Daily

The Eden Project is dominated by two huge biomes – which are effectively the largest greenhouses in the world. The Humid Tropics Biome recreates the conditions and plant life of a lush rainforest while the Warm Temperate biome is Mediterranean in style.

* Project has 2 million visitors a year
* See coffee plants, palm trees and pineapples

Location
Follow signs from A390 at St Austell & A30 Bodmin bypass

Opening
Summer 9.30am–6pm
Winter 10am–4.30pm

Admission
Adult £10, Child £4, Concs £7.50

Contact
Bodelva, St Austell PL24 2SG

t 01726 811900
w edenproject.com
e info@edenproject.com

221 St Ives

Tate St Ives

2 hrs Daily

St Ives has been famous as an artist's colony since the early C20 and the opening of Tate St Ives in 1993 provides the opportunity to view modern art in the surroundings and atmospere which inspired them. The gallery also manages the Hepworth Museum and Sculpture Garden.

* Spectacular coastal setting
* Also visit Barbara Hepworth's home

Location
St Ives town centre

Opening
Mar–Oct, 10am–5.30pm
Nov–Feb, Tue–Sun 10am–4.30pm

Admission
Adult £4.25, Child free, Concs £2.50

Contact
Porthmeor Beach, St Ives TR26 1TG

t 01736 796226
w tate.org.uk/stives
e information@tate.org.uk

Tintagel Castle

1 hr   Daily

This is the legendary home of King Arthur and Merlin, and its spectacular setting with the crashing waves on three sides serves to add fuel to the story. The ruins that stand today are the remnants of a castle built by Earl Richard of Cornwall, brother of Henry III.

* Some of the best sea views in Cornwall
* Put your foot in 'Arthur's Footprint'

Location
½ mile track from village, no vehicles beyond village

Opening
Mar 24–Jul 14, 10am–5pm
Jul 15–Aug 27, 10am–7pm
Aug 28–Sep, 10am–6pm
Oct 10am–5pm,
Nov–Mar 10am–4pm

Admission
Adult £3.20, Child £1.60, Concs £2.40

Contact
Tintagel PL34 0HE

t 01840 770328
w english-heritage.
   org.uk/membership

Royal Cornwall Museum

2 hrs   Daily

A permanent display on the history of Cornwall from the Stone Age to the present day. Also contains a renowned collection of minerals, and ceramics, collections of ancient Egyptian, Greek, and Roman antiquities and a changing display of fine and decorative art.

* Diverse range of temporary exhibitions
* Exhibition of Cornish natural history

Location
Truro town centre

Opening
Mon–Sat, 10am–5pm. Closed Sun & Bank Hols

Admission
Adult £4.00, Child free, Concs £2.50

Contact
River Street, Truro TR1 2SJ

t 01872 272205
w royalcornwallmuseum.org.uk
e enquiries@royal-cornwall-muse
   um.freeserve.co.uk

Devon

224 Barnstaple

Arlington Court

3 hrs+ Apr–Oct

Arlington Court houses the treasures amassed during the travels of Miss Rosalie Chichester. These include model ships, tapestries, pewter and shells. The stable block contains a magnificent collection of horse-drawn vehicles which offer carriage rides around the grounds.

* 'Batcam' films bat colony from May to September
* Spectacular gardens and extensive parkland

Location
Follow signs off A39, 8 miles N of Barnstaple

Opening
House Apr–Oct 10.30am–5.30pm closed Sat
Garden Jun–Sep daily

Admission
Adult £6.20, Child £3

Contact
Arlington, Barnstaple EX31 4LP

t 01271 850296
w nationaltrust.org.uk
e arlingtoncourt@nationaltrust.org.uk

225 Barnstaple

Marwood Hill Gardens

Fine 2 hrs+ Easter–Oct

Marwood Hill Gardens covers 20 acres and has year round interest. Camellias and rhododendrons are planted on the walk along the north side of the walled garden, including three borders of herbaceous peonies. The Lower Garden has a series of small lakes.

* Bog garden houses a National Collection of Astilbes
* Walk between gardens pass plantings of bamboo

Location
4 miles N of Barnstaple

Opening
Daily dawn–dusk
Closed Dec 25

Admission
Adult £3 Child free

Contact
Barnstaple EX31 4EB

t 01271 342528
w marwoodhillgardens.co.uk
e malcolmpheroah@supernet.com

226 Beer

Pecorama Millennium Garden

3 hrs+ Easter–Oct

This unusual garden is one of a number of activities on this hillside site overlooking Beer. Stunning designs include a roof garden enclosed by a ruined tower, a moat garden, rainbow garden, sun and moon garden – all with appropriately colour plants and foliage.

* Miniature railway with steam and diesel locomotives
* Peco model railway exhibition

Location
Follow signs from Beer turning on A3052

Opening
Apr 5–Oct 30, Mon–Fri 10–5.30pm
Sat 10–1pm. Open Easter Sunday & Sun, May 30–Sep 5, 10–5.30pm

Admission
Prices vary, phone for details

Contact
Beer, nr Seaton EX12 3NA

t 01297 20580
w peco-uk.com
e pecorama@amserve.com

227 Bovey Tracey

Devon Guild of Craftsmen

2 hrs Easter–Oct

This is the South West's leading gallery and craft show-rooms with work selected from around 240 makers, many with national and international reputations. Riverside Mill, the Guild's showcase, features frequently changing exhibitions.

* Craft shop and popular cafe
* Riverside Mill dates from 1850

Location
Follow signs for Bovey Tracey, 2 miles from A38

Opening
Daily 10am–5.30. Closed winter Bank Hols

Admission
Free

Contact
Riverside Mill, Bovey Tracey TQ13 9AF

t 01626 832223
w crafts.org.uk
e devonguild@crafts.org.uk

228 Budleigh Salterton

Bicton Park Botanical Gardens

3 hrs+   Daily

Bicton has sweeping lawns, water features, English borders and a formal Italian garden that survived the Capability Brown period. Its palm house is one of the world's most beautiful garden buildings. The museum contains an enormous collection of rural memorabilia.

* Exhibition of traction engines, and vintage machinery
* Bicton Orchid is one of easiest to grow as a houseplant

Location	Contact
Off M5 at junction 30, follow signs via Newton Poppleford	East Budleigh, Budleigh Salterton EX9 7BJ
Opening	t 01395 568465
Summer: 10am–6pm	w bictongardens.co.uk
Winter: 10am–5pm. Closed Dec 25/26	e info@bictongardens.co.uk
Admission	
Adult £4.95, Child £3.95, Concs £3.95	

229 Buckfastleigh

Buckfast Butterfly Farm & Dartmoor Otter Sanctuary

2 hrs   Easter–Oct

This unusual attraction offers an educational experience for animal lovers. See free-flying moths and butterflies from around the world in the indoor tropical garden. Otters swim in large glass enclosures to ensure spectacular underwater views.

* Butterfly habitat constructed to maximise viewing
* British, Asian & North American otters on show

Location	Contact
Follow signs from A38 at A384 to Buckfastleigh	Buckfastleigh TQ11 0DZ
Opening	t 01364 642916
Good Friday–end Oct, 10am–5.30pm	w ottersandbutterflies.co.uk
	e info@ottersandbutterflies.co.uk
Admission	
Adult £4.95, Child £3.50, Concs £4.50	

230 Buckfastleigh

Buckfast Abbey

3 hrs+   Daily

Buckfast Abbey is the only English medieval monastery to have been restored after the Dissolution and used again for its original purpose. This active Benedictine community provides an insight into monastic life and remarkable church architecture in a peaceful setting.

* Impressive marble flooring
* Original building dates from 1018

Location	Contact
Off A38, follow signs on A384	Buckfastleigh TQ11 0EE
Opening	t 01364 645590
Summer 9am–5.30pm	w buckfast.org.uk
Winter 9am–5pm	e enquiries@buckfast.org.uk
Admission	
Free	

231 Cullompton

Coldharbour Mill & Working Wool Museum

4 hrs+   Feb–Dec

This 200-year-old waterside mill houses working spinning and weaving machines, and steam engines restored to their former glory. Coldharbour Mill is also home to the 'New World Tapestry' considered to be the longest in the world (267ft/81m).

* Guided tours available
* Steam engines can be seen running on Bank Holidays

Location	Contact
2 miles off junction 27 of M5. Follow signs to Willand and the museum	Uffculme, Cullompton EX15 3EE
Opening	t 01884 840960
Feb–Dec, 10.30am–5pm	w coldharbourmill.org.uk
	e info@coldharbourmill.org.uk
Admission	
Adult £5.50, Child £2.50	

232 Dartmouth

Dartmouth Castle

1 hr   Daily

Built by C14 merchants (led by mayor John Hawley) to protect themselves from invasion, this brilliantly positioned defensive castle juts out into the narrow entrance to the Dart Estuary. It is said that Hawley was the inspiration for Chaucer's Shipman in *The Canterbury Tales*.

* Hand-on exhibition brings 600 years of history to life
* Complete Victorian gun battery

Location
1 mile SE of Dartmouth on B3025

Opening
Apr–Oct 10am–6pm (Oct 5pm)
Nov–Mar Wed–Sun 10am–4pm

Admission
Adult £3.20, Concs £2.40, Child £1.60
Under 5s free

Contact
Castle Road Dartmouth TQ6 0JN

t 01803 833588
w english-heritage.org.uk
e Dartmouth@english-heritage.org.uk

233 Exeter

Exeter Cathedral

½ hr   Easter–Oct

This magnificent Gothic cathedral was largely rebuilt in the C13 though the imposing towers remain from the earlier Norman structure. The cathedral has played an important historical role through the ages, particularly in the C17.

* Elaborately carved choir stalls of particular note
* Visited by William the Conqueror

Location
Just off the High Street in the city centre

Opening
Daily. Guided tours Apr–Oct

Admission
Free, donations encouraged

Contact
The Cloisters, Exeter EX1 1HS

t 01392 214219/01392 2255573
w exeter-cathedral.org.uk
e admin@exeter-cathedral.org.uk

234 Exeter

Killerton House

2 hrs+   Easter–Oct

An elegant C18 house in a hillside garden. The house has many treasures including the famous Killerton costume collection. The garden features a Victorian rock garden and an interesting ice house. There are fine views across the Devon countryside from the lawns.

* Costume collection extends to over 9,000 items
* Costume display changes every year

Location
6 miles from Exeter off B3181

Opening
Mar 9–Sep 2, 11am–5pm (closed Tue)
Open daily in Aug

Admission
House & Garden
Adult £5.80, Child (5–16) £2.85

Contact
Broadclyst, Exeter EX5 3LE

t 01392 881345
w nationaltrust.org.uk
e killerton@smtp.ntrust.org.uk

235 Exeter

Powderham Castle

3 hrs+   Easter–Oct

Visit a succession of magnificent halls and state rooms filled with lavish furnishings, tapestries and historic portraits of the Courtenay family, whose home this has been for over 600 years. Powderham Castle is situated in beautiful parkland beside the Exe estuary.

* Fantastic grand staircase once part of Medieval Hall
* Rides around deer park

Location
8 miles from Exeter on A379 to Dawlish

Opening
Apr 4–Oct 1, Sun–Fri 10am–5.30pm

Admission
Adult £6.90, Child £3.90, Concs £6.40

Contact
Kenton, Exeter EX6 8JQ

t 01626 890243
w powderham.com
e caslte@powderham.co.uk

236 Great Torrington

Dartington Crystal

3 hrs+   Daily

Internationally known for handmade contemporary glassware. Discover the history of glass and of the company in the visitor centre while visitors to the factory can watch the craftsmen at work. The factory shop is thought to be the biggest glass shop in the world.

* See Dartington's innovative glass designs
* Have your hand or foot cast

   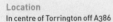

Location
In centre of Torrington off A386

Opening
Mon–Fri 9am–5pm, Sat 10am–5pm
Sun 10am–4pm. No factory tour at weekends. Check for Bank Hols

Admission
Prices vary, phone for details

Contact
Great Torrington EX38 7AN

t 01805 626242
w dartington.co.uk
e tours@dartington.co.uk

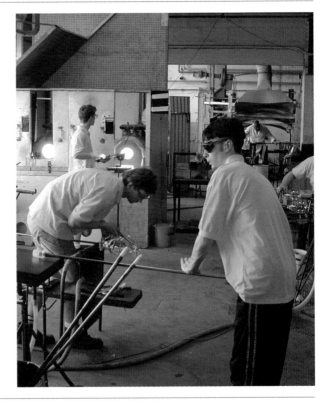

237 Great Torrington

RHS Garden Rosemoor

3 hrs+   Daily

RHS Garden Rosemoor has become a garden of national importance. To the huge range of plants collected by its former owner, the RHS has added features such as the formal garden, herbaceous borders, herb and cottage gardens. Also Mediterranean and winter gardens.

* Extensive rose garden is most popular feature
* Extensive stream and lakeside planting

Location
Junction 27 of M5, A361 to South Molton. Follow signs.

Opening
Daily except Christmas Day
Apr–Sep 10am–6pm
Oct–Mar 10am–5pm

Admission
Adult £5, Child (6-16) £1

Contact
Great Torrington EX38 8PH

t 01805 624067
w rhs.org.uk
e rosemooradmin@rhs.org.uk

238 Okehampton

Okehampton Castle

3 hrs+   Daily

The impressive ruins of this, the largest castle in Devon, stand on the banks of a river in the foothills of Dartmoor. The central keep is still impressive atop its motte, and there are excellent walks through the woodlands surrounding the castle.

* Free audio tape tour available
* Beautiful picnic grounds

Location
1 mile SW of town centre

Opening
Apr–Sep 10am–6pm, Oct–Mar 10am–5pm

Admission
Adult £2.50, Child £1.50, Concs £1.90

Contact
Catle Lodge, Okehampton EX20 1JB

t 01837 52844
w english-heritage.org.uk
e okehampton@english-heritage.org.uk

239 Newton Abbott

Tuckers Maltings

2 hrs+   Easter–Oct

Britain's only working malthouse open to the public, making malt from barley for beer. With its working Victorian machinery, Tuckers Maltings is an education for all ages with video and audio. See and taste real ale from the in-house brewery.

* Guided tours last one hour
* Speciality beer shop open all year

Location
3 mins walk from Newton Abbot railway station

Opening
Good Friday–Oct (closed Sun except Jul & Aug)

Admission
Adult £5.25, Child £3.25, Concs £4.75

Contact
Teign Road, Newton Abbott TQ12 4AA

t 01626 334734
w tuckersmaltings.com
e info@www.tuckersmaltings.com

240 Plymouth

Plymouth Dome

2 hrs   Daily

Over 400 years of Plymouth's great history is brought to life in this high-tech visitor centre. Walk through an Elizabethan street, find out about Drake, Cook and the *Mayflower*, operate a ship's radar and link up a satellite and study weather patterns.

* Walk the gun deck of a galleon
* See the devastation of the Blitz

Location
Follow signs from city centre for Hoe

Opening
Apr–Oct daily 10am–5pm
Nov–Mar Tues–Sat 10am–4pm

Admission
Adult £4.50, Child £3, Concs £3.50

Contact
The Hoe, Plymouth PL1 2NZ

t 01752 603300
w plymouthdome.com
e plymouthdome@plymouth.gov.uk

241 Plymouth

Royal Albert Memorial Museum

2 hrs   Daily

This outstanding collection of local and national importance ranges from local archaeological finds to natural history displays from around the world as well as works of art. The impact of geology on Devon and its people is explored in the 'Geology at Work Gallery'.

* Fascinating building to commemorate Prince Albert
* Display of clocks, watches and timekeeping

Location
Queen Street is just off High Street in city centre

Opening
Daily 10am–5pm. Closed Sun & Bank Hols

Admission
Free

Contact
Queen Street, Exeter EX4 3RX

t 01392 665858
w exeter.gov.uk
e ramm@exeter.gov.uk

242 South Molton

Quince Honey Farm

2 hrs+   Easter–Oct

In this world renowned honey farm you can stand and watch bees in complete safety. The unique design of the indoor apiary allows close-up viewing. The glass booths expose the working colonies without interfering with the bees' natural lifestyle.

* One of the largest honey farms in the country
* See the complete story of the production of honey

Location
From centre of South Molton on Barnstable Road

Opening
Easter–Sep 9am–6pm, Oct 9am–5pm

Admission
Adults £3.50, Child £2, Concs £2.60

Contact
South Molton EX36 3AZ

t 01769 572401
w quincehoney.co.uk
e info@quincehoney.co.uk

243 Tavistock

Morwellham Quay Museum

4 hrs+   Daily

Despite being 23 miles from the sea, Morwellham Quay was the Empire's greatest copper port in the time of Queen Victoria. Today the 1860s are recreated with a Tamar ketch moored at the quay, shops, cottages and costumed staff to act as guides.

* Take a tram underground to explore a coppermine
* Explore the farm, wildlife reserve and parkland

    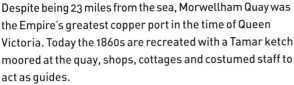

Location
4 miles from Tavistock on River Tamar

Opening
Easter–Oct 10am–5.30pm
Nov–Easter 10am–4.30pm

Admission
Summer Adult £6, Child £4.20,

Concs. £5.80
Winter £5, £3, £4

Contact
Morwellham, Tavistock PL19 8JL

t 01822 832766
w morwellham-quay.co.uk
e enquiries@morwellham-quay.co.uk

244 Tiverton

Tiverton Castle

1 hr   Easter–Sep

Built in the C12 as the home of the Earl of Devon, the building now exhibits aspects of architecture from medieval to modern. Visitors can climb to the roof for views of the town and surrounding hillside, try on some English Civil War armour, and stroll round the gardens.

Location
A361 to Tiverton and follow signs

Opening
Easter–late June + Sep, Sun & Thu & Bank Hols. July–Aug, Sun–Thu 2.30–5.30pm

Admission
Adults £4, Child (7–16) £2

Contact
Park Hill, Tiverton EX16 6RP

t 01884 253 200
w tivertoncastle.com
e tiverton.castle@ukf.net

245 Torquay

'Bygones'

  2 hrs+ **Daily**

This life-size Victorian street with shops and period rooms also features a giant model railway and railwayana collection, an interactive and illuminated children's fantasy land, a multi-sensory First World War trench with militaria collection and a real Anderson shelter.

* Housed in a former cinema
* Christmas is a winter wonderland in Victorian street

Location
Town centre, direction St Mary Church

Opening
Jul–Aug Mon–Thu 10am–9.30pm
Fri–Sun 10am–6pm,
Apr–May + Sep–Oct 10–6pm,
Nov–Feb 10am–4pm

Admission
Adults £4.50, Concs £3.95, Child £3

Contact
Fore Street, St Marychurch
Torquay TQ1 4PR

t 01803 326108
w bygones.co.uk
e info@bygones.co.uk

246 Torquay

Torquay Museum

  1 hr **Daily**

Devon's oldest museum (1845) holds an impressive collections of natural history – both local and from across the world. There are also displays of Torquay pottery, pictorial archives, the life of Agatha Christie and a model of an old Devon farmhouse.

* Regular temporary exhibitions and events programme
* Over 300,000 natural history specimens in store

Location
Near Torquay harbour, a short walk from the clocktower

Opening
Mon–Sat 10am–5pm
Sun (Easter–Oct) 1.30–5pm

Admission
Adult £3, Child £1.50, Concs £2

Contact
529 Babbacombe Road,
Torquay TQ1 1HG

t 01803 293975
w torquaymuseum.org
e info@torquaymuseum.org

247 Totnes

Berry Pomeroy Castle

  1 hr **Apr–Oct**

The Pomeroy family came from France with William the Conqueror and set up home on land bordering the Dart in 1267. The castle followed from that time. A mansion was added in the Elizabethan period but was damaged in the Civil War, the castle has been largely abandoned since.

* Stands on steep wooded hillside
* Rumoured to be the most haunted castle in Britain

Location
2 miles E of Totnes off A385

Opening
Apr–Sep daily 10am–6pm (Oct 5pm)

Admission
Adult £2.80, Child £1.40, Concs £2.10

Contact
Totnes TQ9 6NJ

t 01803 866618
w english-heritage.org.uk

248 Totnes

Totnes Castle

   1 hr Apr–Oct

Totnes Castle sits high on a hill above the town, commanding the approaches from three valleys. One of the best surviving examples of a Norman motte and bailey castle. The C11 wood structure was replaced by a stone keep in the C13 and C14.

* The keep has survived in excellent condition
* Keep surrounded by a curtain wall – now crumbling

Location
On a hill overlooking Totnes

Opening
Apr–Sep daily 10am–6pm
Oct 10am–5pm

Admission
Adult £1.80, Child 90p, Concs £1.40

Contact
Castle Street, Totnes TQ9 5NU

t 01803 864406
w english-heritage.org.uk

Devon | Dorset

249 Totnes

Woodlands Leisure Park

3 hrs+   Easter–Oct

Action rides to suit everyone from bravest down: watercoasters, rapid runs and a 500-metre toboggan run. There are 14 different play zones for the big kid in everyone. Five floors of indoor entertainment as well as animal centres, both indoors and out.

* UK's biggest indoor venture centre
* Falconry centre with flying displays

Location
On A3122 between Totnes
& Dartmouth

Opening
Mar 26–Oct, daily + school hols

Admission
Prices vary, phone for details

Contact
Blackawton, Totnes TQ9 7DQ

t 01803 712598
w woodlandspark.com
e fun@woodlandspark.com

250 Beaminster

Mapperton Gardens

Fine   1 hr+   Easter–Oct

These terraced valley gardens surround a delightful Tudor/Jacobean manor house, stable blocks, dovecote and All Saints Church. Used as location in Jane Austen's *Emma*, *Restoration* and *Tom Jones*. There is also a shop with plants, pots and gift items and a delightful cafe.

* Spring plant sale

Location
15 mins from Crewkerne via A303
to Beaminster on the B3163

Opening
Garden Mar 1–Oct 31, 2pm–6pm
House Weekdays, Jun 2–Jul 11,
May 26/ 25, 2–4.30pm

Admission
Prices vary, phone for details

Contact
Mapperton, Beaminster DT8 3NR

t 01308 862645
w mapperton.com
e office @mapperton.com

251 Yelverton

Buckland Abbey

3 hrs+   Easter–Oct

Originally a small but influential Cistercian monastery. The house, which incorporates the remains of the 13th-century abbey church, has rich associations with Sir Francis Drake and contains memorabilia from that time. Unusual herb garden and beautiful estate walks.

* Magnificent monastic barn
* Exhibition of Buckland's 700 year history

Location
11 miles N of Plymouth

Opening
Mar 27–Oct 31 daily 10.30–5.30pm
(closed Thu). Nov 1–Dec 19, Sat & Sun
2–5pm (closed Dec 25–mid Feb)
Feb 14–Mar 31, Sat & Sun 2–5pm

Admission
Adult £5.30, Child £2.60

Contact
Yelverton PL20 6EY

t 01822 853607
w nationaltrust.org.uk
e bucklandabbey@nationaltrust.
org.uk

252 Blandford

Hall & Woodhouse Brewery

1 hr   Easter–Oct

The brewery visitor centre tells the story of Hall & Woodhouse through the ages. Devise your own beer recipes, enjoy a virtual tour of the brewery, read the guide to beer tasting and view a personal collection of brewery artefacts and old advertising materials

* Fascinating insight into this 225-year-old brewery
* Beer can be bought at the brewery shop

Location
Follow signs from centre of Blandford

Opening
Visitor Centre: 10:30am– 5:30pm,
Mon-Sat. Brewery tours all year
round – phone to check times and
reserve a place

Admission
Free to visitor centre, tours charged

Contact
Blandford, St. Mary DT11 9LS

t 01258 452 141
w hall-woodhouse.co.uk
e enquiries@hall-woodhouse.co.uk

253 Bournemouth

Dorset Belle Cruises

Fine   1 hr+   Daily

Take a glorious coastal and harbour cruise on a number of routes linking Bournemouth, Swanage and Poole Quay as well as Brownsea Island and the Isle of Wight. Specialist cruises are also available along this stunning coastline.

* Jurassic Heritage Coastal Tours
* Fireworks and magnificent sunset cruises

Location
Boats depart from Bournemouth pier, Swanage or Poole

Opening
Seasonal timetable available, check website or phone for details

Admission
Prices vary, phone for details

Contact
Pier Approach,
Bournemouth BH2 5AA

t 01202 558550
w dorsetbelles.co.uk
e info@dorsetbelles.co.uk

254 Bournemouth

Oceanarium Bournemouth

2 hrs   Daily

A visit to the aquarium provides an encounter with marine life from across the globe. This is a fully interactive experience with feeding demos and talks, a walk-through underwater tunnel and exhibits to help you discover more about this fascinating underwater world.

* Gift shop and cafe open to the public

Location
Follow signs to Bournemouth beaches & piers

Opening
Daily 10am–5pm Closed Dec 25

Admission
Adult £6.25, Child £3.95
Concs £4.95/£3.95

Contact
Pier Approach,
Bournemouth BH2 5AA

t 01202 311993
w oceanarium.co.uk
e info@oceanarium.co.uk

255 Bovington

Tank Museum

3 hrs+   Daily

There are few places in the world where you can touch a Second World War tank. There are even fewer that have tanks that are in fully restored, running condition. Here are examples of tanks from both World Wars to the modern day, along with a good deal of post-war equipment.

* Indoor collection of 150 vechiles from 26 countries
* Vechile rides and live demonstrations

Location
Off the A352, between Dorchester & Wareham, near Wool. Follow signs from Bere Regis

Opening
Daily 10am–5pm (except Dec 25 & 26)

Admission
Prices vary, phone for details

Contact
Bovington BH20 6HG

t 01929 405096
w tankmuseum.co.uk
e info@tankmuseum.co.uk

256 Dorchester

Kingston Maurward Gardens

2 hrs+   Daily

Kingston Maurward Gardens are set deep in Hardy's Dorset and are listed on the English Heritage register of gardens. The 35 acres of classical C18 parkland and lawns sweep majestically down to the lake from the Georgian House.

* National Collections of penstemons and salvias
* Edwardian formal & walled demonstration gardens

Location
1 mile E of Dorchester off the A35

Opening
Daily Jan 5–Dec 19
10am–5.30pm or dusk if earlier.
Closed during Christmas break

Admission
Adult £4, Child £2.50

Contact
Dorchester DT2 8PY

t 01305 215003
w www.kmc.ac.uk
e administration@kmc.ac.uk

257 Dorchester

Dorset County Museum

1 hr+   Apr–Nov

Visit Dorset's main general museum. Sixteen display rooms exploring aspects of local history, literature, archaeology, fine art and natural science. Winner of the Best Museum of Social History category in the 1998 Museum of the Year awards.

* Interactive audio guide

Location
Town centre, follow museum signs

Opening
Nov–Apr, open 6 days 10am–5pm
May–Oct, daily 10am–5pm

Admission
Adults £3.90, Conc £2.60

Contact
High West Street,
Dorchester DT1 1XA

t 01305 262735
w dorsetcountymuseum.org
e nicky@dor-mus.demon.co.uk

---

258 Dorchester

The Dinosaur Museum

1 hr+   Daily

Dedicated to dinosaurs, this award-winning museum is a treat. Audio-visual displays portray the earth millions of years ago. One fascinating exhibit explores the question of what life would be like today if the dinosaurs had not become extinct.

* Winner of the Dorset 'Family Attraction' award
* Top 10 'Hands on Museum in Britain'

Location
Centre of Dorchester

Opening
Easter–Oct, 9.30am–5.30pm
Nov–Mar, 10am–4.30pm

Admission
Adults £5.50 Child £3.95

Contact
Icen Way, Dorchester DT1 1EW

t 01305 269880
w thedinosaurmuseum.com
e info@thedinosaurmuseum.com

259 Dorchester

The Keep Military Museum of Devon & Dorset

1 hr+   Daily

Learn stories of courage, tradition and sacrifice of those who served in the regiments of Devon and Dorset for over 300 years. Experience spectacular views from the battlements of Dorchester and surrounding countryside, brought to life by the novels of Thomas Hardy.

* Modern interactive and creative displays

Location
On A35 Bridport road on western edge of Dorchester

Opening
Apr-Sep Mon-Sat 9.30-5pm Sun (July & Aug) 10-4pm. Oct-Mar, Tues-Sat 9-5

Admission
Adult £3, Child £2, Concs £2

Contact
Bridport Road, Dorchester DT1 1RN
t 01305 264066
w keepmilitarymuseum.org
e keep.museum@talk21.com

260 Dorchester

Minterne Gardens

1 hr   Mar-Nov

The C18 gardens and woodlands were landscaped in the style of Capability Brown. A chain of small lakes, cascades and streams lead to woodland which in spring is ablaze with an important collection of Himalayan rhododendrons, azaleas and autumn coloured acers.

Location
On the A352 10 miles N of Dorchester, 2 miles out of Cern Abbas

Opening
Daily Mar 1-Nov 10, 10am-7pm

Admission
Adult £3.00, Child free

Contact
Minterne Magna, Dorchester DT2 7AU
t 01300 341370

261 Dorchester

The Tutankhamun Exhibition

1 hr   Daily

This exhibition recreates the original Tutankhamun artefacts found when the pharoah's tomb was reopened. The artefacts are displayed in a model of the tomb chamber as it looked in 1922 when local archaeologist Howard Carter unearthed it.

* A permanent exhibition of the World Heritage Organisation

Location
3 mins walk from Dorchester centre

Opening
Easter-Oct, 9.30am-5.30pm.
Nov-Easter, daily 9.30am-5pm.
Weekends open 10am,
Sun close 4.30pm

Admission
Adult £5.50, Child £3.95, Concs £4.75

Contact
High West Street,
Dorchester DT1 1UW
t 01305 269571
w tutankhamun-exhibition.co.uk
e info@tutankhamun-exhibition.co.uk

262 Dorchester

Maiden Castle

Fine   1 hr   Daily

Maiden Castle is the largest Iron Age hill fort in Europe, covering an area of 47 acres. 'Maiden' derives from the Celtic 'Mai Dun' meaning 'great hill'. It is an amazing place; even after more than 2,000 years, the earthworks are immense, some ramparts rising to 6 metres.

* Archeological finds from digs are in the Dorchester Museum
* Sheep grazed area

Location
Off the A354, 2 miles SW of Dorchester

Opening
Open all year at reasonable times

Admission
Free

Contact
English Heritage Customer Services,
PO Box 569, Swindon SN2 2YP
t 0870 333 1181
w english-heritage.org.uk/southwest

263 Lyme Regis

The Philpot Museum Lyme Regis

1 hr   Daily

Lyme's lively local history is well represented by
a rich collection of maritime and domestic objects,
and illustrated by paintings, prints and photographs.
The area is famed for fossils and the town's literary
connections, including Jane Austen and John Fowles.

* South West Museum of the Year Award 1999

Location
Centre of town, next to Guildhall

Opening
Apr–Oct, Mon–Sat 10am–5pm, Sun
11–5pm, Nov–Mar Sat & Sun only
(daily in school hols) closed Dec 24–26

Admission
Adult £2, Child free, Concs £1.50/free

Contact
Lyme Regis DT7 3QA

t 01297 443370
w lymeregismuseum.co.uk
e info@lymeregismuseum.co.uk

---

264 Poole

Brownsea Island National Trust

3 hrs+   Mar–Oct

Just a short boat trip from Poole or Bournemouth,
the charm of the landscape, the variety of wildlife and
an intriguing heritage make Brownsea a fascinating
place to visit. It offers magnificent views of the Purbeck
Hills and Studland Bay, with a study centre.

* Exhibition of island information and photographs
* Dorset Wildlife Trust Nature Reserve

Location
By boat from Poole, Bournemouth,
Swanage or Sandbanks

Opening
Mar 27–Oct 31, from 10am. Closing
time varies

Admission
Adult £3.70, Child £1.60

Contact
Poole Harbour BH13 7EE

t 01202 707744
w nationaltrust.org.uk/brownsea
e office@brownseaisland.fsnet.co.uk

265 Poole

Waterfront Museum

1 hr   Daily

Discover a wealth of intriguing items in the Waterfront Museum where 2,000 years of history about trading in Poole and the area is on view, housed in a fine 18th century warehouse adjoining the medieval town cellars with a historic street scene.

* Artifacts from Studland Bay wreck
* Scaplens Court Museum open opposite in August

Location	Admission
End of High Street in town centre	Free
Opening	**Contact**
Nov–Mar, Mon–Sat 10am–3pm	4 High Street, Poole BH15 1BW
Sun 12 noon–3pm	t 01202 262600
Apr–Oct, Mon–Sat 10am–5pm	e museums@poole.gov.uk
Sun 12 noon–5pm	

266 Portland

Portland Castle

1 hr+   Daily

Portland Castle was built by Henry VIII as part of his ambitious scheme of coastal defences against the French and Spanish. It has survived largely unaltered since the C16, making it one of the best preserved examples of Henry's castles.

* Audio guides around the castle
* Contemporary heritage gardens

Location	Contact
Royal Naval Dockyard at Portland	Castletown, Portland Harbour, Weymouth DT5 1AZ
Opening	
Mar 1–Oct 31, daily 10am–6pm	t 01305 820539
Nov 1–Apr 30, Fri–Sun 10am–5pm	w english-heritage.org.uk
Admission	
Adult £3.50, Child £1.80, Concs £2.70	

267 Sherborne

Sherborne Abbey

1 hr+   Daily

This former cathedral is home to a flourishing community of Benedictine monks. It was the monks who carried out a major rebuilding in the C15 and gave the abbey one of its chief glories, the earliest great fan-vaulted roof in Europe.

* Sherborne School is part of abbey complex

Location	Contact
Centre of Sherborne	Abbey Close, Sherborne DT9 3LQ
Opening	t 01935 812 452
Summer 8am–6pm	w sherborneabbey.org
Winter 8am–4pm	e abbey@sherbourne.net.konect.co.uk
Admission	
Free, donations encouraged	
Guided tour Adult £2.50	

268 Sherborne

Sherborne Castle

2 hrs+   Apr–Oct

Built by Sir Walter Raleigh in 1594 and set in 20 acres of beautiful landscaped gardens around a 50-acre lake, Sherborne Castle has been home to the Digby family since 1617 and contains a fine collection of pictures, porcelain, furniture and decorative arts.

* Capability Brown lake

Location	Admission
1 mile E of Sherborne, follow signs from A30	Adult £6, Child free, Concs £5.50
Opening	**Contact**
Apr–Oct, daily (inc. Bank Hols) except	Sherborne Castle Estates,
Mon & Fri, 11am–4.30pm	Cheap Street, Sherborne DT9 3PY
Sat 2:30pm–4.30pm	t 01935 813182
	w sherbornecastle.com
	e enquiries@sherbornecastle.com

269 Studland

Studland Beach & Nature Reserve

3 hrs+   Easter–Oct

Fine sandy beaches stretch for 3 miles from South Haven Point to the chalk cliffs of Handfast Point and Old Harry Rocks. Along the way are Shell Bay and a designated naturist area. The heathland behind the beach is a National Nature Reserve.

Location
Across B'mth & Swanage motor road ferry or via Corfe Castle on the B3351

Opening
Daily

Admission
Parking charges vary through seasons, please telephone for details

Contact
Countryside Office, Studland, Swanage BH19 3AX
t 01929 450259
w nationaltrust.org.uk
e studlandbeach@nationaltrust.org.uk

270 Swanage

Swanage Railway

2 hrs+   Daily

This award-winning railway currently operates on the six mile track between Swanage and Norden, through the beautiful Isle of Purbeck, passing the magnificent ruins of Corfe Castle. At present, there is extension work taking place to the north of Norden.

Location
Station in centre of Swanage, a few mins walk from the beach

Opening
Trains daily Apr–Oct. Weekends only rest of year. Daily Dec 26–31

Admission
Adult £7, Child £5, Concs £5

Contact
Station House, Swanage BH19 1HB
t 01929 425800
w swanagerailway.co.uk
e general@swanrail.freeserve.co.uk

271 Tolpuddle

The Tolpuddle Martyrs Museum

1 hr   All year

Explore the harrowing tale of the Martyrs' arrest, trial and punishment, leading to the foundation of modern day trade unionism. The museum is a modern, informative, and educational exhibition, using interactive touch screen displays telling the story in text and images.

* Tolpuddle Martyrs' Festival 3rd Sun in July

Location
In the centre of Tolpuddle

Opening
Summer, Tue–Sat 10am–5.30pm
Sun 11am–5.30pm (4pm in Winter)
open Bank Hols, ex Dec 24-26 & Jan 1

Admission
Free

Contact
TUC Memorial Cottages,
Tolpuddle, Dorchester DT2 7EH

t 01305 848 237
w www.tolpuddlemartyrs.org.uk
e jpickering@tuc.org.uk

272 Wareham

Monkey World

2 hrs+   Daily

Monkey World is a sanctuary for rescued primates from all over the world. Living at the park is the largest group of chimpanzees outside Africa. Orangutans, gibbons and many more primates inhabit spacious enclosures in a natural woodland setting.

* Adoption scheme

Location
Located between Bere Regis
and Wool, 1 mile from Wool station

Opening
Daily 10am–5pm (6pm Jul & Aug)

Admission
Adult £7, Child £5.50, Concs £5.50

Contact
Longthorns, Wareham BH20 6HH

t 01929 462537
w www.monkeyworld.org
e apes@monkeyworld.org

273 Wareham

Corfe Castle

1 hr+   All year

One of Britain's more majestic ruins, this castle once controlled the gateway through the Purbeck Hills and in its time served as a fortress, prison and home. Many fine Norman and early English features remain.

* Special events including historical reenactments
* Guided tours available

Location
On the A352 Wareham to Swanage road

Opening
Daily except Dec 25/26

Admission
Adult £4.70, Child £2.30

Contact
The National Trust, The Square, Corfe Castle, Wareham BH20 5EZ

t 01929 481294
w nationaltrust.org.uk
e corfecastle@nationaltrust.org.uk

274 Wareham

Lulworth Castle

3 hrs+   Daily

Lulworth Castle was built between 1608 and 1610 but caught fire in 1929 and became a virtual ruin. In the 1970s restoration work began and the exterior is now as it was before the fire. This is a unique building which tells the story of its history and of the family who lived here.

* Lulworth Country Fair & International Horse Trials
* August jousting shows

Location
3 miles SW of Wareham, follow signs

Opening
Summer 10.30am–6pm
Winter 10.30am–4pm
Closed Sat & Dec 24 to early Jan

Admission
Adults £6, Child £3.50, Concs £5

Contact
East Lulworth, Wareham BH20 5QS

t 01929 400 352
w www.lulworth.com
e estate.office@lulworth.com

275 Weymouth

Brewers Quay

3 hrs+   Daily

Redeveloped Victorian brewery at the heart of Weymouth's Old Harbour, offering speciality shopping, entertainment and eating out. Step back in time at the 'Timewalk & Brewery Days' attraction.

Location
On harbour, 5 mins from town centre

Opening
Daily 10am–5.30pm

Admission
Free entry to complex.
Timewalk attraction Adult £4.50, Child £3.25, Concs £4.00

Contact
Hope Square, Weymouth DT4 8TR

t 01305 777 622
w brewers-quay.co.uk
e brewersquay@yahoo.co.uk

Dorset	Gloucestershire

276 Weymouth

Deep Sea Adventure

3 hrs   All year

Experience the world of underwater exploration from C17 to the present day. Discover the history of Weymouth's Old Harbour, alongside compelling tales of shipwreck and survival. Fascinating exhibitions including 'Scuba Diving through the Years' and 'The *Titanic*'.

* Sharkeys Play and Party Warehouse for up to 11yrs
* Creative workshops, paint your own pottery

Location
A35 into Weymouth, follow signs

Opening
Summer 9.30–8pm Winter 9.30–7pm
Closed Dec 25/26& Jan 1 (last entry 1½ hrs before close)

Admission
Adult £3.75, Child £2.75

Contact
9 Custom House Quay, Old Harbour, Weymouth DT4 8BG

t 0871 222 5760
w deepsea-adventure.co.uk
e enquires@deepsea-adventure.co.uk

277 Berkeley

Edward Jenner Museum

1 hr+   Mar–Nov

This was the beautiful Georgian home of Edward Jenner (1749–1823), the discoverer of vacination against smallpox, who also studied birds, fossils and balloons. There is also an exhibition of modern immunology with the aim of promoting wider public understanding.

* Explore the science of Jenner's work
* See how Smallpox has been eradicated

Location
1½ miles W of A38 midway between Bristol & Gloucester

Opening
Apr–Sep Tue–Sat & Bank Hol Mons
12.30pm–5.30pm, Sun 1–5.30pm
Oct Sun only 1pm–5.30pm
Closed Nov–Mar

Admission
Adult £3.50, Child £2.80, Concs £2.80

Contact
Church Lane, Berkeley GL13 9BH

t 01453 810 631
w jennermuseum.com
e manager@jennermuseum.com

278 Wimborne

Kingston Lacy House

3 hrs+   Mar–Nov

Kingston Lacy was home to the Bankes family for over 300 years. All four floors are open to visitors and contain lavish interiors. The Edwardian laundry gives a fascinating insight into life below stairs 100 years ago. Formal gardens and parkland surround the house.

* Special snowdrop days in January
* Events throughout the year

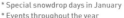

Location
1½ miles from Wimborne on B3082

Opening
House Mar–Nov, Wed–Sun & Bank Hols, 11am–5pm
Garden Mar–Nov, daily 10.30am–6pm, Nov 5–Dec 19, Fri, Sat & Sun 10.30–4pm

Admission
Prices vary, phone for details

Contact
Wimborne BH214EA

t 01202 883402
w www.nationaltrust.org.uk
e kingstonlacy@nationaltrust.org.uk

279 Bourton-on-the-Hill

Bourton House Gardens

1 hr   May–Oct

Bourton House is an C18 Cotswold manor house and C16 tithe barn. Its 3-acre garden, which has been created over the last 20 years, features extravagant borders, exotic plants and fantastic topiary. Much variety including raised alpine troughs and a shade house.

* Fountains and ponds fed by original spring
* Tithe barn has exhibition of local art

Location
On A44, 2 miles W of Moreton-in-Marsh

Opening
May–Aug, Wed–Fri 10am–5pm
Sep–Oct, Thu–Fri only

Admission
Adult £4.50, Child free

Contact
Bourton-on-the-Hill, nr Moreton-in-Marsh GL56 9AE

t 01386 700754
w bourtonhouse.com
e cd@bourtonhouse.com

      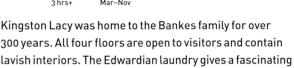

280 Bourton-on-the-Water

Cotswold Motor Museum & Toy Collection

  ½ hr Feb–Nov

A veritable treasure of yesteryear. Though the main focus is on motoring with a fine collection of classic cars motorcycles and caravans, the museum has its very own toy collection including teddy bears and aeroplanes plus a rare collection of pedal cars.

* Largest collection of historic motoring signs
* Home to TV character 'Brum'

Location
Bourton town centre at junction with Sherborne Street

Opening
Feb–Nov daily 10am–6pm

Admission
Adult £2.75, Child £1.95 Family £8.60

Contact
Cotswold Motor Museum & Toy Museum, The Old Mill, Sherbourne Street, Bourton-on-the-Water, Cheltenham GL54 2BY

t 01451 821255
w cotswold-motor-museum.com
e motormuseum@csma-netlink.co.uk

281 Cheltenham

Cheltenham Art Gallery & Museum

    1 hr All year

This collection has been built up over the last 100 years by generous residents who have donated their collections. There are nationally important Arts & Crafts movement displays. One room is dedicated to Edward Wilson who travelled with Scott to Antartica.

* Started with donation of 43 important paintings in 1897
* Oriental gallery with Chinese pottery and costume

Location
Cheltenham town centre

Opening
Mon–Sat 10am–5.20pm, Sun 2pm–4.20pm. Closed Bank Hols

Admission
Free, donations appreciated

Contact
Clarence Street, Cheltenham GL50 3JT

t 01242 237431
w cheltenham.art.gallery.museum
e artgallery@cheltenhammuseum.gov.uk

282 Cheltenham

Holst Birthplace Museum

   1 hr Feb–Dec

This Regency terrace house is where Gustav Holst, composer of *The Planets Suite* was born in 1874. The story of the man and his music is told alongside a fascinating display of personal belongings, including his piano. The museum is also a fine period house.

* Working Victorian kitchen and laundry
* Regency drawing room and Edwardian nursery

Location
In the Pitville area of Cheltenham, opposite Pitville Park

Opening
Tue–Sat 10am–4pm (closed Jan) Tours by appointment only in Jan

Admission
Adult £2.50, Child £2, Concs £2

Contact
4 Clarence Road, Cheltenham GL52 2AY

t 01242 524 846
w holstmuseum.org.uk
e holstmuseum@btconnect.com

283 Chipping Campden

Hidcote Manor Gardens

  2 hrs+ Mar–Oct

One of England's great gardens created early in the C20 by the horticulturist Major Lawrence Johnston. A series of small gardens separated by walls and hedges of different species. The varied style of the outdoor 'rooms' ensure an interesting visit at any time.

* New glasshouse visitor centre & audio guides
* Rare and unusual plants from around the world

Location
4 miles NE of Chipping Campden, off B4081

Opening
27 Mar–31 Sep Mon–Wed, Sat & Sun 10.30am–6pm. 1 Oct 10.30am–5pm Last entry 30mins before close Shop & Restaurant open Nov–mid Dec 12 noon–4pm Sat & Sun

Admission
Adult £6.20, Child £3.10

Contact
Hidcote Bartrim, Chipping Campden GL55 6LR

t 01386 438333
w nationaltrust.org.uk/hidcote
e hidcote@nationaltrust.org.uk

284 Cinderford

Dean Heritage Centre

2 hrs+   Daily

This is the museum of the Forest of Dean, situated by a mill pond in a wooded valley, with woodland walks, adventure playground and picnic site. The centre displays social and industrial history, and exhibits include a beam engine and a water-wheel.

* Traditional charcoal burning demonstrations anually
* Various woodland craft workshops also at this site

Location
In the Forest of Dean on the B4227 at Soudley

Opening
Apr–Oct 10am–5.30pm
Nov–Mar 11am–4pm
Closed Dec 24–26 and Jan 1

Admission
Adult £4.00, Child £2.50, Concs £3.50

Contact
Camp Mill, Soudley,
Cinderford GL14 2UB

t 01594 822170
w deanheritagemuseum.com
e deanmuse@btinternet.com

285 Chipping Campden

Kiftsgate Court Garden

½ hr   Apr–Sep

A series of interconnecting gardens each with its distinct character including the sheltered lower garden that recreates the atmosphere of the Mediterranean. There are many unusual plants that have been collected by the garden's creators – three generation of women.

* Newly added water garden
* Views stretch to the Bredon and the Malvern Hills

Location
SE of Mickleton and 4 miles NE of Chipping Campden off B4081

Opening
Apr–Sep Wed, Thu, Sun & Bank Hol Mons 2pm–6pm
Jun–Jul Mon, Wed, Thu, Sat & Sun 12noon–6pm

Admission
Adult £5, Child £1.50

Contact
Chipping Campden GL55 6LN

t 01386 438777
w kiftsgate.co.uk
e info@kiftsgate.co.uk

286 Gloucester

Clearwell Caves – Ancient Iron Mines

1 hr+   All year

Mining in the Forest of Dean is believed to have started over 7,000 years ago as people migrated back into the area after the last ice age. Large scale iron ore mining continued until 1945. Visitors are allowed to walk into some of the oldest underground workings in Britain.

* See first hand how miners struggled to 'win' ore
* Nine caverns open, deep level visits by appointment.

Location
1½ miles S of Coleford

Opening
Mar–Oct 10am–5pm
Nov–Dec (Christmas Fantasy)
Jan–Feb weekends only

Admission
Adult £4, Child £2.50, Concs £3.50

Contact
Clearwell Caves & Ancient Iron Mines, nr Coleford, Royal Forest of Dean, Gloucester GL16 8JR

t 01594 832535
w clearwellcaves.com
e jw@clearwellcaves.com

287 Gloucester

Gloucester City Museum & Art Gallery

1 hr   All year

This museum is nearly 150 years old and in that time it has acquired a fine collection of art, archaeological, geological and natural history items. Many local people have donated their collections and these include paintings by Rembrandt and Turner.

* Hands-on and interactive computer displays
* Free to Gloucester residents

Location
Gloucester city centre at junction with Parliament Street

Opening
Tue–Sat 10am–5pm.
Closed Dec 25/26, 31 & Jan 1

Admission
Adult £2, Concs £1

Contact
Brunswick Road GL1 1HP

t 01452 396131
w glos-city.gov.uk
e culture@gloucester.gov.uk

288 Gloucester

Gloucester Folk Museum

1 hr+   All year

Housed in splendid Tudor and Jacobean buildings which date from the C16 and C17. Displays include local history, such as the Siege of Gloucester (1643), Severn fishing and farming and an attractive garden. Craft industries including pin-making, toys and games and shoemaking.

* Exhibition of domestic life – kitchen & laundry
* Displays of a dairy, ironmongers and carpenters

Location
Gloucester city centre, nr the docks

Opening
Tues–Sat 10am–5pm

Admission
Adult £2, Child free, Concs £1

Contact
99–103 Westgate Street GL1 1PG

t 01452 396467
w livinggloucester.co.uk
e folk.musuem@glos.gov.uk

289 Gloucester

John Moore Countryside Museum

½ hr+   Apr–Oct

A natural history collection of woodland wildlife, displayed to honour the writings on nature conservation of the late John Moore, a local writer and naturalist. The museum is housed in an historic C15 timber-framed building, part of restored medieval merchant's cottages.

* Programme of temporary exhibitions
* John Moore was one of the earliest conservationists

Location
On A38 by Tewkesbury Abbey

Opening
Apr–Oct Tue–Sat 10am–1pm & 2–5pm
Open all Bank Hol Mons
(open Sat only in winter)

Admission
Adult £1.25, Child 75p, Concs £1

Contact
41 Church Street,
Tewkesbury GL20 5SN

t 01684 297174
w gloster.demon.co.uk/jmcm
e myecrofte@aol.com

290 Gloucester

National Waterways Museum

2 hrs   All year

Housed in the historic Gloucester docks, the museum charts the story of Britain's canals with a nationally important collection. You enter through a replica lock complete with running water and the exhibits show what it was like to live and work on the waterways.

* See Gloucester's role as an important dock
* Over 5,000 items on display from tiny to gigantic

Location
Follow signs for 'Historic Docks'

Opening
Daily 10am–5pm. Closed Christmas Day

Admission
Adult £5, Child £4, Concs £4

Contact
Llanthony Warehouse, Gloucester Docks GL1 2EH

t 01452 318200
w nwm.org.uk
e bookingsnwm|@ thewaterwaystrust.co.uk

291 Gloucester

Soldiers of Gloucestershire Museum

1 hr+   All year

Housed in the Customs House in Gloucester's historic docks, the museum tells the story of how two regiments (one an infantry regiment of the regular Army, the other a territorial Yeomanry cavalry regiment) have brought honour to Gloucestershire and its surrounds.

* The Gloucestershire Regiment (regular Army)
* The Royal Gloucestershire Hussars (territorials)

Location
Follow signs to 'Historic Docks'

Opening
Daily 10am–5pm (closed winter Mons & Christmas) last entry 4.30pm

Admission
Adult £4.25, Child £2.25, Concs £3.25 Family £13, under fives free

Contact
Gloucester Docks GL1 2HE

t 01452 522682
w glosters.org.uk
e rhqrgbw@milnet.uk

292 Lower Slaughter

Old Mill Museum

½ hr+   Daily

A C19 flour mill on the banks of the River Eye is home to a museum and an organic ice cream parlour renowned for its handmade ice cream. Owned by jazz singer Gerald Harris, the mill has been extensively restored and has become a popular Cotswold attraction.

* Free ice cream tasting Apr–Oct
* Voted 'Most beautiful village in the Cotswolds'

Location
Off A429 S of Stow-on-the-Wold

Opening
Daily 10am–6pm, when clocks change 10–dusk. Closed Dec 18–25

Admission
Adults £1.25, Child 50p

Contact
Mill Lane, Lower Slaughter GL54 2HX

t 01451 820052
w oldmill-lowerslaughter.com
e info@oldmill-lowerslaughter.com

293 Moreton-in-Marsh

Batsford Arboretum

1 hr+   All year

With over 1,600 different trees and species from all over the world, Batsford Arboretum has colour throughout the year – from winter snowdrops to daffodils followed by cherry blossom and magnolias, to summer bamboo and a glorious display of golden autumnal colour.

* One of the largest private collections in the country
* Diverse range of birds and animals often seen

Location
Off A44 W of Moreton-in-Marsh

Opening
Mid Nov–Feb 1, weekends 10–4.00pm, Feb 1–mid Nov, daily 10am–5pm, Dec 26 & Jan 1, 11am–3pm

Admission
Adult £5, Child £1, Concs £4

Contact
Batsford Park, nr Moreton-in-Marsh GL56 9QB

t 01386 701441
w batsarb.co.uk
e admin@batsarb.co.uk

294 Moreton-in-Marsh

Sezincote Gardens

1 hr+   Jan–Nov

Built by in a Moghul architectural style, a mixture of Hindu and Muslim, Sezincote is a very unusual English house. The gardens are fascinating and include canals, Moghul paradise gardens and a small Indian style pavilion. The water gardens contain many rare plants.

* Indian bridge decorated with Brahmin bulls
* Sezincote is from Cheisnecote, 'the home of the oaks'

WC

Location
1½ miles W of Moreton-in-Marsh A44

Opening
House May–Jul & Sep Thu & Fri 2.30pm–6pm
Gardens Jan–Nov Thu, Fri & Bank Hol Mon 2–6pm or dusk if earlier

Admission
Gardens Adult £3.50 Child £1
House & Garden £5 (no children)

Contact
nr Moreton-in-Marsh GL56 9AW

t 01386 700444
w gloucestershire.gov.uk

295 Moreton-in-Marsh

Wellington Aviation Museum

1 hr   Daily

Near a training school for Bomber Command during the Second World War, the museum now contains an extensive collection of artefacts from the war years including a Vickers-Armstrong Wellington bomber. A separate tail section shows the famous Barnes-Wallis structure.

* Thousands of documents to investigate
* Collection of aviation and military art

WC

Location
On A44 NE of Cheltenham

Opening
Tue–Sun 10am–12.30pm & 2pm–5pm
Jan–Feb open weekends only

Admission
Adult £2, Child £1

Contact
British School House,
Moreton-in-Marsh GL56 0BG

t 01608 650323
w wellingtonaviation.org

296 North Cerney

Cerney House Gardens

1 hr   Apr–Jul

This beautiful 'secret' garden sits high above the Churn Valley in the heart of the Cotswolds. It has many features including a lovely Cotswold walled garden with lots of old-fashioned roses, a well-labelled herb garden and kitchen garden, as well as plenty of scenic views.

* Next to Chedworth Roman Villa
* Walks available in surrounding woodland

WC

Location
On A435 Cheltenham road. Turn left opposite Bathurst Arms

Opening
Apr–Jul Fri 10am–5pm. Closed on Sat, Mon & Thurs

Admission
Adult £3, Child £1

Contact
North Cerney GL7 7BX

t 01285 831205
w cerneygardens.com
e cerneygardens@hotmail.com

297 Painswick

Painswick Rococo Garden

2 hrs   Jan–Oct

The rococo style was a short but important design period more often associated with art or architecture. Few such gardens survive and its mixture of formal and informal creates a unique effect. Characterised by winding paths, the garden is full of fascinating features.

* Plunge pool, geometric kitchen garden and maze
* An interesting mixture of building styles

WC

Location
Off A46, then B4073 ½ miles N of Painswick

Opening
Jan–Oct 11am–5pm

Admission
Adult £4, Child £2, Concs £3.50

Contact
Painswick GL6 6TH

t 01452 813204
w rococogarden.co.uk
e info@rococogarden.co.uk

298 Tetbury

Chavenage House

2 hrs   Apr–Sep

This wonderful Elizabethan manor house, with Cromwellian connections, has changed little in 400 years. The house is noted for Cromwell's room, the main hall with its magnificent stained glass windows, the ballroom and the Oak Room.

* Set in beautiful gardens
* A favourite with filmmakers

WC

Location	Contact
On B4014, 1½ miles NW of Tetbury	nr Tetbury GL8 8XP
Opening	t 01666 502329
Apr–Sep Thu, Sun + Bank Hols 2–5pm	w chavenage.com
Admission	e info@chavenage.com
Adult £5, Child £2.50	

299 Tetbury

Tetbury Police Museum

½ hr   All year

This museum is housed in the town's original Police office and cells of a former magistrate's court. The building is Victorian with an interesting collection of artefacts from the Gloucestershire Constabulary. An under court room display demonstrates what a trial would have been like.

* See early police batons, helmets and gas-masks
* Extensive photographic collection

WC

Location	Contact
5 mins walk from town centre	The Old Court House, 63 Long Street, Tetbury GL8 8AA
Opening	
9am–3.00pm	t 01666 504670
Mon–Fri (ex Bank Hols)	w tetbury.com/policemuseum
Admission	e tetburycouncil@virgin.net
Free, donations appeciated	

300 Tetbury

Westonbirt Arboretum

2 hrs+   All year

Westonbirt is one of the finest collections of trees in the world today with 18,000 trees and shrubs in 600 acres of landscaped countryside. There is also an extensive array of wild flowers, fungi, birds and animals on display throughout the year.

* International Festival of Gardens Jun-Sep
* Finest autumn leaf colour display in Europe

Location	Contact
3 miles S of Tetbury on A433 to Bath	Westonbirt, nr Tetbury GL8 8QS
Opening	t 01666 880220
Open every day of the year 10am–5pm	w forestry.gov.uk
Admission	e westonbirt@forestry.gsi.gov.uk
Adults £6.00, Child £1.00, Concs £5.00	

301 Tewkesbury

Tewkesbury Museum

½ hr   Apr–Oct

The museum reflects human activity in the area over the last 5,000 years. Roman finds include a skeleton, metalwork, pottery and coins. Fine collection of medieval material from Holm Castle. Later periods cover all aspects of civic, social and industrial life.

* Photos of reenactment of Battle of Tewskbury
* Large-scale fairground models (made in Tewkesbury)

Location	Contact
Junction 9 off M5, same building as the Tourist Information Centre	64 Barton Street, Tewkesbury Gl20 5 PX
Opening	t 01684 292901
Apr–Oct Mon-Sat 10am–5pm	w mysite.freeserve.com/tewkes-burymuseum
Admission	e museum@tewkgl20.fsnet.co.uk
Adult £1, Child 50p, Concs 75p	
Family £2.50	

302 Uley

Owlpen Manor House & Gardens

2 hrs+   Apr–Sep

This Tudor manor house (1450–1616) stands at the centre of a clutch of medieval buildings, with a splended great hall. The terraced garden is a rare survival of an early formal garden, re-ordered in 1723 with magnificent yew topary, old roses and box parterres.

* Queen Margaret of Anjou said to haunt the manor
* Contains collection of furniture, textiles and paintings

Location	Contact
1 mile E of Uley, off B4066	nr Uley, Dursley GL11 5BZ
Opening	t 01453 860261
1 Apr–30 Sep 2pm–5pm. Closed Mon	w owlpen.com
(ex Bank Hols)	e sales@owlpen.com
Admission	
Adult £4.80 Child (4–14) £2	
Family £13.50. *Garden only* £2.80	

303 Westbury-on-Severn

Westbury Court Garden

Fine   1 hr   Mar–Oct

Originally laid out at the turn of the C17, this is the only restored Dutch water garden in the country. It was also the National Trust's first garden restoration, it was restored in 1971 and is planted with species dating from before 1700.

* Replica C17 panelling installed in pavilion
* Parterre and vegetable plots reinstated to C17 style

Location	Admission
8 miles SW of Gloucester on A48	Adult £3.50, Child £1.70
Opening	National Trust members free
1 Mar–31 Oct , Wed–Sun & Bank Hol	**Contact**
Mons 10am–5pm (last entry 4.30pm)	Westbury-on-Severn GL14 1PD
Jul–Aug daily	t 01452 760461
	w nationaltrust.org.uk
	e jerry.green@nationaltrust.org.uk

304 Winchcombe

Sudeley Castle & Gardens

2 hrs+   Mar–Oct

Sudeley Castle is steeped in history. With royal connections spanning a thousand years, it has played an important role in the turbulent and changing times of England's past and has played host to Henry VIII, Elizabeth I and King Charles I – the latter during the Civil War.

* Home and tomb of Queen Katherine Parr.
* Spoiled in the Civil War, resoration began in 1837

Location	*Gardens* £5.15, £2.90, £4 + £1 extra
8 miles NE of Cheltenham on B4632	for Bank Hols & Sun May–Aug
Opening	**Contact**
Castle Apr–Oct 11am–5pm	Winchcombe GL54 5JD
Gardens Mar–Oct 10.30am–5.30pm	t 01242 602308
Admission	w sudeleycastle.co.uk
Castle Adult £6.85, Child £3.85, Concs £5.85	e marketing@sudeley.org.uk
+ £1 extra for Bank Hols & Sun May–Aug	

305 Barrington

Barrington Court

2 hrs+   Mar–Oct

An enchanting formal garden laid out in a series of walled rooms, including the white garden, the rose and iris garden and the lily garden. The working kitchen garden has espaliered apple, pear and plum trees trained along high stone walls.

* Tudor manor house restored in the 1920s

Location
5 miles NE of Ilminster on A358

Opening
Mar & Oct, Thu–Sun 11am–4.30pm
Apr–Sep daily (except Wed)
11am–5.30pm

Admission
Adult £5.50, Child £2.50

Contact
Barrington TA19 0NQ

t 01460 241938
w nationaltrust.org.uk
e barringtoncourt@
    nationaltrust.org.uk

306 Bath

The American Museum & Gardens

3 hrs+   Mar–Dec

Learn how Americans lived from the time of the early European settlers to the American Civil War. Rooms include a replica C18 tavern where all visitors are given a piece of home cooked gingerbread. Wonderful collection of quilts, native American objects and folk art.

* Extensive gardens
* See website for exhibition programme

Location
Off A36 S of Bath at Claverton
(5 mins drive from city)

Opening
Mar 20–Nov 28, 12–5.30pm. Closed
Mon ex Bank Hols 11am–5.30pm

Admission
Adult £6.50, Child £4

Contact
Claverton Manor, Bath BA2 7BD

t 01225 460503
w americanmuseum.org
e info@americanmuseum.org

307 Bath

Bath Aqua Theatre of Glass

1 hr   All year

In this living/working museum glass is produced for church windows, art projects and for private commissions. You can see the beautiful aquamarine glass being blown in the theatre during regular public demonstrations.

* Signed and dated pieces available in shop
* Exhibition of old and new stained glass

Location
5 mins walk W out of city centre

Opening
Daily 10am–1pm & 1.45pm–5pm
Preferred viewing times 10.15, 11.15,
12.15, 2.15, 3.15, last demo at 4pm.

Admission
Adults £3, Child £1.50, Concs £2

Contact
105–107 Walcot Street,
Bath BA1 5BW

t 01225 428146
w bathaquaglass.com
e bathaquaglass@hotmail.com

308 Bath

Holburne Museum of Art

1 hr+   Feb–mid Dec

This jewel among Bath's splendid array of museums and galleries displays the treasures collected by Sir William Holburne. Superb English and continental silver, porcelain, maiolica, glass and Renaissance bronzes. Paintings include works by Turner and Gainsborough.

* Regular specialist exhibitions & lectures
* Book and gift shop open to the public free

Location	Contact
5 mins walk from Pultney Bridge at end of Great Pultney Street	Great Pulteney Street, Bath BA2 4DB
Opening	t 01225 466669
Tue–Sat, 10am–5pm (including Bank Hols) Sun 2.30–5.30pm	w bath.ac.uk/holburne
	e holburne@bath.ac.uk
Admission	
Prices vary, phone for details	

309 Bath

Bath Abbey – Heritage Vaults Museum

1 hr   All year

Situated on the south side of Bath's C15 Abbey (itself built on the site of a Saxon abbey), the vaults have been beautifully restored to provide an interesting seting for objects that have survived from the abbey's fascinating past.

Location	Contact
South side of abbey, city centre	Bath BA1 1LT
Opening	t 01225 422462
Mon–Sat, 10am–4pm	w bathabbey.org
Closed Sun, Dec 25/26, Jan 1 & Good Friday, last entry 3.30pm	e office@bathabbey.org
Admission	
Adults £1, Concs free	

310 Bath

Bath Postal Museum

3 hrs+   Daily

The first letter sent with a stamp (the Penny Black) was sent from this building in 1840. The former post office now illustrates 4,000 years of communication, including Egyptian clay tablets, various writing implements and the story of the first airmail sent from Bath to London.

* Special exhibitions
* Pillar boxes through the ages

Location	Contact
In Broad Street, city centre	8 Broad Street, Bath BA1 5LJ
Opening	t 01225 460333
Mon–Sat, 11am–5pm daily (ex Sun) Oct–Mar close 4.30pm	w bathpostalmuseum.org
	e info@bathpostalmuseum.org
Admission	
Adults £2.90, Child £1.50, Concs £2.40	

311 Bath

Bath Balloon Flights

1 hr   Apr–Oct

Balloons launch from Royal Victoria Park, close to the city centre. Booking ahead is essential and all flights are subject to suitable weather. Flight direction is obviously wind dependent, but central start point ensures fantastic views of city and surroundings.

* Bookings available for singles, couples and groups
* Champagne served during flight

Location
Royal Victoria Park is 5 mins walk from the city centre

Opening
Apr–Oct (office open all year round)

Admission
Prices vary, phone for details

Contact
8 Lambridge, London Road, Bath BA1 6BJ

t 01225 466888
w bathballoons.co.uk
e flights@bathballoons.co.uk

312 Bath

N0.1 Royal Crescent

1 hr   Feb–Nov

Bath is famous the world over for its Georgian architecture and No.1 Royal Crescent is part of what is possibly its most striking example. The house has been restored, redecorated and furnished to show how it would have looked when first built in 1767 by John Wood.

* One of a stunning crescent of 30 Georgian houses
* Gift shop

Location
5 mins walk from centre via The Circus

Opening
Feb 15–Oct 25, Tue–Sun 10.30am–5pm
Oct 26–Nov 30, 10.30am–4pm
Closed Mon ex Bank Hols

Admission
Adult £4, Concs £3.50

Contact
Bath BA1 2LR

t 01225 428126
w bath-preservation-trust.org.uk
e no1@bptrust.demon.co.uk

313 Bath

The Jane Austen Centre

1 hr   Daily

Jane Austen is perhaps the best loved of Bath's many famous residents and visitors. She spent two long periods here at the end of C18 and start of C19 and the city featured in her work. The museum features period costume and exhibits that explore Jane's life in Bath.

* Accolade Winner 2002
* The Best of its Kind 2003

Location
City centre N of Queen Square

Opening
Mon–Sat 10am–5.30pm
Sun 10.30am–5.30pm

Admission
Adults £4.65, Child £2.50, Concs £4.15

Contact
40 Gay Street, Bath BA1 2NT

t 01225443000
w janeausten.co.uk
e info@janeausten.co.uk

314 Bath

Museum of Costume & Assembly Rooms

1 hr   All year

The story of fashion over the last 400 years is brought to life with one of the world's finest collections of fashionable dress – more than 150 dressed figures illustrating changing styles for both men and women. Each of the museum's 30,000 items is original.

* Free audio-guides in seven languages
* New exhibition for 2004 'Jane Austen Film & Fashion'

Location
City centre, just off The Circus

Opening
Nov–Mar, 11am–5pm, Apr–Oct 11am–6pm, (last exit 4pm/5pm)
Closed Dec 25/26 & Jan 1

Admission
Adult £6, Child £4, Concs £5

Contact
Bennett Street, Bath BA1 2QH

t 01225 477789
w museumofcostume.co.uk
e costume_bookings@bathnes.gov.uk

315 Bath

Roman Baths & Pump Rooms

2 hrs+   Daily

This is Bath's most famous attraction. Britain's only natural hot spring flourished between C1 and C5 and the remains are among the finest in Europe. Walk where Romans walked on ancient stone pavements around the steaming pool.

* Taste the water in C18 Pump Room above the Temple
* Displays include sculpture, coins & jewellery

Location
City centre near Abbey

Opening
Jan–Feb, Nov–Dec 9.30am–4.30pm
Mar–June, Sep–Oct 9am–5pm
July–Aug 9am–9pm
Closed Dec 25/26
Last exit 1 hr after close

Admission
Adult £9, Child £5, Concs £8

Contact
Abbey Church Yard, Bath BA1 1LZ

t 01225 477785
w romanbaths.co.uk
e romanbath_bookings@bathnes.gov.uk

316 Bath

Sally Lunn's Refreshment House & Museum

1 hr   Daily

Sally Lunn's famous bun is still served from what is Bath's oldest building (c. 1482). The museum shows remains of Roman, Saxon and medieval buildings on the site. The ancient kitchen used by Sally Lunn in the late C17 can also be seen.

* Three themed refreshment rooms
* Historic Trencher dinner is served from 6pm

Location
Between Abbey Green & North Parade

Opening
Mon–Sat 10am–6pm, Sun 11am–6pm.
Closed Dec 24–26 & Jan 1

Admission
Adult 30p, Concs free

Contact
4 North Parade Passage,
Bath BA1 1NX

t 01225 461634
w sallylunns.co.uk
e info@sallylunns.co.uk

317 Bath

Victoria Art Gallery

3 hrs+   Daily

This fine gallery houses the region's permanent collection of British and European art from C15 to the present day. The gallery has one of the best temporary exhibition programmes in the region ranging from prints to sculpture.

*Regular workshops and holiday activities
* National touring exhibitions & major retrospectives

Location
City side of Pulteney Bridge

Opening
Daily (ex Mon) 10am–5.30pm
Sat 10am–5pm Sun 2pm–5pm
Closed Bank Hols

Admission
Free

Contact
Bridge Street, Bath BA2 4AT

t 01225 477233
w victoriagal.org.uk
e victoria_enqiries@bathnes.gov.uk

318 Bath

William Herschel Museum

1 hr+   Feb–Nov

The home of C18 astronomer and musician William Herschel from which he made important discoveries such as Uranus and infrared radiation. The museum is furnished in the style of the period and is representative of Bath's famous mid-Georgian townhouses.

* Attractive Georgian garden
* Eduction programmes available on request

Location
5 mins walk W of city centre

Opening
Feb 10–Nov 30, daily 2–5pm ex Wed,
weekends 11am–5pm

Admission
Adult £3.50, Child £2
Groups on request even when closed

Contact
New King Street, Bath BA1 2BL

t 01225 311342
w bath-preservation-trust.org.uk
e debbie@herschelbpt.fsnet.co.uk

319 Bath

Thermae Bath Spa

2 hrs+   Daily

Bath's newest and most spectacular attraction. A unique opportunity to bathe in natural thermal waters enjoyed by the Romans 2,000 years ago. Thermae Bath Spa is a state-of-the-art building with four bathing pools, steam rooms and full range of spa treatments. Booking advised.

* No membership or joining fee required
* Spa visitor centre

Location
100 yards from historic Roman Baths

Opening
Opening early 2004. Please ring for confirmation
Daily 9am–10pm
Closed Dec 25/26/31 & Jan 1

Admission
Prices vary, phone for details

Contact
The Hetlin Pump Room
Hot Bath Street, Bath BA1SJ

t 01225 33 1234 / 780308
w thermaebathspa.com
e info@thermaebathspa.com

320 Cheddar

Cheddar Gorge & Caves

3 hrs+   Daily

The highest inland limestone cliffs in Britain and the famous cathedral-like caves form a 360-acre nature reserve owned by Lord Bath (of Longleat). The gorge walk is worth the effort for the fantastic views across Somerset from the top.

* New 'Cheddar Man and the Cannibals' attraction
* Open top bus tour runs through gorge Apr–Sept

Location
Follow signs from junction 22 on M5 & A38 or take B3135 from A37 and the east

Opening
Jul–Aug 10am–5pm
Sep–Jun 10.30am–4.30pm

Admission
Explorer ticket for all attractions
Adult £8.90, Child £5.90

Contact
Cheddar BS27 3QF

t 01934 742343
w cheddarcaves.co.uk
e info@cheddarcaves.co.uk

321 Dunster

Dunster Castle

3 hrs+   April–Oct

Dramatically sited on top of a wooded hill, there has been a castle here at least since Norman times. The present building was remodelled between 1868–72. A sheltered terrace to the south is home to the National Collection of strawberry trees and Britain's oldest lemon tree.

* C13 gatehouse survives
* Surrounded by beautiful parkland for walking

Location
Off A39, 3 miles SE from Minehead

Opening
Castle Mar 20–Oct 23, 11am–5pm
Oct 24–Nov 31, 11–4pm (ex Thur, Fri)
Garden & Park daily (not Dec 25/26)

Admission
Castle Adult £6.80, Child £3.40
Garden & Park £3.70, £1.60

Contact
Dunster, nr Minehead TA24 6SL

t 01643 821314
w nationaltrust.org.uk
e dunstercastle@nationaltrust.org.uk

322 Farleigh Hungerford

Farleigh Hungerford Castle

2 hrs+   Daily

The ruins of this C14 castle lie in the beautiful valley of the River Frome. A free audio guide tells the story of the castle and its occupants during the Middle Ages and its sinister past. The impressive castle has a chapel that contains wall paintings and stained glass.

* Important collection of death masks in chapel crypt
* Programme of living history throughout the year

Location
8 miles SE of Bath off A36

Opening
April–Oct, daily 10am–6pm, Nov–Mar
Wed–Sun 10am–4pm
Closed Dec 24-26 & Jan 1

Admission
Adult £2.50, Child £1.30, Concs £1.90

Contact
Farleigh Hungerford, nr Trowbridge
BA3 6RS

t 01225 754026
w english-heritage.org.uk/southwest
e customers@english-heritage.org.uk

323 Glastonbury

Glastonbury Abbey

2 hrs   Daily

The abbey is set in 36 acres of peaceful parkland in the centre of this ancient market town. One of the oldest religious sites Great Britain, visited so legend has it, by Joseph of Arimathea and Saints David and Patrick. Believed by many to be the burial site of King Aurthur.

* Visitor centre with award-winning museum
* Period-dressed guides in summer months

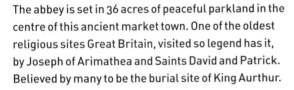

Location
Take A39 from junction 23 of M5,
follow signs once in Glastonbury

Opening
Jan-Aug, daily 9am–6pm (or dusk if
earlier) Mar–May & Sep–Nov, 9–6pm
Dec-Feb 10am–dusk

Admission
Adults £3.50, Child £1.50, Concs £3

Contact
Abbey Gatehouse, Magdalene Street,
Glastonbury BA6 9EL

t 01458 832267
w glastonburyabbey.com
e info@glastonburyabbey.com

324 Sparkford

Haynes Motor Museum

3 hrs+   Daily

The museum contains a unique collection of hundreds of classic, veteran and vintage cars and motorcycles – all in full working order and as original as possible. Features the famous red collection of 1950s and 1960s sports cars.

* Fabulous collection of American sports cars
* 70-seater video theatre

Location
½ mile N of Sparkford on A359

Opening
Mar-Oct, daily 9.30am–5.30pm
& Nov-Feb 10am–4pm
Closed Dec 25/26 & Jan 1

Admission
Adult £6.50, Child £3.50, Concs £5

Contact
Sparkford BA22 7LH

t 01963 440804
w haynesmotormuseum.co.uk
e info@haynesmotormuseum.co.uk

325 Street

The Shoe Museum

1 hr+ Daily

A fascinating collection of shoes, showcards and machinery from Street's famous shoemakers C&J Clark who were among the first in Britain to introduce machinery and sponsor inventions. The shoe collection displays footwear worn in Britain from Roman times.

* Adjacent to Clarks Shopping Village

Location	Contact
A39 to Street from junction 23 of M5, follow signs for Clarks Village	C&J Clark, High Street, Street BA16 0YA
Opening	t 01458 842169
Daily except Dec 24–Jan 4	e janet.targett@clarks.com
Admission	
Free	

326 Taunton

Hestercombe Gardens

2 hrs+ Daily

Hestercombe is a unique combination of a Georgian landscape created by Bampfylde in the 1750s, Victorian terraces and Edwardian gardens designed by Lutyens and Jekyll. The landscaped park (40 acres) has walks, lakes, temples and woods and stunning views.

* Jekyll's original planting faithfully restored

Location	Contact
4 miles N of Taunton & 1 mile NW of Cheddon Fitzpaine	Cheddon Fitzpaine, Taunton TA2 8LG
Opening	t 01823 413923
Daily 10am–6pm	w hestercombegardens.com
Admission	e info@hestercombegardens.com
Adult £5.20, Child £1.30	

327 Wookey Hole

Wookey Hole Caves & Papermill

1 hr+ Daily

One of Britain's most spectacular complex of caves cut into the Mendip Hills. The story of the famous Witch of Wookey is a highlight of the cave tour. The C19 papermill has demonstrations of handmade papermaking with the opportunity for visitors to make their own.

* Magical mirror maze and penny arcade
* Museum of the caves traces back millions of years

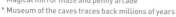

Location	Contact
Junction 22 of M5 & follow signs A39 from Bath to Wells	Wookey Hole, nr Wells BA5 1BB
Opening	t 01749 672243
Mar–Oct 10am–5pm, Nov–Feb 10.30am–4.30pm Closed Dec 17–25	w wookey.co.uk
Admission	e witch@wookey.co.uk
Adults £8.80, Child £5.50	

328 Williton

The Bakelite Museum

1 hr+   Mar–Sep

Set in peaceful Somerset countryside, and housed within a historic watermill, this is the largest collection of vintage plastics in Britain. Exhibits from the inter-war period, stylish Art Deco plus hundreds of the domestic items with which we all grew up.

* Thousands of quirky and rare items on show
* 'Before Bakelite' - a display of Victorian plastics

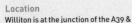

Location
Williton is at the junction of the A39 & A358, NW of Taunton

Opening
Mar–Sept 10.30am–6pm
Only Thurs–Sun in school term

Admission
Adult £3.50, Child £2, Concs £3

Contact
Orchard Mill, Williton TA44NS

t 01984 632133
w bakelitemuseum.co.uk
e info@bakelitemuseum.co.uk

329 Yeovil

Fleet Airarm Museum

3 hrs+   Daily

Now one of the largest aviation museums in the world, situated alongside an operational naval air station. Today the museum covers 6½ acres and has more than 40 aircraft on display including Concorde. The museum has an excellent simulated tour of HMS *Ark Royal*.

* 40 further aircraft in store or renovation
* 'Fly' by simulated helicopter to flightdeck of *Ark Royal*

Location
1 mile off A303/A37 roundabout

Opening
Apr–Oct 10am–5.30pm
Nov–Mar 10am–4.30pm
Closed Dec 24/25/26

Admission
Adult £8.50, Child £5.75, Concs £6.75

Contact
PO Box D6, RNAS, Yeovilton
Illchester BA22 8HT

t 01935 840565
w fleetairarm.com
e info@fleetairarm.com

330 Yeovil

Montacute House & Gardens

3 hrs+   Mar–Oct

A glittering Elizabethan house, with splendid Renaissance features. The magnificent state rooms, including a long gallery (the largest of its type in England), are full of fine C17 and C18 furniture and period portraits from the National Portrait Gallery.

* Featured in the film *Sense and Sensibility*
* Parkland & gardens including historic rose garden

Location
On A30, 5 miles W of Yeovil

Opening
House Mar 19–Oct 31, 11am–5pm
(except Tues)
Garden Apr–Oct 11am–6pm, Nov–Mar 11am–4pm

Admission
House & Gardens Adult £6.90, Child £3.40
Gardens only £3.70, £1.70

Contact
Montacute, nr Yeovil TA16 6XP

t 01935 823289
w nationaltrust.org.uk
e montacute@nationaltrust.org.uk

331 Yeovil

Tintinhull House & Gardens

1 hr   March–Sep

This small manor house (mainly C17 farmhouse with Queen Anne facade) stands in beautiful formal garden created by Mrs Phyllis Reiss. The garden is divided into seven 'rooms' by clipped yew hedges and walls. Includes pool garden, fountain garden and kitchen garden.

* Striking mixed borders and colour schemes

Location
Tintinhull is just off A303 south of Yeovil, follow signs from village

Opening
Mar 23–Sep 28, Wed–Sun
12noon–6pm, plus Bank Hols

Admission
Adult £4.20, Child £2.10

Contact
Farm Street, Yeovil BA22 9PZ

t 01935 822545
w nationaltrust.org.uk
e tintinhull@nationaltrust.org.uk

Wiltshire

332 Amesbury

Stonehenge

1 hr   Easter–Oct

Stonehenge is a ring of upright stones set in a circle – each stone towering about 19 feet (6m). Its original purpose is unclear, but theories range from a temple made to worship ancient deities to an astronomical observatory. Others claim that it was a sacred burial site.

* World Heritage site
* Audio tours in nine languages

Location
2 miles W of Amesbury on junction of A303 & A360

Opening
Mar 16–May 31, 9.30–6.00pm, Jun 1–Aug 31, 9–7pm. Sep 1–Oct 15, 9.30–6pm Oct 16–Mar 15, 9.30–4pm Closed Dec 24–26 & Jan 1

Admission
Adult £5, Child £2.50, Concs £3.80

Contact
Stonehenge Information Line

t 01980 624715
w english-heritage.org.uk/stonehenge

333 Amesbury

Woodhenge

15 mins   All year

Woodhenge is thought to be a Neolithic ceremonial monument (dating from about 2,300 BC) and consisted of concentric rings of wooden posts possibly forming a roofed building or wooden Stonehenge-type monument.

* Six rings of timber posts marks the original site
* Alligned to the midsummer sunrise

Location
Just off the A345, 1½ miles N of Amesbury

Opening
All year any reasonable time

Admission
Free

Contact
Amesbury Tourist Information

t 01980 622833
w english-heritage.org.uk

334 Corsham

Corsham Court

1 hr+   Daily

Corsham Court is based on an Elizabethan house dating from 1582. It was bought by Paul Methuen to house a collection of C16 and C17 paintings and, after alterations to the house in C19, more Italian Old Masters and works of art were added.

* Works by Van Dyck, Carlo Dolci and Reynolds
* Picture gallery boasts a rare ornate ceiling

Location
Signposted 4 miles W of Chippenham from the A4 Bath road

Opening
20 Mar–Sep 30, daily ex Mon & Fri (open Bank Hols) 2pm–5.30 pm Oct 1–Mar 19, Sat & Sun 2pm–4.30pm (last entry 30 mins before close) Closed Dec

Admission
House & Garden Adult £5, Child £2.50

Contact
Corsham SN13 0BZ

t 01249 701610
w corsham-court.co.uk
e enquiries@corsham-court.co.uk

335 Devizes

Broadleas Gardens

1 hr+   Apr–Oct

Lady Anne Cowdray's valley garden, bought in 1946, has been created and developed since the early 1960s. Treasures include a secret garden, winter garden, a woodland a sunken rose garden and a silver border packed with plants which are unusual or rarely seen.

*Afternoon teas on Sundays

Location
A360 road to Salisbury, garden 1 mile S of Devizes

Opening
Apr–Oct, 2pm–6pm, Sun, Wed & Thu

Admission
Adult £4, Child £1.50

Contact
Broadleas Gardens Charitable Trust Limited, Broadleas, Devizes SN10 5JQ

t 01380 722035

336 Salisbury

Salisbury Cathedral

1 hr   All year

Salisbury is one of the finest medieval cathedrals in Britain. Started in 1220 it was completed by 1258, with the spire, the tallest in England (404ft/123m) added a generation later. It also boasts the largest and best preserved cathedral close in Britain.

* Voluntary guide tours of cathedral & Chapter House
* Chapter House contains rare surviving original Magna Carta

Location
Centre of city

Opening
7.15am–6.15pm Times vary depending on services, please phone for details

Admission
Recommended voluntary donation
Adults £3.80, Child £2, Concs £3.30

Contact
Visitor Services, 33 The Close, Salisbury SP1 2EJ

t 01722 555120
w www.salisburycathedral.org.uk
e visitor@salcath.co.uk

337 Salisbury

Larmer Tree Gardens

2 hrs   Apr–Oct

These gardens were created by General Pitt Rivers in 1880 and have been restored over the last 10 years. An open air theatre, Roman temple, Nepalese carved buildings and water features cover the land. Ornamental pheasants and peacocks also roam the gardens.

* Concerts and fairs during the summer
* Larmer Tree Festival in July

Location
On the B3081 off A354 Salisbury to Blandford road.

Opening
Apr–Oct, Sun–Thurs 11am–4pm

Admission
Adult £3.75, Child £2.50

Contact
Tollard Royal, Salisbury SP5 5PT

t 01725 516228
w larmertreegardens.co.uk
e enquires@rushmore/estate.co.uk

338 Salisbury

Salisbury & South Wiltshire Museum

1 hr+   All year

The museum holds material from major archaeological sites in Salisbury and South Wiltshire. Exhibitions cover the entire range of the museum's interests which, in addition to archaeology, include fine and decorative arts, costume, and social history.

* Tempoary exhibitions all year round and giftshop
* A collection of Turner watercolours

Location
In Cathedral Close, opposite the West Front

Opening
Mon–Sat 10am–5pm
Sun in Jul & Aug 2pm–5pm

Admission
Adult £3.50, Child £1, Concs £2.30

Contact
The King's House, 65 The Close, Salisbury SP1 2EN

t 01722 332151
w salisburymuseum.org.uk
e museum@salisburymuseum.org.uk

339 Stourhead

Stourhead Gardens

3 hrs+   All year

The garden was designed by Henry Hoare II. Classical temples, including the Pantheon and the Temple of Apollo, are set around the central lake at the end of a series of vistas which change as the visitor moves around the paths and through the magnificent mature woodland.

* Palladian mansion and gift shop
* King Alfred's Tower, a 50m-high red-brick folly

Location
Just off A303 at Mere

Opening
Gardens all year
House Apr–Oct. Closed Wed, Thurs

Admission
Gardens or House Adult £5.40 Child £3
Both Adult £9.40 Child £4.50

Contact
Stourhead Gardens,
nr Warminster BA12 6QD

t 01747 842020
w national-trust.org.uk
e stourhead@nationaltrust.org.uk

---

340 Swindon

STEAM – Museum of the Great Western Railway

2 hrs+   Daily

This museum tells the story of the men and women who built, operated and travelled on the Great Western Railway. The museum celebrates Isambard Kingdom Brunel and the thousands of ordinary people who made the GWR one of the world's greatest railway networks.

* Special evens running throughout the year
* Featuring world famous GWR locomotives

Location
Follow signs from Swindon town centre

Opening
Open all year round
except Dec 25/26 & Jan 1

Admission
Adult £5.95, Child £3.80, Concs £3.90

Contact
Kemble Drive, Swindon SN2 2TA

t 01793 466 646
w steam-museum.org.uk
e steampostbox@swindon.gov.uk

---

341 Tisbury

Pythouse Walled Garden

1 hr   Easter–Oct

Visit the restoration of a beautiful C18 walled garden with views across Vale of Wardor and the Dorset and Somerset borders. Hidden treasures exposed so far have included a cellared boiler room, forcing room, dipping pond and a heated propogation house.

* Display gardens and pick your own crops
* Specialist plant nursery

Location
Road from Semley to Tisbury nr Newtown

Opening
Wed–Sat 10am–4pm
Other days by appointment

Admission
Free

Contact
Hatch, Tisbury SP3 6PA

t 01747 870444
e tpminter@compuserve.com

342 Warminster

Longleat

All day   Daily

Longleat is set in more than 900 acres of Capability Brown landscaped parkland with further woodlands, lakes and farmland. Longleat House is one of the best examples of high Elizabethan architecture as well as being famous for its safari park, mazes and murals.

* World's longest hedge maze
* Featured in TV's *Lion Country* and *Animal Park*

Location	Contact
Off the A36 between Bath & Salisbury (A362 Warminster to Frome road)	The Estate Office, Longleat, Warminster BA12 7NW
Opening All attractions: daily Mar 27–Oct 31 phone for details of opening times	t 01985 844400 w www.longleat.co.uk e enquiries@longleat.co.uk
Admission Prices vary, phone for details	

343 Westbury

Westbury White Horse & Bratton Camp

3 hrs+   All year

This famous landmark in west Wiltshire has views of the Wiltshire and Somerset countryside. Cut into a chalk hillside in 1778, the white horse is thought to rest on the site of an older horse that commemorated the defeat of the Danes by King Alfred at Ethandun in AD 878.

*Neolithic barrow or burial mound

Location	Contact
Between Westbury and B3098	Westbury Tourist Information Centre
Opening All year, any reasonable time	t 01373 827158 w english-heritage.org.uk
Admission Free	

344 Wilton

Wilton House

2 hrs+   Apr–Oct

Wilton House contains many state rooms including the Double Clube room, which houses a world famous collection of Van Dyck paintings. Other attractions include the old riding school, Tudor kitchen, Victorian laundry and a 'Times Past, Times Present' exhibition.

* Gardens and parkland bordered by the River Nadder

Location	
3 miles W of Salisbury, situated on A30, off A36. 10 miles from A303	£5.50, Concs £8 *Grounds only* £4.50/£3.50
Opening *Grounds* daily. *House* Apr 2–Oct 31, Tues–Sun ex Bank Hols, 10.30–5.30pm	**Contact** The Estate Office, Wilton, Salisbury SP2 0BJ
Admission *House & Grounds* Adult £9.75, Child	t 01722 746720 w wiltonhouse.com e tourism@wiltonhouse.com

Snape Maltings, Suffolk

Eastern

Bedfordshire Cambridgeshire Essex
Hertfordshire Norfolk Suffolk

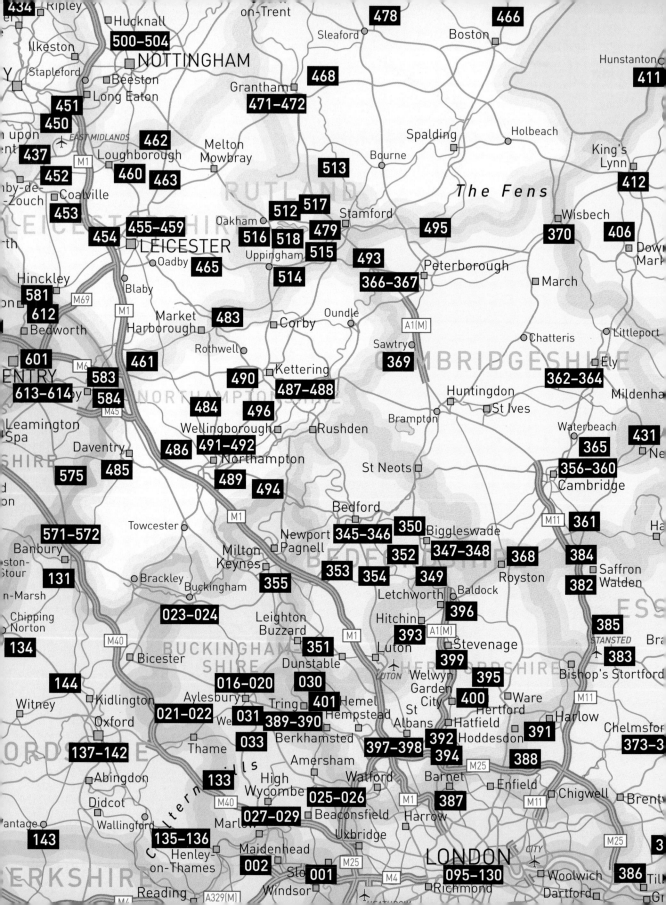

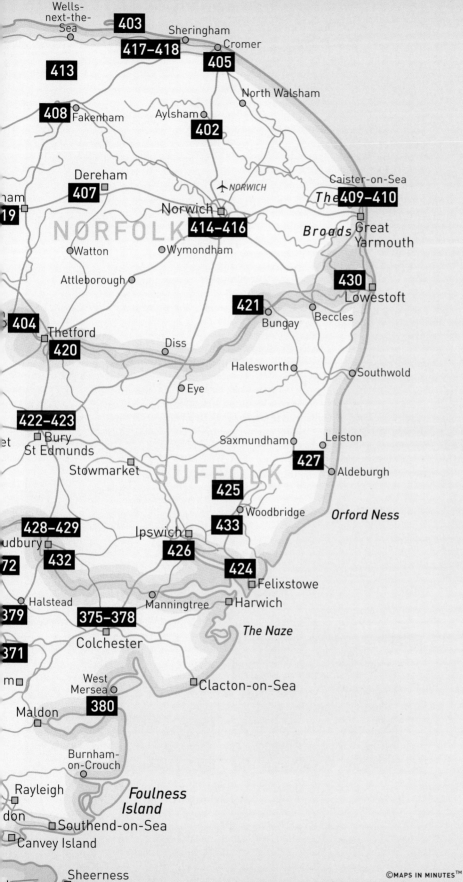

Wells-
next-the-
Sea
403
Sheringham
417–418
Cromer
405
413
North Walsham
408 Fakenham
Aylsham
402
Dereham
407
ham
✈ *NORWICH*
19
Norwich
NORFOLK
414–416
Watton
Wymondham
Attleborough
Caister-on-Sea
The **409–410**
Broads Great
Yarmouth
430
Lowestoft
421
Bungay Beccles
404
Thetford
420
Diss
Halesworth
Southwold
Eye
422–423
Bury
St Edmunds
Stowmarket
SUFFOLK
Saxmundham Leiston
427
Aldeburgh
425
Orford Ness
Woodbridge
428–429
433
udbury
Ipswich
432
426
424
72
Felixstowe
Halstead Manningtree Harwich
379
375–378 *The Naze*
Colchester
371
West
m Mersea
Clacton-on-Sea
380
Maldon
Burnham-
on-Crouch
Rayleigh
Foulness
Island
don
Southend-on-Sea
Canvey Island
Sheerness
Isle of Sheppey Herne Margate

345 Bedford

Bedford Museum

1 hr+   All year

Housed in the former Higgins and Sons Brewery, Bedford Museum is situated within the picturesque gardens of Bedford Castle. The courtyard and galleries offer a rich and varied range of exhibits. Take a journey through the human and natural history of Bedfordshire.

* Treasures and curiosities include Blackbeard's sword
* 'Old Billy' the record breaking longest-lived horse

Location
Well signposted from town centre, near embankment

Opening
Tue–Sat 11am–5pm
Sun & Bank Hols 2pm–5pm

Admission
Adult £2.20, Child & Concs Free

Contact
Castle Lane, Bedford MK40 3XD

t 01234 353323
w bedfordmuseum.org
e bmuseum@bedford.gov.uk

346 Bedford

Cecil Higgins Art Gallery

1 hr+   All year

The gallery is housed in a Victorian mansion, once home to the Higgins family who were wealthy brewers. Adjoining this is a modern gallery housing an internationally renowned collection of watercolours, prints and drawings, ceramics, glass and lace.

* Rooms include items from the Handley-Read collection
* Furniture by Victorian architect William Burges

Location
Just off the Embankment and High Street

Opening
Tue–Sat 11am–5pm
Sun & Bank Hols 2pm–5pm

Admission
Adult £2.20, Child & Concs free

Contact
Castle Lane, Bedford MK40 3RP

t 01234 211222
w cecilhigginsartgallery.org
e chag@bedford.gov.uk

347 Biggleswade

The English School of Falconry

3 hrs+   All year

The family-run centre is sited at Shuttleworth Old Warden Park to create a woodland setting as near as possible to the birds' natural surroundings. The centre is home to over 300 birds of various species including falcons, hawks, eagles, vultures, and owls.

* Three flying displays daily
* Hands-on experience

Location
Old Warden is 2 miles W of A1 where it bypasses Biggleswade

Opening
Nov–Mar 10am–4pm
Apr–Oct 10am–5pm

Admission
Adult £6, Child £4

Contact
Old Warden Park, Biggleswade SG18 9EA

t 01767 627527
w birdsofpreycentre.co.uk
e enquiries@birdsofpreycentre.co.uk

348 Biggleswade

Swiss Garden

2 hrs   All year

A visit to this garden takes you back to the early C19, when an interest in ornamental gardening and picturesque architechture was combined with a passion for 'Swiss Vogue'. The Swiss garden is a beautiful example from a great period of English gardening.

* Atmospheric grotto and fernery
* At the centre is a tiny thatched Swiss cottage

Location
Located within Shuttleworth, Old Warden Park. Off the A1 at Biggleswade

Opening
Mar–Sep Mon–Friday 1pm–5pm
Sun 10am–5pm
Jan, Feb & Oct Sun only 10am–5pm

Admission
Adult £3, Child & Concs £2

Contact
Old Warden Park, Biggleswade
SG18 9ER

t 01767 627666
w shuttleworth.org/swissgarden

349 Henlow

Stondon Motor Museum

2 hrs   All year

This museum is one of the largest private collections in the country with over 400 exhibits. It includes veteran cars dating from 1890–1990, housed in five different halls, some exhibits are for sale. An exclusive collection of Rolls Royce and Bentley vehicles is a feature of the museum.

* Full size replica of Captain Cook's HM Bark *Endeavour*
* Large free car park

Location
At Lower Stondon near Henlow off the A600

Opening
Daily 10am–5pm

Admission
Adult £6, Child £3, Concs £5

Contact
Station Road, Lower Stondon, Henlow
SG16 6JN

t 01462 850339
w transportmuseum.co.uk
e info@transportmuseum.co.uk

350 Biggleswade

Shuttleworth Collection

2 hrs+   All year

This world famous collection of aircraft, started by Richard Shuttleworth, depicts the history of flight from 1900–1940s and ranges from a 1909 Bleriot to a Second World War Spitfire. Cars, motorcycles and carriages are exhibited alongside the aircraft in eight hangars.

* Regular flying displays during the summer
* Clayton and Shuttleworth steam traction engine

Location
Shuttleworth Old Warden Aerodrome is 2 miles W of A1 where it bypasses Biggleswade

Opening
Apr–Oct 10am–5pm
Nov–Dec 10am–4pm
Jan–Mar Wed–Sun 10am–4pm

Admission
Adult £7.50, Child free, Concs £6

Contact
Old Warden Park, Biggleswade
SG18 9EP

t 01767 627288
w www.shuttleworth.org
e collection@shuttleworth.org

351   Leighton Buzzard

Ascott House

2 hrs+   Mar–Aug

Ascott is a black-and-white C19 house set in 30 acres of grounds. It houses Anthony de Rothschild's collection of art, French and English furniture and oriental porcelain. The garden has unusual trees, flower borders, topiary, a sundial, Italian garden and fountain statuary.

* Houses one of the foremost collections of Chinese three-colour wares ceramics in the world

Location
On the A418 betweem Aylesbury and Leighton Buzzard, E of Wing

Opening
16 Mar–30 Apr and 1–31 Aug daily except Monday 2pm–6pm
May 4–Jul 29 Tue–Thurs only 2–6pm

Admission
Adult £6, Child £3

Contact
Wing, Leighton Buzzard LU7 0PP
t 01296 688242
w ascottestate.co.uk
e info@ascottestate.co.uk

352   Shefford

Hoo Hill Maze

1 hr+   All year

Set within an orchard, this hedge maze measures 300 square feet and 7 feet high (30m^2 x 2m). Visitors are invited to picnic in the orchard, where there is also an open area. An adult garden maze is currently being constructed.

* All three species of woodpecker present
* Abundance of daffodils in the Spring

Location
Off the A507 and A600 close to Shefford

Opening
Daily 10am–5pm

Admission
Adult £3, Child & Concs £2

Contact
Hoo Hill Maze, Hitchin Road, Shefford SG17 5JD
t 01462 813475

353 Marston Moretaine

Forest Centre & Marston Vale Country Park

3 hrs+   All year

Stretching over 600 acres, the park has a mosaic of habitats from wetlands to woodlands – lakes and lagoons. It is home to a wealth of wildlife – in particular wild birds. Discover some of the new inhabitants who can be viewed from paths, boardwalks and bird hides.

* Walkway and cycleway with sunning views
* Forest Centre hands-on exhibition

Location
Off A421 at Marston Moretaine

Opening
Summer 10am–6pm
Winter 10am–4pm

Admission
Free, *Wetlands* Adult £2, Child & Concs £1.25

Contact
Station Road, Marston Moretaine MK43 0PR

t 01234 767037
w marstonvale.org
e info@marstonvale.org

354 Silsoe

Wrest Park Gardens

2 hrs+   Apr–Sep

Come and enjoy the magnificent gardens inspired by the great gardens of Versailles and the Loire Valley in France. Woodland walks and stunning formal gardens are complimented by the reflective expanses of water and wonderful stone and lead statuary.

* Domed baroque pleasure pavilion
* Chinese and Roman architecture

Location
¾ mile E of Silsoe off A6, 10 miles S off Bedford

Opening
Apr–Sep Sat, Sun & Bank Hols
10am–5pm

Admission
Adult £4, Child £2, Concs £3

Contact
Silsoe MK45 4HS

t 01525 860152
w english-heritage.org.uk

Bedfordshire | Cambridgeshire

355 Woburn

Woburn Abbey

3 hrs+   Jan–Oct

A palatial C18 mansion founded in 1145 as a religious house for a group of Cistercian monks. In 1547 Edward VI gave Woburn Abbey to Sir John Russell who became the 1st Earl of Bedford. Tours include Queen Victoria's bedroom and the state dining room.

* Woburn's treasures are acknowledged worldwide
* Home to the Dukes of Bedfordshire for over 400 years

Location
Located on the edge of the village of Woburn

Opening
Daily Mar 14–Oct 31 11am–4pm
Sat & Sun only Jan–Mar

Admission
Adult £9, Child £4.50, Concs £8

Contact
Woburn MK17 9WA

t 01525 290666
w woburnabbey.co.uk
e enquiries@woburnabbey.co.uk

356 Cambridge

Cambridge & County Folk Museum

1 hr   All year

The museum is housed in the former White Horse Inn, a C16 timber-framed building in the oldest part of the city. Founded in 1936, the museum provides a fascinating insight into the history of Cambridge capturing the lives of everyday people from C17 to the present day.

* 30,000 objects collected over 60 years

Location
Junction 13 of M11 signs to city centre

Opening
Apr–Sep, Mon–Sat 10.30am–5pm
Sunday 2–5pm
Oct–Mar, Tue–Sat & Mon during school holidays
Closed Dec 24–Jan 1

Admission
Adults £2.50, Child 75p, Concs £1.50

Contact
2/3 Castle Street, Cambridge CB3 0AQ

t 01223 355159
w folkmuseum.org.uk
e info@folkmuseum.org.uk

357 Cambridge

Fitzwilliam Museum

3 hrs+   All year

This is the art museum of the University of Cambridge with public access to its collection of international repute. Antiquities from ancient Egypt, rare printed books, Chinese jades and paintings by Titian, Canaletto, Rubens, Monet and Picasso. Fine collection of C20 art.

* Collection of Japanese ceramics
* Exhibition of medals since the Renaissance

Location
Approx 500 yards from city centre

Opening
Tue–Sat, 10am–5pm
Sunday, 2.15–5pm. Closed Mon except Summer Bank Hols

Admission
Free

Contact
Trumpington Street, Cambridge CB2 1RB

t 01223 332900
w fitzmuseum.cam.ac.uk
e fitzmuseum-enquiries@lists.cam.ac.uk

358 Cambridges

King's College

½ hr+   All year

King's is one of the oldest colleges in Cambridge, founded in 1441 by Henry VI. It is also the premier tourist attraction primarily due to the stunning architecture of its perpendicular chapel and its impressive interior that includes the painting Adoration of the Magi by Rubens.

Location
Take junction 11 or 12 from M11 follow signs for centre parking or park+ride

Opening
Term time, Mon–Sat 9.30am–3.30pm
Sun 1.15–2.15pm & 5–5.30pm
Out of term, Mon–Sat 9.30am–4.30pm
Sun 10am–5pm (closed Dec 24–Jan 3)

Admission
Adult £4, Child £3

Contact
King's College, Cambridge CB2 1ST

t 01223 331212
w kings.cam.ac.uk/visitors

359 Cambridge

Museum of Archaeology & Anthropology

2 hrs+   All year

Established in 1884, the museum displays renowned archaeological and anthropological collections from around the world. Highlights include world prehistory and local archaeology; historical and geographical display of the social anthropology collection.

* Faculty's current research interests displayed
* New created photographic collection on-line

Location
City centre between Pembroke Emmanuel College

Opening
Tue–Sat 2–4.30pm

Admission
Free

Contact
Downing Street, Cambridge CB2 3DZ

t 01223 333516
w museum-server.archanth.cam.ac.uk/museum.html
e cumaa@hermes.cam.ac.uk

360 Cambridge

Cambridge University Botanic Garden

3 hrs   All year

This tranquil 40-acre garden offers year round interest to visitors. Over 10,000 labelled plant species in beautifully landscaped settings, including rock garden, lake, glasshouses, winter garden, woodland walk, and nine National Collections.

* Important collections of native English plants
* Founded by mentor of Charles Darwin

Location
1 mile S of city centre

Opening
Nov–Jan 10am–4 pm
Feb–Oct 10am–5pm
Mar–Sep 10am–6pm

Admission
Adult £2.50, Child £2, Concs £2

Contact
Cory Lodge, Bateman Street,
Cambridge CB2 1JF

t 01223 336265
w botanic.cam.ac.uk
e enquiries@botanic.cam.ac.uk

361 Duxford

Imperial War Museum Duxford

3 hrs+   All year

This former Battle of Britain airfield is now home to 180 historic aircaft including biplanes, Spitfires, Concorde and Gulf War jets – many of which still regularly fly. The 7 acres of indoor exhibition space also house one of the country's finest collections of military vehicles.

* 'D-Day Experience' complete with video story
* Flying displays held throughout the summer

Location
Off junction 10 of M11

Opening
Summer Mar–Sep, 10am–6pm
Winter 10am–4pm

Admission
Adult £6.50, Child free, Concs £4.50

Contact
Duxford CB2 4QR

t 01223 835 000
w iwm.org.uk/duxford
e duxford@iwm.org.uk

362 Ely

Ely Cathedral

3 hrs+   All year

Begun by William the Conqueror, this magnificent cathedral stands on the site of a monastery founded in 673 by St Ethelreda. Essentially Romanesque, there is a blend of architectural styles complemented by many beautiful objects in stone, wood and glass.

* Extensive renovation completed in 2000

Location
Ely city centre

Opening
Summer 7am–7pm
Winter 7.30am–6pm Mon–Sat
Sun 7.30–5pm

Admission
Adult £4.80, Concs £4.20, Free on Sun

Contact
Chapter House, The College,
Ely CB7 4DL

t 01353 667735
w cathedral.ely.anglican.org
e receptionist@cathedral.ely.
    anglican.org

363 Ely

Stained Glass Museum

1 hr   All year

The museum offers a unique insight into the story of stained glass, an artform practised in Britain for at least 1,300 years. This Trust, set up in the 1970s to rescue and preserve stained glass, now houses a National Collection of British stained glass.

* Work by William Morris on display
* Opportunity to design your own pattern

Location
Inside Ely Cathedral

Opening
Mon–Fri, 10.30–5pm Sat 10.30–5.30
(5pm in Winter) Sun 12–6 (4.30 Winter)
Closed Dec 25/26 & Good Friday

Admission
Adult £3.50, Child £2.50, Conc £2.50

Contact
Ely Cathedral, Ely CB7 4DL

t 01353 660347
w stainedglassmuseum.com
e Admin@stainedglassmuseum.com

364 Ely

Oliver Cromwell's House

1 hr+   Easter–Oct

Home to Ely's most famous former resident, Cromwell's carefully restored house now contains Civil War exhibitions including weapons and armour. It also has illustrations of everyday C17 life and a history of the Fenlands and its transformation from marsh to farmland.

* C15 inglenook fireplace restored to working order
* Kitchen area has display of C17 recipes and ingredients

Location
Ely town centre next to St Mary's Church

Opening
Summer Apr–Oct, 10am–5.30pm
Winter Mon–Fri, 11am–4pm
Sat 10am–5pm, Sun 11.15–4pm

Admission
Adult £3.50, Concs £3

Contact
29 St Mary's Street, Ely CB7 4HF

t 01353 662062
w eastcambs.gov.uk/html/ochouse
e tic@eastcambs.gov.uk

365 Lode

Anglesey Abbey

3 hrs   All year

This site of a former Augustinian priory (many C12 stonework features remain) was brought to its current splendour by Lord Fairhaven in the first half of the C20, Fairhaven purchased the vast collection of paintings, planned the elaborate gardens and purchased the mill.

* Watermill can be seen working on 1st & 3rd Saturdays
* One of country's finest collections of historic statuary

Location
6 miles NE of Cambridge on B1102

Opening
Summer, *Gardens* Apr–Nov
10.30–5.30pm *Mill* 1–5pm
Winter, *Gardens* 10.30–4.30
Mill Sat–Sun 11–3.30pm

Admission
Summer Adult £6.60, Child £3.30

Gardens only £4.10/ £2.05
Winter £3.40/£1.70

Contact
Lode CB5 9EJ

t 01223 810080
w nationaltrust.org.uk/angleseyabbey
e angleseyabbey@nationaltrust.
    org.uk

366 Peterborough

Peterborough Cathedral

1 hr   All year

Today's cathedral is essentially the third abbey, founded in 1118 (the first dates from 655). It suffered badly at the hands of Oliver Cromwell, but many of its unique features remain to be admired today. The west front is a remarkable example of medieval archtitecture.

* The interior remains largely unchanged in 800 years
* Burial place for two queens

Location
Follow signs for city centre from junction 16/17 of A1M

Opening
Daily 8.30am–5.15pm, Sun 12–5pm
Closed Dec 25/26

Admission
Free, donations encouraged

Contact
Little Prior's Gate, Minster Precincts, Peterborough PE1 1XS

t 01733 560964
w peterborough-cathedral.org.uk
e a.watson@peterborough-cathedral.org.uk

367 Peterborough

Nene Valley Railway

3 hrs+   All year

A 15-mile round trip through the beautiful Nene Park from Wansford to Peterborough. One of Britain's leading steam railways is home for a wide range of British and European engines and carriages, both steam and diesel.

* Train galas in March, June and September
* Talking Timetable 01780 784404

Location
Off the southbound A1 at Stibbington between the A47 & A605 junctions

Opening
Daily 9am–4.30
Closed Dec 24–Jan 1

Admission
Adults £10, Child £5, Concs £7.50

Contact
Wansford Station, Stibbington, Peterborough PE8 6LR

t 01780 784444
w nvr.org.uk
e nvrorg@aol.com

368 Royston

Wimpole Estate

3 hrs+   Mar–Nov

First built in 1643 and much altered by subsequent owners, Wimpole has developed into the largest country house in Cambridgeshire. The 360 acres of beautiful parkland is the product of four celebrated designers including Capability Brown.

* Parkland includes restored lakes and gothic tower
* Good walks available through woodland & rolling hills

Location
8 miles SW of Cambridge
junction 12 off M11/junction 9 off A1(M)

Opening
Mar–Nov, Tue–Sun (not Fri ex during Aug & Good Friday) & Bank Hol Mons 1–5pm (Bank Hol Mons\ 11am–5pm)
Farm open weekends Nov–Mar

Admission
Adult £6.60, Child £3.20

Contact
Wimpole Hall, Arrington, Royston SG8 0BW

t 01223 207257
w wimpole.org
e wimpolehall@nationaltrust.org.uk

369 Sawtry

Hamerton Zoo Park

2 hrs+ All year

Opened as a conservation sanctuary in 1990, Hamerton's 15 acres of parkland provide a safe home for a fascinating array of beautiful creatures from around the world, including many endangered species and some that are extinct in the wild.

* Spacious indoor-outdoor enclosures for monkeys
* Opportunity to handle many different animals

Location
On the A14, turn off to B660 at junction 15 onto A1M follow signs

Opening
Daily 10.30am–6pm (4pm in winter)
Closed Dec 25

Admission
Adult £6, Child £4, Concs £5

Contact
Hamerton, nr Sawtry PE28 5RE

t 01832 293362
w hamertonzoopark.com
e office@hamertonzoopark.com

370 Wisbech

Peckover House & Gardens

3 hrs+ Mar–Nov

This outstanding Victorian garden includes an orangery, summer-houses, roses, herbaceous borders, fernery, croquet lawn and reed barn. The townhouse, built *c*.1722, is renowned for its very fine plaster and wood rococo decoration.

* Restored Victorian library
* One of the finest walled town gardens in England

Location
From A47 to Wisbech town centre, follow signs

Opening
Gardens Mar 21–Oct 31, daily (ex Fri)
House Mar 21–Apr 29, Wed–Sun &
Bank Hols, 1.30pm–4.30pm
May–Aug, Wed, Thur, Sat, Sun.
Sept–Oct, Wed, Sat, Sun

Admission
House Adult £4.25, Child £2
Gardens £2.75, £1.50

Contact
North Brink, Wisbech PE13 1JR

t 01945 583463
w peckoverhouse.com
e info@peckoverhouse.com

371 Braintree

Braintree District Museum

2 hrs   All year

Situated in an old Victorian school the musuem tells the story of Braintree district and its place in history. The people of the area developed ideas which shaped C20 life. Exhibits interpret local industrial heritage, in particular the production of fabrics for state occasions.

* Specialities include the history of man-made textiles
* Textile collection

Location	Contact
Just off market square, Braintree	Market Square, Braintree CM7 3YG
Opening	t 01376 325266
All year Mon–Sat 10am–5pm,	w enjoybraintreedistrict.co.uk
Sun during Nov and Dec	e jean@bdcmuseum.demon.co.uk
Admission	
Adult £2, Concs £1	

372 Castle Hedingham

Colne Valley Railway

2 hrs+   Mar–Oct

Take a ride on a period country railway. A pretty line, relocated station buildings, signal boxes and bridges all lovingly restored and rebuilt. A large collection of vintage steam and diesel engines, carriages and wagons is available to explore.

* Seven steam engines and 40 carriages and wagons
* Colne Valley Farm Park

Location	Contact
Located on right hand side of A1017	Yeldham Road, Castle Hedingham
1 mile from Castle Hedingham	CO9 3DZ
Opening	t 01787 461174
Mar–Oct 11am–5pm	w colnevalleyrailway.co.uk
dates vary, phone for details	e info@colnevalleyrailway.co.uk
Admission	
Adult £6, Child £3, Concs £5	

373 Chelmsford

Chelmsford Museum & Essex Regiment Museum

1 hr+   All year

The museum is set in a Victorian mansion where visitors may follow the story of Chelmsford from the ice ages, via the Roman town, to the present day. See also the superb Essex regiment museum housing many military artefacts.

* Bright & colourful Victorian pottery from Hedingham
* Period dress and room settings

Location	Contact
In Oaklands Park, off Moulsham Street	Oaklands Park, Chelmsford CM2 9AQ
Opening	t 01245 615100
Mon–Sat 10am–5pm	w chelmsfordmuseums.co.uk
Sun 2pm–5pm	e oaklands@chelmsfordbc.gov.uk
Admission	
Free	

374 Chelmsford

RHS Garden Hyde Hall

Fine   3 hrs   All year

40 years of work has transformed a windswept hill with just six mature trees, to the present day garden of 24 acres. It contains the National Collection of viburnum and an attractive garden of 8 acres including woodland and a large collection of modern roses.

* Rope walk of climbing and pillar roses
* Ornamental ponds with lilies and fish

Location	Contact
From Rettendon follow flower	Rettendon, Chelmsford CM3 8ET
signposts	t 01245 400256
Opening	w rhs.org.uk/gardens/hydehall
All year 10am–dusk	e hydehall@rhs.org.uk
Admission	
Adult £4.50, Child £1	

375 Colchester

Beth Chatto Gardens

2 hrs+   All year

These gardens began in 1960 when the site was an overgrown wasteland between two farms. Faced with difficult conditions and with dry and damp soil in both sun and shade, the owners have put into practice what is now referred to as ecological gardening.

* Remarkable drought resistant garden
* Water garden and woodland

Location
Located on A133. Approx 4 miles E of Colchester and a ¼ mile E of Elmstead Market

Opening
Mar–Oct Mon–Sat 9am–5pm
Nov–Feb Mon–Fri 9am–4pm

Admission
Adult £3.50, Child free

Contact
Elmstead Market, Colchester CO7 7DB

t 01206 822007
w bethchatto.co.uk
e info@bethchatto.fsnet.co.uk

---

377 Colchester

Tymperley's Clock Museum

½ hr+   Apr–Oct

This C15 timber-framed house, was home to William Gilberd, scientist and physician to Elizabeth I, and now home to a fine collection of clocks and watches. View part of the famous Bernard Mason collection, one of the largest collections of clocks in Britain.

* Clocks made in Colchester between 1640 and 1840
* 1645 lantern clock by William Bacon

Location
Situated in Trinity Street off Culver Street East

Opening
Apr–Oct Tue–Sat 10am–1pm and 2pm–5pm

Admission
Free

Contact
14 Rygate, Colchester CO1 1YG

t 01206 282939
w colchestermuseums.org.uk
e marie.taylor@colchester.gov.uk

---

376 Colchester

Colchester Zoo

6 hrs   All year

Colchester Zoo has some of the best cat and primate collections in Europe. See a white tiger eye to eye in White Tiger Valley, or get closer to the zoo's chimpanzees at Chimp World. Other enclosures include Penguin Shores and Serengeti Plains for African lions.

* Playa Patagonia – sealion underwater experience
* Tiger campaign earned a Platinum Certificate

Location
Take the A1124 exit from the A12

Opening
Summer 9.30am–5.30pm
Winter 9.30am–1 hr before dusk

Admission
Adult £10.99, Child £6.99, Concs £6.99

Contact
Maldon Road, Stanway, Colchester CO3 0SL

t 01206 331292
w colchester-zoo.co.uk
e enquiries@colchester-zoo.co.uk

378   Colchester

Colchester Castle Museum

2 hrs   All year

The museum covers 2,000 years of the most important events in British history. Once the capital of Roman Britain, Colchester has experienced devastation by Boudica, invasion by the Normans and a siege during the English Civil War.

* The castle has been a library and a gaol for witches
* 2250 BC Dagenham idol

Location
Situated in Castle Park at the eastern end of the High Street

Opening
Mon–Sat 10am–5pm
Sun 11am–5pm

Admission
Adult £4.25, Concs £2.80

Contact
High Street, Castle Park, Colchester
CO1 1TJ

t 01206 282939
w colchestermuseums.org.uk
e marie.taylor@colchester.gov.uk

379   Halstead

Hedingham Castle

½ hr+   Apr–Oct

This is one of the best preserved Norman keeps in England. Built in 1140, it possesses four floors including a magnificent banqueting hall with a minstrels' gallery and Norman arch. It is approached by a Tudor bridge, built in 1496 to replace the drawbridge.

* Woodlands and lake with a pretty C18 dovecote
* 1920s bog garden contains camellias and azaleas

Location
Situated in Castle Hedingham, ½ mile from A1017 between Cambridge & Colchester

Opening
Apr–Oct Thu, Fri & Sun 11am–4pm
Special school holiday opening 10am–5pm, phone for details

Admission
Adult £4, Child £3, Concs £3.50

Contact
Halstead CO9 3DJ

t 01787 460261
w hedinghamcastle.co.uk
e hedinghamcastle@aspects.net.co.uk

380 East Mersea

Cudmore Grove Country Park

1 hr   All year

Cudmore Grove is at the eastern end of Mersea Island, with fine views across the Colne and Blackwater estuaries. Walk the sea wall, explore the shore and watch for wildlife. Behind the sandy beach is a tranquil area of cliff top and grassland.

* Wildside walk and bird hides
* Ranger-led guided walks available by request

Location
Take B1025 S of Colchester & Mersea Island. Take left hand fork to East Mersea – signposted

Opening
8am–dusk

Admission
£1 per hour per car, £2 per day per car

Contact
Bromans Lane, East Mersea CO5 8UE

t 01206 383868
w essexcc.gov.uk
e cudmoregrove@essexcc.gov.uk

381 Pitsea

The Motorboat Museum

2 hr+   Feb–Dec

This museum is devoted to the history and evolution of sports and leisure motorboats, with over 31 exhibits of motorboats from 1873 to present. From the state-of-the-art offshore powerboats to the early days of steamers, trace the history of these wonderful crafts.

* Collection of inboard and outboard motors
* Carstais collection

Location
Well signposted from Pitsea

Opening
Thu–Mon 10–4.30pm, daily during school holidays.

Admission
Free

Contact
Wat Tyler Country Park, Basildon SS16 4UH

t 01268 550 077
w basildon.gov.uk

382 Saffron Walden

Mole Hall Wildlife Park

2 hrs   Easter–Oct

This family-owned wildlife park was first opened to the public in 1963 and has continued to grow. The collection of animals and birds contains many exotic species including otters, primates including chimpanzees, owls, birds and many more.

* Butterfly pavilion
* Animal adoption scheme

    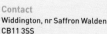

Location
Signposted from B1383 & junction 8 of M11

Opening
Easter–Oct daily 10.30am–dusk

Admission
Adult £5, Child £3.50, Concs £4

Contact
Widdington, nr Saffron Walden CB11 3SS

t 01799 540400
w molehall.co.uk
e enquiries@molehall.co.uk

383 Stansted

Mountfitchet Castle & Norman Village

2 hrs   Mar–Nov

This is a Norman motte and bailey castle and village, re-constructed on its original ancient site. Vivid exhibition of village life at the time of the conquest includes houses, exhibition, seige tower and church. Computerised figures give historical information.

* Iron-Age fort, Roman, Saxon and Viking settlements

Location
2 miles from Junction 8 of the M11

Opening
Mar–Nov Mon–Sun 10am–5pm

Admission
Adult £8, Child £5, Concs £5.50

Contact
Stansted CM24 8SP

t 01279 813237
w www.mountfitchetcastle.com
e mountfitchetcastle1066@btinternet.com

384 Saffron Walden

Audley End House & Gardens

3 hr+   Apr–Sep

The house was built by the first Earl of Suffolk, Lord Treasurer to James I, on the scale of a great royal palace. Parts of the house were demolished in the early C18 and what remains is one of the most significant Jacobean houses in England.

* Historic kitchen and dry laundry
* Landscaped garden walks

Location
1 mile W of Saffron Walden on B1383 (M11 exits 8 and 9, northbound only, and 10)

Opening
Apr–Sep Wed–Sun 11am–6pm

Admission
Adult £8, Child £4, Concs £6

Contact
Saffron Walden CB11 4JT
t 01799 522399
w english-heritage.org.uk

385 Stansted

The House on the Hill Toy Museum

2 hrs   All year

This is the largest privately owned toy museum in the world with over 30,000 items on display. The artefacts range from the Victorian era right through to the 1980s, and are the collection of one man who started in 1946 by buying a Hornby train set with his pocket money.

* Dolls and dolls' houses & rock 'n' roll memorabilia
* End-of-the-pier amusement machines

Location
Situated 2 miles from Junction 8 of the M11

Opening
Daily 10am–4pm

Admission
Adult £4, Child £3.20, Concs £3.50

Contact
Stansted CM24 8SP
t 01279 813237
w mountfitchetcastle.com
e mountfitchetcastle1066@btinternet.com

386 Tilbury

Tilbury Fort

2 hrs   All year

The finest surviving example of C17 military engineering in England, Tilbury Fort remains largely unaltered. Today, exhibitions, the powder magazine and bunker-like 'casemates', demonstrate how the fort protected the city. Visitors can even fire an anti-aircraft gun.

* Regular military collectors fairs
* Designed by Charles II's chief engineer

Location
Located 5 miles E of Tilbury off A126

Opening
Apr–Sep daily 10am–6pm
Oct–Nov daily 10am–5pm
Dec–Apr Wed–Sun 10am–4pm

Admission
Adult £3, Child £1.50, Concs £2.50

Contact
Tilbury, RM18 7NR

t 01375 858489
w english-heritage.org.uk

387 Barnet

Museum of Domestic Design & Architecture

1 hr   All year

The museum (MoDA) houses one of the most important and comprehensive collections of late C19 and C20 decorative design for the home. MoDA offers a wide ranging programme alongside its permanent exhibition, 'Exploring Interiors: Decoration of the Home 1900–1960'.

* Wallpapers and textiles from 1870s–1960s
* Crown Wallpaper archive

Location
Underground Oakwood, from where there is a university shuttle bus. Or M25 junction 24 onto A111 for 3 miles

Opening
Tue–Sat 10am–5pm, Sun 2pm–5pm

Admission
Free

Contact
Middlesex University, Cat Hill, Barnet EN4 8HT

t 020 8411 5244
w moda.mdx.ac.uk
e moda@mdx.ac.uk

388 Waltham Abbey

Royal Gunpowder Mills

3 hrs+   All year

The world of explosives is uncovered with a range of interactive and static displays which follows the trail back to the 17th century. This unique museum traces the evolution of gunpowder technology and reveals the impact it had on the history of Great Britain.

* Muskets, rifles, pistols, machine guns!
* Munitionettes – photo exhibits of women in Second World War

Location
1 mile from junction 26 of M25, A121

Opening
Apr 24–Sep 26 Sat, Sun & Bank hols 11am–5pm (last entry 3.30pm)

Admission
Adult £5.50, Child £2.50, Concs £4.50

Contact
Beaulieu Drive, Waltham Abbey EN9 1JY

t 01992 707370
w royalgunpowdermills.com
e info@royalgunpowdermills.com

389 Berkhamsted

Ashridge Estate

1 hr+   All year

This estate, situated along the main ridge of the Chiltern Hills, offers a variety of picturesque walks, supporting a variety of wildlife in the commons, woodlands and chalk downland. The focal point is the Duke of Bridgewater Monument, erected in 1832.

* Splendid views from Ivinghoe Beacon
* Visitor Centre with exhibition room

Location
Between Northchurch & Ringshall just off B4506

Opening
All year

Admission
Estate free
Monument Adult £1.20, Child 60p

Contact
Ringshall, Berkhamsted HP4 1LT

t 01442 851227
w nationaltrust.org.uk
e ashridge@nationaltrust.org.uk

Berkhamsted Castle

2 hrs+   All year

Berkhamsted Castle is a good example of a motte and bailey castle where the original wooden defences were later rebuilt in stone. It consists of a large bailey and a motte to one side, on which there are traces of a stone tower. The only double-moated Norman castle in the UK.

* Built in late C11 by Robert of Mortain
* Further improvements were made by King John

Location
Adjacent to Berkhamsted station

Opening
Apr–Oct 10am–6pm
Nov–Mar 10am–4pm

Admission
Free

Contact
Berkhamsted HP4 1LJ

t 01442 871737
w english-heritage.org.uk
e customers@english-heritage.org.uk

Paradise Wildlife Park

2 hrs+   All year

The park is a special place, with a relaxed and friendly atmosphere. It has a range of animals from monkeys to lions, zebras to tigers and cheetahs to camels. What makes it unique is the fact that you can get really close, meeting and feeding many of the animals.

* Brazilian tapirs and reptilemania
* Hollywood Stunt Parrot Show

Location
Junction 25 of M25 onto A10, signposted from Broxbourne

Opening
Mar–Oct Mon–Sun 9.30am–6pm
Nov–Feb Mon–Sun 10am–5pm

Admission
Adult £9, Child & Concs £7

Contact
White Stubbs Lane, Broxbourne EN10 7QA

t 01992 470 490
w pwpark.com
e info@pwpark.com

392 Hatfield

Mill Green Museum & Mill

1 hr+   All year

This museum is housed in what was for centuries the home of the millers who worked in the adjoining watermill. The watermill is fully restored and operational. It probably stands on the site of one of four Hatfield mills listed in the *Domesday Book*.

* Waterwheel in action every day
* Watch milling of organic flour on Tue, Wed & Sun

Location
Located in Mill Green, between Hatfield and Welwyn Garden City

Opening
Tue–Fri 10am–5pm
Sat, Sun & Bank Hols 2pm–5pm

Admission
Free

Contact
Mill Green, Hatfield AL9 5PD

t 01707 271362
w hertsmuseums.org.uk/millgreen
e museum@welhat.gov.uk

393 Hitchin

Hitchin Museum

1 hr   All year

The museum recounts Hitchin's history through imaginative displays. It holds hold the Hertfordshire Yeomanry Collection and a costume collection covering 200 years. There is a Victorian chemist's shop and physic garden of medicinal plants and shrubs.

* Programme of special exhibitions and events
* Researc enqueries welcome

Location
Signposted from town centre, on A505 & A602

Opening
Mon, Tue, Thu–Sat 10am–5pm

Admission
Free

Contact
Paynes Park, Hitchin SG5 1EQ

t 01462 434476
w north-herts.gov.uk

394 Hatfield

Hatfield House

2hrs+   Easter–Sep

This Jacobean house stands in its own great park and is the home of the Marquess of Salisbury. The state rooms are rich in paintings, furniture, fine tapestries and historic armour. Superb examples of Jacobean craftsmanship can be seen throughout the house.

* Beautifully carved wooden grand staircase
* Rare stained-glass window in the private chapel

Location
Signed from junction 4 of A1(M)
Entrance opposite Hatfield train station

Opening
Easter–Sep *House* open daily 12 noon–4pm. *Garden* daily 11am–5.30pm

Admission
Adult £7.50, Child £4

Contact
Hatfield AL9 5NQ

t 01707 287 010
w hatfield-house.co.uk
e s.jessup@hatfield-house.co.uk

395 Knebworth

Knebworth House

3 hrs+   All year

The Lytton family have lived at Knebworth for 500 years. Queen Elizabeth I stayed here, Charles Dickens acted in private theatricals in the house and Winston Churchill's painting of the banqueting hall hangs in the room where he painted it.

* Constance Lytton fought for votes for women in 1900s
* The stately home of rock music

Location
29 miles N of London off junction A1(M) at Stevenage

Opening
Mar 27–Sep 26 Sat Sun & Bank Hols 12 noon–5pm
Daily Apr 3–18 May 29–Jun 6 Jul 3–Aug 31

Admission
Adult £8.50, Child & Concs £8

Contact
Knebworth SG3 6PY

t 01438 812 661
w knebworthhouse.com
e info@knebworthhouse.com

396 Letchworth

Letchworth Museum & Art Gallery

1 hr+   All year

The museum opened in 1914 to house the collections of the Letchworth Naturalists' Society. Today it shows examples of local wildlife in realistic settings including the famous Letchworth black squirrel and the two art galleries house changing exhibitions.

* Iron Age Chieftain's burial display
* Many examples of Roman pottery and jewellery

Location
In Letchworth town centre, opposite cinema

Opening
Mon, Tue, Thu, Fri & Sat 10am–5pm

Admission
Free

Contact
Broadway, Letchworth SG6 3PF

t 01462 685 647
w north-herts.gov.uk
e letchworth.museum@north-herts.gov.uk

397 St Albans

Museum of St Albans

1 hr · All year

Founded in 1898, the museum tells the story of St Albans from the departure of the Romans to the present day. Find out about Alban, Britain's first Christian martyr, and the abbey that grew up around the site of his martyrdom. Complete with many temporary exhibits.

* Objects illustrate everyday life in Victorian St Albans
* Special exhibitions from Barbie dolls to the Egyptians

Location
400 yards from the centre of town

Opening
All year Mon–Sat 10am–5pm
Sun 2pm–5pm

Admission
Free

Contact
Hatfield Road, St Albans AL1 3RR

t 01727 819340
w stalbansmuseums.org.uk
e a.coles@stalbans.gov.uk

398 St Albans

The Verulamium Museum

1 hr+ · All year

Discover the life and times of a major Roman city at St Albans. This is the museum of everyday life in Roman Britain. Displays and activities include recreated Roman rooms, hands-on discovery areas and some of the best mosaics and wall plasters outside the Mediterranean.

* Excavation video and accessible collections
* Roman soldiers second weekend of every monrh

Location
Signposted from St Albans

Opening
Mon–Sat 10am–5.30pm
Sun 2pm–5.30pm

Admission
Adult £3.30, Child & Concs £2

Contact
St Michaels, St Albans AL3 4SW

t 01727 751 810
w stalbansmuseums.org.uk
e a.coles@stalbans.gov.uk

399 Stevenage

Stevenage Museum

1 hrs+   All year

Explore the new Millennium Galleries, see a rare Vincent motorbike and a roman coin hoard. Discover the story of Stevenage from prehistoric times up to the present day through hands-on displays, films and special exhibitions.

* The Story of Stevenage – prehistory to 1700
* Varied programme of events

Location
Located underneath St.Andrew &
St.Georges Church – signposted from
town centre

Opening
Mon–Sat 10am–5pm
Sun 2pm–5pm. Closed Bank Hols

Admission
Free, exhibitions may charge

Contact
St George's Way, Stevenage SG1 1XX

t 01438 218881
w stevenage.gov.uk/museum
e museum@stevenage.gov.uk

400 Welwyn

Shaw's Corner

1 hr+   Mar–Oct

This Edwardian villa was the home of George Bernard Shaw from 1906 till his death in 1950. The rooms remain much as he left them, with many literary and personal effects and many touches evoking the individuality and genius of this great dramatist.

* An Edwardian Arts & Crafts-influenced house
* Kitchen and outbuildings evocative of early C20 life.

Location
Junction 4 of the A1(M) signposted
from B653 & B656

Opening
Mar 20–Oct 31 Wed–Sun & Bank Hols
House 1pm–5pm
Garden 12 noon–5.30pm

Admission
Adult £3.80, Child £1.90

Contact
Ayot St Lawrence
Welwyn AL6 9BX

t 01438 820307
w nationaltrust.org.uk/shawscorner
e shawscorner@nationaltrust.org.uk

401 Tring

Walter Rothschild Zoological Museum

1 hr+   All year

This collection, started in 1890 by Walter Rothschild, contains thousands of birds, mammals, reptiles, fish, insects and even dressed fleas. The Victorian setting gives it a unique atmosphere and it's a fascinating insight into the life of a classic English eccentric.

* Come face to face with a giant anaconda
* Part of the Natural History Museum since 1937

Location
Tring is on A41, 12 miles W of Hemel
Hempstead and 33 miles N of London.
Museum is off Tring High Street

Opening
Mon–Sat 10am–5pm, Sun 2pm–5pm

Admission
Free

Contact
Akeman Street, Tring HP23 6AP

t 020 7942 6171
w nhm.ac.uk/museum/tring
e tring-enquiries@nhm.ac.uk

Norfolk

402 Aylsham

Blickling Hall, Garden & Park

3 hrs+   Mar–Oct

One of England's great Jacobean houses, it is famed for its spectacular long gallery, superb library and fine collections of furniture, pictures and tapestries. The gardens are full of colour all year, and the extensive parkland features a lake and a series of beautiful walks.

* Superb Jacobean plaster ceiling in the long gallery
* Formal woodland and wilderness garden

Location
N of B1354, 1½ miles NW of Aylsham
on A140

Opening
Mar 20–Oct 31 Wed–Sun
Hall 1pm–4.30pm
Garden & Park 10.15am–5.15pm

Admission
Adult £6.90, Child free
Garden only £3.90, free

Contact
Blickling, Norwich NR11 6NF
t 01263 738030
w nationaltrust.org.uk
e blickling@nationaltrust.org.uk

403 Blakeney

Blakeney Point

3 hrs   All year

One of Britain's foremost bird sanctuaries, the point is a 3½-mile long sand and shingle spit, noted for its colonies of breeding terns and for the rare migrants that pass through in spring and autumn. Both common and grey seals can also be seen.

* Information centre at Morston Quay provides further details
* Restricted access during main bird breeding season

Location
Morston Quay, Blakeney and Cley are
all off A149 Cromer to Hunstanton road

Opening
All year, all times

Admission
Free

Contact
The Warden, 35 The Cornfield,
Langham, Holt NR25 7DQ
t 01263 740480 (Apr–Sep)
  01263 740241 (Oct–Mar)
w nationaltrust.org.uk
e blakeneypoint@nationaltrust.org.uk

404 Brandon

Grimes Graves

fine   1 hr   All year

These flint mines, dating back 4,000 years, were found in 1870. They were named by the Anglo-Saxons after the pagan god Grim. The mines provided materials needed to make tools and weapons. Visitors can descend 10 metres by ladder into one excavated shaft.

* Unfortunately NO UNDER FIVES allowed down shaft
* Site of Special Scientific Interest

Location
Located 7 miles NW of Thetford off
A134

Opening
Apr–Sep daily 10am–6pm
Oct daily 10am–5pm
Nov–Mar Wed–Sun 10am–4pm
Closed every day 1pm–2pm

Admission
Adult £3.50, Child £1.50, Concs £2

Contact
Brandon, Lynford IP26 5DE
t 01842 810656
w english-heritage.org.uk

405 Cromer

Cromer Museum

3 hrs+   All year

Visit the Victorian fisherman's cottage illuminated by gaslight and imagine what it was like to live here at the end of the C19. Uncover the history of this Victorian seaside resort and see the West Runton elephant, Britain's oldest elephant fossil.

* Atmosphere is 'cottage' and displays are simple
* Learn the daring rescues of the Cromer boatmen

Location
In Tucker Street, opposite the E end
of Cromer Parish Church

Opening
Mon–Sat 10am–5pm
From Apr 11 onwards Sun 2pm–5pm

Admission
Adult £1.80, Child 90p, Concs £1.40

Contact
Tucker Street, Cromer NR27 9HB
t 01263 513543
w norfolk.gov.uk
e cromer.museum@norfolk.gov.uk

406 Downham Market

Denver Windmill

1–3 hrs   All year

Visit a working windmill set on the edge of the Fens. Recently restored, this unique set of buildings allows visitors to explore the story of windmilling in England and of the people who lived and worked at the windmill since it was built in 1835.

* Tours to the very top of the windmill tower
* See the mill working – wind and the miller permitting!

Location	Admission
Signposted from A10	Adult £3.50, Child £2, Concs £3
Opening	**Contact**
Apr–Oct Mon–Sat 10am–5pm	Denver, Downham Market PE38 0EG
Sun 12 noon–5pm	
Nov–Mar Mon–Sat 10am–4pm	t 01366 384009
Sun 12 noon–4pm	w denvermill.co.uk
	e enquires@denvermill.co.uk

407 Dereham

Roots of Norfolk

4 hrs+   Mar–Nov

Set in 50 acres of beautiful countryside, this collection of rural Norfolk life is housed in a Georgian workhouse dating from 1777. There is a traditional farm, worked by heavy horses. Explore village life, agriculture and the workhouse through hands–on displays.

* Recent £3.5 million refurbishment
* A display of large diesel and steam engines

Location	Contact
3 miles NW of Dereham, follow signs	Gressenhall, Dereham NR20 4DR
Opening	t 01362 860563
Mar–Nov daily 10am–5pm	w norfolk.gov.uk/tourism/museums
	e gressenhall.museum@norfolk.gov.uk
Admission	
Adult £5.45, Child £4.35, Concs £4.95	

408 Fakenham

Thursford Collection

2 hrs   Easter–Sep

An Aladdin's cave of old road engines and mechanical organs of magical variety all gleaming with colour. Live musical shows featuring nine mechanical pipe organs and starring Robert Wolfe in the Wurlitzer Show. Old farm buildings, transformed into a small village.

Location
A148 between Fakenham & Holt

Opening
Easter–Sep Sun–Fri 12 noon–5pm

Admission
Adult £5.10, Child £2.60

Contact
Thursford, Fakenham NR21 0AS
t 01328 878 477
e admin@thursfordcollection.co.uk

409 Great Yarmouth

Elizabethan House Museum

1 hr   Apr–Oct

A C16 building with rooms reflecting the lives of families who have lived there. Of particular interest are a Tudor bedroom and dining-room, Victorian kitchen, scullery and parlour, and the Conspiracy Room, where the trial and execution of King Charles I were allegedly plotted.

* Special children's room with replica toys
* Hands-on activities

Location
In Great Yarmouth on 'Historic South Quay'

Opening
Apr–Oct Mon–Fri 10am–5pm
Sat & Sun 1.15pm–5pm

Admission
Adult £2.60, Child £1.30, Concs £2

Contact
4 South Quay, Great Yarmouth NR30 2QH
t 01493 855746
w nationaltrust.org.uk

410 Great Yarmouth

Tolhouse Museum

1 hr+   Apr–Oct

This C13 museum is one of the oldest civic buildings in the country. Once Great Yarmouth's courtroom and gaol, it illustrates aspects of local history, including the dungeons in which Victorian figures can be seen lurking in their cells. Brass rubbings can be made.

* Audio guide brings to life the stories and characters
* Museum of local history

Location
Great Yarmouth, near 'Historic South Quay'

Opening
Apr–Oct Mon–Fri 10am–5pm
Sat & Sun 1.15pm–5pm

Admission
Adult £2.60, Child £1.30, Concs £2

Contact
Tolhouse Street, Great Yarmouth NR30 2SH
t 01493 858900
w norfolkmuseumservice.org.uk
e yarmouth.museums@norfolk.gov.uk

411 Hunstanton

Hunstanton Sea Life Centre

1 hr+ **All year**

At this sanctuary you will see otters, penguins and more than 30 permanent displays all showcasing the diversity of life under the waves. The centre also provides a safe haven for sick, injured or orphaned seal pups which are cared for at the sanctuary.

* Penguin sanctuary, home to rare Humboldt penguins
* Seal adoption programme

Location
Take the A140 from Kings Lynn to Hunstanton and follow the signs

Opening
Mon–Sun 10am–4pm.
Times may vary during winter, phone for details

Admission
Adult £6.50, Child £4.50

Contact
Southern Promenade,
Hunstanton PE36 5BH

t 01485 533 576
w sealsanctuary.co.uk

---

412 King Lynn

Sandringham

3 hrs **Apr–Oct**

The country retreat of Her Majesty The Queen and His Royal Highness The Duke of Edinburgh. Sandringham is a friendly and informal place and visits include ground floor rooms within the house, a museum within the stable blocks and beautiful grounds.

* Nature trails and woodland walks in the Country Park
* Collection of vintage Royal motor vehicles

Location
Signposted from Kings Lynn

Opening
Apr–Sep
House 11am–4.45pm Oct 11am–3pm
Museum 11am–5pm Oct 11am–4pm
Gardens 10.30am–5pm Oct 11am–4pm

Admission
House, Garden & Museum Adult 6.50,
Child £4, Concs £5. *Garden and Museum* £4.50, £2.50, £3.50

Contact
Estate Office, Sandringham, PE35 6EN
t 01553 612 908
w sandringhamestate.co.uk
e visits@sandringhamestate.co.uk

Little Walsingham

Walsingham Shirehall Museum & Abbey Grounds

1 hr+   All year

Walsingham is one of the main centres for Christian pilgrimage in England, it has been an important site since 1061 and in 1153 an Augustinian Priory was founded in the village. It was destroyed in 1538, but the remains and site of the original shrine can still be seen.

* Picturesque and tranquil grounds
* Shirehall Museum – unaltered 'hands-on' courtroom

Location
4 miles NE of Fakenham off A149

Opening
Daily 10am–4pm

Admission
Adut £3, Child £1.50, Concs £1.50

Contact
Common Place, Little Walsingham
NR22 6BP

t 01328 820510 / 820259
e walsingham.museum@farmline.com

Norwich

Felbrigg Hall, Garden & Park

2 hrs+   Mar–Oct

This handsome house owes much of its splendour to William Windham II. The interior was remodelled in the 1750s to provide a sumptuous setting for his art treasures. The state rooms contain superb C18 furniture and paintings, and there is an outstanding library.

* The orangery has a fine display of camellias in spring
* Walled garden, extensive parkland, lake and woods

Location
In Felbrigg, 2 miles SW of Cromer, off
the B1346. Signposted from A140 & A148

Opening
Mar 20–Oct 31 Sat–Wed
Hall 11am–5pm
Garden 11am–5.30pm

Admission
Hall, Garden & Park Adult £6.30, Child £3
Garden only £2.60, £1

Contact
Felbrigg, Norwich NR11 8PR

t 01263 837444
w nationaltrust.org.uk
e felbrigg@ntrust.org.uk

415 Norwich

Norwich Cathedral

1 hr+   All year

This is a magnificent Norman building. The nave roof bosses, illustrating The Bible from Creation to the Day of Judgment, and the Saxon Bishop's throne are unique features. The cloisters are the largest monastic cloisters in the country, and spire the second highest.

* Nurse Edith Cavell is buried here
* Famous collection of medieval carvings

Location
Signposted from Norwich city centre

Opening
Mid Sep–mid May 7.30am–6pm
Mid May–mid Sep 7.30am–7pm

Admission
Free, although donations welcome

Contact
62 The Close, Norwich NR1 4EH

t 01603 218 321 / 218300
e vis-proffice@cathedral.org.uk
w cathedral.org.uk

416 Norwich

Sainsbury Centre for Visual Arts

1 hr   All year

In an internationally renowned building designed by Norman Foster, discover the delights of the Sainsbury art collection. There are over 1,200 items in the collection which spans thousands of years and many cultures. Alongside African masks are works by Picasso and Bacon.

* Degas' Little Dancer
* Giacometti's Standing Woman

Location
On University campus – signposted

Opening
Tue–Sun 11am–5pm

Admission
Adult £2, Concs £1

Contact
University of East Anglia
Earlham Road, Norwich NR4 7TJ

t 01603 593 199
w uea.ac.uk/scva
e scva@uea.ac.uk

417 Sheringham

Henry Ramey Upcher Lifeboat Museum

½ hr   Easter–Sep

This is a private pulling and sailing lifeboat donated by the Upcher family to the Sheringham fishermen. Built in 1894, she remained in service until 1935. During that time, she saved over 300 lives. The boat is on display in her original shed in her original condition.

* Display of contemporary photographs
* Built by Lewis 'Buffalo' Emery

Location
On the seafront at Sheringham

Opening
Easter–Sep 12.30pm–4.30pm

Admission
Free

Contact
West Slipway, Sheringham NR26 8JT

t 01263 821392
0778 083873

418 Sheringham

The Muckleburgh Collection

2 hrs   Apr–Nov

This is a collection of military vehicles, many of which are in full working order. Further displays feature the Royal Flying Corps and the modern armed forces. Several aero engines and missiles are on show. Frequent live tank demonstrations take place.

* The Meteor is on loan from the Imperial War Museum.
* Gama Goat Rides – in a USA Personnel Carrier

Location
Signposted from A149 W of Cromer, 3 miles W of Sheringham

Opening
Daily Apr–Nov 10am–5pm

Admission
Adult £5.50, Child £3, Concs £4.50

Contact
Weybourne Military Camp, Holt NR25 7EG

t 01263 588 210
w muckleburgh.co.uk
e info@muckleburgh.co.uk

---

419 Swaffham

Castle Acre Priory

1 hr   All year

The priory's ruins span seven centuries and include a C12 church with an elaborately decorated great west front which still rises to its full height, a C15 gatehouse and a porch and prior's lodging. Visit the recreated herb garden, growing both culinary and medicinal herbs.

* Regular events held throughout the year
* One of the first Cluniac priories in England

Location
¼ mile W of village of Castle Acre, 5 miles N of Swaffham

Opening
Apr–Sep daily 10am–6pm
Oct daily 10am–5pm
Nov–Mar Wed–Sun 10am–4pm

Admission
Adult £4, Child £2, Concs £3

Contact
Stocks Green PE32 2XD

t 01760 755394
w english–heritage.org.uk
e castleacre-priory@english-heritage.org.uk

---

420 Thetford

Ancient House Museum

½ hr   All year

This magnificent Tudor merchant's house was built about 1490. Discover Thetford's connection with an Indian Prince, the Maharajah Duleep Singh. The museum, founded by the Maharajah's second son, displays original family photographs and other items.

* Thetford treasure – Roman jewellery and spoons
* Replicas of the treasure made by Peter Shorer

Location
Near bus station in Thetford

Opening
All year Mon–Sat 10am–5pm
Jul & Aug only Sun 2pm–5pm

Admission
Sep–Jun Free. Jul–Aug Adult £1, Child 60p, Concs 80p

Contact
White Hart Street, Thetford IP24 1AA

t 01842 752599
w www.norfolkgov.uk/tourism
e mus@norfolk.gov.uk

421 Bungay

Norfolk & Suffolk Aviation Museum

2 hrs   All year

The museum constitutes an impressive collection of aircraft and equipment. It also houses the Royal Observer Corps Museum, the 446th (H) Bomb Group Museum, the RAF Bomber Command Museum and the Air Sea Rescue and Coastal Command Museum.

* 40 aircraft within seven buildings
* Aircraft from pre First World War to present day

Location	Contact
On B1062, off A143, 1 mile W of Bungay	The Street, Flixton NR35 1NZ
Opening	t 01986 896644
Apr–Oct Sun–Thu 10am–5pm	w aviationmuseum.net
Nov–Mar Tue Wed & Sun 10am–4pm	e lcurtis@aviationmuseum.net
Dec 15–Jan 15 closed	
Admission	
Free	

422 Bury St Edmunds

Ickworth House

2 hrs+   Mar–Nov

Ickworth is an elegant Italianate house set within spectacular English parkland. The central rotunda and curving wings were intended to house treasures collected from all over Europe. Today, the state rooms display works by Titian, Velasquez and Gainsborough.

* Noted for its Georgian silver and Regency furniture
* Enchanting gardens and woodland walks

Location	Admission
On A143, 2 miles S of Bury St Edmunds signposted from A14	Adult £6.10, Child £2.75
Opening	**Contact**
House Mar–Sep 1pm–5pm, Oct–Nov 1pm–4.30pm closed Wed & Thu	Bury St Edmunds IP29 5QE
Garden Jan–Feb 10am–4pm daily	t 01284 735 270
Mar–Oct 10am–5pm daily	w nationaltrust.org.uk
Nov–Dec 10am–4pm Mon–Fri	e julia.vinson@nationaltrust.org.uk

423 Bury St Edmunds

Manor House Museum

1 hr+   All year

The museum, a Georgian townhouse in Bury St Edmunds' Great Churchyard, houses a superb series of collections. The displays feature some of the finest clocks and watches to be found anywhere in the world, costumes and textiles from C17 to the present day.

* Hear the polyphon longcase clock
* 1920s costume collection

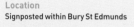

Location
Signposted within Bury St Edmunds

Opening
Wed–Sun 11am–4pm

Admission
Adult £2.50, Child £2

Contact
5 Honey Hill, Bury St Edmunds
IP33 1RT

t 01284 757076 / 757074
w stedmundsbury.gov.uk/manorhse
e manor.house@stedsbc.gov.uk

424 Felixstowe

Landguard Fort

1 hr   Apr–Oct

Originally built during the C16, the remains of this fort date back to the C18. What remains now are parts of the walls and casemate rooms within, dating from the fort of 1744 and later changes made during Queen Victoria's reign. It overlooks the Orwell Estuary.

* Some hoists for raising ammunition are still *in situ*
* Submarine minefield observation position

Location
On Viewpoint Road, Languard Point, off A14

Opening
Apr daily 10am–5pm
May–Sep daily 10am–6pm
Oct daily 10am–5pm

Admission
Adult £3, Child £1, Concs £2.50

Contact
49 Looe Road, Felixstowe IP11 9QB

t 01394 277767
w english-heritage.org.uk

425 Framlingham

Framlingham Castle

1 hr+   All year

This is a fine example of a late C12 castle. It has 13 hollow towers connected by a large curtain wall, 42 feet high and 8 feet thick (13 x 2.5m), similar to those at Dover and Windsor castles. The castle has fulfilled a number of roles including fortress, prison, poorhouse and school.

* Walk along the impressive wall walk
* Explore the outer courts, moat and mere

Location
In Framlingham on B1116

Opening
Apr–Sep 10am–6pm
Oct 10am–5pm
Nov–Mar 10am–4pm

Admission
Adult £4, Concs £3, Child £2

Contact
Framlingham, Woodbridge IP13 9BP

t 01728 724189
w english-heritage.org.uk

426 Ipswich

Ipswich Transport Museum

1 hr   Mar–Nov

The museum has the largest collection of transport items in Britain devoted to just one town. Everything was either made or used in and around Ipswich. The collection, started in 1965, consists of around 100 major exhibits, and numerous smaller transport related items.

* Timetables, photographs, maps, tickets and uniforms
* Varied programme of events as avertised

Location
SE of Ipswich near junction 57 of A14

Opening
Mar–Nov Sun and Bank Hols 11am–4pm, school hols Mon–Fri 1pm–4pm

Admission
Adult £3, Child £1.75, Concs £2.50

Contact
Old Trolleybus Depot, Cobham Road, Ipswich IP3 9JD

t 01473 715666
w ipswichtransportmuseum.co.uk
e enquiries@ipswichtransportmuseum.co.uk

427 Leiston

Long Shop Steam Museum

1 hr+   Apr–Oct

The Long Shop was built in 1852 as Britain's first production lines for steam engines. Traction engines, steamrollers, electric trolleybuses and even ammunition were also produced here. Learn how the Victorians worked and explore our industrial heritage.

* Discover the amazing range of Garrett products
* A collection of unique and fascinating exhibits

Location
In Leiston town centre, off A12 at Saxmundham

Opening
Apr–Oct, Mon–Sat 10am–5pm
Sun 11am–5pm

Admission
Adult £3.50, Child £1, Concs £3

Contact
Main Street, Leiston IP16 4ES

t 01728 832189
w www.longshop.care4free.net
e longshop@care4free.net

428 Long Melford

Kentwell Hall

2 hr+   All year

A mellow red brick mansion, Kentwell offers a glimpse into the Tudor period. Includes a paved mosaic maze, fine moated gardens and a working rare breeds farm. The hall is also home to re-creations of Tudor and wartime domestic life.

* Kentwell pioneered domestic living history events
* Working Tudor kitchen and magnificent hall

Location
just off A134 between Bury St Edmunds & Sudbury

Opening
From Apr 4 12 noon–5pm
times vary, phone for details

Admission
Adult £6.95, Child £4.45, Concs £5.95

Contact
Long Melford CO10 9BA

t 01787 310 207
w kentwell.co.uk
e info@kentwell.co.uk

429 Long Melford

Long Melford Hall

1 hr   Apr–Oct

One of East Anglia's most celebrated Elizabethan houses, little changed externally since 1578 and with a beautiful panelled banqueting hall. There is a Regency library, as well as Victorian bedrooms and good collections of furniture and porcelain.

* Small collection of Beatrix Potter memorabilia
* Garden contains a charming banqueting house

Location
In Long Melford off A134, 14 miles
S of Bury St Edmunds, 3 miles N
of Sudbury

Opening
Apr Sat & Sun 2pm–5.30pm
May–Sep Wed–Sun 2pm–5.30pm
Oct Sat & Sun 2pm–5.30pm

Admission
Adult £4.50, Child £2.25

Contact
Long Melford, Sudbury CO10 9AA

t 01787 880286
w nationaltrust.org.uk
e e.melford@nationaltrust.org.uk

430 Lowestoft

Lowestoft Maritime Museum

1 hr+   Easter–Oct

The museum specialises in the history of the Lowestoft fishing fleet and early commercial activities, from early days of sail, to steam through to modern diesel vessels. Methods of fishing are also recorded including the art of herring driftnet fishing.

* Fine exhibition of the evolution of lifeboats
* Collection of shipwright's and cooper's tools

Location
Under the Lighthouse on Whaplode Road in Sparrow's Nest Park

Opening
May–Oct 10 and Easter hols
daily 10am–5pm

Admission
Adult 75p, Child 25p, Concs 50p

Contact
Whapload Road, Lowestoft NR32 1XG

t 01502 561963

431 Newmarket

National Horseracing Museum

1 hr+   Apr–Oct

The story of the people and horses involved in racing from Royal origins to Lester Piggott, Frankie Dettori and other modern-day heroes. Highlights include the head of Persimmon, a great Royal Derby winner in 1896 and the colourful jackets of 'Prince Monolulu'.

* Exciting programme of temporary exhibits
* Minibus tours – behind-the-scenes at Newmarket

Location
Centre of Newmarket, well signposted

Opening
Apr–Oct Tue–Sun 11am–4.30pm
Jul–Aug daily 11am–5pm

Admission
Adult £4.50, Child £2.50, Concs £3.50

Contact
99 High Street, Newmarket CB8 8JL

t 01638 667333
w nhrm.co.uk
e museum@nhrm.freeserve.co.uk

432 Sudbury

Gainsborough's House

1 hr   All year

This is the birthplace of Thomas Gainsborough RA (1727–88). The Georgian fronted townhouse with attractive walled garden, displays more of the artist's work than any other gallery. The collection is shown together with C18 furniture and memorabilia.

* Varied exhibitions of contemporary art
* Includes works by Hubert Gravelot and Francis Hayman

Location	**Admission**
In centre of Sudbury	Adult £3.50, Child & Concs £1.50
Opening	**Contact**
Mon–Sat 10am–5pm	46 Gainsborough Street, Sudbury
Bank Hols & Sun before Bank Hols 2pm–5pm	CO10 2EU
	t 01787 372 958
	w gainsborough.org
	e mail@gainsborough.org

433 Woodbridge

Orford Castle

1 hr+   All year

Originally a keep and bailey castle with a walled enclosure and a great tower. Henry II constructed the building we see today as a coastal defence during the C12. The unique polygon keep survives almost intact with three immense towers.

* The building records are the earliest in the kingdom
* Audio tours of 50mins

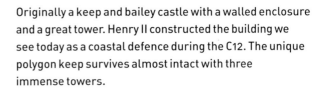

Location	**Admission**
In Orford on B1084, 20 miles NE of Ipswich	Adult £4, Child £2, Concs £3
Opening	**Contact**
Apr–Sep daily 10am–6pm	Orford, Woodbridge IP12 2ND
Oct daily 10am–5pm	t 01394 450472
Nov–Mar daily 10am–5pm	w english-heritage.org.uk

Stanage Edge, Derbyshire

East Midlands

Derbyshire Leicestershire Lincolnshire
Northamptonshire Nottinghamshire Rutland

Counties / Regions
- STAFFORDSHIRE
- WORCESTERSHIRE
- WARWICKSHIRE
- GLOUCESTERSHIRE
- OXFORDSHIRE
- BUCKINGHAMSHIRE
- BEDFORDSHIRE
- HERTFORDSHIRE
- NORTHAMPTONSHIRE
- LEICESTERSHIRE
- RUTLAND
- CAMBRIDGESHIRE
- The Fens
- WEST MIDLANDS
- BIRMINGHAM
- COVENTRY
- LEICESTER

Towns and Places
Uttoxeter, Rugeley, Cannock, Lichfield, Burton upon Trent, Long Eaton, Grantham, Spalding, Holbeach, King's Lynn, Wisbech, Bourne, March, Peterborough, Stamford, Oundle, Corby, Kettering, Rushden, Oakham, Uppingham, Melton Mowbray, Loughborough, Ashby-de-la-Zouch, Coalville, Hinckley, Nuneaton, Tamworth, Sutton Coldfield, Brownhills, Walsall, Solihull, Bedworth, Rugby, Market Harborough, Blaby, Oadby, Rothwell, Sawtry, Brampton, Huntingdon, St Ives, St Neots, Cambridge, Ely, Chatteris, Littleport, Waterbeach, Milden(hall), Saffron Walden, Bishop's Stortford, STANSTED, Harlow, Hoddesdon, Hertford, Ware, Hatfield, St Albans, Hemel Hempstead, Berkhamsted, Tring, Aylesbury, Dunstable, Leighton Buzzard, Luton, LUTON (airport), Welwyn Garden City, Hitchin, Letchworth, Baldock, Royston, Biggleswade, Bedford, Newport Pagnell, Milton Keynes, Buckingham, Brackley, Towcester, Northampton, Wellingborough, Daventry, Leamington Spa, Warwick, Stratford-upon-Avon, Shipston-on-Stour, Chipping Norton, Moreton-in-Marsh, Stow-on-the-Wold, Evesham, Pershore, Cheltenham, Carterton, Witney, Kidlington, Oxford, Bicester, Stevenage, Welwyn, Chelms(ford)

Grid index numbers (as printed in boxes)
558–560, 442–444, 445, 451, 565, 437, 452, 453, 450, 454, 455–459, 460, 462, 463, 471–472, 513, 495, 412, 406, 370, 365, 361, 384, 382, 385, 383, 391, 395, 400, 399, 396, 393, 349, 354, 353, 352, 350, 345–346, 347–348, 368, 355, 351, 030, 401, 389–390, 031, 016–020, 021–022, 023–024, 131, 144, 132, 134, 279, 280, 292, 293–295, 296, 281–282, 285, 283, 298, 573, 304, 624, 568–570, 576–577, 611, 617, 619–620, 554–555, 602–610, 599, 563, 564, 553, 591, 585–593, 600, 598, 594–597, 579, 582, 578, 613–614, 574, 601, 575, 583, 584, 485, 486, 489, 494, 491–492, 487–488, 484, 496, 490, 483, 461, 581, 612, 366–367, 493, 369, 514, 515, 465, 479, 516, 518, 512, 517, 366–364, 362–364, 571–572

Motorways
M5, M6, M1, M40, M42, M45, M69, M11, A1(M)

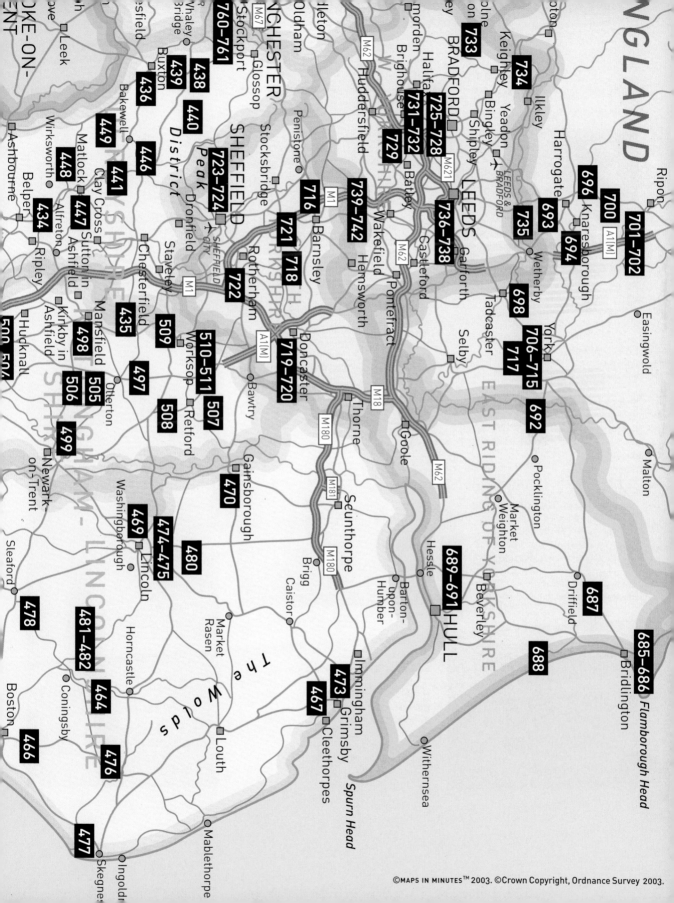

434 Alfreton

Wingfield Manor

1 hr+   All year

Mary Queen of Scots was imprisoned three times in this C15 manor house. Now an imposing ruin, the building was begun by Ralph, Lord Cromwell, Chancellor of England, around 1441. Over the entrance are carved twin money bags, symbolising Cromwell's status.

* Impressive undercroft of the hall, with a vaulted roof
* *Peak Practice* and Zeffirelli's *Jane Eyre* were filmed here

Location
On B5035, 5 miles S of South Wingfield

Opening
Apr–Sep Wed–Sun 10am–6pm
Oct Wed–Sun 10am–5pm
Nov–Mar Sat–Sun 10am–4pm

Admission
Adult £3.20, Child £1.60, Concs £2.40

Contact
Garner Lane, South Wingfield
D55 7NH

t 01773 832060
w english-heritage.org.uk

435 Bolsover

Bolsover Castle

1 hr+   All year

Bolsover Castle is a C17 house, built on the site of a Norman fortress, and is a wonderful place to meander and muse. Sir Charles Cavendish, son of Bess of Hardwick, started the construction of the little castle in 1612.

* Symbolic and erotic wall-paintings restored in 1970s
* The Venus fountain garden has been restored

Location
In Bolsover, on A632, 6 miles E of Chesterfield

Opening
Apr–Sep daily 10am–6pm
Oct daily 10am–5pm
Nov–Mar Thu–Mon 10am–4pm

Admission
Adult £6.20, Child £3.10, Concs £4.60

Contact
Castle Street, Bolsover S44 6PR

t 01246 822844
w english-heritage.org.uk
e bolsover.castle@english-heritage.
   org.uk

436 Buxton

Buxton Museum & Art Gallery

1 hr+   Easter–Sep

This building once housed the Victorian Peak Hydropathic Establishment and is packed with many local treasures. It is the venue for numerous county and national exhibitions of art. A visit to the Sir William Boyd Dawkins room is like stepping into the past.

* Explore geology, archaeology and history of the Peaks
* Time tunnel, complete with sounds and smells

Location
In Buxton marketplace

Opening
Easter–Sep Tue–Fri 9.30am–5.30pm,
Sat 9.30am–5pm,
Sun & Bank Hols 10.30am–5pm

Admission
Free

Contact
Terrace Road, Buxton SK17 6DA

t 01298 24658
w www.derbyshire.gov.uk
e buxton.museum@derbyshire.
   gov.uk

437 Castle Donington

Donington Grand Prix Collection

2–4 hrs   All year

Take a spin around the largest collection of Grand Prix cars and journey through motor sport history. Exhibits include a 1999 Ralf Schumacher Williams, a 1997 David Coulthard McLaren and the car in which Ayrton Senna won the 1993 European Grand Prix at Donington Park.

* The world's only complete collection of Vanwalls
* Henry Seagrave's 1922 3-litre GP Sunbeam

Location
M1 junction 23a / 24, access from NW via A50

Opening
Daily 10am–5pm

Admission
Adult £7, Child £2.50, Concs £5

Contact
Donington Park, Castle Donington
DE74 2RP

t 01332 811027
w doningtoncollection.com
e enquiries@doningtoncollection.
co.uk

438 Castleton

Blue John Cavern

1 hr   All year

An historic cavern containing the first known mined deposits of the Blue John mineral for which the area is famous. It was worked by the Romans more than 2,000 years ago. Tours take visitors through many colourful caves, including the crystallised and waterfall caverns.

* Exhibition of C19 miners' working implements

Location
2 miles W of Castleton

Opening
Summer daily 9.30am–5.30pm
Winter daily 9.30am–dusk

Admission
Adult £6.50, Child £3.50, Concs £4.50

Contact
Castleton S33 8WP

t 01433 620638 / 620642
w bluejohn-cavern.co.uk
e lesley@bluejohn.gemsoft.co.uk

439 Castleton

Peak Cavern

1 hr   All year

Explore the mystery of the Devil's Arse and step into the unique world of Peak Cavern, with its unusual rock formations, eerie sounds of running water and echoes of a bygone age. The cavern's imposing entrance chamber is the largest natural cave entrance in the British Isles.

* Riverside walk past historic miners' cottages
* Guided tours and rope-making demonstrations

Location
On the A6187, between Haterssage and Whaley Bridge

Opening
Apr–Oct daily 10am–5pm
Nov–Mar Sat–Sun 10am–5pm

Admission
Adult £5.50, Child £3.50, Concs £4.50

Contact
Peak Cavern Road, Castleton,
Hope Valley S33 8WS

t 01433 620285
w devilsarse.com
e info@peakcavern.co.uk

440   Castleton

Peveril Castle

1 hr   All year

Built shortly after the Norman Conquest of 1066 by one of King William's most trusted men, the elegant tower of this stronghold still stands to its original height. The castle, perched high above the pretty village of Castleton, offers breathtaking views of the Peak District.

* Some of the earliest herringbone masonry
* Sir Walter Scott based a book on the castle

Location
On S side of Castleton, on A6187, 15 miles W of Sheffield

Opening
Daily Apr–Sep 10am–6pm
Oct 10am–5pm.
Nov–Mar Wed–Sun 10am–4pm

Admission
Adult £2.50, Child £1.30, Concs £1.90

Contact
Market Place, Castleton S33 8WQ

t 01433 620613
w english-heritage.org.uk

441   Crich

The National Tramway Museum

3 hrs+   Mar–Dec

Visit the museum to see a variety of trams, including open, closed, double-deck, single-deck, horse drawn, steam and vintage electric from all the corners of the globe. Electric trams also run through Period Street, and on to open countryside, giving panoramic views.

* Exhibition hall houses impressive displays
* Dramatic 'tram at night' experience

Location
8 miles from M1 junction 28 , via A38, A6, A61 and A52

Opening
Mar–Nov daily 10am–5.30pm
Nov & Dec Sat–Sun 10.30am–4pm

Admission
Adult £8, Child £3.50, Concs £6.50

Contact
Crich Tramway Village, Matlock DE4 5DP

t 0870 7587267
w tramway.co.uk
e info@tramway.co.uk

442 Derby

Melbourne Hall & Gardens

2 hrs   Apr–Sep

An historic house and garden that was once the home of Prime Minister William Lamb, who as Lord Melbourne gave his name to the Australian city. It has interesting and extensive gardens which contain a wrought iron arbour made around 1710 by Robert Bakewell of Derby.

* Formal garden with yew tunnel
* Best surviving example of work by London and Wise

Location
7 miles S of Derby

Opening
House Aug daily 2–4.30pm
Gardens Apr–July, Sep Wed, Sat–Sun & Bank Hols 1.30–5.30pm,

Admission
House Adult £3, Child £ 1.50, Concs £2.50
Gardens Adult £3, Child £2

Contact
Church Square, Melbourne DE73 1EN

t 01332 862502
w melbournehall.com
e melbhall@globalnet.co.uk

443 Derby

Pickford's House

1 hr   All year

This Grade I listed building was built in 1770 by architect Joseph Pickford. Other houses in Friar Gate were also designed by Pickford, but no. 41 is the only one open to the public and it demonstrates what domestic life was like in C18 and early C19.

* Georgian bedroom and dressing room of about 1815
* The kitchen has been reconstructed to about 1830

Location
Derby city centre

Opening
All year Mon 11am–5pm,
Tue–Sat 10am–5pm,
Sun & Bank Hols 2–5pm

Admission
Free

Contact
41 Friar Gate, Derby DE1 1DA

t 01332 255363
w derby.gov.uk/museums
e pickford.house@derby.gov.uk

444 Derby

Royal Crown Derby Visitor Centre

2 hrs   All year

Tour the working factory and watch the production of tableware and giftware, from clay through to the finished hand-decorated product. The museum is full of treasures going back to 1750 and there are demonstrations of skills such as flower-making, painting and gilding.

* Working factory tour available on weekdays
* Museum, demonstration studio and factory shop

Location
On A415, nr Derby city centre

Opening
Mon–Sat 9.30am–4pm,
Sun 10.30am–4pm

Admission
Adult £2.95, Child & Concs £2.75
Tour Adult £4.95, Child & Concs £4.75

Contact
194 Osmaston Road, Derby DE23 8JZ

t 01332 712800
w royal-crown-derby.co.uk
e enquiries@royal-crown-derby.
co.uk

445 Swadlincote

Beehive Farm Woodland Lakes

4–6 hrs   All year

Using specially laid out trails, visitors can explore the beauty of this woodland landscape on foot or horseback. Alternatively, they can simply enjoy the atmosphere of the three tranquil fishing lakes – Horseshoe, Botany Bay and Jubilee.

* Woodland, meadow and wetland habitats
* Animal farm

Location
In Rosliston, nr Burton on Trent

Opening
Daily 9.30am–5pm, Sun 9.30–4pm

Admission
Adult £1, Child 50p

Contact
Lullington Road, Rosliston, Swadlincote DE12 8HZ

t 01283 762920
w beehivefarm-woodlandlakes.co.uk
e info@beehivefarm-woodlandlakes.
co.uk

446 Matlock

Chatsworth House

4–6 hrs   All year

©Chatsworth House Trust

The 'Palace of the Peak' contains one of Europe's finest collections of treasures, displayed in more than 30 rooms, from the grandeur of the 1st Duke's hall and state apartments with their rich decoration and painted ceilings, to the C19 library and dining room.

* Works by Rembrandt, Gainsborough and Freud
* Maze, rose, cottage and kitchen gardens

Location
8 miles N of Matlock, off B6012

Opening
House 11am–5.30pm
Garden 11am–6pm

Admission
House Adult £9, Child £3.50, Concs £7,
Garden Adult £5.50, Child £2.50,
Concs £4

Contact
Bakewell DE45 1PP

t 01246 565300
w chatsworth.org

447 Matlock Bath

Masson Mills Working Textile Museum

1 hr+   All year

Sir Richard Arkwright built these mills as his showpiece on the banks of the River Derwent in 1783. Beautifully restored, Masson Mills house a working textile museum containing a unique and comprehensive collection of authentic historic working textile machinery.

* Internationally famous Grade II listed buildings
* Experience over 200 years of industrial history

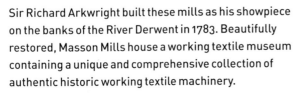

Location
On A6, ½ mile S of Matlock Bath

Opening
Mon–Fri 10am–4pm, Sat 11am–5pm,
Sun 11am–4pm

Admission
Adult £2.50, Child £1.50, Concs £2

Contact
41 Derby Road, Matlock Bath DE4 3PY

t 01629 581001.
w massonmills.co.uk

448 Middleton by Wirksworth

National Stone Centre

2 hrs+   All year

Deep in the heart of the Derbyshire Dales, this dramatic site is steeped in industrial history, but the centre tells the full story of stone. Through artefacts such as 330 million-year-old fossils and tropical reefs, it covers its history, the science and technology and its use in art.

* Gem panning
* Fossil rubbing

Location
On B5035, S of Matlock, between
Cromford & Carsington

Opening
Summer 10am–5pm
Winter 10am–4pm

Admission
Adult £1.80, Child 90p, Concs £1.20

Contact
Porter Lane, Middleton by Wirksworth
DE4 4LS

t 01629 824833
w nationalstonecentre.org.uk
e nsc@nationalstonecentre.org.uk

449 Monyash

Arbor Low Stone Circle & Gib Hill Barrow

  1 hr All year

A fine Neolithic monument, comprising a recumbent stone circle of white limestone slabs surrounded by a large ditch. This arrangement has led some people to describe the circle as resembling a clock face, but it is not known whether the stones were ever upright.

* Gib Hill takes its name from its use as a hanging hill
* Arbor Low dates to Neolithic / early Bronze Age

Location	Admission
½ mile W of A515, 2 miles S of Monyash	Farmer who owns right of way to property may levy a charge
Opening	**Contact**
Summer 10am–6pm	t 01629 816200
Rest of year 10am–5pm	w english-heritage.org.uk

450 Ashby de la Zouch

Ashby de la Zouch Castle

  1 hr+ All year

In the C15, Edward IV gave this property to Lord Hastings, who converted what was then a fortified manor house into a grand castle, adding a chapel and the Hastings Tower. Now partly ruined, the tower remains, soaring to the great height of 80ft.

* Wonderful views across Leicestershire
* The setting for jousting scenes in the film *Ivanhoe*

Location	Admission
In Ashby de la Zouch, 12 miles S of Derby, on A511	Adult £3.20, Child £1.60, Concs £2.40
Opening	**Contact**
Apr–Sep daily 10am–6pm	South Street, Ashby de la Zouch
Oct daily 10am–5pm	LE65 1BR
Nov–Mar Wed–Sun 10am–4pm	t 01530 413343
	w english-heritage.org.uk
	e customers@english-heritage.org.uk

451 Ticknall

Calke Abbey

  3 hrs+ Apr–Oct

This baroque mansion, built in 1701and set in stunning parkland, has become famous as an English country house in decline. Little restored, it contains the natural history collection of the Harpur Crewe family, as well as interiors essentially unchanged since the 1880s.

* Magnificent C18 state bed
* Grounds feature beautiful walled garden

Location	Admission
10 miles S of Derby, on A514, at Ticknall, between Swadlincote & Melbourne	*House* Adult £5.90, Child £2.90
	Garden Adult £3.20, Child £1.60
Opening	**Contact**
House Apr–Oct Sun–Wed 1–5.30pm	Ticknall, Derby DE73 1LE
Garden Apr–Oct Sun–Wed 11am–5pm	t 01332 863822
	w nationaltrust.org.uk
	e calkeabbey@nationaltrust.org.uk

452 Coalville

Manor House at Donington

  1 hr+ All year

Donington-le-Heath Manor House was built in the late C13 and renovated early in C17. Visitors can see restored rooms and displays on medieval life. The house is set in recently recreated C17-style gardens with herbaceous borders, herb gardens an orchard and a maze.

* Re-enactment, hands-on and demonstrations
* Temporary exhibitions on a wide range of subjects

Location	Admission
1 mile S of Coleville, signposted from M1 junction 22, on A50	Free
Opening	**Contact**
Apr–Sep daily 11.30am–5pm	Donington-le-Heath, Coalville LE67 2FW
Oct–Nov & Mar daily 11.30am–3pm	t 01530 831259
Dec–Feb Sat–Sun 11.30am–3pm	w leics.gov.uk/museums

453 Coalville

Snibston Discovery Park

6 hrs   Feb–Dec

A popular museum, Snibston is situated on the site of a former colliery. The museum displays a rich collection of historic objects telling the story of transport, mining and quarrying, engineering and the fashion industry. A visit includes a tour of the historic colliery buildings.

* Train ride along the newly restored colliery railway
* A sculpture trail

Location
On A511, on the edge of Coalville town centre

Opening
Daily 10am–5pm
Closed in early Jan, ring for details

Admission
Adult £5.50, Child £3.50, Concs £3.75

Contact
Ashby Road, Coalville LE67 3LN

t 01530 278444
w leics.gov.uk/museums/snibston
e snibston@leics.gov.uk

454 Desford

Tropical Birdland

2 hrs+   Easter–Oct

Created in 1982, this exotic bird lover's dream is set in beautiful surroundings and features over 85 species of our feathered friends. You can walk through aviaries, visit the chick room, see spectacular free-flying birds, take a woodland stroll and visit the koi ponds.

Location
Just off M1 at junction 22

Opening
Easter–Oct, daily 10am–5pm

Admission
Adult £4 Child £3, Concs £3.50

Contact
Lindridge Lane, Desford, Leicester LE9 9N

t 01455 824603
w www.tropicalbirdland.co.uk
e info@tropicalbirdland.co.uk

455 Leicester

Jewry Wall

1 hr   All year

One of Leicester's most famous landmarks, this rare example of Roman walling has survived for nearly 2,000 years. Originally part of the Roman public baths, it separated the exercise hall, which stood on the site of St Nicholas Church, from the rest of the baths.

* Archaeologists discovered remains of Roman baths
* Museum tells the story of Leicester from the Iron Age

Location
In St Nicholas Street, W of St Nicholas Church

Opening
Apr–Sep Mon–Sat 10am–5pm, Sun 1pm–5pm
Oct–Mar Mon–Sat 10am–4pm
Sun 1pm–4pm

Admission
Free

Contact
St Nicholas Circle, Leicester LE1 4LB

t 0116 2254971
w english-heritage.org.uk

456 Leicester

Kirby Muxloe Castle

1 hr+   Sat & Sun

The construction of this picturesque, moated, brick castle was started in 1480 by William, Lord Hastings. He was later beheaded on the orders of Richard III and the castle was left unfinished. The gun-ports here are among the earliest in England.

* Regular English Civil War re-enactments
* Moat, drawbridge and portcullis

Location
4 miles W of Leicester off B5380, close to M1 junction 21A, northbound exit

Opening
Apr–Oct Sat, Sun & Bank Hols 12noon–5pm

Admission
Adult £2.20, Child £1.10, Concs £1.70

Contact
Main Street, Kirby Muxloe, Leicester

t 01162 386886
w english-heritage.org.uk
e customers@english-heritage.org.uk

457 Leicester

National Space Centre

4–6 hrs   All year

This centre is dedicated to space science and astronomy. From its futuristic Rocket Tower discover the stories, personalities and technology of the past and present, and explore our current understanding of space and how it affects our future.

* Five themed galleries with hands-on activities
* Space theatre show

Location
Just off A6, 2 miles N of city centre

Opening
Term time Tue–Sat 10am–3.30
Sat–Sun 10am–4.30pm
School Hols Mon 12noon–4.30pm
Tue–Sun 10am–4pm

Admission
Adult £8.95, Child £6.95

Contact
Exploration Drive, Leicester LE4 5NS

t 0870 6077223
w spacecentre.co.uk
e info@spacecentre.co.uk

458 Leicester

Newarke Houses Museum

1 hr+   All year

Composed of two historic houses, Wygston's Chantry House and Skeffington House, this museum holds many collections, including clocks, toys, greeting cards and coins. The ground floor has a recreated Victorian street scene and a room setting of the 1600s.

* See the clothes of Britain's heaviest man
* Attractive gardens are worth walking round

Location
Opposite De Montfort University

Opening
Apr–Sep Mon–Sat 10am–5pm
Sun 1pm–5pm
Oct–Mar Mon–Sat 10am–4pm
Sun 1pm–4pm

Admission
Free

Contact
The Newarkes, Leicester LE2 7BY

t 0116 2254980
w leicestermuseums.ac.uk

459 Leicester

New Walk Museum

1 hr+ All year

The museum's permanent collections include the Ancient Egypt Gallery and the Natural History Room, with dinosaur skeletons and interesting fossils. It is also a major art gallery with a collection of German Expressionist and European art dating from the C15.

* Decorative arts gallery
* Colourful story of the Royal Leicestershire Regiment

Location
Short walk from city centre

Opening
Mon–Sat 10am–4pm Sun 1pm–4pm

Admission
Free

Contact
53 New Walk, Leicester LE1 7EA

t 0116 2254900
w leicester.gov.uk/museums
e museums@leicester.gov.uk

460 Loughborough

Great Central Railway

2 hrs+ All year

Main line steam trains run every weekend throughout the year. Re-create the experience of the famous expresses of the steam age. See freight and parcel train demonstrations or relax in the comfort of classic corridor trains, which are steam-heated in winter.

* Steam through the glorious Leicester countryside
* Driver's view of bridges, trains and hidden sidings

Location
SE of Loughborough town centre

Opening
Trains run at weekends all year and midweek Jun–Aug, phone for details

Admission
Adult £11, Child & Concs £7.50

Contact
Great Central Road,
Loughborough LE11 1RW

t 01509 230 726
w gcrailway.co.uk
e booking_office@gcrailway.co.uk

461 Lutterworth

Stanford Hall

1 hr Sun

Stanford, on the river Avon, has been the home of the Cave family since 1430. In the 1690s, Sir Roger Cave commissioned Smiths of Warwick to pull down the old manor house and build the present hall, which is a superb example of their work.

* Motorcycle museum, housed in the stables
* A collection of royal Stuart portraits

Location
Just off the M1 / M6 interchange, nr A14

Opening
Easter–Sep Sun
House 1.30–5.30pm
Grounds 12noon–5.30pm

Admission
House & Grounds Adult £5, Child £2
Grounds Adult £3, Child £1
Motorcycle Museum Adult £1, Child 35p

Contact
Lutterworth LE17 6DH

t 01788 860250
w stanfordhall.co.uk

462 Loughborough

Whatton Gardens

1 hr Wed

The gardens and park are early C19. The house was built in 1876 and the garden is laid to lawn punctuated with Irish yews. Other highlights include the Chinese garden with oriental statuary, the kitchen garden, an ice house now used as a grotto and the Bogey Hole.

* Ornate stone loggia with Quattrocento carving
* Arboretum and small lake

Location
Off A6, between Hathern and Kegworth

Opening
Apr–Sep Wed 11am–4pm

Admission
Adult £2.50, Child free

Contact
Whatton House, Loughborough
LE12 5BG

t 01509 842268 / 842302
e whatto@compuserve.com

Lincolnshire

463 Newtown Linford

Bradgate Country Park

3 hrs+   All year

With 850 acres of heathland, small woods, herds of deer and the River Lin, this is Leicestershire's largest country park. It also includes the ruins of Bradgate House, the birthplace of Lady Jane Grey, who was famously Queen of England for nine days.

* Old John Tower folly

Location
3 miles from M1 junction 22, signposted on A50

Opening
Dawn to dusk

Admission
Free, charges for car park and visitor centre

Contact
Deerbarn Buildings, Newtown Linford LE6 0HE

t 0116 2362713

464 Alford

Claythorpe Watermill & Wildfowl Gardens

1 hr+   Easter–Oct

Situated at the tip of the Lincolnshire wolds, Claythorpe is home to over 500 birds and visitors are able to experience their environment and habitat first hand. Visit the Old Bakery, which depicts the history of the site's milling and baking industry.

* Enchanted Woods in which fairy tales come to life
* Otters, red squirrels and wallabies

Location
Signposted off A16

Opening
Easter–Oct Mon–Sun 10am–5pm

Admission
Adult £3.95, Child £2.95, Concs £3.50

Contact
Aby, nr Alford LN13 0DU

t 01507 450687
w claythorpewatermill.
  fsbusiness.co.uk
e info@claythorpewatermill.co.uk

465 Wigston

Wigston Framework Knitters Museum

1 hr   All year

The museum is unique, because when the last master hosier, Edgar Carter, died in 1952, the workshop was locked and left. Inside were eight hand frames for making gloves and fancy ribbed tops, with all the needle moulds and tools.

* Original frames, needle moulds and tools

Location
4 miles S of Leicester on B582, off A5199

Opening
Sun, first Sat of every month & Bank Hols 2pm–5pm

Admission
Adult £1, Child 50p

Contact
42-44 Bushloe End, Wigston LE18 2BA

t 0116 288 3396

466 Boston

Sibsey Trader Windmill

1 hr   Apr–Oct

Built in 1877 in typical Lincolnshire style, to replace a small post mill, this is one of the few six-sailed mills remaining in England. It's not exceptionally tall, but the slender tower and surrounding flat landscape create the impression that it's bigger than it really is.

* Grade 1 listed working windmill
* Fresh, organic, stoneground flour available

Location
Off A16, 5 miles N of Boston, 1/2 mile W of Sibsey

Opening
Apr–Oct Tue & Sat 10am–6pm
Sun 11am–6pm
Bank Hols 10am–6pm

Admission
Adult £2, Child £1, Concs £1.50

Contact
Frith Ville Road, Sibsey PE22 0SY

t 01205 750036 / 460647
w sibsey.fsnet.co.uk
e traderwindmill@sibsey.fsnet.co.uk

467 Cleethorpes

Cleethorpes Humber Estuary Discovery Centre

1 hr   All year

Visit this exhibition and observatory to learn more about Cleethorpes and the Humber Estuary through an excting hands-on exhibition. Explore the Lincolnshire coast and discover the ancient, submerged forest that is buried along Cleethorpes beach.

* Discover the famous Cleethorpes saltmarsh
* The centre is on the edge of an important habitat

Location
From A180 & A16 follow signs for the lakeside

Opening
Jan–Jun, Sep & Oct 10am–5pm
Jul & Aug 10am–6pm,
Nov–Dec 10am–4pm

Admission
Adult £1.95, Child £1.30

Contact
Lakeside, Kings Road, Cleethorpes DN35 0AG

t 01472 323232
w cleethorpesdiscoverycentre.co.uk
e lynne.emery@nelincs.gov.uk

469 Doddington

Doddington Hall

1 hr+   May–Sep

The hall was built in 1600 by the Elizabethan architect Robert Smithson. The mansion, with its contemporary gatehouse and walled garden, retains its Elizabethan exterior and has never been sold, passing through four families by marriage.

* Interior has a Georgian elegance
* Portrait of Sir Francis Delavel painted by Reynolds

Location
In the centre of Doddington, 6 miles W of Lincoln

Opening
Gardens Feb–Apr Sun 2–6pm
Hall & Gardens May–Sep Wed, Sun & Bank Hols 2–6pm

Admission
Adult £5.20, Child £2.60

Contact
Doddington, Lincoln N6 4RU

t 01522 694308
w doddingtonhall.com

468 Colsterworth

Woolsthorpe Manor

2 hrs   Mar–Oct

This C17 farmhouse was the birthplace and home of the scientist, Sir Isaac Newton. Visitors can see his childhood scribblings on the walls. A gnarled old apple tree in the garden may be a descendant of the famous specimen which helped Newton with his work.

* An interactive science discovery centre
* Replica of principle of differential calculus

Location
From A1, take B676 at Colsterworth roundabout, turn right at second crossroads and follow signposts

Opening
Jul & Aug Wed–Sun 1–6pm
Apr, May & Sep Wed–Sun 1–5pm
Mar & Oct Sat & Sun 1–5pm

Admission
Adult £3.60, Child £1.80

Contact
23 Newton Way, Woolsthorpe-by-Colsterworth, nr Grantham NG33 5NR

t 01476 860338
w nationaltrust.org.uk

©National Trust Photographic Library/Tessa Musgrave

470 Gainsborough

Gainsborough Old Hall

2 hrs   All year

This is a large C15 timber-framed medieval house, with a magnificent Great Hall and brick tower built on the site of an earlier C13 manor house. In 1483 King Richard lll stayed at the Old Hall and in 1451 King Henry Vlll was a guest.

* Special events throughout the year
* Lectures on first Tuesday of each month

Location
Town centre, off Parnell Street

Opening
Easter–Oct Mon–Sat 10am–5pm
Sun 2–5.30pm
Nov–Easter Mon–Sat 10am–5pm

Admission
Adult £3.20, Child £1.95, Concs £1.95

Contact
Parnell Street, Gainsborough
DN21 2NB

t 01427 612669
w lincolnshire.gov.uk/
   gainsboroughholdhall
e gainsboroughholdhall@
   lincolnshire.gov.uk

---

471 Grantham

Belton House

6 hrs   Mar–Nov

A stunning example of Restoration country house architecture, Belton was built in 1685-88 and later altered by James Wyatt. The interiors contain fine plasterwork and wood-carving, as well as collections of paintings, furniture, tapestries and silverware.

* Formal gardens, orangery and landscape park
* Edward VIII often came to stay before his abdication

Location
On A607 3miles NE of Grantham, signposted from A1

Opening
House Mar–Nov Wed–Sun 12.30–5pm
Garden Mar–Nov Wed–Sun
11am–5.30pm
Nov–Dec Sat & Sun 12noon–4pm

Admission
Adult £6.50, Child £3

Contact
Grantham NG32 2LS

t 01476 566116
w nationaltrust.org.uk
e belton@nationaltrust.org.uk

---

472 Grantham

Grantham Museum

½ hr   Mon–Sat

The museum interprets the archaeology and social history of Grantham and includes exhibits on famous residents such as Sir Isaac Newton and Margaret Thatcher, who has given many personal items to the museum. There is also a section on the Dambusters.

* Dambusters mission planned here
* 1851 Great Exhibition gold medal winning doll

Location
Central Grantham

Opening
Mon–Sat 10am–5pm

Admission
Free

Contact
St Peter's Hill, Grantham NG31 6PY

t 01476 568783
w lincolnshire.gov.uk/
   granthammuseum
e grantham.museum@
   lincolnshire.gov.uk

473 Grimsby

National Fishing Heritage Centre

2 hrs   Mar–Oct

The centre tells the story of the area's fishermen, their boats and the waters they fished in. The dangers and hardships of life at sea are explained and there is a reconstruction of a 1950s sea voyage, complete with authentic aromas and a moving deck.

* Collection of historic vessels in adjacent dock
* Reconstruction of streets and alleys of 1950s Grimsby

Location
Next to Alexandra Dock, 2 min walk from town centre

Opening
Mar–Oct Mon–Fri 10am–4pm
Sat–Sun & Bank Hols
10.30am–5.30pm

Admission
Adult £4.95, Child £3.85

Contact
Alexandra Dock, Grimsby DN31 1UZ

t 01472 323345
w nelincs.gov.uk
e ann.hackett@nelincs.gov.uk

474 Lincoln

Lincoln Medieval Bishop's Palace

1 hr   All year

Standing in the shadow of Lincoln Cathedral, the palace acted as the administrative centre of the largest diocese in medieval England and now forms an impressive bishop's house. Don't miss the East Hall, with its stunning vaulted undercroft, or the chapel.

* The palace was 'modernised' in the 1430s
* Panorama of the Roman, medieval and modern city

Location
S side of Lincoln Cathedral

Opening
Apr–Sep daily 10–6pm
Oct 10am–5pm
Nov–Mar Wed–Sun 10am–4pm

Admission
Adult £3.20, Child £1.60, Concs £2.40

Contact
Minster Yard, Lincoln LN2 1PU

t 01522 527468
w english-heritage.org.uk

475 Lincoln

Usher Gallery

1 hr+   Tue–Sat

Set in the beautiful grounds of the Temple Gardens, the gallery houses a collection of fine and decorative arts. The original Usher bequest of clocks and watches, porcelain, silver, enamels, miniatures and coins remains the core of the gallery's permanent collection.

* Neo-classical sculpture to contemporary portraiture
* C17-C20 glass, including English drinking glasses

Location
Lincoln city centre

Opening
Tue–Sat & Bank Hols 10am–5pm
Sun 2.30–4.30pm

Admission
Free, charges for special exhibitions

Contact
Lindum Road, Lincoln LN2 1NN

t 01522 527980
w lincolnshire.gov.uk
e usher.gallery@lincolnshire.gov.uk

476 Old Bolingbroke

Bolingbroke Castle

1 hr   All year

Bolingbroke Castle is a prime example of C13 castle design, complete with a large gatehouse, round towers and a moat. Today the castle is a ruin, with only the ground floors of the towers and the lower parts of the walls remaining.

* Regular re-enactments
* The birthplace of King Henry IV

Location
In Old Bolingbroke, 16 miles N of Boston, signposted from A155

Opening
Apr–Sep daily 9am–9pm
Oct–Mar daily 9am–7pm

Admission
Free

Contact
Old School, Cameron Street, Hecklington NG34 9RW

t 01529 461499
w lincsheritage.org
e info@lincsheritage.org

477 Skegness

Skegness Natureland Seal Sanctuary

2 hrs   All year

The sanctuary houses seals, penguins and tropical birds. There are reptiles in an aquarium and a display of free-flying tropical butterflies. Natureland is well known for rescuing abandoned seal pups and visitors can view the hospital unit and large seascape pool.

* Family Attraction of the Year 2000

   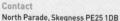

Location
Signposted from town centre

Opening
Jun–Sep 10am–5pm,
Oct–May 10am–4pm

Admission
Adult £4.75, Child £3.10, Concs £3.80

Contact
North Parade, Skegness PE25 1DB

t 01754 764345
w skegnessnatureland.co.uk
e natureland@fsbdial.co.uk

478 Sleaford

Cogglesford Watermill

1 hr   All year

This watermill on the banks of the River Slea has a fascinating history. Millers have produced flour on the site for over a thousand years and the mill was a major meeting place for local farmers and traders. Discover the story of William Almond, a prosperous miller.

* Ingenious labour-saving sack hoists
* Special working days held throughout the year

Location
½ mile from centre of Sleaford,
nr A153

Opening
Easter–Sep Mon–Fri 12noon–4pm
Sat–Sun & Bank Hols 11am–4.30pm
Oct–Easter Sat–Sun 12noon–4pm

Admission
Free

Contact
East Road, Sleaford

t 01529 414294
w tic.alan.co.uk
e tic@n-besteven.gov.uk

479 Stamford

Burghley House

3 hrs   Mar–Oct

Built between 1555 and 1587 by William Cecil, Lord Treasurer to Queen Elizabeth I, Burghley was based on designs of other great houses of the period, but has European influences. Externally, it is largely as it was when completed by Cecil's masons.

* Paintings include work by John Frederick Herring
* Sculpture park

Location
1½ miles from Stamford, well signed

Opening
House Mar–Oct Mon–Sun 11am–5pm
Sculpture Park Mon–Sun 10am–5pm

Admission
Adult £7.80, Child £3.50, Concs £6.90

Contact
Stamford PE9 3JY

t 01780 752451
w burghley.co.uk
e burghley@burghley.co.uk

480 Spilsby

Lincoln Aviation Centre

4 hrs   All year

This aircraft museum is based on a 1940s bomber airfield and has a number of exhibits, ranging from the original control tower and war-time blast shelter to Barnes Wallis' bouncing bomb and squadron and airfield photographs.

* Avro Lancaster bomber NX611 'Just Jane'
* RAF Escaping Society

Location
On the A155, between Revesey & East Kirkby

Opening
Easter–Oct Mon–Sat 9.30am–5pm
Nov–Easter Mon–Sat 10am–4pm

Admission
Adult £5, Child £1.50, Concs £4.50

Contact
East Kirkby Airfield, nr Spilsby
PE23 4DE

t 01790 763207
w lincsaviation.co.uk
e enquiries@lincsaviation.co.uk

481 Tattershall

Tattershall College

½ hr   All year

The remains of a grammar school for church choristers, built in the mid C15 by Ralph, Lord Cromwell, who also built nearby Tattershall Castle. The college was used as a school in the late C17 and then converted into a malting house and granary in 1790.

* One of the earliest brick buildings in Lincolnshire
* Part of a unique complex of medieval buildings

Location
In Tattershall, on A153, 14 miles NE of Sleaford

Opening
Daily 10am–5pm

Admission
Free

Contact
Old School, Cameron Street, Hecklington NG34 9RW

t 01529 461499
w lincsheritage.org
e info@lincsheritage.org

482 Tattershall

Tattershall Castle

1 hr   All year

A large medieval fortified and moated red brick tower, built for Ralph Cromwell, Lord Treasurer of England. The building was restored by Lord Curzon in 1911–14 and contains four great chambers with enormous Gothic fireplaces, tapestries and brick vaulting.

* Spectacular views from the battlements

Location
On S side of A153, 15 miles NE of Sleaford, 10miles SW of Horncastle

Opening
Apr–Sep Mon–Wed Sat–Sun 11am–5pm
Mar, Nov–Dec, Sat–Sun 12noon–4pm

Admission
Adult £3.50, Child £1.80

Contact
Tattershall, Lincoln LN4 4LR

t 01526 342543
w nationaltrust.org.uk
e tattershallcastle@nationaltrust.org.uk

Deene Park

2 hrs   Jun–Aug

Deene park is a largely C16 house incorporating a medieval manor. It's built around a courtyard and had important rooms added during the reign of George III. It was the seat of the 7th Earl of Cardigan who led the charge of the Light Brigade at Balaklava in 1854.

* Crimean War exhibition of uniforms and memorabilia
* Beautiful gardens and parkland

Location
6 miles NE of Corby, off A43

Opening
Jun–Aug Sun & Bank Hols 2–5pm

Admission
Adult £6, Child £2.50

Contact
Corby NN17 3EW

t 01780 450278
w deenepark.com
e admin@deenepark.com

Cottesbrooke Hall & Gardens

2 hrs+   May–Sep

Architecturally magnificent Queen Anne house with a renowned picture collection, featuring sporting and equestrian subjects. Other collections include fine furniture and porcelain. Cottesbrooke is reputed to be the model for Jane Austen's Mansfield Park.

* HHA / Christies Garden of the Year 2000
* Guided tours of the house are available

Location
At A14 junction 1 head S on A5199, signposted for Cottesbrooke

Opening
May & Jun, Wed–Thu & Bank Hols, 2–5.30pm
Jul, Aug & Sep, Thu & Bank Hols 2–5.30pm

Admission
Hall & Gardens Adult £6, Child £3
Gardens Adult £4, Child £2

Contact
Cottesbrooke, Northampton NN6 8PF

t 01604 505808
w cottesbrookehall.co.uk
e hall@cottesbrooke.co.uk

Canons Ashby House

1 hr+   Apr–Sep

Constructed in the mid-C16, this charming house has survived substantially unaltered since 1710. The interior contains wall paintings and Jacobean plasterwork, with rich panelling in the Winter Parlour. Edward Dryden's formal gardens have been restored.

* Remains of an Augustinian priory
* Orchard containing varieties of typical C16 apple trees

Location
Between Northampton and Banbury

Opening
Apr–Sep Sat–Wed 1–5pm
Oct Sat–Wed 12 noon–4pm

Admission
Adult £5.60, Child £2.80

Contact
Daventry NN11 3SD

t 01327 860044
w nationaltrust.org.uk
e canonsashby@nationaltrust.org.uk

Sywell Country Park

1 hr+   All year

This country park is based on a former water supply reservoir and the surrounding pastureland. The original Edwardian pump house buildings and valve tower survive, along with a collection of exotic trees in a small arboretum below the dam.

* Nationally renowned coarse fishery
* Bird hides and arboretum

Location
1 mile from A45 off Northampton to Mensbury road

Opening
Summer 9am–6pm
Winter 9am–5pm

Admission
Free, charges for car park

Contact
Washbrook Lane, Ecton NN6 0QX

t 01604 810970
w northhamptonshire.gov.com
e sywell@northhamptonshire.gov.uk

487 Kettering

Boughton House

2–4 hrs   Aug–Sep

Known as the English Versailles due to the French-style additions made in 1695, this 500-year-old Tudor monastic building houses an impressive collection of C16 carpets, C17 and C18 furniture, tapestries, porcelain and paintings, including works by El Greco and Caracci.

* Over 40 Van Dyck paintings.
* Armoury and ceremonial coach

Location
Just off A43, 3 miles N of Kettering

Opening
House Aug–Sep daily 2–4.30pm
Grounds May–Sep Sat–Thu 1–5pm

Admission
Adult £6, Child & Concs £5

Contact
Kettering NN14 1BJ

t 01536 515 731
w boughtonhouse.org.uk
e llt@boughtonhouse.org.uk

488 Kettering

Rushton Triangular Lodge

1 hr   Apr–Oct

This triangular building was designed and built by Sir Thomas Tresham in 1593 as a testament to his Catholicism, for which he had been imprisoned. Consequently, the lodge is emblazoned with references to the number three and the Holy Trinity.

* Colourful house adorned with dates and emblems
* Three windows, three floors, three roof gables

Location
1 mile W of Rushton, on A6, on unclassified road 3 miles from Desborough

Opening
Apr–Sep daily 10am–6pm
Oct daily 10am–5pm

Admission
Adult £2, Child £1, Concs £1.50

Contact
Rushton, Kettering NN14 1RP

t 01536 710761
w english-heritage.org.uk

489 Market Harborough

Kelmarsh Hall & Gardens

2 hrs+   Apr–Sep

This early C18 Palladian style house was designed by James Gibbs. It includes a Chinese room with hand-painted wallpaper, interesting gardens, a lake and woodland walks. A herd of British white cattle roam the parkland.

* Managed by the Kelmarsh Trust
* Regular courses in arts, crafts and music

Location
On A508 at Kelmarsh village

Opening
House Apr–Aug Sun & Bank Hols 2.30–5pm
Gardens Apr–Sep Mon–Thu 2.30–5pm

Admission
Adult £4, Child £2, Concs £3.50

Contact
Kelmarsh, Northampton NN6 9LU

t 01604 686543
w kelmarsh.com
e enquiries@kelmarsh.com

490 Market Harborough

Rockingham Castle

3 hrs   Apr–Sep

Still the centre of an agricultural community, the castle also remains a family home and the owners' collection of C20 pictures adds a personal flavour. Poised above the Welland Valley, with views over five counties, the ramparts enclose 12 acres of sweeping lawns.

* Formal and informal gardens
* Circular rose garden on the site of the old keep

Location
1 mile N of Corby, off A427

Opening
Apr–Jun & Sep Sun & Bank Hols
12 noon–5pm
Jul & Aug Sun, Tue, Thu & Bank Hols
12 noon–5pm

Admission
Adult £6, Child £4, Concs £5.50

Contact
Market Harborough LE16 8TH

t 01536 770240
e rockinghamcastle@lineone.net

491 Northampton

Holdenby House, Gardens & Falconry Centre

2 hrs   Apr–Sep

Across the fields from Althorp lies Holdenby, a house whose royal connections go back over 400 years. Its history is complemented by a regal collection of birds of prey, including the only naturally reared male black eagle on display anywhere.

* Based on the remaining kitchen wing of the old palace
* Built in 1583 by Sir Christopher Hatton

Location
6 miles NW of Northhampton, off
A5199 or A428

Opening
Apr–Aug Sun–Fri 1–5pm
Sep Sun 1–5pm

Admission
Gardens & Falconry Centre
Adult £4.50, Child £3, Concs £4

Contact
Holdenby, Northampton NN6 8DJ

t 01604 770074
w holdenby.com
e enquiries@holdenby.com

492 Northampton

Northampton Museum & Art Gallery

1 hr   All year

Reflecting the town's proud standing as Britain's boot and shoe capital, the Northampton Museum & Art Gallery features the world's largest collection of footwear. Other displays include British and Oriental pottery and porcelain and a display of fine glassware.

* Programme of temporary exhibitions and events
* The town's history from the Stone Age to the present day

Location
Northampton town centre

Opening
Mon–Sat 10am–5pm, Sun 2–5pm

Admission
Free

Contact
4–6 Guildhall Road
Northampton NN1 1DP

t 01604 858111
w northampton.gov.uk/museums
e museums@northampton.gov.uk

493 Oundle

Lyveden New Bield

1 hr+   All year

This incomplete Elizabethan garden lodge remains unaltered since building work stopped 400 years ago. Designed in the shape of a cross, with fascinating archictectural stonework, the lodge is set in beautiful countryside adjoining the remains of a moated garden.

* Designed by Sir Thomas Tresham
* Elizabethan water gardens open by arrangement

Location
4 miles SW of Oundle on A427, 3 miles E of Brigstock, leading off A6116

Opening
Wed–Sun 9am–5pm

Admission
Adult £2.50, Child £1.20

Contact
nr Oundle, Peterborough PE8 5AT

t 01832 205358
w nationaltrust.org.uk/lyveden
e lyvedennewbield@nationaltrust.org.uk

494 Towcester

Canal Museum

2–4 hrs   Oct–Sep

Housed in an old corn mill on the Grand Union Canal are exhibits from two centuries of canal history, including a reconstructed narrowboat, with all its traditional furniture and equipment. Trips can be taken through the mile-long Blisworth Tunnel.

* Cruise along the Grand Union Canal
* Courses in narrowboat decoration and ropework

Location
S of Northampton, 10 mins from M1 junction 15 and A5, on Grand Union Canal S of Blisworth Tunnel

Opening
Oct–Mar Tue–Sun 10am–4pm
Apr–Sep Mon–Sun 10am–5pm

Admission
Adult £3, Child £2.50, Concs £2.50

Contact
Stoke Bruerne, Towcester NN12 7SE

t 01604 862 229
w waterwaystrust.co.uk
e canal.museum@waterwaystrust.co.uk

495 Wansford

Prebendal Manor House

2 hrs+   May–Sep

This C13 Grade 1 listed manor house is the oldest surviving dwelling in Northamptonshire and is steeped in history. The recreated medieval gardens are unique to the area and are the largest in Europe. Visit the C16 dovecote and the large C18 tithe barn museum.

* Rare breeds of sheep and pigs and medieval farming
* Explore the history of the Prebends

Location
A few miles from A1 and A605, signposted from nearby villages

Opening
May, Jun & Sep, Wed, Sun & Bank Hols, 1–5.30pm
Jul & Aug, Wed, Thu & Sun & Bank Hols 1–5.30pm

Admission
Adult £4.50, Child £2

Contact
Nassington, Peterborough PE8 6QG

t 01780 782575
w prebendal-manor.demon.co.uk
e info@prebendal-manor.demon.co.uk

496 Wellingborough

Irchester Country Park

4–6 hrs   All year

Explore a network of trails running across 83 hectares of mixed woodland and observe the wealth of wildlife, including woodpeckers and sparrowhawks. A Forestry Centre of Excellence, the park balances conservation with timber production and recreation.

* Ironstone railway museum
* Accessible trails and orienteering trail

Location
2 miles S of Wellingborough, on B570, in the Nene Valley

Opening
Park Daily 24 hrs
Car park 9am–5pm

Admission
Free, £1.50 for car park

Contact
Gypsy Lane, Little Irchester Wellingborough NN9 7DL

t 01933 276866
w northamptonshire.gov.uk
e irchester@northamptonshire.gov.uk

Sherwood Forest Country Park & Visitor Centre

2 hrs   All year

A good place to begin any exploration of Sherwood Forest is the visitor centre. Find out what life would have been like for outlaws, kings and commoners in Sherwood Forest during the Middle Ages. Enjoy the trails and discover the forest yourself.

* See the Major Oak, Robin Hood's hiding place
* Forests of the World exhibition

Location
In Edwinstowe village, off B6034

Opening
Visitor Centre summer 10am–5pm
winter 10am–4pm
Park dawn to dusk

Admission
Free, charges for car park

Contact
Edwinstowe, nr Mansfield NG21 9HN

t 01623 823202
w sherwoodforest.org.uk
e sherwood.forest@nott-cc.gov.uk

Mansfield Museum & Art Gallery

1 hr   All year

Explore the history of Mansfield and the surrounding area. Permanent displays illustrate the social, industrial and natural history of the area, while the Buxton watercolours reveal a Mansfield that has long since disappeared.

* Pottery pieces from Derby, Pinxton and Mansfield
* Varied programme of temporary exhibitions

Location
5 mins walk from market place

Opening
Mon–Sat 10am–5pm

Admission
Free

Contact
Leeming Street, Mansfield NG18 1NG

t 01623 463088
w mansfield.gov.uk
e mansfield-museum@hotmail.com

Newark Air Museum

2 hrs   All year

The museum's impressive collection currently stands at over 65 aircraft and cockpit sections, including transport, training and reconnaissance aircraft and helicopters and a diverse selection of jet fighters and bombers.

* Post-war air-to-air missile display
* History of RAF Winthorpe, wartime bomber training

Location
Easily accessible from A1, A46, A17, A1133 and Newark bypass

Opening
Mar–Oct 10am–5pm
Nov–Feb 10am–4pm

Admission
Adult £4.75, Child £3, Concs £4

Contact
Winthorpe Showground, Newark
NG24 2NY

t 01636 707170
w newarkairmuseum.co.uk
e newarkair@lineone.net

500 Nottingham

Angel Row Gallery

1–2 hrs   All year

This is a one of the region's leading contemporary art and craft galleries, with a programme of exhibitions that covers a whole range of art, including painting, photography, video and installations. The gallery also runs wokshops and hosts talks by leading artists.

Location
Central Nottingham

Opening
Mon–Sat 10am–5pm
Wed 10am–7pm

Admission
Free

Contact
Central Library Building, 3 Angel Row ,
Nottingham NG1 6HP
t 0115 9152869
w angelrowgallery.com
e angelrow.marketing@
nottinghamcity.gov.uk

501 Nottingham

Galleries of Justice

2–3 hrs   All year

A tour through three centuries of crime, punishment and law. Located in the Shire Hall, it includes Victorian courtrooms, an C18 prison, exercise yard, cave cells, a women's prison with bath house and laundry, medieval cave system and an Edwardian police station.

* Costumed interpreters bring the experience to life
* Series of temporary exhibitions

Location
Central Nottingham, nr Broadmarsh
Shopping Centre

Opening
Tue–Sun & Bank Hols 10am–5pm

Admission
Adult £6.95, Child £5.25, Concs £5.95

Contact
Shire Hall, High Pavement,
Lace Market, Nottingham NG1 1HN
t 0115 9520555
w galleriesofjustice.org.uk

502 Nottingham

The Lace Centre

½ hr   All year

Nottingham is famous for its lacemaking heritage and Nottingham lace is a rich, varied fabric, knitted, twisted or embroidered in the UK by a member of the British Lace Federation. The Lace Centre is housed in a C14 medieval house in the heart of the city.

* Weekly bobbin lace demonstrations
* Hands-on experiences on Thursday afternoons

Location
Opposite Nottingham Castle

Opening
Jan–Mar daily 10am–4pm
Apr–Dec Mon–Sat 10am–5pm
Sun 11am–4pm

Admission
Free

Contact
Severns Building, Castle Road,
Nottingham NG1 6AA
t 0115 9413539
e nottinghamlace@btopenworld.com

503 Nottingham

Tales of Robin Hood

1–2 hrs   All year

The swashbuckling adventures of Robin Hood have inspired storytellers for more than 700 years. Explore the world of this infamous and endearing outlaw and experience medieval life, legend and adventure by fleeing through the forest to escape the evil Sheriff.

* Regular Robin Hood events
* Medieval banquets are held on Fridays and Saturdays

Location
In the city centre, next to the castle,
signposted from M1

Opening
Daily 10am–5.30pm

Admission
Adult £6.95, Child £4.95, Concs £5.95

Contact
30-38 Maid Marian Way,
Nottingham NG1 6GF
t 0115 9483284
w robinhood.uk.com
e robinhoodcentre@mail.com

504 Nottingham

Nottingham Castle

1–2 hrs   All year

Situated high above the city, Nottingham Castle was originally constructed by William the Conqueror, demolished after the Civil War and then rebuilt in the C17. As well as displays about its turbulent history, the castle has paintings, sculptures, china and silverware.

* Network of caves and passageways beneath the castle
* Robin Hood statue

Location
Central Nottingham

Opening
Daily 10am–4.30pm

Admission
Weekdays free
Sat–Sun & Bank Hols Adult £2,
Child & Concs £1

Contact
Lenton Road, Nottingham NG1 6EL

t 0115 9153700
w nottinghamcity.gov.uk

506 Ollerton

Rufford Abbey

4 hrs   All year

This ruined, former Cistercian monastery was founded in C12, but following its dissolution in 1536, its lands were granted to George Talbot, 4th Earl of Shrewsbury. The Talbot family then went on to transform the buildings into a country house.

* Stable block houses a modern ceramics gallery
* The gardens were re-established in the late 1970s

Location
2 miles S of Ollerton, off A614

Opening
Apr–Oct 10am–5pm
Nov–Mar 10am–4pm

Admission
Free, Sat–Sun & Bank Hols £1.50
for car park

Contact
Ollerton, nr Newark NG22 9DF

t 01623 822944
w notting hamshiretourism.co.uk

505 Ollerton

Holocaust Centre, Beth Shalom

2–3 hrs   All year

Beth Shalom is set in two acres of beautiful gardens and provides a range of facilities for visitors to explore the history and implications of the Holocaust. The main features are its red brick memorial building, permanent exhibition on the Nazi period and memorial gardens.

* Art and photography exhibitions about the Holocaust
* Survivors regularly speak at the centre

Location
Large buildings on right between
Laxton and Ollerton

Opening
Jan–Nov Wed–Sun 10am–5pm

Admission
Adult £6, Child & Concs £4

Contact
Laxton, nr Ollerton NG22 0PA

t 01623 836627
w holocaustcentre.net
e office@bethshalom.com

©National Trust Photographic Library/Andrew Butler

507 Retford

Mattersey Priory

½ hr   All year

These are the remains of a small Gilbertine monastery on the banks of the River Idle, which was founded for six canons in 1185. For nearly four centuries the monks lived in their secluded village, until the smaller monastries were dissolved in 1536 and it closed.

Location
1 mile E of Mattersey, off B6045,
½ mile down rough drive

Opening
Daily dawn to dusk

Admission
Free

Contact
English Heritage, 44 Durngate,
Northampton NN1 4UH

t 0870 3331181
w english-heritage.org.uk

508 Southwell

Southwell Workhouse

1 hr+   Mar–Nov

The lives of the poor and destitute in the C19 and C20 are revealed at Southwell workhouse. Explore the building and its history, including the segregated staircases and rooms, and unlock the stories of the people who lived and worked there.

* Play the Master's Punishment game
* Meet some of the 'characters' who lived here

Location
13 miles from Nottingham on A612,
8 miles from Newark on A617 & A612

Opening
Mar 24–Nov Thu–Mon 12noon–5pm
Aug 11am–5pm

Admission
Adult £4.40, Child £2.20

Contact
Upton Road, Southwell NG25 0PT

t 01636 817250
w nationaltrust.org.uk
e theworkhouse@
nationaltrust.org.uk

Nottinghamshire

509 Worksop

Clumber Park

2–3 hrs   All year

Part of Nottinghamshire's famed 'Dukeries', at Clumber Park there are over 3,800 acres of parkland, peaceful woods, open heath and rolling farmland with a superb serpentine lake at their heart. Although the house was demolished in 1938, many features of the estate remain.

* Outstanding Gothic Revival chapel
* Walled kitchen garden

Location
4 miles SE of Worksop

Opening
Park Apr–Sep 9am–7pm
Oct–Mar daily 9am–5pm
Garden Apr–Sep Wed–Sun
10.30am–5.30pm
Oct Wed–Sun 10.30am–4pm

Admission
Free, £3.80 per car

Contact
The Estate Office, Clumber Park,
Worksop S80 3AZ

t 01909 476592
w nationaltrust.org.uk/clumberpark
e clumberpark@nationaltrust.org.uk

510 Worksop

Harley Gallery

1 hr   All year

The Harley Foundation, set up as a charitable trust in 1977 by the late Ivy, Duchess of Portland, is based in the Ducal Estate of Welbeck. As well as offering studio space to artists and craftspeople, it also funds an art gallery and programme of exhibitions.

* Historical gallery exhibiting decorative and fine art
* Full programme of events

Location
5 miles S of Worksop on the A60

Opening
Jan 17–Dec Tue–Sun & Bank Hols
10am–5pm

Admission
Free

Contact
Welbeck, Mansfield Road, Worksop
S80 3LW

t 01909 501700
w harleygallery.co.uk
e info@harley-wellbeck.co.uk

511 Worksop

Mr Straw's House

1 hr+   Apr–Nov

This modest, semi-detached, Edwardian house provides a fascinating insight into early C20 everyday life. The interior has remained unaltered since the 1930s and features contemporary wallpaper, Victorian furniture and household objects.

* Displays of family costumes
* A typical suburban garden

WC

Location
Follow signs to Bassetlaw General
Hospital, signposted from Blyth Road

Opening
Apr–Nov Tue–Sat 11–4.30pm

Admission
Pre-booked timed ticket only
Adult £4.30, Child £2.15

Contact
7 Blyth Grove, Worksop S81 0JG

t 01909 482380
w nationaltrust.org.uk
e mrstrawshouse@
nationaltrust.org.uk

Rutland

Drought Garden & Arboretum

½ hr   All year

Designed by the late Geoff Hamilton with refurbishment by Nick Hamilton, this garden–on a south-facing clay slope at Barnsdale–has survived dry summers and penetrating frost. The arboretum shows the species of trees planted around the reservoir.

* Accolade Winner 2002
* The Best of its Kind 2003

Location	Admission
Accessed from A606 Oakham–Stamford road. Turn into Barnsdale car park at Rutland Water	Free
Opening All year, 24 hrs	**Contact** Barnsdale, Rutland Water t 01572 653026 w ruttlandwater.net

Clipsham Yew Tree Avenue

1½ hrs   All year

The Yew Tree Avenue is a unique collection of 150 clipped yew trees, most over 200 years old, which was once the drive to Clipsham Hall. The topiary was begun in 1870 by Amos Alexander, the estate's head forester, who lived in the gate lodge at the foot of the avenue.

* Clipping each autumn by Forestry Commission
* Muntjac may be seen crossing the avenue

Location	Contact
Less than 1 mile E of Clipsham on Castle Bytham road	Forest Enterprise, North Hants Top Lodge, Fineshade NN17 3BB
Opening All year daily	t 01780 444394 w forestry.gov.uk e northants@forestry.gsi.gov.uk
Admission Free	

Lyddington Bede House

1 hr   Apr–Sept

Lyddington Bede House was originally a wing of a medieval rural palace belonging to the bishops of Lincoln. In 1600, the building was converted into an almshouse and remained a home for pensioners until the 1930s.

* Great Chamber features a beautiful ceiling cornice
* Bedesmen's rooms with tiny windows and fireplaces

Location	Admission
In Lyddington, 6 miles N of Corby, 1 mile E of A6003, next to the church	Adult £3.20, Child £1.60, Concs £2.40 Prices for events vary
Opening Apr–Sep 10am–6pm Oct 10am–5pm	**Contact** Bluecoat Lane, Lyddington LE15 9LZ t 01572 822438 w english-heritage.org.uk

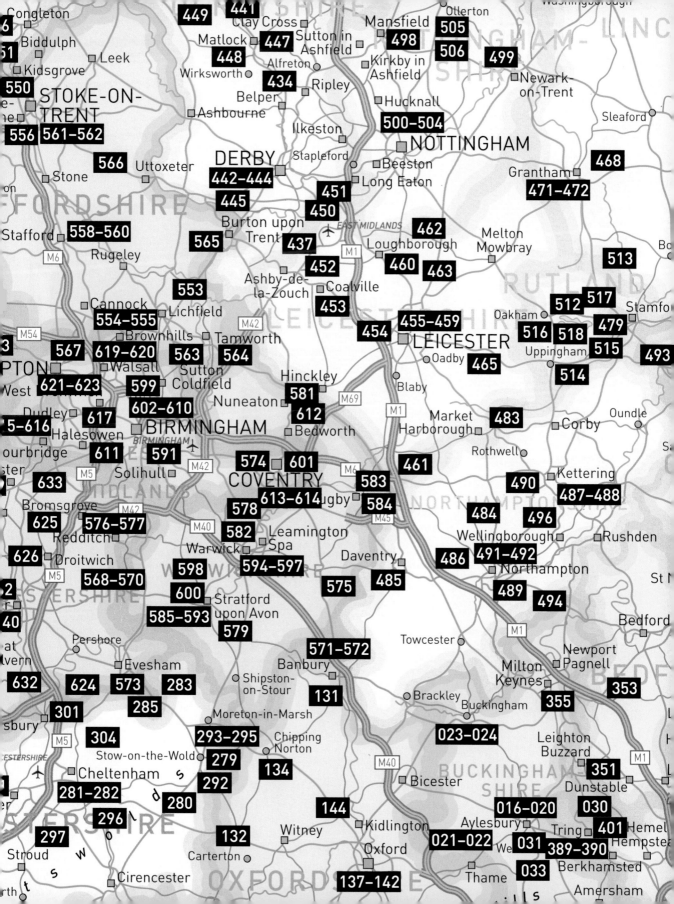

519 Bromyard

Brockhampton Estate

1 hr   All year

This 1,700–acre estate still maintains farms and has extensive areas of woodland, including ancient oak and beech. Visitors can enjoy a variety of walks through both park and woodland. At the heart of the estate lies Lower Brockhampton House, a late C14 moated manor house.

* Timber-framed gatehouse and ruined chapel
* Woodland is home to interesting range of wildlife

Location
2 miles E of Bromyard on A44

Opening
House Mar 12noon–4pm
Apr–Sep 12noon–5pm
Oct 12noon–4pm
Estate open all year dawn to dusk

Admission
Adult £3.20, Child £1.60

Contact
Greenfields, Bringsty WR6 5TB

t 01885 488099 / 482077
w nationaltrust.org.uk
e brockhampton@nationaltrust.org.uk

520 Bromyard

Bromyard Heritage Centre

½ hr   Apr–Oct

Based in an C18 stable block, Bromyard Heritage Centre displays aspects of Bromyard's past, together with an extensive exhibition of hops and hop growing. This traces the growing and picking cycle and changing methods of cultivation since C15.

* Host to highly successful Year of the Hop exhibition
* Exhibition of rural & urban developments in the town

Location
Signposted from A44

Opening
Apr–Oct Mon–Sat 10am–4pm

Admission
Free

Contact
Rowberry Street, Bromyard HR7 4DU

t 01885 482341
w visitorlinks.com

521 Hereford

The Cider Museum

1 hr   All year

Explore the story of traditional cider making: how apples were harvested, milled and pressed, and how the resulting juice was fermented to produce cider. You can also walk through a reconstructed farm ciderhouse and see the 300-year-old travelling cider maker's 'tack'.

* Visit the original champagne cider cellars
* See the distillation process being used for cider brandy

Location
In W Hereford, off A438

Opening
Apr–Oct daily 10am–5pm
Nov–Dec daily 11am–3pm
Jan–Mar Tue–Sun 11am–3pm

Admission
Adult £2.70, Child & Concs £2.20

Contact
21 Ryelands Street, Hereford HR4 0LW

t 01432 354 207
w cidermuseum.co.uk
e info@cidermuseum.co.uk

522 Hereford

Hereford Cathedral, Mappa Mundi & Chained Library

2 hrs   All year

Housed within the cathedral's C15 south west cloister and the new library building is an exhibition that uses models and original artefacts to reveal the secrets of Mappa Mundi, the largest and most elaborate complete pre-C15 world map in existence.

* The world's largest chained library – 1,500 rare books
* Working stonemasons yard and cathedral shop

Location
Hereford town centre

Opening
Summer Mon–Sat 10am–4.15pm
Sun 11am–3.15pm
Winter Mon–Sat 11am–3.15pm

Admission
Adult £4.50, Child & Concs £3.50

Contact
5 College Cloisters, Cathedral Close, Hereford HR1 2NG

t 01432 374200
w herefordcathedral.co.uk
e visits@herefordcathedral.co.uk

523 Hereford

The Old House

½ hr   All year

Originally completed in 1621, by the end of C19 the building had been taken over by a local bank that later became part of Lloyds Bank. Lloyds moved out in 1928 and donated the house to the city. The Old House is now a museum recreating C17 life.

* One of the finest examples of Jacobean architecture
* Virtual tours for those that can't climb stairs

Location
Centre of High Town, signposted

Opening
Apr–Sep Tue–Sat 10am–5pm
Sun & Bank Hols 10am–4pm

Admission
Free

Contact
High Town, Hereford HR1 2AA

t 01432 260694

524 Hereford

The Weir

1 hr+   Jan–Oct

A delightful riverside garden, particularly spectacular in early spring and with fine views over the River Wye and the Black Mountains. The late C18 house (not open to the public) sits on top of steep slopes that fall away to the river.

* Walks through beech woodland high above the river
* Created by the Parr family in the 1920s

Location
5 miles W of Hereford, signposted from A438

Opening
Jan 17–Jan 31 Sat–Sun 11am–4pm
Feb Wed–Sun 11am–6pm
Mar daily 11am–6pm
Apr–Oct Wed–Sun & Bank Hols 11am–6pm

Admission
Adult £3.50, Child £1.75

Contact
Swainshill, nr Hereford HR4 7QF

t 01981 590509
w nationaltrust.org.uk
e theweir@ntrust.org.uk

525 Kington

Hergest Croft Gardens

2 hrs+   Apr–Oct

In the heart of the Welsh Marches, with stunning views towards the Black Mountains, Hergest Croft was created over 100 years by three generations of the Banks family. There are hidden valleys, woodland glades, open parkland and flower borders for year-round beauty.

* National Collection of birch and maples
* Rhododendrons and azaleas

Location
Signposted on A44 from Kington

Opening
Apr 3–Oct 31 daily 12.30–5.30pm

Admission
Adult £4.50, Child free

Contact
Kington HR5 3EG

t 01544 230160
w hergest.co.uk
e gardens@hergest.co.uk

526 Leominster

Berrington Hall

2½ hrs   Mar–Oct

With sweeping views to the Brecon Beacons, this elegant Henry Holland house was built in the late C18 and is set in parkland designed by Capability Brown. A rather austere external appearance belies a surprisingly delicate interior.

* Beautiful ceilings and a spectacular staircase hall
* Good collection of furniture and paintings

Location
3 miles N of Leominster

Opening
Mar 6–Apr 4 Sat–Sun 12noon–4.30pm
Apr 5–Oct 31 Sat–Wed 1–4.30pm

Admission
Adult £4.80, Child £2.40

Contact
Leominster HR6 0DW

t 01568 615721
w nationaltrust.org.uk
e berrington@nationaltrust.org.uk

527 Leominster

Croft Castle

2 hrs   Mar–Oct

Re-opened in 2003 after a major refurbishment programme, with additional showrooms to complement the fine Georgian interior and period furnishings. The gardens and park offer pleasant walks and magnificent views.

* Joint tickets with Berrington Hall available
* Beautiful period walled garden

Location
5 miles NW of Leominster

Opening
Mar 6–Mar 28 Sat–Sun 1–5pm
Apr 1–Sep 30 Wed–Sun 1–5pm
Oct 2–Oct 31 Sat–Sun 1–5pm

Admission
House & Garden Adult £4.40, Child £2.20
Garden Adult £3.10, Child £1.55

Contact
nr Leominster HR6 9PW

t 01568 780246
w nationaltrust.org.uk
e croftcastle@nationaltrust.org.uk

528 Leominster

Hampton Court Gardens

Fine   3 hrs   All year

With the stunning backdrop of a late medieval castle and surrounded by acres of parkland, Hampton Court has much to offer. Water features highly and there are canals, island pavilions, a waterfall and a sunken garden, plus two very different walled gardens.

* A maze of a thousand yews
* Organically managed site

Location
A417 nr junction with A49

Opening
Times vary, phone for details

Admission
Adult £5, Child £3, Concs £4.75

Contact
Hope under Dinmore,
Leominster HR6 0PN

t 01568 797 777
w hamptoncourt.org.uk
e office@hamptoncourt.org.uk

529 Ludlow

Wigmore Castle

Fine   2 hrs   All year

One of the most remarkable ruins in England, Wigmore Castle was abandoned pre-C17 and left to deteriorate naturally. Today, it has been buried up to first floor level by fallen upper floors, but its towers and curtain walls survive to their full height.

* WARNING: The castle has steep steps to the summit which are hazardous in icy conditions

Location
8 miles W of Ludlow on A4110

Opening
Dawn to dusk

Admission
Free

Contact
English Heritage West Midlands,
112 Colmore Row,
Birmingham B3 3AG

t 0121 6256820
w english-heritage.org.uk
e customers@english-heritage.org.uk

530 Ross-on-Wye

Goodrich Castle

1 hr   All year

This fortified baronial palace stands majestically on a red sandstone crag, commanding the passage of the River Wye into the picturesque wooded valley of Symonds Yat. Much of the stone used was quarried from the rock around the base of the castle, creating a deep moat.

* Cannon that destroyed the castle in 1645 is now on display
* Views over River Wye and Symonds Yat

Location
5 miles S of Ross-on-Wye off A40

Opening
Apr–Sep daily 10am–6pm
Oct daily 10am–5pm
Nov–Mar Wed–Sun
10am–1pm & 2–4pm

Admission
Adult £3.70, Child £1.90, Concs £2.80

Contact
Ross-on-Wye HR9 6HY

t 01600 890538
w english-heritage.org.uk

531 Symonds Yat

Amazing Hedge Puzzle

1 hr   Easter–Oct

Planted over 20 years ago by brothers Lindsay and Edward Heyes, the fun of the Amazing Hedge Puzzle has made it one of Herefordshire's most popular private tourist attractions. Learn about mazes through history and the myths surrounding them in the maze museum.

* Hands-on displays allow you to build your own maze
* Set in the beautiful countryside of the Wye Valley

Location
Follow signs on B4164, off A40
between Ross-on-Wye & Monmouth

Opening
Good Friday–Sep daily 11am–5pm
Mar & Oct Sat–Sun 11am–4pm
Daily during half-terms

Admission
Adult £3.50, Child £2, Concs £2.50

Contact
Jubilee Park, Symonds Yat West,
Ross-on-Wye HR9 6DA

t 01600 890360
w mazes.co.uk

532 Worcester

Worcester City Art Gallery & Museum

2 hrs   All year

Worcester's principal art gallery and museum hosts a unique programme of contemporary art exhibitions, as well as being home to a historic picture collection. It also has an intriguing selection of historical objects, including a C19 chemist shop and a Worcester sauce machine.

* The Worcestershire Soldier exhibit opened in 2003
* Display areas change regularly

Location
Near station, off A449 to
Kidderminster

Opening
Mon–Fri 9.30am–5.30pm
Sat 9.30–5pm

Admission
Free

Contact
Foregate Street, Worcester WR1 1DT

t 01905 25371
w cityofworcester.gov.uk
e artgalleryandmuseum@
   cityofworcester.gov.uk

533 Bishop's Wood

Boscobel House & The Royal Oak

2 hrs+   Mar–Nov

A refuge for Charles II before he fled to France, this timber-framed farmhouse was later converted into a hunting lodge. It was called Boscobel after the Italian 'bosco bello', meaning 'in the midst of fair woods' and reflecting the woodland that once surrounded it.

* Its true use is thought to have been to hide Catholics
* Escape from Worcester and farm exhibition

Location
8 miles NW of Wolverhampton, on minor road between A41 & A5

Opening
Mar–Sep daily 11am–6pm, Oct daily 11am–5pm, Nov Wed–Sun 11am–4pm

Admission
Adult £4.40, Child £2.20, Concs £3.30

Contact
Brewood, Bishop's Wood ST19 9AR

t 01902 850244
w english-heritage.org.uk
e bascobelhouse@english-heritage.org.uk

534 Bridgnorth

Dudmaston

2 hrs+   Mar–Oct

A late C17 house with intimate family rooms containing fine furniture and Dutch flower paintings, as well as important contemporary paintings and sculpture. The gardens are a mass of colour in spring and include a wooded valley or dingle.

* C20 art includes Nicholson, Moore and Hepworth
* Oak-panelled study opened to view in 2003

Location
4 miles SE of Bridgnorth, on A442

Opening
House Mar 30–Sep 28 Tue–Wed & Sun 2–5.30pm
Garden Mon–Wed & Sun 12 noon–6pm

Admission
Adult £4.10, Child £2

Contact
Quatt, nr Bridgnorth WV15 6QN

t 01746 780866
w nationaltrust.org.uk
e dudmaston@nationaltrust.org.uk

535 Bridgnorth

Severn Valley Railway

3 hrs+   All year

A full-size standard-gauge line running regular steam-hauled passenger trains between Kidderminster and Bridgnorth, a distance of 16 miles. For most of the way, the route follows the meandering course of the River Severn closely.

* Crosses impressive Victoria Bridge
* Passengers may break the journey at any station

Location
Stations in Kidderminster, Bridgnorth & Bewdley

Opening
May–Sep daily, Oct–Apr Sat–Sun
Full timetable available on web site

Admission
See web site for full details

Contact
The Railway Station, Bewdley DY12 1BG

t 01299 403 816
w svr.co.uk

536 Broseley

Benthall Hall

1 hr+   Apr–Sep

Situated on a plateau above the gorge of the Severn, this C16 stone house has mullioned and transomed windows and a stunning interior with carved oak staircase, decorated plaster ceilings and oak panelling. There is also an interesting Restoration church.

* Carefully restored plantsman's garden
* Old kitchen garden

Location
On B4375, 1 mile NW of Broseley,
1 mile SW of Ironbridge

Opening
Apr–Jun Tue–Wed, Bank Hols & Sun of Bank Hols
Jul–Sep Tue, Wed, Sun & Bank Hols
House 2–5.30pm
Gardens 1.30–5.30pm

Admission
Adult £4, Child £2

Contact
Broseley TF12 5RX

t 01952 882159
w nationaltrust.org.uk

537 Church Stretton

Acton Scott

3 hrs   Apr–Oct

Experience daily life on an upland farm at the turn of the century. The waggoner and his team of heavy horses work the land with vintage farm machines. Every day you can see milking by hand and butter making in the dairy. You will also see the farrier and the blacksmith.

* Lambing, shearing, cider making etc in season
* Children's holiday activities

Location
Off A49, 17 miles S of Shrewsbury,
14 miles N of Ludlow

Opening
Mar 30–Oct 31 Tue–Sun & Bank Hols
10am–5pm

Admission
Adult £4.25, Child £2, Concs £3.75

Contact
nr Church Stretton SY6 6QN

t 01694 781306
w actonscottmuseum.co.uk
e acton.scott.museum@
shropshire-cc.gov.uk

538 Craven Arms

Secret Hills – Shropshire Hills Discovery Centre

2 hrs+   All year

A stylish and imaginative new building with a grass roof set within 25 acres of the Onny Meadows. Designed to improve understanding of the landscape, culture and heritage of the area, the centre provides a base for year-round entertainment and hands-on activities.

* Craft gallery and activities area
* Find out about earthquakes

Location
Off A49, 7 miles N of Ludlow

Opening
Apr–Oct daily 10am–4.30pm
Nov– Mar daily 10am–3.30pm

Admission
Adult £4.25, Child £2.75

Contact
School Road, Craven Arms SY7 9RS

t 01588 676000 / 676040
w shropshire-cc.gov.uk/discover.nsf
e secrethills@shropshire-cc.gov.uk

539 Ludlow

Ludlow Castle

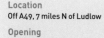

1 hr   All year

A dramatic medieval ruined castle, set in glorious Shropshire countryside. Walk through the castle grounds, see the ancient houses of kings, queens, princes, judges and the nobility and get a glimpse of the lifestyle of medieval society.

* Host to the popular Ludlow festival
* Many events throughout the year

Location
On A49, in town centre

Opening
Jan Sat–Sun 10am–4pm
Feb–Mar & Oct–Dec daily 10am–4pm
Apr–Jul & Sep daily 10am–5pm
Aug daily 10am–7pm

Admission
Adult £3.50, Child £1.50, Concs £3

Contact
Castle Square, Ludlow SY8 1AY

t 01584 873355
w ludlowcastle.com
e ludlowcastle@
paperclaydesigns.com

540   Ludlow

Stokesay Castle

1 hr   All year

Strength and elegance are united in this fortified medieval manor house, built by renowned wool merchant Lawrence of Ludlow. In 1291 a 'licence to crenellate' was obtained from Edward I at Hereford for the three-storey south tower.

* Magnificent Great Hall largely untouched
* Timber-framed Jacobean gatehouse

Location
Off A49, 7 miles NW of Ludlow

Opening
Apr–Sep daily 10am–6pm
Oct daily 10am–5pm
Nov–Mar Wed–Sun 10am–4pm

Admission
Adult £4.50, Child £2.30, Concs £3.40

Contact
Craven Arms SY7 9AH

t 01588 672544
w english-heritage.org.uk

541   Market Drayton

Hodnet Hall Gardens

2 hrs   Apr–Sep

Hodnet Hall features over 60 acres of flowers, forest trees, a chain of ornamental pools and a cultivated garden valley providing a natural habitat for waterfowl and other wildlife. The gardens also include a kitchen garden where the produce can be purchased.

* Woodland walks along chain of pools and lakes
* Planted to give colour from early spring to late autumn

Location
On A53, between Shrewsbury & Market Drayton

Opening
Apr–Sep Tue–Sun & Bank Hols
12 noon–5pm, Oct Sun 12noon–5pm

Admission
Adult £3.75, Child £1.75, Concs £3.25

Contact
Hodnet, Market Drayton TF9 3NN

t 01630 685 786
w hodnethallgardens.co.uk
e marlene@
heber-percy.freeserve.co.uk

542 Market Drayton

Wollerton Old Hall Garden

2 hrs   Easter–Sep

Wollerton Old Hall Garden is a three-acre plantsman's garden developed around a C16 house (not open) in rural Shropshire. The strong formal design has created many separate gardens, each with its own character, and there are many rare and unusual plants.

* Present garden developed from 1984
* Difficult-to-obtain perennials available in nursery

Location
Off A53, between Market Drayton & Shrewsbury

Opening
Good Friday–Aug Fri, Sun & Bank Hols 12noon–5pm
Sep Fri 12noon–5pm

Admission
Adult £4, Child £1

Contact
Wollerton, Market Drayton TF9 3NA
t 01630 685760
w wollertonoldhallgarden.com
e info@wollertonoldhallgarden.com

544 Shifnal

Weston Park

2 hrs+   May–Sep

The house was first mentioned in the *Domesday Book* in the C11, but Weston owes its unique character to the developments of the C17, directed by Lady Wilbraham. The beautiful landscaped gardens are the work of Capability Brown, although they were restored in 1991.

* Mary, daughter of George V, honeymooned here
* One of Disraeli's favourite locations

Location
On A5, 3 miles off M54 junction 3

Opening
May–Jun Holidays & Sat–Sun daily 11am–7pm
Jul–Sep 11am–7pm

Admission
Adult £3, Child £2, Concs £2.50

Contact
Weston-under-Lizard, Shifnal TF11 8LE
t 01952 852 100
w weston-park.com
e enquiries@weston-park.com

543 Shifnal

The RAF Museum – Cosford

3 hrs+   All year

Tells the story of man's flight – the sucesses and failures – through one of the largest aviation collections in the UK. Over 70 historic aircraft are displayed in three wartime hangars on an active airfield. The collection spans nearly 80 years of aviation history.

* Visitor Attraction of the Year 2003
* State-of-the-art flight simulator

Location
On A41, less than 1 mile from M54 junction 3

Opening
Daily 10am–6pm (last entry 4pm)
Closed Dec 24–26 & Jan 1

Admission
Free, charges for special events

Under 16s must be accompanied by an adult

Contact
Cosford, Shifnal TF11 8UP
t 01902 376 200
w rafmuseum.org
e cosford@rafmuseum.com

545 Shrewsbury

Attingham Park

2 hrs+ All year

One of the great houses of the Midlands, this elegant mansion was built in 1785 for the first Lord Berwick, to the design of George Steuart, and has a picture gallery by John Nash. The Regency interiors contain collections of silver, Italian furniture and Grand Tour paintings.

* Park with walk by River Tern landscaped by Repton
* Environmental activity room opened in 2003

Location
On B4380, 4 miles SE of Shrewsbury

Opening
House Mar–Nov Fri–Tue 1–4.30pm
Bank Hols 12noon–5pm
Grounds Mar–Oct daily 9am–8pm
Nov–Feb daily 9am–5pm

Admission
House & grounds Adult £5.50, Child £2.75
Grounds only £2.90, £1.35

Contact
Shrewsbury SY4 4TP

t 01743 708123
w nationaltrust.org.uk
e attingham@nationaltrust.org.uk

546 Shrewsbury

Hawkstone Park

4 hours All year

Created in C18, Hawkstone became one of the greatest historic parklands in Europe. The park is centred around the Red Castle and the awe-inspiring Grotto Hill, and features intricate pathways, ravines, arches and bridges, the towering cliffs and follies.

* Woodland full of ancient oaks
* The attraction has won numerous awards

Location
Off A49, between Shrewsbury & Whitchurch

Opening
Times vary, phone for details

Admission
Adult £5.50, Child £3.50, Concs £4.50

Contact
Weston-under-Redcastle, Shrewsbury SY4 5UY

t 01939 200611
w hawkstone.co.uk
e info@hawkstone.co.uk

547 Shrewsbury

Shrewsbury Museum & Art Gallery

1 hrs+ All year

The museum occupies two of Shrewsbury's finest buildings – a C16 timber-framed former merchant's warehouse and a stone and brick building of about 1616. Displays include social history, geology, costume, ceramics and fine art.

* Excavated material from Viroconium
* See pre-Roman and medieval Shrewsbury

Location
City centre

Opening
Jan–Mar & Oct–Dec Tue–Sat
10am–4pm
Apr & May Tue–Sat & Bank Hols
10am–4pm
Jun–Sep Tue–Sat 10am–5pm
Sun–Mon 10am–4pm

Admission
Free

Contact
Barker Street, Shrewsbury SY1 1QH

t 01743 361 196
w shrewsburymuseums.com
e museums@
shrewsbury-atcham.gov.uk

©English Heritage Photographic Library/Jonathan Bailey

548 Shrewsbury

Wroxeter Roman City

1 hr   All year

The largest excavated Roman British city to have escaped development, Wroxeter was originally home to 6,000 people. The most impressive ruins are the C2 municipal baths and the remains of a huge dividing wall. Local finds are on display in the visitor centre.

* The fourth largest Roman settlement in Britain

Location
On B4380, 5 miles E of Shrewsbury

Opening
Apr–Sep daily 10am–6pm
Oct daily 10am–5pm
Nov–Mar daily 10am–1pm & 2–4pm

Admission
Adult £3.70, Child £1.70, Concs £2.80

Contact
Wroxeter, Shrewsbury SY5 6PH

t 01743 761330
w english-heritage.org.uk

549 Telford

Ironbridge Gorge Museums

1–6 hrs   All year

There are ten award-winning museums spread along what is often called 'the valley that changed the world'. That valley, beside the River Severn, is still spanned by the world's first iron bridge. See the products that set industry on its way and the machines that made them.

* Various workshops, including ceramic and iron working
* Engenuity – hands-on design and tech experiences

Location
5 miles S of Telford, signposted from M54 junction 4

Opening
Daily 10am–5pm – some areas close in winter

Admission
Passport ticket to all ten attractions
Adult £12.95, Child £8.25, Concs £11.25

Contact
Ironbridge, Telford TF8 7DQ

t 01952 884 391
w ironbridge.org.uk
e visits@ironbridge.org.uk

550 Burslem

Ceramica

1½ hrs+   All year

Ceramica is an interactive experience in the heart of the English Potteries and the centre of the ceramic industry. Learn how clay is transformed into china and the important part ceramics play in everyday life. Discover the past, present and future of ceramics in the displays.

* See a reconstruction of the inside of a bottle oven
* Josiah Wedgwood's kiln, discovered by Channel 4's *Time Team*

Location
In town centre, beside A50

Opening
Mon–Sat 9.30am–5pm
Sun 10.30am–4.30pm

Admission
Adult £3.50, Child & Concs £2.50

Contact
Market Place, Burslem,
Stoke-on-Trent ST6 3DS

t 01782 832001
w ceramicauk.com
e info@ceramicauk.com

551 Hanley

The Potteries Museum & Art Gallery

2 hrs   All year

Discover the story of Stoke-on-Trent's people, industry, products and landscapes through displays of pottery, community history, archaeology, goelogy and wildlife. There is also a large collection of paintings, drawings, prints, costume and glass.

* World's finest collection of Staffordshire ceramics
* A collection of more than 650,000 objects

Location
A500 junction 15 , signposted from
town centre

Opening
Mar–Oct Mon–Sat 10am–5pm
Sun 2–5pm
Nov–Feb Mon–Sat 10am–4pm
Sun 1–4pm

Admission
Free

Contact
Bethesda Street, Hanley ST1 3DW

t 01782 232323
w stoke.gov.uk/museums
e museums@stoke.gov.uk

552 Halfpenny Green

Halfpenny Green Vineyards

1 hr   All year

Information boards describe many of the French, German and hybrid varieties of vine planted here and visitors to Halfpenny Green can follow the self-guided vineyard trail. After touring the vineyard, inspect the winery and taste the wines.

* Award-winning wines
* Vineyard trail and craft centre

Location
Off B4176, nr Halfpenny Green Airfield

Opening
Daily 10.30am–5pm

Admission
Free, charges for tours

Contact
Tom Lane, Halfpenny Green DY7 5EP

t 01384 221122
w halfpenny-green-vineyards.co.uk
e sales@halfpenny-green-vine-yards.co.uk

553 Lichfield

Erasmus Darwin's House

1 hr   All year

An elegant C18 house near Lichfield Cathedral, this was home to Charles Darwin's grandfather, Erasmus, a renowned doctor, philosopher, inventor, scientist and poet. Period furnishings, an audio-visual and interactive displays tell the story of this remarkable man.

*Cellar tours by arrangement
* Conference facilities

Location
In town centre, nr cathedral

Opening
Thu–Sat 10am–4.30pm
Sun & Bank Hols 12noon–4.30pm

Admission
Phone for details

Contact
Beacon Street, Lichfield WS13 7AD

t 01543 306 260
w erasmusdarwin.org
e erasmus.d@virgin.net

554 Lichfield

Wall Roman Site (Letocetum)

1 hr   Apr–Oct

Wall was an important staging post on the Roman military road to North Wales. It provided overnight accommodation and a change of horse for travelling Roman officials and imperial messengers. The foundations of a hotel and bathhouse can be seen.

* Many excavated finds displayed in the museum
* Audio tour with Gallas the Roman soldier

Location
Off A5, nr Lichfield

Opening
Apr–Sep 10am–6pm
Oct 10am–5pm

Admission
Adult £2.60, Child £1.30, Concs £2

Contact
Watling Street, nr Lichfield WS14 0AW

t 01543 480768
w english-heritage.org.uk

555 Lichfield

Lichfield Heritage Centre

1 hr+   All year

The centre gives an account of Lichfield's varied history. It is home to the Staffordshire Millennium Embroideries, which are displayed in their own gallery, as well as fine examples of city, diocesan and regimental silver, ancient charters and archives.

* Audio-visual presentations
* Collection of photographs of Lichfield, old and new

Location
In town centre

Opening
Daily 10am–5pm

Admission
Adult £3.50, Child £1, Concs £2.50

Contact
Market Square, Lichfield WS13 6LG

t 01543 256 611
w lichfieldheritage.org.uk
e info@lichfieldheritage.org.uk

556 Longton

Gladstone Working Pottery Museum

2 hrs+   All year

Discover the story of the Potteries at Gladstone, the only factory remaining from the days when coal–burning bottle ovens made the world's finest English bone china. This is a unique working museum that allows visitors to see how C19 potters worked.

* Traditional skills and original workshops
* Cobbled yard and huge bottle kilns

Location
From M6, follow A500, take A50 to Longton

Opening
Daily 10am–5pm

Admission
Adult £4.95, Child £3.50, Concs £3.95

Contact
Uttoxeter Road, Longton, Stoke-on-Trent ST3 1PQ

t 01782 319232
w stoke.gov.uk/gladstone
e gladstone@stoke.gov.uk

557 Market Drayton

Dorothy Clive Garden

1 hr+   Apr–Oct

A wide range of unusual plants can be seen in this lovely garden. Features include a quarry garden with a waterfall, a woodland garden and a scree and water garden. The summer borders are spectacular and the autumn crocus and dwarf cyclamen breathtaking.

* Lovely views of three counties
* Japanese maples add to autumn colours

Location
On the A51, between Nantwich & Stone

Opening
Mar 13–Oct 31 daily 10.30am–5.30pm

Admission
Adult £3.80, Child £1, Concs £3.30

Contact
Willoughbridge, Market Drayton TF9 4EU

t 01630 647237
w dorothyclivegarden.co.uk

558 Milford

Shugborough

3 hrs+   Mar–Sep

In 1693 the original manor house was demolished and a three-storey house was built. This survives and forms the centre of the house today, but between 1745 and 1748 the architect Thomas Wright transformed the property into a magnificent Georgian mansion.

* Living history museum with costumed servants
* Fully working Georgian farm complete with animals

Location
6 miles from M6 junction 13

Opening
Mar–Sep Tue–Sun 11am–5pm

Admission
Adult £6, Concs £4

Contact
Shugborough, Milford ST17 0XB

t 01889 881388
w staffordshire.gov.uk
e shugborough.promotions @staffordshire.gov.uk

559 Stafford

The Ancient High House

½ hr+   All year

Stafford's Ancient High House has been one of the most important buildings in the town for over 400 years. Its late Elizabethan architecture makes it particularly distinctive among its C20 neighbours. Rooms are displayed in period settings, illustrating its varied history.

* The Staffordshire Yeomanry Museum
* Samples of C18 and C19 restored wallpapers

WC

Location
In town centre

Opening
Tue–Sat 10am–4pm

Admission
Free, charges for some events

Contact
Greengate Street, Stafford ST16 2JA

t 01785 619131
w staffordbc.gov.uk
e ahh@staffordbc.gov.uk

560 Stafford

Stafford Castle

3 hrs+   All year

Built by William the Conqueror to subdue rebellious local people, Stafford Castle has dominated the landscape throughout 900 years of turbulent history. Visitors today will find a more peaceful setting – follow the castle trail, explore the castle ruins and take in the panoramic view.

* Try on armour and chainmail
* Host of archaeological finds

WC

Location
Off A518, 1 mile SW of Stafford

Opening
Apr–Oct Tue–Sun & Bank Hols
10am–5pm
Nov–Mar Sat–Sun 10am–4pm

Admission
Free

Contact
Castle Bank, Newport Road, Stafford
ST16 1DJ

t 01785 257698
w staffordbc.gov.uk
e castlebc@btconnect.com

561 Stoke-on-Trent

Biddulph Grange Garden

1 hr+   Mar–Dec

A rare survival of a high Victorian garden, restored by the National Trust. The garden is divided into a series of themed spaces, including a Chinese temple, Egyptian court, pinetum, dahlia walk, glen, avenues and many other settings.

* Inspiration of the C19 horticulturist James Bateman
* The Egyptian garden contains obelisks of topiary yew

Location	Admission
Off A527, N side of Biddulph	Adult £4.80, Child £2.40
Opening	Contact
Mar 20 & 21 11am–5.30pm	Grange Road, Biddulph,
Mar 27–Oct 31 Wed–Fri	Stoke-on-Trent ST8 7SD
12noon– 5.30pm Sat–Sun	t 01782 517999
11am–5.30pm	w nationaltrust.org.uk
Nov–Dec 19 Sat–Sun 12noon–4pm	

562 Stoke-on-Trent

Spode Museum & Visitor Centre

1 hr+   All year

Visitors will see a collection of Spode ceramics, including teaware, dessert ware and dinnerware, as well as beautiful ornamental pieces. The display includes items from the late 1700s to 1833, illustrating the genius of Josiah Spode I and II.

* Display includes designs for the royal family
* Fully guided factory tours available

Location	Contact
From M6 junction 15 take A500, go left at 2nd roundabout, then follow signs	Church Street, Stoke-on-Trent ST4 1BX
Opening	t 01782 744011
Mon–Sat 9am–5pm Sun 10am–4pm	w spode.co.uk
Bank Hols 9am–5pm	e spodemuseum@spode.co.uk
Admission	e visitorcentre@spode.co.uk
Free	

563 Tamworth

Middleton Hall

2–3 hrs   Apr–Oct

The hall has an interesting architectural history, with its oldest buildings dating from 1300 and others dating from C16 the early C19. Attractions include the 11-bay Georgian west wing and the impressive C16 Great Hall, the restoration of which was completed in 1994.

* 24 embroideries, depicting history of Sutton Coldfield
* Links with Lady Jane Grey, Elizabeth I and Jane Austen

Location	Contact
On A4091, 4 miles S of Tamworth, between Belfry & Drayton Manor Park	Middleton, Tamworth B78 2AE
Opening	t 01827 283 095
Apr–Oct Sun 2–5pm	w middletonhalltrust.co.uk
Bank Hols 11am–5pm	e middletonhall@btconnect.com
Admission	
Adult £2.50, Child free, Concs £1.50	

564 Tamworth

Tamworth Castle

1 hr   All year

This is a Norman shell-keep castle with intact apartments from C12 to C19. Fifteen period rooms are open to visitors, including the Great Hall, dungeon and haunted bedroom. There is also a permanent exhibition on Norman castles.

* The Tamworth Story is an interactive local history exhibit
* Living images also known as 'talking heads'

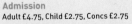

Location	Admission
Take A51 & A453 through town centre, signposted from A51	Adult £4.75, Child £2.75, Concs £2.75
Opening	Contact
Tue–Sun 12noon–5.15pm	The Holloway, Ladybank
Autumn / winter times differ, please telephone for details	Tamworth B79 7NA
	t 01827 709629 / 709626
	w tamworth.gov.uk
	e heritage@tamworth.gov.uk

565 Tutbury

Tutbury Castle

2 hr   Easter–Sep

Built in the 1070s for one of William the Conqueror's barons, Tutbury Castle has been involved in some of the most dramatic events in English history. A bloody place of siege and battle, on three occasions it acted as a prison for Mary Queen of Scots.

* Authentic Tudor privy garden and mediaeval herbery
* Secret staircase recently uncovered to the Great Hall

Location
Exit M1 junction 24a or M6 junction 15, nr A50

Opening
Easter Sun–Sep 19 Wed–Sun
11am–5pm

Admission
Adult £3.50, Child £3, Concs £3

Contact
Tutbury, Burton-on-Trent DE13 9JF

t 01283 812129
w tutburycastle.com
e info@tutburycastle.com

---

566 Uttoxeter

Croxden Abbey

1 hr   All year

A C12 Cistercian abbey and its imposing church, the remains are intertwined with modern features, including a road separating the north transept and east end of the church from the rest. Otherwise, the buildings survive remarkably intact.

* Ruins dominated by west front of the abbey's church
* C13 detail, particularly in the chapterhouse

Location
Off A522, 5 miles NW of Uttoxeter

Opening
Daily 10am–5pm

Admission
Free

Contact
w english–heritage.org.uk

---

567 Wolverhampton

Moseley Old Hall

2 hrs+   Mar–Dec

An Elizabethan house, famous for its associations with the fugitive King Charles II who hid there in 1651. Faced with brick in the 1870s, inside it remains as Charles would have known it, with timber framing, oak panelling, period furniture and ingenious hiding places.

* Knot garden recreated in the C17 style
* Exhibition of Charles II's escape after Battle of Worcester

Location
4 miles N of Wolverhampton, S of the M54 between A449 and A460

Opening
Mar 20–Oct 31 Wed Sat–Sun 1–5pm
Nov 1–Dec 19 Sun 1–4pm

Admission
Adult £4.60, Child £2.30

Contact
Moseley Old Hall Lane, Fordhouses, Wolverhampton WV10 7HY

t 01902 782808
w nationaltrust.org.uk
e moseleyoldhall@nationaltrust.org.uk

568 Alcester

Coughton Court

3 hrs   Mar–Oct

This beautiful Tudor house has been a family home since 1409. There is a fine collection of family portraits, furniture and a fascinating exhibition about the Gunpowder Plot. The gatehouse and courtyard are complemented by an Elizabethan knot garden.

* Stunning displays of roses and herbaceous plants
* There are two churches to visit

Location
On A435, 2 miles N of Alcester

Opening
Mar & Oct Sat–Sun 11.30am–5pm
Apr–Jun & Sep Wed–Sun 11.30am–5pm
Jul–Aug Tue–Sun 11.30am–5pm

Admission
Adult £8.25, Child £4.15

Contact
nr Alcester B49 5JA

t 01789 400777
w coughtoncourt.co.uk
e office@throckmortons.co.uk

569 Alcester

Kinwarton Dovecote

1 hr   Apr–Oct

Beside Kinwarton Church is a field full of archaeological interest, in particular an impressive circular C14 dovecote, which still houses doves. Visitors will see an unusual pivoted ladder from which access to the nesting boxes is possible.

Location
S of B4089, 1 mile NE of Alcester

Opening
Apr–Oct daily 9am–6pm

Admission
£1

Contact
Kinwarton, nr Alcester B49 5DN

t 01743 708100
w nationaltrust.org.uk
e kinwartondovecote@ntrust.org.uk

570 Alcester

Ragley Hall

5 hrs   Apr–Sep

Ragley Hall is set in 27 acres of beautiful formal gardens. The home contains baroque plasterwork, the stunning C20 mural, The Temptation, and a collection of paintings, china and furniture. In addition to the beautiful house, there are the formal gardens and parkland.

* Ever-changing gardens
* Game fair and other events throughout the year

Location
Off Alcester bypass, signposted at A46 junction

Opening
House Apr–Sep Thu–Sun & Bank Hols 12noon–5.30pm
Park & gardens Apr–Sep Thu–Sun & Bank Hols 10am–6pm

Admission
Adult £7.50, Child £4.50, Concs £6.50

Contact
Alcester B49 5NJ

t 01789 762090
w ragleyhall.com
e info@ragleyhall.com

571 Banbury

Farnborough Hall

2 hrs+   Apr–Oct

A beautiful, honey-coloured stone house, richly decorated in the mid-C18 and the home of the Holbech family for over 300 years. The interior plasterwork is quite outstanding and the charming grounds contain C18 temples, a terrace walk and an obelisk.

* Terrace walk open by prior appointment only

Location
6 miles N of Banbury, W of A423

Opening
Apr 7–Sep 25 Wed & Sat 2–6pm
May Mon & Sat 2–6pm

Admission
Adult £3.80, Child £1.90

Contact
Banbury OX17 1DU

t 01295 6900002
w nationaltrust.org.uk
e farnboroughhall@nationaltrust.org.uk

572 Banbury

Upton House

1 hr+   Apr–Dec

Once owned by Walter Samuel, 2nd Viscount Bearsted and chairman of Shell 1921–46, Upton contains an outstanding collection of English and continental Old Master paintings, including works by Hogarth, Stubbs, Guardi, Canaletto, Brueghel and El Greco.

* Exhibition of Shell paintings and publicity posters
* Tapestrie, French porcelain and Chelsea figures

Location
On A422, 7 miles NW of Banbury, 12 miles SE of Stratford-upon-Avon

Opening
House Apr 3–Oct 31 Mon–Wed Sat–Sun 1–5pm
Garden Apr 3–Dec 19 Sat–Sun

Admission
Adult £6.50, Child £3.50

Contact
nr Banbury OX15 6HT

t 01295 670266
w nationaltrust.org.uk
e uptonhouse@nationaltrust.org.uk

573 Broadway

Snowshill Manor

2 hrs+   Mar–Oct

The terraces and ponds of this Arts and Crafts garden were designed by Charles Wade in collaboration with M.H. Baillie Scott. It's a lively mix of architectural features, cottage flowers, bright colours and delightful scents.

* Cottage and organic garden also on display

Location
Signposted from Broadway

Opening
Mar 19–Oct Wed–Sun & Bank Hols 11.30am–5.30pm

Admission
Adult £6.40, Child £3.20

Contact
Snowshill, Broadway WR12 7JU

t 01386 852410
w nationaltrust.org.uk
e snowshillmanor@nationaltrust.org.uk

574 Coventry

Brandon Marsh Nature Centre

1 hr+   All year

A visit to Brandon Marsh Nature Centre starts at the visitor centre, opened by Sir David Attenborough in 1998. This contains displays, hands-on activities and information about the nature reserve, which covers 220 acres and features many lakes and bird hives.

* Warwickshire Wildlife Trust Centre

Location
Off A45

Opening
Mon–Sat 9am–4.30pm
Sun 10am–4pm

Admission
Adult £2.50, Child £1, Concs £1.50

Contact
Brandon Lane, Coventry CV3 3GW

t 024 76308999
w wildlifetrust.org.uk
e admin@warkswt.cix.co.uk

575 Gaydon

Heritage Motor Centre

3 hrs   All year

The Heritage Motor Centre is home to the largest collection of classic, vintage and veteran British cars in the world. There are 200 vehicles on display, charting the history of the British car industry from the turn of the century to the present day.

* 1963 Morris Mini Cooper
* Regular programme of events

Location
2 mins from M40 junction 12

Opening
Daily 10am–5pm

Admission
Adult £8, Child £6, Concs £7

Contact
Banbury Road, Gaydon CV35 0BJ
t 01926 641188
w heritage-motor-centre.co.uk
e enquiries@
heritage-motor-centre.co.uk

576 Henley-in-Arden

Henley-in-Arden Heritage & Visitor Centre

1 hr   Easter–Oct

Henley-in-Arden's history is recorded in the town's oldest house, part of which is C14. Exhibits include a model of the Norman castle which once stood on the mount and information on the ancient Market Cross and the tradition of town criers.

* Chronicle of the origins of the famous ice cream
* Tales of industrial, social and sporting life in the town

Location
In town centre

Opening
Easter–Oct Tue–Fri 10.30am–4.30pm
Sat–Sun 2.30–4.30pm

Admission
Free

Contact
Joseph Hardy House, 150 High Street,
Henley-in-Arden B95 5BS
t 01564 795919
w henley-in-arden-heritage.co.uk
e henleyheritage@lineone.net

577 Henley-in-Arden

The Saxon Sanctuary

½ hr   All year

Warwickshire's oldest church is known as the Saxon Sanctuary. Its tower saw in the last millennium and the drama of English history has swept through it ever since. Every age has left its own story, so a visit to St Peter's Church is a real adventure.

* The tomb of Francis Smith, 1604
* Millennium exhibition in the barn-roofed Lady Chapel

Location
Take A3400 from Stratford-upon-Avon
N for 4½ miles

Opening
Daily 9am–dusk

Admission
Free

Contact
Stratford Road, Wootton Wawen,
Henley-in-Arden B95 6BD
t 01564 792659
w saxonsanctuary.org.uk
e saxon@btopenworld.com

578 Kenilworth

Kenilworth Castle

2 hrs+   All year

The largest castle ruin in England and the scene of many sieges and murders, Kenilworth Castle has been linked with some of the most important names in English history. Explore its impressive Norman keep, Tudor gardens and John of Gaunt's Great Hall.

* Walks to Old Kenilworth and ruined abbey
* Elizabethan festival and Shakespeare performances

Location
In town centre

Opening
Apr–Sep 10am–6pm
Oct 10am–5pm
Nov–Mar 10am–4pm

Admission
Adult £4.50, Child 2.30, Concs £3.40

Contact
Castle Mews, Kenilworth CU8 1NE
t 01926 852078
w english-heritage.org.uk

579 Kineton

Compton Verney Art Gallery

2hrs+   Mar–Oct

An innovative art gallery, in a C18 mansion, designed by Robert Adam and set in 114 acres of Capability Brown landscape. The Peter Moores collections include artefacts from Naples 1450-1800, China 3000 BC–AD 1500 and a collection of British folk art.

* Major temporary exhibitions
* Projects for schools and groups

Location
Off B4086, between Kineton & Stratford-upon-Avon

Opening
March–Oct daily 10am–5pm

Admission
Adult £5

Contact
Compton Verney CV35 9HZ

t 01926 645500
w comptonverney.org.uk
e info@comptonverney.org.uk

581 Nuneaton

Arbury Hall

½hr+   Bank Hols

This Elizabethan house was built on the site of a C12 Augustinian priory. Transformed in C18 to become a fine example of Gothic Revival architecture, the house contains collections of antique furniture, pictures, glass and china. Many rooms are open to the public.

* Delightful landscaped gardens, wooded walks and lake
* Chimney piece based on tomb of Aymer de Valence

Location
Signposted from Nuneaton

Opening
Sun & Mon of Bank Hols only 2–6pm

Admission
House & Gardens Adult £6.50, Child £3
Gardens Adult £4.50, Child £2.50

Contact
Nuneaton CV10 7PT

t 0247 6382804
e brenda.newell@arburyhall.net

580 Knowle

Baddesley Clinton

3 hrs+   Mar–Nov

This moated manor house dates from C15 and indeed little has changed since 1634. During the Elizabethan era it was a haven for persecuted Catholics and there are three priest-holes. The garden includes stewponds, a lake and a nature walk.

* 70-seater restauraunt
* Quiz for children

Location
W of A4141, between Warwick & Birmingham, 7 miles NW of Warwick

Opening
Mar 3–Nov 7 Wed–Sun 1.30–5pm

Admission
Adult £6.20, Child £3.10

Contact
Rising Lane, Baddesley Clinton, Knowle, Solihull B93 0DQ

t 01564 783294
w nationaltrust.org.uk
e baddesleyclinton@nationaltrust.org.uk

©National Trust Photographic Library/Andrew Butler

582   Royal Leamington Spa

Royal Pump Rooms

1 hr   All year

The historic Royal Pump Rooms have been redeveloped and now include an art gallery and museum. Visitors can explore life in a Victorian spa town, relax in the magnificent Turkish Room and discover the water treatments used at the Royal Pump Rooms.

* Historic Hammam room
* Temporary exhibition space and interactive gallery

Location	Contact
Town centre	The Parade, Royal Leamington Spa CV32 4AA
Opening	t 01926 742700
Tue, Wed, Fri–Sat 10.30am–5pm	w royal-pump-rooms.co.uk
Thu 1.30–8pm Sun 11am–4pm	e prooms@warwickdc.gov.uk
Admission	
Free	

583   Rugby

HM Prison Service Museum

1 hr   Feb–Dec

Visit this museum to find out about punishment and imprisonment, from medieval times to the present day. See Oscar Wilde's cell door, part of Holloway's treadmill and escape tools, as well as a sampler embroidered with a female prisoner's hair and prisoner artwork.

* The last gibbet irons used in England
* The flogging block from notorious Newgate

Location	Contact
On B4057, nr Stretton Under Fosse	Newbold Revel, Rugby CV23 0TH
Opening	t 01788 834168
Feb–Dec Mon–Fri 9am–8pm	w hmprisonservice.gov.uk
Admission	e museum@breathemail.net
Free	

584   Rugby

Rugby Art Gallery

1 hr+   All year

This gallery contains a collection of paintings, prints and drawings by well known British artists such as Sir Stanley Spencer, L.S. Lowry, Percy Wyndham Lewis, Paula Rego, Barbara Hepworth, Bridget Riley and Lucian Freud.

* Rugby's collection of modern art
* Roman artefacts and local social history objects

Location	Contact
Signposted from town centre	Little Elbarow Street, Rugby CV21 3BZ
Opening	t 01788 533721
Tue & Thu 10am–2pm, Wed & Fri	w rugbygalleryandmuseum.org.uk
10am–5pm, Sat 10am–4pm, Sun &	e rugbyartgallery&museum@rugby.
Bank Hols 1–5pm	gov.uk
Admission	
Free	

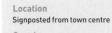

585 Stratford-upon-Avon

Anne Hathaway's Cottage

1 hr   All year

Anne Hathaway's cottage was home to Shakespeare's wife before they married in 1582. Besides being the place where the teenage Shakespeare courted his future bride, the Hathaway home is regarded as the quintessential English country cottage.

* Inhabited by Hathaway family until C19
* Shakespeare tree garden, maze, orchard and brook

Location	Admission
1 mile from Stratford town centre	Adult £5, Child £2, Concs £4
Opening	**Contact**
Nov–Mar daily 10am–4pm,	Cottage Lane, Shottery CV37 9HH
Apr–May & Sep–Oct Mon–Sat	
9.30am–5pm Sun 10am–5pm	t 01789 292100
Jun–Aug Mon–Sat 9am–5pm	w shakespeare.org.uk
Sun 9.30am–5pm	e info@shakespeare.org.uk

586 Stratford-upon-Avon

The Falstaffs Experience

½ hr   All year

Situated along the cobbled courtyard of the magnificent Shrieves House, Falstaffs is a museum like no other. As you enter the C16 building, you learn of some remarkable tales about the history of both Stratford and England. This is also Stratford's most haunted building.

* Labyrinth of theatrical settings
* Genuinely haunted museum with heady atmosphere

Location	Contact
Town centre	The Shrieves House Barn,
Opening	Sheep Street, Stratford-upon-Avon
Daily 10.30am–5.30pm	CV37 6EE
Admission	t 01789 298070
Adult £3.75, Child £2.50, Concs £3	w falstaffsexperience.co.uk
	e info@falstaffsexperience.co.uk

587 Stratford-upon-Avon

Hall's Croft

1 hr   All year

One of the finest half-timbered, gabled houses in Stratford-upon-Avon, named after Dr John Hall, who married Shakespeare's daughter, Susanna. Dr Hall was a pioneering medical practitioner and displays in the house reflect his wealth and status in the community.

* Outstanding paintings and furniture
* Exhibition of medical artefacts from C16 and C17

Location	Admission
Nr town centre	Adult £3.50, Child £1.70, Concs £3
Opening	**Contact**
Nov–Mar 11am–4pm	Old Town, Stratford-upon Avon CV37
Apr–May & Sep–Oct 11am–5pm	
Jun–Aug Mon–Sat 9.30am–5pm	t 01789 292107
Sun 10am–5pm	w shakespeare.org.uk
	e info@shakespeare.org.uk

588 Stratford-upon-Avon

Harvard House

1 hr   May–Sep

Harvard House was home to Katherine Rogers, mother of John Harvard, whose bequest founded Harvard University. Built in 1596, the property is a fine example of an Elizabethan townhouse. It boasts the most ornately timber-framed frontage in Stratford.

* Home to the first museum of British pewter
* Many architectural features of interest

Location	Contact
In town centre	High Street, Stratford-upon-Avon
Opening	t 01789 204507
May–Sep Fri–Sun & Bank Hols	w shakespeare.org.uk
11am–4pm	e info@shakespeare.org.uk
Admission	
Adult £2, Child free	

589 Stratford-upon-Avon

Holy Trinity Church

½ hr+   All year

Visit Shakespeare's grave and the graves of Anne Hathaway, Dr John Hall and his wife Susanna Shakespeare and Thomas Nash in the chancel of Holy Trinity Church. Also in the chancel are 26 fine C15 carved misericords.

* Beautiful church situated on banks of River Avon
* Church is approached along an avenue of lime trees

Location	*Shakespeare's Grave* **Adult £1, Child & Concs 50p**
Signposted from Stratford town centre	
Opening	**Contact**
Mar–Oct Mon–Sat 8.30am–6pm	Old Town, Stratford-upon-Avon
Sun 2–5pm, Nov–Feb Mon–Sat	CV37 6BG
9am–4pm Sun 12noon–5pm	
Admission	t 01789 266316
Church **free**	w stratford-upon-avon.org.uk
	e office@stratford-upon-avon.org.uk

590 Stratford-upon-Avon

Nash's House & New Place

1 hr   All year

This building belonged to Thomas Nash, a rich property owner who married Elizabeth Hall, Shakespeare's granddaughter. In addition to the exceptional collection of C17 tapestries and oak furniture, Nash's House also contains exhibits on the history of Stratford-upon-Avon.

* Stratford's first Shakespeare festival
* Elizabethan style knot-garden

Location	Contact
Signposted from town centre	Chapel Street, Stratford-upon-Avon
Opening	CV37 6EP
Nov–Mar 11am–4pm, Apr–May &	t 01789 292325
Sep–Oct 11am–5pm Jun–Aug Mon–Sat	w shakespeare.org.uk
9.30am–5pm Sun 10am–5pm	e info@shakespeare.org.uk
Admission	
Adult £3.50, Child £1.70, Concs £3	

©National Trust Photographic Library/Keith Hewitt

591 Stratford-upon-Avon

Packwood House

2 hrs   Mar–Nov

The original C16 house was restored between the world wars by Graham Baron Ash. The interior contains a fine collection of C16 textiles and furniture. The gardens have renowned herbaceous borders and a famous collection of yews.

* A curious feature is the large number of sundials
* Glorious gardens

Location	Admission
On A3400, 2 miles E of Hockley Heath	Adult £5.40, Child £2.70
Opening	**Contact**
House Mar 3–Nov 7 Wed–Sun 12noon–4.30pm	Lapworth, Solihull B94 6AT
Garden Mar 3–Nov 7 Wed–Sun 11am–4.30pm	t 01564 783294
	w nationaltrust.org.uk
	e packwood@nationaltrust.org.uk

592 Stratford-upon-Avon

Shakespeare's Birthplace

1 hr   All year

Experience the Tudor world of William Shakespeare by visiting the house where, in 1564, he was born. Shakespeare's Birthplace provides an insight into his childhood. Family rooms have been recreated with furniture, utensils and wall hangings from the period.

* Exhibitions tell the story of the house
* Exhibits of rare period items including *First Folio* 1623

Location	Admission
Signposted from town centre	Adult £6.50, Child £2.50, Concs £5.50
Opening	**Contact**
Nov–Mar Mon–Sat 10am–4pm	Henley Street, Stratford-upon-Avon CV37 6QW
Sun 10.30–4pm	
Apr–May & Sep–Oct Mon–Sat 10am–5pm Sun 10.30am–5p	t 01789 201823
Jun–Aug Mon–Sat 9am–5pm	w shakespeare.org.uk
Sun 10.30am–4pm	e info@shakespeare.org.uk

593 Stratford-upon-Avon

The Shakespeare Countryside Museum & Mary Arden's House

1 hr+   All year

Mary Arden was the mother of William Shakespeare and this site contains her family home. Comprising two C16 farmhouses – Mary Arden's house itself and Palmer's farm – these houses, outbuildings and the adjoining land demonstrate life on a Tudor working farm.

* Falconry displays
* Rare breeds farm

Location	Admission
3 miles outside Stratford	Adult £5.50, Child £2.50, Concs £5
Opening	**Contact**
Jun–Aug Mon–Sat 9.30am–5pm	Station Road, Wilmcote CV37 9UN
Sun 10am–5pm	
Apr–May & Sep–Oct Mon–Sat 10am–5pm Sun 10.30am–5pm	t 01789 293455
Nov–Mar Mon–Sat 10am–4pm	w shakespeare.org.uk
Sun 10.30am–4pm	e info@shakespeare.org.uk

594 Warwick

The Doll Museum

1 hr   All year

Based in Oken's House, which dates from late C15, this museum is situated in one of the most picturesque buildings in Warwick. Displays include the collections of the late Joy Robinson, who founded the museum in 1953, and other dolls, toys and games.

* Watch a video of the mechanical toys on display
* Play spinning tops and hopscotch

Location	Contact
Beside tourist information centre	Oken's House, Castle Street, Warwick CV34 4BP
Opening	
Apr–Oct Mon–Sat 10am–5pm	t 01926 495546 / 412500
Sun 11.30–5pm	w warwickshire.gov.uk/museum
Nov–Mar Sat 10am–4pm	e museum@warwickshire.gov.uk
Admission	
Adult £1, Child 70p, Concs 70p	

595 Warwick

Lord Leycester Hospital

1 hr   All year

The buildings of the Warwick Guilds were converted into a retreat for old soldiers and this continues to the present day. The 'Brethren', as the inhabitants are known, still wear their blue gowns and flat Tudor hats on ceremonial occasions.

* Museum of Queen's Own Hussars in Chaplain's Hall
* Masters garden

Location	Admission
Nr tourist information centre	Adult £3.40, Child £2.40, Concs £2.90
Opening	**Contact**
Tue–Sun & Bank Hols 10am–5pm	High Street, Warwick CV34 4BH
	t 01926 491422

596 Warwick

St John's House

1 hr+   All year

A charming Jacobean house dating from about 1620, St John's became a branch of the Warwickshire Museum in 1961 and houses the social history collection. The galleries have themes such as costume, domestic life and school life, and are changed frequently.

* Museum of Royal Warwickshire Regiment
* Ever-changing display of costume

Location	Contact
Signposted from town centre	Warwick CV34 4NF
Opening	t 01926 4120041
May–Sep Tue–Sat & Bank Hols	w warwickshire.gov.uk/museum
10am–5pm Sun 2.30–5pm	e museum@warwickshire.gov.uk
Admission	
Free	

597 Warwick

Warwickshire Museums

1 hr+   All year

The Warwickshire Museum Service is housed in the C17 market hall. This is one of the few buildings in central Warwick that survived a huge fire in the town in 1694. Displays of geology, biology and archaeology illustrate the natural and historical heritage of the county.

* The famous Sheldon tapestry map of Warwickshire
* 180 million-year-old plesiosaur from the Jurassic Period

Location	Contact
In town centre	Market Place, Warwick CV34 4SA
Opening	t 01926 412827
May–Sep Tue–Sat 10am–5pm	w warwickshire.gov.uk
Sun and Bank Hols 11.30–5pm	e museums@warwickshire.gov.uk
Oct–Apr Tue–Sat 10am–5pm	
Admission	
Free	

598 Wellesbourne

Charlecote Park

2 hrs+   Mar–Dec

The mellow brickwork and great chimneys of Charlecote sum up the essence of Tudor England. There are associations with both Queen Elizabeth and Shakespeare – he knew the house well and is alleged to have been caught poaching the estate deer.

* Contains objects from Beckford's Fonthill Abbey
* Formal garden and Capability Brown deer park

Location
1 mile W of Wellesbourne, 5 miles
E of Stratford, on N side of B4086

Opening
House Mar 6–Nov 2 Fri–Tue noon–5pm
Park & Gardens Mar 6–Nov 2 Fri–Tue
10.30am–6pm Nov 7–Dec 19 Sat & Sun

Admission
Adult £6.40, Child £3.20

Contact
Warwick CV35 9ER

t 01789 470277
w nationaltrust.org.uk
e charlecote.park@
nationaltrust.org.uk

599 Aston

Aston Hall

1 hr   Easter–Oct

A fine Jacobean house, built between 1618 and 1635 by Sir Thomas Holte, featuring elaborate plasterwork ceilings and friezes, a magnificent carved oak staircase and a spectacular 136foot (40m) Long Gallery. Period rooms contain fine furniture, paintings, textiles and metalwork.

* Biennial candlelight event
* Regular programme of events

Location
M6 junction 6, 3 miles N of city centre

Opening
Easter–Oct Tue–Sun & Bank Hols
11.30am–4pm

Admission
Free

Contact
Trinity Road, Aston,
Birmingham B6 6JD

t 0121 3270062
w birmingham.gov.uk

600 Wellesbourne

Wellesbourne Watermill

2 hrs   Easter–Sep

Visitors to this historic watermill can see the mill's machinery being driven by one of the country's largest wooden waterwheels. There are regular demonstrations of how stoneground flour is milled. Coracles are used on the millpond, which is a tranquil haven for wildlife.

Location
On B4086, between Kineton &
Stratford-upon-Avon

Opening
Easter–Sep Thu–Sun & Bank Hols
10am–5pm

Admission
Adult £3.50, Child £2.50, Concs £3

Contact
Kineton Road, Wellesbourne
CV35 9HG

t 01789 470237
w wellesbournemill.co.uk
e andrew@mill.spacomputers.com

601 Baginton

Midland Air Museum

2 hrs   All year

Exhibits range from the Avro Vulcan bomber through more than 30 other historic aircraft, both civil and military, aero engines and other artefacts, to a wide range of memorabilia. The Heritage Centre houses a collection of material relating to Sir Frank Whittle.

* Giant Armstrong Whitworth Argosy freighter of 1959
* Meteor, Vulcan, Hunter, Starfighter and Phantom

Location
Off A45, between roundabout
& Baginton

Opening
Apr–Oct Mon–Sat 10am–5pm
Sun 10am–6pm
Nov–Mar daily 10am–5pm

Admission
Adult £4, Child £2.25, Concs £3.25

Contact
Coventry Airport, Baginton,
Coventry CV8 3AZ

t 02476 301033
w midlandairmuseum.org.uk
e midlandairmuseum@aol.com

602 Birmingham

Birmingham Eco Park

2 hrs   All year

The Eco Park is a demonstration of the principles of sustainability and provides a stimulating and educational environment. Explore ponds, woodland, flowering meadows and heathland. Frogs, herons, dragonflies, sparrowhawks and foxes are regularly seen here.

* Wildlife and permaculture gardens
* Colourful combination of gardens

Location	Admission
From inner ring road take A45 to Heybarnes Circus roundabout, signposted from there	Free
	Contact
Opening	258a Hobmoor Road, Smallheath, Birmingham B10 9HH
Tue–Thu 12noon–4pm	
Sat 10am–4pm	t 0121 785 0553
	w eco-park.org.uk
	e ecopark@bbcwildlife.org.uk

603 Birmingham

Birmingham Museum & Art Gallery

2 hrs   All year

This magnificent building houses one of the world's finest collections of Pre-Raphaelite art, as well as displays of silver, sculpture, ceramics, archaeology and social history. British watercolours and Arts and Crafts movement work is also on show.

* Permanent collection of the famous Pre-Raphaelites
* Fine and applied art collections

Location	Contact
Adjacent to Council House, signposted from the end of New Street	Chamberlain Square, Birmingham B3 3DH
Opening	t 0121 3032834
Mon–Thu & Sat 10am–5pm	w bmag.org.uk
Fri 10.30am–5pm Sun 12.30–5pm	e bmag_enquiries@birmingham. gov.uk
Admission	
Free	

604 Birmingham

Cathedral Church of St Philip

½ hr   All year

A dramatic and elegant building at the heart of the city, this is a notable C18 church and a rare example of English baroque style. It contains renowned, massive Pre-Raphaelite stained glass windows by Edward Burne-Jones.

* Italianate domed tower
* Designed and built by Thomas Archer in 1715

Location	Contact
City centre	Colmore Row, Birmingham B3 2QB
Opening	t 0121 2364333
Daily 7.30am–7pm	e enquiries@ birminghamcathedral.com
Admission	
Suggested donation £1	

605 Birmingham

Ikon Gallery

1 hr   All year

One of Europe's leading contemporary art galleries, Ikon exhibits the best in international and British art in a changing programme of exhibitions and events. A variety of media are represented, including sound, video, mixed media, photography, painting, sculpture and installation.

* Exhibitions in Ikon's events room and tower room
* Situated in a converted neo-gothic school building

Location	Contact
15 mins from city centre, signposted from Victoria Square	1 Oozells Square, Brindleyplace, Birmingham B1 2HS
Opening	t 0121 2480708
Tue–Sun & Bank Hols 11am–6pm	w ikon-gallery.co.uk
Admission	e art@ikon-gallery.co.uk
Free	

606 Birmingham

Museum of the Jewellery Quarter

1hr+ Apr–Oct

Visit a real jewellery factory that has changed little since the early part of the last century. The museum tells the story of jewellery making in Birmingham from its origins in the Middle Ages to the present day, and includes an explanation of jewellery-making techniques.

* Free entry includes a guided tour of the factory

Location	Contact
Adjacent to Jewellery Quarter Clock & Jewellery Quarter Station	75-79 Vyse Street, Birmingham B18 6HA
Opening Apr–Oct Tue–Sun 11.30am–4pm	t 0121 554 3598 w bmag.org.uk
Admission Free	

608 Birmingham

Royal Birmingham Society of Artists Gallery

2 hrs All year

One of the oldest art societies in the UK, the Royal Birmingham Society of Artists was given royal status in 1868 by Queen Victoria and played an important part in the Pre-Raphaelite movement. The gallery exhibits the work of members and local designers.

* Regularly changing programme of exhibitions
* Craft gallery, including ceramics, jewellery and more

Location	Contact
Follow New Hall Street to Brook Street	4 Brook Street, St Paul's Square, Birmingham B3 1SA
Opening Mon–Wed & Fri 10.30am–5.30pm Thu 10.30am–7pm Sat 10.30am–5pm	t 0121 236 4353 w rbsa.org.uk e secretary@rbsa.org.uk
Admission Free	

607 Birmingham

National Sea Life Centre

3 hrs All year

A unique insight into the lives of a myriad creatures – from shrimps to sharks. The unique, one-million-litre tropical ocean display has a Hawaiian volcanic theme, and the completely transparent 360 degree submarine tunnel provides a home for two giant green turtles.

* Programme of talks and feeding demonstrations
* Brand new feature for 2004

Location	Admission
Between National Indoor Arena & International Convention Centre	Adult £8.95, £Child £6.95, Concs £7.50
Opening Summer Daily 10am–5pm Winter Mon–Fri 10am–4pm Sat & Sun 10am–5pm	**Contact** The Waters Edge, Brindleyplace, Birmingham B1 2HL t 0121 643 6777 / 633 4700 w sealifeeurope.com e slcbirmingham@ merlinentertainments.biz

609 Birmingham

Think Tank

4 hrs   All year

Think Tank is an invigorating science attraction which examines the past, investigates the present and explores what the future may bring. Learn about the canal, road and railway networks that connected Birmingham to the rest of Britain.

* Unravel the mysteries of the body
* Medical tour covers techniques and instruments

Location
Follow blue banners, 15 mins walk from New Street

Opening
Daily 10am–5pm

Admission
Adult £6.95, Child £4.95, Concs £5.50

Contact
Curzon Street, Birmingham B4 7XG
t 0121 2022222
w thinktank.ac
e findout@thinktank.ac

610 Birmingham

Tolkien's Birmingham

2 hrs   Apr–Sep

J.R.R. Tolkien garnered inspiration from childhood haunts in Birmingham. The imagery he skilfully created can be attributed to various places and buildings in the city. See where Tolkien dreamt up *The Hobbit* and *Lord of the Rings* for yourself or choose a guided tour.

* In-depth knowledge from specialist tour guide
* Appropriate clothing must be worn, including footwear

Location
Various areas of Birmingham

Opening
Leaflet for self-guided tours from Sarehole Mill

Admission
Apr–Sep by appointment
Phone for details of guided tours

Contact
t 0121 4444046
w birminghamheritage.org.uk
e balti1@compuserve.com

611 Bournville

Cadbury World

3 hrs   All year

Chocolate through the centuries – from Aztec rainforests to Victorian England. Learn about the Cadbury family and their early triumphs and struggles to develop the business. Follow the journey of chocolate from its origins as cocoa to liquid chocolate in the factory.

* Learn how chocolate is used to make famous brands
* Chocolate Coronation Street!

Location
Signposted from M42

Opening
Times vary, phone for details

Admission
Adult £8.75, Child £6.60, Concs £7
Pre-booking recommended

Contact
Linden Road, Bournville, Brimingham B30 2LD
t 0121 4514159
w cadburyworld.co.uk
e cadbury.world@csplc.com

612 Castle Bromwich

Castle Bromwich Hall Gardens

  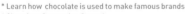
2 hrs+   Apr–Oct

This unique example of an English baroque garden is being restored to the period 1680–1740. The 10-acre walled garden contains rare and interesting period plants, vegetables and herbs. Classical patterned parterres can be seen at the end of the Holly Walk.

* C19 holly maze
* Restored summer house and green house

Location
Signposted from M6 junction 5

Opening
Apr–Oct Tue–Thu 1.30–4.30pm
Sat, Sun & Bank Hols 2–6pm

Admission
Adult £3.50, Child £1.50, Concs £2.50

Contact
Chester Road, Castle Bromwich, Birmingham B36 9BT
t 0121 7494100
w cbhgt.colebridge.net
e Admin@cbhgt.colebridge.net

613 Coventry

Coventry Cathedral

1 hr+   All year

Coventry Cathedral was bombed and destroyed in 1940, during the Second World War. The striking new cathedral, designed by Basil Spence, was consecrated in 1962 and is filled with work from leading artists of the time, including John Hutton's screen Saints and Angels.

* Sutherland's Christ in Glory in the Tetramorph
* Works by Elizabeth Frink, John Piper and Ralph Beyer

Location
Central Coventry

Opening
9am–5.30pm (services permitting)

Admission
Free

Contact
1 Hilltop, Coventry CV1 5AB

t 02476 521200
w coventrycathedral.org.uk
e information@
coventrycathedral.org.uk

614 Coventry

Herbert Art Gallery & Museum

1 hr   All year

As a focus for Coventry's cultural heritage, the museum offers a fascinating visit. Enjoy the Godiva City exhibition – one thousand years of the city's history, told through historical treasures and artefacts, interactive games and archive film.

* Archaeological finds from Saxon and medieval times
* Objects from Coventry's Asian communities

Location
Central Coventry, nr Cathedral, next to Tourist Information Centre

Opening
Mon–Sat 10am–5.30pm
Sun 12noon–5pm

Admission
Free

Contact
Jordan Well, Coventry CV1 5QP

t 0247 6832381
w coverntrymuseum.org.uk
e artsandheritage@coventry.gov.uk

615 Dudley

Black Country Living Museum

3 hrs+   All year

The museum occupies an urban heritage park in the shadow of Dudley Castle. Historic buildings from around the Black Country have been moved and rebuilt to create a tribute to the traditional skills and enterprise of the people that lived in the heart of industrial Britain.

* Tramcars and trolleybuses transport visitors
* Costumed demonstrators and working craftsmen

Location
On A4037, 3 miles from M5 junction 2

Opening
Mar–Oct 10am–5pm
Nov–Feb Wed–Sun 10am–4pm

Admission
Adult £9.60, Child £5.50, Concs £8.50

Contact
Tipton Road, Dudley DY1 4SQ

t 0121 5579643
w bclm.co.uk
e info@bclm.co.uk

616 Dudley

Dudley Museum & Art Gallery

½ hr+   All year

This museum contains a collection of C17, C18 and C19 British and European paintings, furniture and ceramics, together with oriental ceramics, Japanese netsuke and inro, Bilston enamels, commemorative medals, and Greek, Roman and Egyptian pottery.

* Geological collection of fossils, rock and minerals
* Regular and varied art exhibitions

Location
Off Priory Street, nr bus station

Opening
Mon–Sat 10am–4pm

Admission
Free

Contact
St James' Road, Dudley DY1 1HU

t 01384 815575
w dudley.gov.uk
e museums@museums.gov.uk

617 Edgbaston

Birmingham Botanical Gardens & Glasshouses

2 hrs+   All year

The gardens originally opened in 1832 and today tropical, Mediterranean and desert glasshouses stand in 15 acres of beautiful gardens. This fine collection of plants includes over 200 trees and the National Bonsai Collection.

* Designed by JC Loudon, a leading garden planner
* Sculpture trail, waterfowl and exotic birds

Location
Signposted from Edgbaston

Opening
Mon–Sat 9am–5pm
Sun 10am–5pm

Admission
Adult £5.50, Child £3

Contact
Westbourne Road, Edgbaston, Birmingham B15 3TR

t 0121 454 1860
w birminghambotanicalgardens. org.uk
e admin@birminghambotanical gardens. org.uk

618 Kingswinford

Broadfield House Glass Museum

2 hrs   All year

The museum has a collection of British glass, much of which was made locally, from C18 tableware to Victorian cameo vases to modern sculptural pieces. Permanent displays and temporary exhibitions celebrate the art of glassmaking. There is also a glassmaking studio.

* Watch and wonder at the glassblowers' skills
* The Glass Dance windows made by David Prytherch

Location
Off A491, between Stourbridge & Wolverhampton

Opening
Tue–Sun & Bank Hols 10am–4pm

Admission
Free

Contact
Compton Drive, Kingswinford DY6 9NS

t 01384 812745
w glassmuseum.org.uk
e glass.museum@dudley.gov.uk

619 Walsall

New Art Gallery

2 hrs   All year

This Arts Lottery-funded gallery opened in 2000 and is said to be one of the most exciting art galleries to be built in the UK in the last 20 years. Traditional art is showcased in the Garman Ryan Collection, donated by Lady Kathleen, widow of sculptor Sir Jacob Epstein.

* Building designed by Caruso St John Architects
* Exhibitions dedicated to best of contemporary art

Location
A454 on Wolverhampton Street

Opening
Tue–Sat & Bank Hols 10am–5pm
Sun 12noon–5pm

Admission
Free

Contact
Gallery Square, Walsall WS2 8LG

t 01922 654400
w artatwalsall.org.uk
e info@artatwalsall.org.uk

620 Walsall

Walsall Leather Museum

2 hrs   All year

Located in the heart of Britain's saddlery and leather goods trade, this fascinating museum tells the story of Walsall's leather workers, past and present. Regular demonstrations of traditional leather crafts take place in historic workshops.

* Collection of contemporary designer leather work
* Regular exhibitions and special events

Location
On A4148

Opening
Mar–Oct Tue–Sat 10am–5pm
Sun 12noon–5pm
Nov–Apr Tue–Sat 10am–4pm
Sun 12noon–4pm

Admission
Free

Contact
Littleton Street West, Walsall WS2 8EQ

t 01922 721153
w walsall.gov.uk/leathermuseum
e leathermuseum@walsall.gov.uk

621 Wolverhampton

Bantock House & Park

1 hr+   All year

This Grade II listed family home was built in 1788. The ground floor has recently been restored to its Edwardian splendour, while the upstairs features superb displays of enamels, Japanned ware and steel jewellery, with lots of hands-on activities for all ages.

* Gottle of Gear, a tribute to ventriloquism
* Programme of changing exhibitions

Location
Signposted from Wolverhampton ring road

Opening
Nov–Mar Fri–Sun 12noon–4pm
Apr–Oct Tue–Sun 10am–5pm

Admission
Free

Contact
Finchfield Road, Wolverhampton
WV3 9LQ

t 01902 552195
w wolverhampton.gov.uk

622 Wolverhampton

Wightwick Manor

2 hrs   Mar–Dec

This is a fine example of a house built and furnished in the Arts and Crafts movement style. The house features many original William Morris wallpapers and fabrics, Pre-Raphaelite paintings, Kempe glass and tiles by de Morgan.

* Beautiul garden designed by Thomas Mawson
* Talks and tours bring the house to life

Location
Off A454, beside the Mermaid Inn, 3miles W of Wolverhampton

Opening
Mar–Dec 24 Thu & Sat 1.30–5pm

Admission
Adult £6, Child £3
Timed ticket and guided tour only

Contact
Wightwick Bank, Wolverhampton
WV6 8EE

t 01902 761400
w nationaltrust.org.uk
e wightwickmanor@
nationaltrust.org.uk

623 Wolverhampton

Wolverhampton Art Gallery

1 hr+   All year

The gallery has an innovative programme of temporary exhibitions, alongside a series of workshops and special events. The collection includes British and American pop art as well as traditional C18 and C19 paintings by Gainsborough, Turner and Landseer.

* Contemporary art collection is the finest in the region
* Sensing Sculpture, a tactile sculpture court

Location
Opposite Tourist Information Centre

Opening
Mon–Sat 10am–5pm

Admission
Free

Contact
Lichfield Street, Wolverhampton
WV1 1DU

t 01902 552055
w wolverhamptonart.org.uk
e info@wolverhamptonart.org.uk

624 Broadway

Broadway Tower & Country Park

½ hr+   All year

Built on an ancient beacon site, the tower has a colourful history as – amongst others – home to the renowned printing press of Sir Thomas Phillips and country retreat for Pre-Raphaelite artists, notably the artist, designer, writer, craftsman, and socialist William Morris.

* Today houses exhibition connected with its past
* Said to be one of England's outstanding viewpoints

Location	Contact
Off A44 one mile SE of Broadway	Middle Hill, Broadway WR12 7LB
Opening	t 01386 852 390
Apr–Oct daily 10.30–5pm	w broadway-cotswolds.co.uk
Nov–Mar Sat, Sun 11am–3pm	e broadwaytower1@aol.com
Admission	
Adult £3, Child £1.50, Concs £2.50	

625 Bromsgrove

Avoncroft Museum of Historic Buildings

3 hrs   Mar–Nov

Avoncroft is a fascinating world of historic buildings covering seven centuries, rescued and rebuilt on a beautiful open-air site. You can see craftsmen working in a C19 workshop, furnished historic houses and a variety craft demonstrations.

* Visit rural Victorian England at the Toll Cottage
* See a church, gaol and a working windmill

Location	Contact
2 miles S of Bromsgrove off A38	Stoke Heath, Bromsgrove B60 4JR
Opening	t 01527 831 363
Mar–Oct Tue–Sun 10.30am–4.30	w avoncroft.org.uk
Nov, Sat & Sun 10.30am–4pm	e avoncroft1@compuserve.com
Admission	
Adult £6, Child £3, Concs £5	

626 Droitwich

Hanbury Hall

2 hrs+   All year

Completed in 1701, this homely William & Mary-style house is famed for its beautiful painted ceilings and staircase, and has other fascinating features including an orangery, ice house, pavilions and working mushroom house.

* Tercentenary exhibition opened in 2001
* Garden surrounded by 160 acres of parkland

Location	Contact
Near junction 5 of M5, 5 miles E of Droitwich	School Road, Droitwich WR9 7EA
Opening	t 01527 821 214
Mar 12–Oct 29 Sat–Wed 1pm–5pm	w nationaltrust.org.uk
Admission	e hanburyhall@ nationaltrust.org.uk
Adult £5.40, Child £2.70	

627 Kidderminster

Bodenham Arboretum

2 hrs+   All year

Bodenham Arboretum is a collection of over 2,700 trees set in 156 acres, with 11 pools, 5 miles of footpaths and a working farm with a herd of pedigree Herefords. In addition there is an award-winning 'Earth Visitor Centre' set in the hillside overlooking the Big Pool.

* Christmas Nativity trail
* Laburnum Tunnel is a highlight in late May/June

         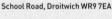

Location	Contact
Signed from Wolverley	Wolverley, Kidderminster DY11 5SY
Opening	t 01562 852 444
Mar 1–Dec daily 11am–5pm	w bodenham-arboretum.co.uk
Jan–Mar Sat & Sun 11am–5pm	
Admission	
Adult £4, Child £1.50	

628 Kidderminster

Harvington Hall

2 hrs   Mar-Oct

A moated medieval and Elizabethan manor house. Many of the rooms still have their original Elizabethan wall-paintings that were discovered under whitewash in 1936. The hall also contains the finest series of priest-holes anywhere in the country.

* Elizabethan malthouse and Georgian chapel in garden
* Moat broadens into a small lake, home to waterfowl

Location
3 miles SE of Kidderminster just off A450 Birmingham to Worcester road

Opening
Mar & Oct Sat & Sun 11.30am-4.30pm
Apr-Sep Wed-Sun 11.30am-4.30pm

Admission
Adult £4.20, Child £3, Concs £3.50

Contact
Harvington, Kidderminster DY10 4LR
t   01562 777 846
w   harvingtonhall.com
e   thehall@harvington.
    fsbusiness.co.uk

629 Kidderminster

Worcestershire County Museum

2 hr   Feb-Nov

The museum is housed in Hartlebury Castle, home to the Bishops of Worcester for over a thousand years. In the former servant's quarters of the north wing a wide range of permanent exhibitions show the past lives of the county's inhabitants, from Roman times to the C20.

* Displays include a Victorian room & transport gallery
* Programme of temporary exhibitions & events

Location
Off the A449, signposted

Opening
Feb-Nov Mon-Thu 10am-5pm
Fri & Sun 2pm-5pm

Admission
Adult £2.50, Child & Concs £1.20

Contact
Hartlebury Castle, Stourport Road, Hartlebury, Kidderminster DY11 7XZ
t   01299 250 416
w   worcestershire.gov.uk
e   museum@worcestershire.gov.uk

Great Malvern Priory

  ½ hr All year

Malvern Priory is one of the greater parish churches in the country. It was founded in 1085 and contains the finest collection of stained glass after York Minster, together with carved miserichords from the C15 and C16 and the largest collection of medieval floor and wall tiles.

* Venue for many concerts
* Newly restored organ for 2004

Location
Just off A449 in Malvern

Opening
Apr–Sep daily 9am–6.30pm
Oct–Mar daily 9am–4.30pm

Admission
Free, donations welcome

Contact
Church Street, Malvern WR14 2AY

t 01684 561020
w greatmalvernpriory.org.uk
e gmpriory@hotmail.com

Malvern Museum

   1 hr Easter–Oct

Displays in five rooms depicting the geological structure of the Malvern Hills, medieval history of the town, the Water Cure, Victorian Malvern, the effects of the Second World War on the town and, more recently, Morgan Motors and radar technology.

* Building was originally the gateway to the priory
* Audio equipment for hire

Location
Centre of Malvern, nr priory church

Opening
Easter–Oct daily 10.30–5pm
Closed Wed during term time

Admission
Adult £1, Child 20p

Contact
The Abbey Gateway, Malvern
WR14 3ES

t 01684 567811

Croome Park

   2 hrs Mar–Dec

Croome was Capability Brown's first complete landscape, making his reputation and establishing a new style of parkland design which became universally adopted over the next 50 years. The park buildings are mostly by Robert Adam and James Wyatt.

* Ten-year restoration plan including water features
* Restoration of park buildings also in progress

    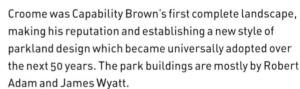

Location
8 miles S of Worcester & E of A38

Opening
Park Mar 5–Oct 31 Wed–Sun
10am–5pm, Nov 3–Dec 19 Wed–Sun
10am–4pm, Open all Bank Hols
10am–4pm

Admission
Adult £3.50, Child £1.70

Contact
NT Estate Office, The Builders' Yard,
High Green, Severn Stoke WR8 9JS

t 01905 371006
w nationaltrust.org.uk
e croomepark@nationaltrust.org.uk

633 Stourbridge

Hagley Hall

1 hr   Limited

Commissioned in 1756 and designed by Sanderson Miller, it was the last of the great Palladian houses to be built. Van Dyck paintings, Chippendale furniture and exquisite rococo plasterwork are displayed throughout the house.

* Surrounded by 350 acres of landscaped deer park
* See where two of the gunpowder conspirators hid

Location
E of Kidderminster, junction 4 of M5, signed from junction of A456 and A491

Opening
Jan–Feb Sun–Fri 2pm–5pm
All Bank Hols and their weekends
Times limited, please phone or check website for details

Admission
Adult £4, Child £1.50, Concs £2.50

Contact
Hagley DY9 9LG
t 01562 882408
w hagleyhallcom
e contact@hagleyhall.info

634 Worcester

The Commandery

1½ hrs   All year

The building was originally founded as a hospital in 1085 by the then Bishop of Worcester, Saint Wulfstan. Over the centuries it has been adapted for different uses while retaining the fabric of its history. It currently houses a variety of historical exhibitions.

* Try on original armour and weapons
* Relive the Battle of Worcester

Location
Just outside city walls at Sidbury Gate

Opening
Mon–Sat 10am–5pm
Sun 1.30–5pm

Admission
Adult £3.95, Child £2.95, Concs £2.95

Contact
Sidbury, Worcester WR1 2HU
t 01905 361821
w worcestercitymuseums.org.uk
e thecommandery@
cityofworcester.gov.uk

635 Worcester

Leigh Court Barn

½ hr+   Apr–Sep

This is a striking example of medieval architecture. At 130 feet long and 36 feet wide (40 x 11m), the barn is the largest cruck structure in the UK. Once part of Leigh Court Manor, the barn has ten bays and two porches

* Originally built for the monks of Pershore Abbey

Location
5 miles W of Worcester on unclassified road off A4103

Opening
Apr–Sep 10am–6pm

Admission
Free

Contact
Leigh, Worcester WR6 5LB
t 01902 765105
w english-heritage.org.uk

636 Worcester

Royal Worcester Porcelain Works

3 hrs+   All year

Recently refurbished and doubled in size, the museum displays the world's largest collection of Worcester Porcelain. See Georgian, Victorian and C20 galleries that showcase how styles dramatically changed through time, using room sets, shop fronts and period scenes.

* One of the world's leading ceramics museums
* Huge variety of porcelain, bone china & earthenware

Location
3 miles from junction 7 of M5, follow signs to city centre – near cathedral

Opening
Mon–Sat 9am–5.30pm Sun 11am–5pm

Admission
Prices vary. See website or phone for details

Contact
Severn Street, Worcester WR1 2NE
t 01905 746 000
w royalworcester.com
e rwgeneral@royal-worcester.co.uk

637 Worcester

Sir Edward Elgar Birthplace Museum

1 hr   Feb–Dec

The cottage and the Elgar Centre together tell the story of Sir Edward Elgar, the composer of many England's best known classical music. Visit his study with his gramaphone. See family photographs and countless mementos including his books and his golf clubs.

* In the Elgar Centre see manuscripts and music scores
* Watch historic film of his final years

Location
3 miles from Worcester on A44 towards Leominster

Opening
Daily 11am–5pm
Closed Dec 23–Feb 1

Admission
Adult £4.50, Child £2, Concs £4

Contact
Crown East Lane, Lower Broadheath WR2 6RH

t 01905 333 224
w elgarmuseum.org
e birthplace@elgarmuseum.org

---

638 Worcester

Spetchley Park Garden

2 hrs   Apr–Sep

Virtually hidden from the road, and largely unaltered in the last century, this lovely 30-acre Victorian paradise boasts an enviable collection of plant treasures from every corner of the globe. Clipped hedges and tumbling borders to olives and pineapple–scented flowers.

* Year round colour
* Unexpected vistas provide views of the Malvern Hills

Location
2 miles E of Worcester on A44, leave M5 at junction 6

Opening
Apr–Sep Tue–Fri 11am–5pm
Sun 2–5pm, Bank Hols 11am–5pm
Deer park closed in Jun

Admission
Adult £4, Child £2

Contact
Spetchley, Worcester WR5 1RS

t 01905 345 213
w spetchleygardens.co.uk

---

639 Worcester

Witley Court

2 hrs   All year

An early Jacobean manor house, Witley Court was converted in the C19 into a vast Italianate mansion with porticoes by John Nash. The spectacular ruins of this once great house are surrounded by magnificent landscaped gardens.

* Huge stone fountains that once shot 120 feet upwards
* £1m garden renovation in last two years

Location
10 miles NW of Worcester on A443

Opening
Apr–Oct daily 10am–6pm (Oct 5pm)
Nov–Mar Wed–Sun 10am–4pm

Admission
Adult £4.60, Child £2.30, Concs £3.50

Contact
Great Witley WR6 6JT

t 01299 896636
w english-heritage.org.uk
e mark.badger@english-heritage.org.uk

---

640 Worcester

Worcester Cathedral

1 hr   All year

Worcester Cathedral has been a place of prayer and worship since 680 AD. The present building was begun in 1084. Its many attractions include: King John's tomb, Prince Arthur's Chantry, the early C12 Chapter House and St Wulstan's crypt.

* Tower open 10am–4.30pm, Sat & summer holidays
* Magnificent Victorian stained glass windows

Location
City centre, off College Street

Opening
Daily 7.30am–6pm,
services three times daily

Admission
Free, donations welcome

Contact
10A College Green, Worcester WR1 2LH

t 01905 28854
w cofe-worcester.org.uk
e info@worcestercathedral.org.uk

Llyn Y Gadair, Gwynedd

Wales

Mid Wales North Wales South Wales

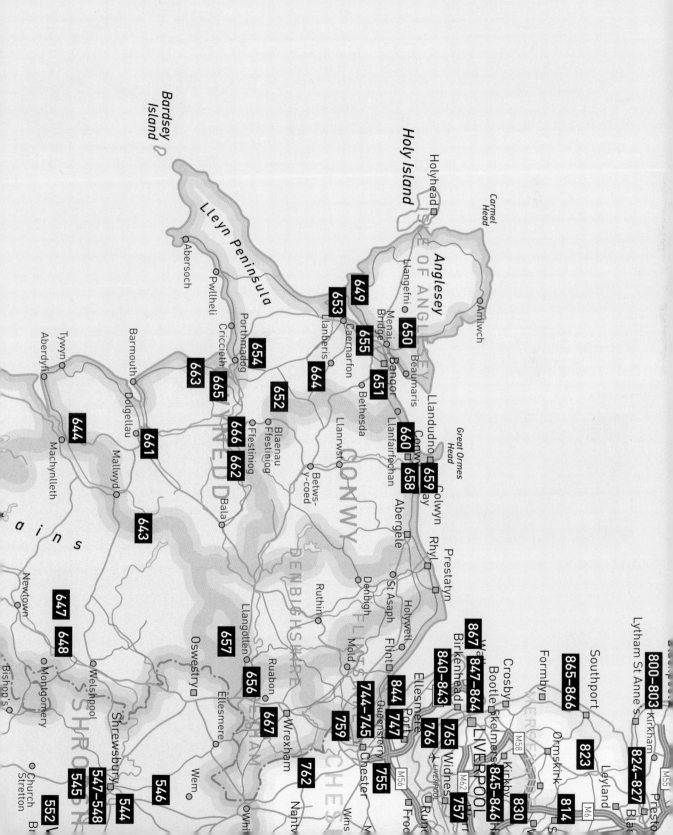

Bardsey Island

Holy Island

Anglesey

Carmel Head

Holyhead

Lleyn Peninsula

ISLE OF ANGLESEY

Llangefni

Menai Bridge

Amlwch

649
653
650
655
651
660

Llanberis

Caernarfon

Beaumaris

Bangor

Bethesda

Llanfairfechan

Conwy

Abersoch

Pwllheli

Criccieth

Porthmadog

654
663
665
664
652

Tywyn

Aberdyfi

Barmouth

Dolgellau

Mallwyd

Machynlleth

644
661
666
662

Llandudno

Great Ormes Head

Colwyn Bay

Rhyl

659
658

Abergele

Prestatyn

Llanrwst

Betws-y-coed

GWYNEDD

Bala

643

CONWY

Ruthin

Denbigh

St Asaph

Holywell

Flint

Newtown

Bishop's

647
648

Montgomery

Welshpool

Llangollen

Oswestry

DENBIGHSHIRE

FLINTSHIRE

Mold

657
656

Ruabon

Ellesmere

Wrexham

667

Church Stretton

Shrewsbury

Wem

552
545
547–548
544
546
762

SHROPSHIRE

WREXHAM

CHESHIRE

Chester

759
744–745
755
757

Queensferry

Widnes

Runc

844
747
766
765

Ellesmere Port

840–843
845–846

Birkenhead

Bootle

Skelmersd

Crosby

Formby

867
847–864

LIVERPOOL

Kirkby

830

Ormskirk

823
814

Southport

865–866

Leyland

Lytham St Anne's

Kirkham

Preston

800–803
824–827

M55
M58
M62
M56
M6

641 Brecon

Brecon Beacons National Park Visitor Centre

  1 hr+ All year

The attractions of the Brecon Beacons National Park range from lush, green, open countryside to historical and cultural heritage. There are attractions to suit all the family, including museums, theatres and family activity centres.

* Centre of internationally renowned festivals
* Selection of guided walks available

Location
The national park Mountain Centre is 5½ miles SW of Brecon

Opening
Mar–Jun and Sep–Oct 9.30am–5pm
Jul–Aug 9.30am–6pm
Nov–Feb 9.30am–4.30pm

Admission
Free, car parking may be charged

Contact
NPVC, Libanus, Brecon, Powys LD3 8ER

t 01874 623366
w breconbeacons.org
e mountaincentre@breconbeacons.org

642 Llannwrda

Dolaucothi Gold Mines

  2 hrs   All year

These unique gold mines are set amid wooded, hillsides overlooking the beautiful Cothi Valley. The Romans, who exploited the site almost 2,000 years ago, left behind a complex of pits, channels, adits and tanks. Mining resumed in the C19 and peaked in 1938.

* Historical tours
* Opportunity to pan for gold

Location
Between Lampeter and Llanwrda on A482

Opening
Apr 2–Nov 2 daily 10am–5pm

Admission
Adult £3, Child £1.50

Contact
Pumsaint, Llanwrda SA19 8US

t 01558 650177
w nationaltrust.org.uk
e dolaucothi@nationaltrust.org.uk

643 Llanwyddyn

Lake Vyrnwy Nature Reserve

   2 hrs+ All year

This man-made lake was completed in 1888. In dry weather, if the water level drops far enough, the ruins of the old submerged village of Llanwyddyn reappear. With various hides, vantage points and nature trails, it is a spectacular place for birdwatching.

* Moorland, woodland and water habitats
* Good birdwatching all year round

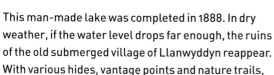

Location
10 miles W of Llanfyllin

Opening
Apr 1–Dec 24 10.30am–5.30pm
Jan 1–Mar 31 Sat–Sun only

Admission
Free

Contact
Brynawel, Llanwyddyn, Powys SY10 0LZ

t 01691 870278
w rspb.org.uk
e vyrnwy@rspb.org.uk

644 Machynlleth

King Arthur's Labyrinth

  2 hrs+ Mar–Nov

Take an underground boat through a waterfall and deep into the spectacular caverns under the mountains where tales of King Arthur are told with stunning sound and light effects. Back above ground, join the Bard's Quest to search for legends lost in the Maze of Time.

* Large craft centre with demonstrations
* Shop sells items on the Arthurian theme

Location
On the A487 between Machynlleth and Dolgellau

Opening
Daily Mar 27–Nov 7 10am–5pm

Admission
Adult £5, Child £3.50, Concs £4.45

Contact
Corris, Machynlleth, Powys SY20 9RF

t 01654 761584
w kingarthurslabyrinth.com
e king.arthurs.labyrinth@corriswales.co.uk

645 Narberth

Colby Woodland Garden

3 hrs   Apr–Oct

This attractive woodland garden has a fine collection of rhododendrons and azaleas. There are beautiful walks through secluded valleys along open and wooded pathways. The house is not open to the public but there is access to the walled garden.

* Regular guided walks with gardener–in–charge

Location
1 mile inland from Amroth, follow signs from A477 (Tenby/Carmarthen)

Opening
Apr–Oct daily 10am–5pm

Admission
Adult £3.40, Child £1.70

Contact
Amroth, Narberth SA67 8PP

t 01834 811885
w nationaltrust.org.uk

646 Rhayader

Gigrin Farm

1 hr+   All year

A family-run, upland sheep farm with wonderful views of the Wye and Elan valleys. It has 400 breeding ewes along with donkeys, ponies, assorted ducks, chickens and a number of pea fowl. In 1994 it became the Official Kite Country Red Kite feeding station.

* Farm & nature trail
* New wetland project

Location
On the A470, ½ mile south of Rhayader

Opening
Daily 1pm–5pm

Admission
Adult £2.50, Child £1, Concs £2

Contact
South Street, Rhayader, Powys LD6 5BL

t 01597 810243
w redkitecentre.co.uk
e kites@gigrin.co.uk

647 Welshpool

Andrew Logan Museum of Sculpture

½ hr+   May–Oct

The museum houses a collection of works by renowned sculptor Andrew Logan, founder of the famous Alternative Miss World contest and international artist *extraordinaire*. This is the only museum in Europe dedicated to a living artist.

* Features art of popular poetry and metropolitan glamour
* Works of art, sculpture, jewellery and more

Location
On the A438 from Welshpool

Opening
Easter Weekend 12–6pm
May–Oct Wed–Sun 12–6pm
Sat–Sun Nov–Dec 12–4pm

Admission
Adult £2, Child & Concs £1

Contact
Berriew, nr Welshpool, Powys SY21 8PJ

t 01686 640689
w andrewlogan.com
e info@andrewlogan.com

648 Welshpool

Powis Castle & Garden

3 hrs   Mar–Oct

This world-famous garden, overhung with enormous clipped yews, shelters rare and tender plants, statues, an orangery and an aviary on the terraces. The medieval castle contains one of the finest collections of paintings and furniture in Wales.

* Collection of Indian treasures at the Clive Museum
* Beautiful interiors dating from 1600–1904

Location
1 mile S of Welshpool signposted from A483

Opening
Mar 21–Oct 31 Thu–Mon
Castle 1pm–5pm
Garden 11am–6pm
(Mar & Oct only 1pm–4pm)

Admission
Adult £8.40, Child £4.20

Contact
Welshpool SY21 8RF

t 01938 551944
w nationaltrust.org.uk
e powiscastle@nationaltrust.org.uk

North Wales

649 Anglesea

Anglesey Sea Zoo

2 hrs+   Feb–Oct

This is Wales' largest marine aquarium, nestling on the shores of the Menai Strait. With over 50 displays, the Sea Zoo has recreated the habitats of the fauna and flora found around Anglesey and North Wales coastline.

* Major seahorse conservation project
* Lobster hatchery

Location
On the A55, cross the Britannia Bridge onto Anglesey and follow the brown lobster signs to Brynsiencyn. Nearest railway station is Bangor, then no. 42 bus

Opening
Daily Feb–Apr 11am–3pm
May–Oct 10am–6pm

Admission
Adult £5.95, Child £4.95, Senior £5.50

Contact
Brynsiencyn, Isle of Anglesey LL61 6TQ
t 01248 430411
w angleseyseazoo.co.uk
e fishandfun@seazoo.demon.co.uk

651 Bangor

Penrhyn Castle

2 hrs+   Apr–Oct

A neo-Norman fantasy castle that sits between Snowdonia and the Menai Strait. The castle is crammed full of curiosities including a one-ton slate bed made for Queen Victoria, elaborate carvings and mock-Norman furniture. The castle contains an outstanding collection of paintings.

* Stable block hosts a variety of museums
* Exotic plant collection and a Victorian walled garden

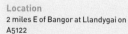

Location
2 miles E of Bangor at Llandygai on A5122

Opening
Mar 27–Oct 31 Wed–Mon 12noon–5pm
Jul & Aug Wed–Mon 11–5pm

Admission
Adult £7, Child £3

Contact
Llandygai, Bangor LL57 4HN
t 01248 353084
w nationaltrust.org.uk
e penrhyncastle@nationaltrust.org.uk

650 Anglesey

Plas Newydd

3 hrs   Easter–Oct

This C18 house built by Wyatt is an interesting mixture of classical and Gothic. Restyled in the 1930s, the house is famous for its association with Whistler, whose work is exhibited. There is also a museum for the 1st Marquess of Anglesey who led the cavalry at the Battle of Waterloo.

* Access to a marine walk on the Menai Strait
* Fine spring garden with Australasian arboretum

Location
Junction 7 & 8 off A55

Opening
Mar 27–Nov 3 Sat–Wed 11am–5.30pm

Admission
Adult £5, Child £2.50

Contact
Llanfairpwll,
Anglesey LL61 6DQ
t 01248 715272/714795
w nationaltrust.org.uk
e plasnewydd@nationaltrust.org.uk

652   Blaenau Ffestiniog

Llechwedd Slate Caverns

2 hrs   All year

Two underground train rides: The 'Miner's Tramway' takes passengers into the mountainside past early Victorian remains and spectacular caverns. The 'Deep Mine' descends on Britain's steepest passenger railway, with a gradient of 1:1.8.

* Explore on foot ten chambers
* Experience life in the 'Victorian Village'

Location
On the A470 between Blaenau Ffestiniog & Dolwyddelan

Opening
Daily from 10am

Admission
Adult £8.25, Child £6.25, Concs £7

Contact
Blaenau Ffestiniog LL41 3NB

t 01766 830 306
w llechwedd-slatecaverns.co.uk
e info@llechwedd-slatecaverns.co.uk

653   Caernarfon

Caernarfon Castle

3 hrs+   All year

Designed to replicate the walls of Constantinople, with its unique polygonal towers, intimidating battlements and colour-banded masonry, the castle dominates the town. In 1969, the castle was the setting for the investiture of Prince Charles as Prince of Wales.

* A World Heritage site
* Houses the museum of the Royal Welch Fusiliers

Location
In Caernarfon town centre on the A55
Nearest station Bangor

Opening
1 Apr–1 Jun daily 9.30am– 5pm
2 Jun–28 Sep daily 9.30am–6pm
29 Sep–26 Oct daily 9.30am–5pm
27 Oct–31 Mar Mon–Sat 9.30am–4pm
Sun 11am– 4pm

Admission
Adult £4.50, Child £3.50, Concs £3.50

Contact
Castle Ditch, Caernarfon, Gwynedd
LL55 2AY

t 01286 677617
w cadw.wales.gov.uk

654   Caernarfon

Welsh Highland Railway

4 hrs +   All year

Take a 12-mile ride, from the coast to the slopes of Snowdon, on North Wales' newest railway. Enjoy the spectacular scenery of lakes, mountains and forest *en route* to the heart of Snowdonia itself.

Location
Main station on St Helens Road in Caernarfon, signed from A487

Opening
Mar–Nov daily, Limited winter service, phone for details

Admission
Adult + 1 child £14
additional children £7 each

Contact
Harbour Station, Porthmadog,
Gwynedd LL49 9NF

t 01766 516073
w festrail.co.uk
e info@festrail.co.uk

©National Trust Photographic Library/Matthew Antrobus

655 Caernarfon

Plas Menai National Watersports Centre

6–7 days   All year

Sailing, canoeing, windsurfing, yachting, powersports, mountain activities – this centre has a fantastic range of activity courses on offer all year round for every level of ability.

* Residential and non-residential courses
* Great low-season savings during the winter

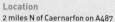

Location
2 miles N of Caernarfon on A487

Opening
Daily all year round

Admission
Different prices for different courses, please telephone or see website for prices

Contact
Llanfairisgaer, Caernarfon, Gwynedd LL55 1UE

t 01248 670964
w plasmenai.co.uk
e plas.menai@scw.co.uk

656 Chirk

Chirk Castle

2 hrs   Mar–Oct

A magnificent Marcher fortress, completed in 1310. The austere exterior belies the comfortable and elegant state rooms inside, with elaborate plasterwork, superb Adam-style furniture, tapestries and portraits. Formal garden of clipped yews, rose garden and climbers.

* Informal area with thatched cottage
* Terrace with stunning views, a classical pavilion

Location
1 mile off A5, 2 miles W of Chirk

Opening
Mar 20–Oct 31 Wed–Sun 12noon–5pm

Admission
Adult £6, Child £3

Contact
Chirk, Wrexham LL14 5AF

t 01691 777701
w nationaltrust.org.uk
e chirkcastle@nationaltrust.org.uk

657 Chirk

Pony & Quad Treks

1–4 hrs   Easter–Oct

Explore the beautiful and spectacular scenery of the Ceiriog Valley and stunning Ceiriog River in North Wales on horseback or quad bike. Horses and ponies for all abilities, off-roading for all tastes.

* Full safety equipment provided
* Full protective clothing available

Location
8 miles from Chirk on B4500

Opening
Easter–Oct 10.30am–4pm

Admission
Pony Trekking day £40, 2 hours £22, 1 hour £14. *Quad Trekking* (over 12 years old) 1 hour £25, 30 mins £15

Contact
Pont-y-Meibion, Pandy, Glyn Ceiriog, Chirk, Llangollen LL20 7HS
t 01691 718333/718413
w ponytreks.co.uk
e enquiry@ponytreks.co.uk

658 Colwyn Bay

Bodnant Garden

1 hr+   Mar–Nov

Situated above the River Conwy and looking across the valley towards the Snowdonia range, this is a garden of exceptional beauty. The garden is in two parts, an upper terraced garden and a lower portion, known as the Dell, which contains the wild garden.

* Wide range of interesting plants
* Garden covers 80 acres

Location
Off the A470 road, 7 miles S of Llandudno & Colwyn Bay

Opening
Mar–Oct 31 daily 10am–5pm

Admission
Adult £5.50, Child £2.70

Contact
Tal y Cafn,
Colwyn Bay LL28 5RE
t 01492 650460
w bodnantgarden.co.uk
e office@bodnantgarden.com

659 Conwy

Conwy Castle

1 hr+   All year

This gritty, dark stoned fortress has the rare ability to evoke an authentic medieval atmosphere. Commanding a rock above the Conwy Estuary, the castle demands as much attention as the dramatic Snowdonia skyline behind it.

* One of the great fortresses of medieval Europe
* Marvellous floodlit night time views

Location
On the B5106 off the A55. Railway station is next to the castle

Opening
1 Apr–1 Jun 9.30am– 5m daily
2 Jun–28 Sep 9.30am–6pm daily
29 Sep–26 Oct 9.30am–5pm daily
27 Oct–31 Mar Mon–Sat 9.30am–4pm
Sun 11am–4pm

Admission
Adult £3.50, Child £3, Concs £3

Contact
Cadw, Conwy LL32 8LD
t 01492 592358
w cadw.wales.gov.uk

660 Conwy

The Royal Cambrian Academy

½ hr+   All year

The most prestigious art institution in Wales, has been in Conwy for over 121 years. Members come from all parts of the UK, but the majority come from Wales. The work shown is a true reflection of contemporary Welsh art.

* Exhibited paintings are for sale
* Exhibitions change regularly

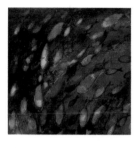 

Location
In the centre of Conwy, just off High Street behind Plas Mawr

Opening
Tue–Sat 11am–5pm Sun 1–4.30pm

Admission
Free

Contact
Crown Lane, Conwy LL32 8AN

t 01492 593413
w rcaconwy.org
e info@rcaconwy.org

---

661 Dolgellau

Quaker Heritage Centre

½ hr   All year

Discover the story of the Quaker community that once lived here. Vigorously persecuted due to their Oath of Allegiance to the king, they bought 40,000 acres of land in America in what became known as Pennsylvania and emigrated there in 1681.

* Pennsylvania still has numerous Welsh names

Location
Town centre, off Sgwar Eldon Square

Opening
Summer Daily 10am–6pm
Winter Thu–Mon 10am–5pm

Admission
Free

Contact
Ty Meirion,
Sgwar Eldon Square, Dolgellau

t 01341 424442
w gwynedd.gov.uk
e amgueddfeydd-museums@
    gwynedd.gov.uk

---

662 Ffestiniog

Hydro Centre – Ffestiniog Power Station

1 hr   Jun–Sep

After a lecture on the generation of electricity, visitors are taken on a tour of Britain's first hydro-electricity station. See the machine hall, generators, turbines, interactive models and displays. Drive to the top of the dam for magnificent views.

* Visitors must be able to climb 160 steep steps
* No children under 4

Location
A487 N of Ffestiniog

Opening
Jun–Sep Sun–Fri 10am–4.30pm
Easter & half terms Sun–Fri
10am–4.30pm

Admission
Adult £2.75, Child £1.50, Concs £2

Visit to Stwlan Dam £3 per car

Contact
Tan-y-Grisiau,
Blaenau Ffestiniog LL41 3TP

t 01766 830465
w fhc.co.uk
e hydrocentre@edisonmission.com

663 Harlech

Harlech Castle

½ hr · All year

Set high on the cliffs overlooking Tremadog Bay, this is the most dramatically sited of all the castles built by King Edward I in his 'iron ring' of fortresses. Magnificent medieval architecture combined with spectacular location justify its status as a World Heritage site.

* Inner walls and towers still stand to full height
* Panoramic views across the bay and to Snowdonia

Location
Harlech town centre

Opening
Apr–May & Oct daily 9.30–5pm
Jun–Sep daily 9.30–6pm
Nov–Mar Mon–Sat 9.30–4pm,
Sun 11am–4pm. Closed Dec 24–26, Jan 1

Admission
Adult £3, Child & Concs £2

Contact
Harlech, Gwynedd LL46 2YII

t 01766 780552
w harlech.com

664 Llanberis

Snowdon Mountain Railway

2 hrs+ · Mar–Nov

This tremendously ambitious feat of engineering is unique in Britain. The rack and pinion railway, which rises to within 66feet (20m) of the summit of the highest mountain in England and Wales (3,560ft/1,085m), was built and opened in 1896.

* 30-minute stay at the top, single tickets available
* Breathtaking views from the train and the summit

Location
Llanberis Station on the A4086, 7.5 miles from Caernarfon. 15 mins drive from A55/A5 junction at Bangor. Nearest station is Bangor

Opening
Daily mid-March–1 Nov
Please telephone for timetable

Admission
Adult £20, Child £15, Concs £17

Contact
Llanberis, Gwynedd LL55 4TY

t 0870 4580033
w snowdonrailway.co.uk
e info@snowdonrailway.co.uk

665 Minffordd

Portmeirion

4 hrs+ · All year

This unique village is set on a private peninsula on the southern shores of Snowdonia. It was created by Welsh architect Clough Williams-Ellis (1883–1978) to demonstrate how a naturally beautiful place could be developed without spoiling it.

* Used as location for cult TV series *The Prisoner*
* Cottages in the village let by Portmeirion Hotel

Location
Signposted off the A487 at Minffordd between Penrhyndeudraeth and Porthmadog

Opening
Daily 9.30am–5.30pm

Admission
Adult £5.70, Child £2.80, Concs £4.60

Contact
Gwynedd, LL48 6ET

t 01766 770000
w portmeirion-village.com
e info@portmeirion-village.com

666 Porthmadog

The Ffestiniog Railway

4 hrs+   All year

Take a 13-mile ride on this historical railway. For 140 years, steam-hauled trains have run from the harbour at Porthmadog to the mountains at Blaenau Ffestiniog, passing farmland and forest, mountains and moors, lakes and waterfalls.

* Regular special events
* Refurbished café/bar at Harbour Station

Location
Next to harbour in Porthmadog on A487.

Opening
Mar–Nov daily, limited winter service, please phone for timetables

Admission
Adult + 1 child £14, additional children £7 each

Contact
Harbour Station, Porthmadog, Gwynedd LL49 9NF

t 01766 516073
w festrail.co.uk
e info@festrail.co.uk

667 Wrexham

Erddig Hall

1 hr+   Mar–Sep

One of the most fascinating houses in Britain, not least because of the close relationship that existed between the family of the house and their servants. The state rooms display most of the original C18 and C19 furnishings, including some exquisite Chinese wallpaper.

* Large walled 18th-century formal garden
* Extensive park with woodland walks

Location
2 miles S of Wrexham, signposted from A525 & A483

Opening
Mar 20–Sep 30 Mon–Wed, Sat & Sun 12noon–5pm
Oct 12 noon–4pm

Admission
Adult £7, Child £3.50

Contact
Wrexham LL13 0YT

t 01978 355314
w nationaltrust.org.uk
e erddig@nationaltrust.org.uk

668 Blaenafon

Big Pit National Mining Museum

3 hrs+   Mar–Nov

This is a real colliery. Kitted out in helmet, cap–lamp and battery pack, you descend 300 feet (90 metres) to another world; a world of shafts, coal faces and levels, of underground roadways, air doors and stables. Interactive exhibitions new for 2004.

* Protective clothing available
* Winding engine–house, blacksmith's workshop

Location
Leave M4 at junction 25a / 26, follow signs from the A465

Opening
Daily Mar–Nov 9.30am–5.00pm
Underground tours run frequently from 10.00am–3.30pm

Admission
Free

Contact
Blaenafon, Torfaen NP4 9XP

t 01495 790311
w nmgw.ac.uk
e bigpit@nmgw.ac.uk

669 Caerleon

Caerleon Roman Baths & Amphitheatre

2 hrs   All year

The site of the 50-acre Roman legionary fortress of Isca, this was the permanent base of the 2nd Augustan Legion in Britain from about AD 75. Impressive remains of the fortress baths, amphitheatre, barracks, and fortress walls.

* Site exhibition
* Open-air events and re-enactments

Location
On the A4042 to Caerleon off M4

Opening
1 Apr–26 Oct 9.30am–5pm daily
27 Oct–31 Mar Mon–Sat 9.30am–5pm
Sun 2pm–5pm

Admission
Adult £2.50, Child & Concs £2

Contact
Broadway, Caerleon, Newport NP18 1AY

t 01633 422518
w cadw.wales.gov.uk

670 Caerphilly

Caerphilly Castle

1 hr+   All year

Caerphilly Castle is one of the most impressive examples of medieval castle building in Great Britain. Spread over some 30 acres of land, this is the second largest castle in the UK after Windsor. In the words of the poet Tennyson, 'It isn't a castle – it's a town in ruins'.

* 45-minute audio tours
* Many summer demonstrations and events

Location
Exit the M4 at junction 32 and take the A470 or A469 for Caerphilly

Opening
1 Apr–1 June 9.30am–5pm
2 Jun–28 Sep 9.30am–6pm
29 Sep–26 Oct 9.30am–5pm
27 Oct–31 Mar Mon–Sat 9.30am–4.30pm
11am–4pm Sun

Admission
Adult £3, Child & Concs £2.50

Contact
Bridge Street, Caerphilly CF83 1JD

t 02920 883143
w cadw.wales.gov.uk
e caerphilly.castle@cadw.co.uk

671 Cardiff

Cardiff Castle

2hrs+   All year

Cardiff Castle is one of Wales' leading tourist attractions. Situated in the very heart of the capital, alongside city-centre shopping and the magnificent Bute Park, the castle's enchanting fairytale towers conceal an elaborate and splendid interior.

* Lavish and opulent interiors
* Set in beautiful grounds

Location
Cardiff city centre

Opening
Daily Mar–Oct 9.30am–6pm
Nov–Feb 9.30am–5pm

Admission
Adult £6, Child & Concs £3.70

Contact
Castle Street, Cardiff CF10 3RB

t 029 20 878100
w cardiffcastle.com
e cardiffcastle@cardiff.gov.uk

---

672 Cardiff

Millennium Stadium Tours

1 hr   All year

Experience the moments before a match when Wales charge down the players' tunnel cheered on by tens of thousands of rugby and football fans. Feel the pre-match tension and the joy of victory in the changing rooms before celebrating in the Cardiff Arms Suite.

* Sit in the royal box and lift a trophy

Location
Cardiff city centre

Opening
Daily 10.00am–5.00pm

Admission
Adult £5, Child £2.50, Concs £3

Contact
Millenium Stadium Shop, Gate 3, Westgate Street, Cardiff CF10 1GE

t 02920 822040
w cardiff-stadium.co.uk

---

673 Cardiff

Museum of Welsh Life

3hrs+   All year

Standing in the grounds of the magnificent St Fagan's Castle, this museum shows how the people of Wales have lived, worked and spent their leisure time over the last 500 years. Over 30 buildings have been moved from various parts of Wales and reassembled here.

* Exhibitions of costume, daily life and farming tools
* Regular festivals of traditional music and dance

Location
4 miles W of Cardiff city centre
Exit junction 33 from the M4

Opening
Daily 10am–5pm

Admission
Free

Contact
St Fagan's, Cardiff CF5 6XB

t 02920 573500
w nmgw.ac.uk
e post@nmgw.ac.uk

MV *Aliquando*

1 hr+   All year

The MV *Aliquando* is a privately owned 10-metre trawler yacht available for hire by the hour or the day in Cardiff Bay or the Bristol Channel. As seen recently on BBC TV's *Casualty*.

* Available for private hire
* Carries a maximum of 8 passengers

Location	Contact
Pick up by arrangement in Penarth or Mermaid Quay, Cardiff Bay	Telephone / e-mail only
Opening	t 07710 025553 / 01446 773253
By arrangement with the owner	e dennis.thebrambles@ btopenworld.com
Admission	
By arrangement with the owner	

Techniquest

2hrs+   All year

This science discovery centre in Cardiff Bay has over 150 hands-on exhibits that will bring science and technology to life. Among the amazing activities, visitors can fire a rocket, launch a hot-air balloon, play a giant keyboard and much more.

* Explore the universe in the planetarium
* Enjoy a fascinating interactive science theatre show

Location	Admission
Exit M4 at junction 33 and follow signs on the A4232	Adult £6.75, Child & Concs £4.65
Opening	**Contact**
Daily Mon–Fri 9.30am–4.30pm	Stuart Street, Cardiff CF10 5BW
Sat, Sun & Bank Hols 10.30am–5.00pm	t 02920 475475
	w techniquest.org
	e info@techniquest.org

National Botanic Garden of Wales

2 hrs+   All year

The first national botanic garden in the UK for over 200 years, it is dedicated to conservation, science, education, leisure and the arts. Set in the former C18 park of Middleton Hall, this 568-acre estate enjoys a pollution-free environment, spectacular views and a rich heritage.

* Outdoor art installations
* Regular calendar of special events

Location	Contact
On the A48 near Carmarthen, signposted from the M4 and A40	Garden of Wales, Llanarthne, Carmarthenshire SA32 8HG
Opening	t 01558 668768
Daily Easter–Oct 25 10am–6pm	w gardenofwales.org.uk
Oct 26–Mar 10 am–4.30pm	e reception@gardenofwales.org.uk
Admission	
Adult £6.95, Child £3.50, Concs £5	

677 Chepstow

Tintern Abbey

1 hr   All year

This Cistercian abbey is one of the greatest monastic ruins of Wales. Since the early C20 every effort has been made to maintain one of the finest and most complete abbey churches in the country. A favourite of many artists.

* Site exhibition
* Audio tour and brail plan

Location
Off the A466 4m N of Chepstow,

Opening
Apr 1–Jun 1, 9.30am–5pm
Jun 2–Sep 28, 9.30am–6pm
Sep 29–Oct 26, 9.30am–5pm
Mon–Sat Oct 27–Mar 31, 9.30am–4pm
Sun 11am–4pm

Admission
Adult £2.50, Child & Concs £2

Contact
Cadw, Welsh Historic Monuments,
Cathays Park, Cardiff CF10 3NQ
t 01291 689251
w cadw.wales.gov.uk
e phillip.stallard.cadw@wales.gsi.gov.uk

678 Neath

Aberdulais Falls

½ hr+   Mar–Dec

For over 400 years this famous waterfall provided the energy to drive the wheels of industry, from copper to tinplate. A unique hydro-electricity scheme makes Aberdulais Falls self-sufficient in environmentally-friendly energy.

* The waterwheel is the largest used in Europe
* Often visited by famous artists such as Turner in 1796

Location
On A4109, 3 miles NE of Neath,
4 miles from junction 43 of M4

Opening
Mar 1–Mar 30 Fri–Sun 11am–4pm
Mar 31–Nov 2 Mon–Fri 10am–5pm
Sat & Sun 11am–6pm
Nov 7–Dec 21 Fri–Sun 11am–4pm

Admission
Adults £3.20, Child £1.60

Contact
Aberdulais,
nr Neath SA10 8EU
t 01639 636674
w nationaltrust.org.uk

679 Rhossili

Rhossili Visitor Centre

3 hrs+   All year

This National Trust visitor centre is situated adjacent to the Warren, the Down, Worm's Head, the beach and coastal cliffs, and provides information about one of the most beautiful areas of Wales. It is very popular with walkers, hand-gliders, para-gliders and surfers.

* Exhibition of local history

Location
Gower Peninsula, from Swansea via
A4118 and then B4247

Opening
Jan–Mar Sat & Sun 11am–4pm
Mar–Oct daily 10.30am–5.30pm
Nov & Dec Wed–Sun 11am–4pm

Admission
Free

Contact
Coastguard Cottages, Rhossili,
Swansea SA3 1PR
t 01792 390707
w nationaltrust.org.uk
e rhossili@nationaltrust.org.uk

680 St David's

St David's Cathedral

1 hr+   All year

This beautiful cathedral is built on the site of St David's C6 monastery. It has been a site of pilgrimage and worship for hundreds of years and continues to serve the local community. It is the only chapter within the UK of which the queen is a member.

* Exhibition of Celtic carved stone
* 90-minute tours

Location
Near the centre of St David's

Opening
Tours Jul & Aug Mon–Fri at 2.30pm
Please book 3 weeks ahead at all
other times

Admission
Free, but suggested donation of £2/£1
Tours Adult £3, Child/Concs £1.20

Contact
R.G.Tarr, 23 Maes-yr-Hedydd,
St David's, Pembrokeshire SA62 6QW
t 01437 720691
w stdavidscathedral.org.uk
e tours@stdavidscathedral.org.uk

681 Swansea

Dylan Thomas Centre

2 hrs+   All year

This centre celebrates the life and work of Dylan Marlais Thomas (Swansea's world-famous son). Refurbished in 1995 to host the British Year of Literature, this splendid building has a permanent exhibition on Dylan Thomas and his life.

* Regular programme of special events
* Award-winning restaurant

Location	Contact
Swansea city centre	Somerset Place, Swansea SA1 1RR
Opening	t 01792 463980
All year Tue–Sun & Bank Hols	w swansea.gov.uk/DylanThomas
10am–5pm	e dylanthomas.lit@swansea.gov.uk
Admission	
Free	

682 Swansea

Egypt Centre

1 hr   All year

Opened in 1998, this museum houses the private collection of renowned pharmacist Sir Henry Wellcome. There are over 3,500 items in the collection, including an Egyptian coffin dating to around 1000 BC, beautiful jewellery and ancient pottery.

* Objects date from thousands of years BC to 500AD

Location	Contact
Follow signs for the University of Wales, Swansea	University of Wales, Singleton Park, Swansea SA2 8PP
Opening	t 01792 295960
Tue–Sat 10am–4pm	w swan.ac.uk/egypt
Admission	e c.a.graves-brown@swansea.ac.uk
Free	

683 Treharris

Llancaiach Fawr Manor

1 hr+   All year

This splendid Tudor, semi-fortified manor house, has been refurbished to its C17 state. Step back in time to the year 1645 where the servants of the household will delight you with tales of their lives during the English Civil War years.

* Listen to the gossip of the day – 300 years ago
* Stroll in the formal gardens

Location	Admission
On the B4254 between Nelson and Gelligaer, about 2½ miles from the A470	Adult £4.50, Child & Concs £3
	Contact
	Nelson, Treharris CF46 6ER
Opening	
Daily Mon–Fri 10am–5pm	t 01443 412248
Sat–Sun 10am–6pm	w caerphilly.gov.uk/visiting
Closed Mon Nov–Feb	

684 Tenby

Tudor Merchant's House

1 hr   Apr–Oct

This late C15 townhouse is characteristic of Tenby's heyday as a thriving trading port. The ground-floor chimney at the rear of the house is a fine vernacular example. The remains of early frescos can be seen on three interior walls.

* Furnished to recreate family life in the Tudor period
* Access to the small herb garden, weather permitting

Location	Admission
Centre of Tenby, off Tudor Square	Adult £2, Child £1
Opening	**Contact**
Apr–Sep Thu–Tue 10am–5pm	Quay Hill, Tenby SA70 7BX
Sun 1–5pm	
Oct Mon, Tue, Thu, Fri 10am–3pm	t 01834 842279
Sun 12 noon–3am	w nationaltrust.org.uk

Yorkshire

East Riding North Yorkshire
South Yorkshire West Yorkshire

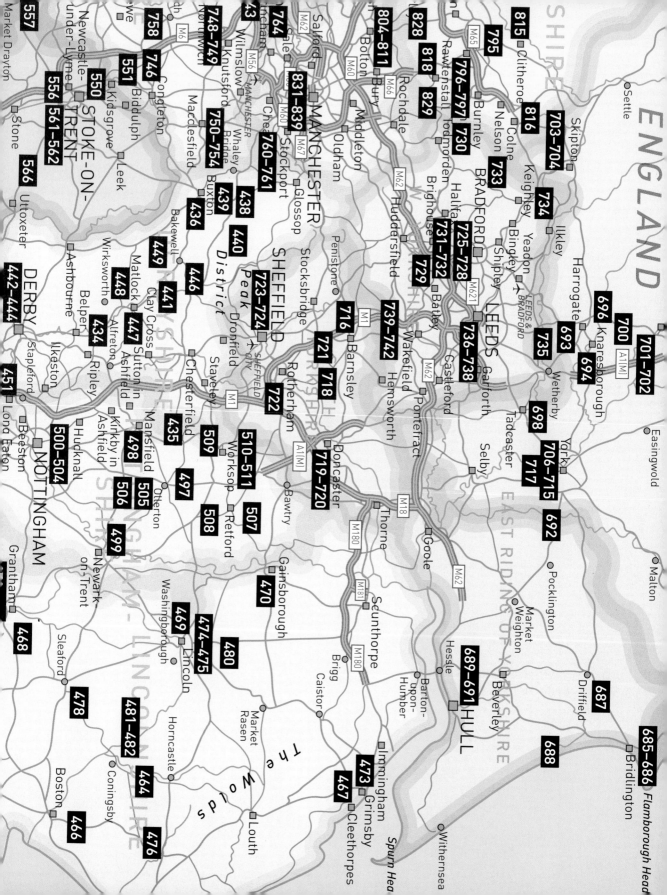

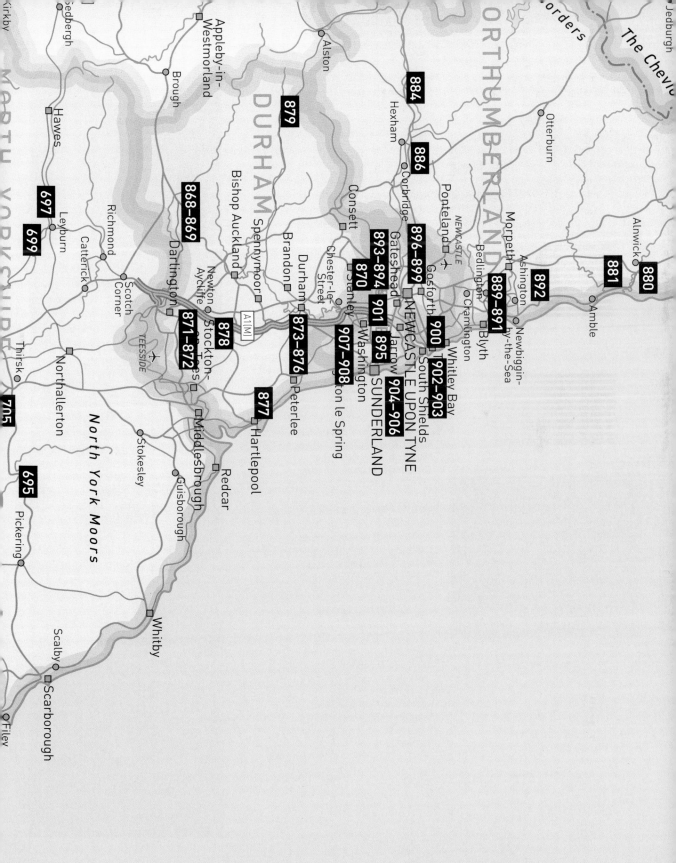

685 Bridlington

Bempton Cliffs Nature Reserve

2 hrs   All year

One of the best places in England to see seabirds. More than 200,000 birds nest on the cliffs, including gannets, puffins, guillemots, razorbills and kittiwakes. Five safe viewing areas are situated along 3 miles of chalk cliffs. First 1 mile suitable for wheelchairs.

* Gannets first colonised cliffs in 1920s
* Puffins can be seen in spring and summer

Location
On cliff road from Bempton, on B1229
from Flamborough to Filey

Opening
Visitor centre Mar–Nov 10am–5pm
Dec–Feb Sat/Sun only 9.30am–4pm

Admission
£3, car park fee for non-members

Contact
c/o 11 Cliff Lane, Bempton,
Bridlington YO15 1JD

t 01262 851179
w rspb.org.uk

686 Bridlington

Sewerby Hall & Gardens

3 hrs   All year

Set in 50 acres of early C19 parkland in a dramatic cliff-top position overlooking Bridlington Bay. The hall contains a magnificent orangery, period rooms and art and photographic galleries. Attractions in the grounds include an old English and rose walled garden.

* Display of Amy Johnson's awards and trophies
* Children's zoo includes monkeys and penguins

Location
From Bridlington, follow signs for
Flambourgh and then Sewerby

Opening
Open all year, times vary
Main season Apr–Sep 10am–5.30pm

Admission
Adult £3.10, Child £1.20, Concs £2.40

Contact
Church Lane, Sewerby, Bridlington
YO15 1EA

t 01262 673769
w sewerby-hall.co.uk
e sewerbyhall@yahoo.com

687 Driffield

Burton Agnes Hall

2 hrs+   Apr–Oct

An Elizabethan hall filled with treasures collected by the Agnes family over four centuries, ranging from the original carving and plasterwork to a large collection of Impressionist and contemporary paintings. Contemporary commissions include tapestry by Kaffe Fassett.

* Life-size board games in garden including a maze
* Walled Elizabethan garden and *potager*

Location
On A614 between Bridlington & York

Opening
Daily Apr–Oct 11am–5pm

Admission
Adult £5.20, Child £2.60, Concs £4.70
Grounds only half price

Contact
Driffield YO25 4NB

t 01262 490324
w burton-agnes.com
e burton.agnes@farmline.com

688 Hornsea

Hornsea Museum

1 hr+   Easter–Sep

This award-winning museum shows how village life has changed in North Holderness from the pre-industrial age of the early C17 through to post Second World War. Sited in a C18 farmhouse.

* Local industrial display, photographic exhibition
* Hornsea pottery collection

Location
Hornsea town centre, off B1242

Opening
Easter–Sep & autumn half term (&
Bank Hol Mon) Tue–Sat 11am–5pm
Sun 2–5pm

Admission
Adult £2, Child £1.50, Concs £1.50

Contact
Burns Farm, 11 Newbegin,
Hornsea HU18 1AB

t 01964 533443
w hornseamuseum.com
e contact@hornseamuseum.com

689   Kingston upon Hull

Ferens Art Gallery

1 hr+   All year

Opened in 1927, the award-winning Ferens Art Gallery combines internationally-renowned permanent collections with exhibitions and live art. The first-class permanent collection of paintings and sculpture spans the medieval period to the present day.

* European Old Masters, particularly Dutch & Flemish
* Masterpieces by, Canaletto, Spencer, Hockney

Location
City centre

Opening
Mon–Sat 10am–5pm
Sun 1.30–4.30pm

Admission
Free

Contact
Queen Victoria Square,
Kingston upon Hull HU1 3RA

t 01482 613902
w hullcc.gov.uk/museums/ferens
e museums@hull.gov.uk

690   Kingston upon Hull

Streetlife Museum of Transport

2 hrs+   All year

Major new developments, opened in 2003, include a new motor car gallery, a major extension of the popular carriage gallery, a larger street-scene with several new shops and a hands-on interactive exhibition area.

* Supported by Heritage Lottery funding

Location
High Street nr Wilberforce House

Opening
Mon–Sat 10am–5 pm
Sun 1.30pm–4.30pm

Admission
Free

Contact
High Street, Kingston upon Hull
HU1 1PS

t 01482 613902
w hullcc.gov.uk/museums/streetlife
e museums@hull.gov.uk

691   Kingston upon Hull

Wilberforce House Museum

1 hr+   All year

Birthplace of William Wilberforce, known worldwide for his fight to abolish slavery. This C17 building retains many interesting features, including the oak-panelled banqueting room. The museum also houses collections of dolls, C19 and C20 costumes and clocks.

* Tools of the trade bear stark witness to inhumanity
* Wilberforce is one of Hull's most famous sons

Location
High Street, next to Streetlife

Opening
Mon–Sat 10am–5pm
Sun 1.30–4.30pm

Admission
Free

Contact
High Sreet, Kingston upon Hull
HU1 1NQ

t 01482 613902
w hullcc.gov.uk/wilberforcehouse
e museums@hull.gov.uk

692   Pocklington

Burnby Hall Gardens

4 hrs   All year

Burnby Hall Gardens is world famous for its National Collection of water lilies, which contains more varieties than anywhere else in Europe. There is also an extensive range of ornamental trees, plants, shrubs and numerous fish and birds.

* Award–winning disabled facilities
* Two large lakes in 10 acres of beautiful gardens

Location
20 mins E of York off A1079

Opening
Apr–Sep daily 10am–5pm
Oct–Mar Mon–Fri 10am–4pm

Admission
Adult £2.70, Child £1.20, Concs £2.20
Gardens free in winter

Contact
August Cottage, 48 Burnby Lane,
Pocklington YO42 2QE

t 01759 302068
w burnbyhallgardens.co.uk
e burnbyhallgardens@hotmail.com

693 Harrogate

RHS Garden Harlow Carr

3 hrs   All year

Created from mixed woodland and pasture land in 1950, Harlow Carr's chief aim was to create a trial ground where the suitability of plants for growing in northern climates could be assessed. The garden has year-round interest for the novice and expert alike.

* Built on site of former spa (sulphur water)

Location	Contact
Off B6162, 1½ miles from Harrogate town centre	Crag Lane, Harrogate HG3 1QB
Opening	t 01423 565418
Daily 9.30am–dusk	w rhs.org.uk./gardens/harlowcarr
	e admin-harlowcarr@rhs.org.uk
Admission	
Adult £4.50, Child £1, Concs £4	
RHS members free	

694 Knaresborough

Knaresborough Castle & Museum

2 hrs   Easter–Sep

Towering over the River Nidd, Knaresborough Castle symbolises the wealth of the medieval kings. Today's remains date from C14, although the moat is from the time of King John. Explore the keep and dungeon and the English Civil War gallery.

* Daily guided tours
* Special events programme throughout the year

Location	Contact
Signed from the centre of Knaresborough	c/o Royal Pump Room Museum, Crown Place, Harrogate HG1 2RY
Opening	t 01423 556188
Good Friday–Sep daily 10.30am–5pm	w harrogate.gov.uk/museums
	e lg23@harrogate.gov.uk
Admission	
Adult £2, Child £1.25, Concs £1.50	

695 Helmsley

Duncombe Park

3 hrs   Easter–Oct

Used as a girl's school for 60 years, Duncombe Park has been restored as a grand family home (200 rooms), housing a fine collection of English and Continental furniture. Naturally landscaped gardens, fine views over valley and moors.

* 450 acres of parkland is National Nature Reserve
* Waymarked walks through woods and river valley

Location	Contact
1 mile from Helmsley centre	Helmsley YO62 5EB
Opening	t 01439 770 213
Daily 11am–5.30pm	w duncombepark.com
House by guided tour only	e info@duncombepark.com
12.30–3.30pm every 30 mins	
Admission	
Adult £6.50, Child £3, Concs £5	

696 Knaresborough

Mother Shipton's Cave

1 hr+   Feb–Nov

Mother Shipton is perhaps England's most famous prophetess, foretelling the Spanish Armada and the Great Fire of London. She lived 500 years ago during the reign of King Henry VIII and Queen Elizabeth I. Cave, petrifying well and 12 acres of historic woodland park.

* Visitor attraction for 300 years
* Free all day parking

Location
Signposted from A1 on A51

Opening
Mar–Oct daily 9.30am–5.45pm
Nov & Feb Sat & Sun 10am–4.30pm
Closed Dec & Jan

Admission
Adult £4.95, Child £3.75, Concs £4.25

Contact
Prophecy House,
Knaresborough HG5 8DD
t 01423 864600
w mothershipton.co.uk
e adrian@mothershipton.co.uk

697 Leyburn

Constable Burton Hall

1 hr+   Mar–Oct

Set in the beautiful countryside of Wensleydale, this extensive romantic garden is surrounded by C18 parkland and a superb John Carr house (not open). Fine trees combine with an interesting collection of alpines and extensive shrubs and roses. New water garden.

* Tulip festival early May (check website for details)
* House tours sometimes available (01677 460225)

Location
3 miles E of Leyburn on A684

Opening
Mar 22–Oct 14 daily 9am–6pm

Admission
Adult £2.50, Child 50p, Concs £2

Contact
Leyburn DL8 5LJ
t 01677 450428
w constableburtonhallgardens.co.uk
e enquiries@constableburtonhall
    gardens.co.uk

698 Malton

Eden Camp
Modern History Museum

4 hrs   All year

In this military museum, historical scenes are reconstructed using movement, lighting, sound, smells and smoke machines. Attractions include an original prisoner of war camp built in 1942. New exhibition areas being opened.

* Covers complete C20 British military history
* Multiple award-winning attraction

Location
At the junction of A64 with A169

Opening
Daily 10am–5pm
Closed Dec 24–2nd Mon in Jan

Admission
Adult £4, Child £3, Concs £3

Contact
Malton YO17 6RT
t 01653 697777
w edencamp.co.uk
e admin@edencamp.co.uk

699 Middleham

Middleham Castle

1 hr Apr–Dec

The commanding views from this impressive fortress cover an area that has been inhabited by prehistoric, Roman, Viking and Norman settlers. The formidable stone keep was one of the largest in England. Many modifications have been made over the centuries.

* Childhood home of Richard III
* *James Herriott's Yorkshire* was filmed in the area

Location
2 miles S of Leyburn on A6108

Opening
Apr–Sep daily 10am–6pm
Oct daily 10am–5pm
Nov–Dec daily 10am–1pm & 2–4pm
Jan–Mar Wed–Sun 10am–1pm & 2–4pm

Admission
Adult £3, Child £1.50, Concs £2.30

Contact
Castle Hill, Middleham, Leyburn DL8 4QR
t 01969 623899
w english-heritage.org.uk

700 Ripley

Ripley Castle & Gardens

2 hrs+ All year

Home to the Ingilby family for over 700 years, the castle is famous as the place where Jane Ingilby held Oliver Cromwell at gunpoint. Impressive collection of arms and armour from the English Civil War. Extensive hot houses, gardens and grounds.

* Guided tours leave front door every 15–30 mins
* Home to the National Collection of hyacinths

Location
3 miles N of Harrogate on the A61

Opening
Jun–Aug daily 10.30am–3.30pm
Sep–May Tue, Thu, Sat, Sun & Bank Hols

Admission
Adult £6, Child £3.50, Concs £5

Contact
The Ripley Castle Estate, Harrogate HG3 3AY
t 01423 770152
w ripleycastle.co.uk
e enquiries@ripleycastle.co.uk

701 Ripon

Fountains Abbey & Studley Royal Estate

2 hrs+ All year

While the spectacular ruins of this C12 Cistercian Abbey are undoubtedly the star attraction, you will also find interesting historic buildings including a 500 strong deer park and Victorian church, as well as an elegant C18 landscape garden with water features and follies.

* Best surviving example of a monastic mill
* Declared a World Heritage site in 1987

Location
4 miles W of Ripon

Opening
Jan Sat–Thu 10am–4pm
Feb–Mar daily 10am–4pm
Apr–Sep daily 10am–6pm
Oct daily 10am–4pm
Nov–Dec Sat–Thu 10am–4pm

Admission
Adult £5.50, Child £3

Contact
Ripon HG4 3DY
t 01765 608 888
w fountainsabbey.org.uk
e webinfo@fmtp.ntrust.org.uk

702 Ripon

Newby Hall & Gardens

4 hrs Apr–Sep

One of England's renowned Adam houses, this is an exceptional example of C18 interior decoration, recently restored to its original beauty. Contents include the Gobelins tapestry room, a renowned gallery of classical statues and some of Chippendale's finest furniture.

* 25 acres of award-winning gardens
* Miniature railway, woodland walk and special events

Location
Off the B6265 between Boroughbridge & Ripon

Opening
Apr–Sep Tue–Sun + Bank Hols 11am–5pm

Admission
Adult £7.20, Child £4.70, Concs £6.20

Contact
Ripon HG4 5AE
t 01423 322 583
w newbyhall.com
e info@newbyhall.com

703 Skipton

Bolton Abbey

2 hrs+   All year

This estate covers 30,000 acres of beautiful countryside in the Yorkshire Dales. There are medieval buildings, C12 priory ruins to explore, and 80 miles of moorland, woodland and riverside footpaths. Guide book and walks leaflet available.

* Landscape was inspiration for Wordsworth & Turner
* Grounds include 6-mile stretch of River Wharfe

Location	Contact
Between Harrogate & Skipton, off A59 on B6160	Skipton BD23 6EX
	t 01756 718009
Opening	w boltonabbey.com
Daily 9am–dusk	e tourism@boltonabbey.com
Admission	
Vehicle pass £4 (occupants free) £2.50 for disabled badge holders	

704 Skipton

Skipton Castle

1 hr+   All year

Over 900 years old, Skipton Castle is one of England's most complete and best-preserved medieval castles – surviving a three-year siege during the English Civil War. Climb from the depths of the dungeons to the very top of the watch tower, and visit the fantastic book shop.

* View banqueting hall, kitchen, bedchambers
* Comprehensive tour sheets

Location	Contact
Centre of Skipton	Skipton BD23 1AQ
Opening	t 01756 792442
Mar–Sep Mon–Sat 10am–6pm,	w skiptoncastle.co.uk
Sun 12 noon–6pm	e info@skiptoncastle.co.uk
Oct–Feb 10am–4pm. Closed Dec 25	
Admission	
Adult £5, Child £2.50, Concs £4.40	

705 Whitby

Captain Cook Memorial Museum

1 hr   All year

The museum houses a collection of exhibits about Cook's Whitby years and his later achievements, and includes unique items of great historical importance. It is located in the old house by the harbourside where Cook was apprenticed in 1746.

* Four floors of rooms to visit in the house
* Temporary exhibit of the lost treasures of Captain Cook

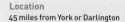

Location	Contact
45 miles from York or Darlington	Grape Lane, Whitby YO22 4BA
Opening	t 01947 601900
Mar Sat & Sun 11am–3pm	w cookmuseumwhitby.co.uk
Apr–Oct daily 9.45am–5pm	e captcookmuseumwhitby@ ukgateway.net
Admission	
Adult £3, Child £2, Concs £2.50	

706 York

The Bar Convent

  1 hr+   Mon–Fri

The oldest working convent in England (established in 1686). The foundress of the order, Mary Ward, was a pioneer of education for women and its members ran a school for 299 years. The Bar Convent museum tells the early history of Christianity in the North of England.

* C18 neo–classical chapel still used for weekly service
* School moved to comprehensive system in 1985

Location	Contact
2 mins walk from train station	17 Blossom Street, York YO24 1AQ
Opening	
Museum tours, Mon–Fri 10.30am & 2.30pm. 10am–5pm for non tours	t 01904 643 238
	w bar-convent.org.uk
	e info@bar-convent.org.uk
Admission	
Adult £3, Child £1, Concs £2	

707 York

Clifford's Tower

  ½ hr   All year

Clifford's Tower is all that remains of York Castle. The original wooden tower was burned down during anti-Jewish riots. The height of the motte was increased and the tower was rebuilt in stone. Today the tower is just a shell, but you can climb to the top for a good view of York.

* Used as prison after English Civil War
* Castle continued to be used for executions until 1896

Location	Contact
Eye of York, opposite York Castle museum	Tower Street, York YO1 9SA
Opening	t 01904 646940
Apr–Sep daily 10am–6pm (Oct 5pm)	w english-heritage.org.uk/ cliffordstower.com
Nov–Mar 10am–4pm	e cliffords.tower@ english-heritage.org.uk
Admission	
Adult £2.50, Child £1.30, Concs £1.90	

708 York

Castle Howard

   2 hrs+   Feb–Nov

One of Britain's finest stately homes, located in the beautiful Howardian hills. The magnificent house is distinguished by its famous dome and inside there are enormous collections of important art treasures. Spectacular gardens form part of 10,000 acre estate.

* Archaelogical dig, uncovering a medieval village
* Outdoor guided tours and historical characters

Location	Contact
15 miles NE of York	Nr York YO60 7DA
Opening	t 01653 648 333
Feb–Oct 11am–4pm	w castlehoward.co.uk
Admission	e house@castlehoward.co.uk
Adult £9.50, Child £6.50, Concs £8.50 3-day passes	

709 York

Fairfax House

³/₄ hr   All year

Designed by John Carr of York, Fairfax House typifies the best of mid-C18 rococo decoration. After years of neglect and decay, the house was restored in the 1980s and the house is furnished with a superb collection of Georgian furniture.

* Restoration of stucco ceiling took 20,000 man hours
* Regular changing exhibitions

Location
City centre near Jorvik Centre

Opening
Mon–Thu & Sat 11am–5pm, Fri guided tour only 11am & 2pm, Sun 1.30–5pm, Closed Jan 7–Feb 14

Admission
Adult + 1 child £4.50, each additional Child £1.75, Concs £3.75

Contact
Castlegate, York YO1 9RN

t 01904 655543
w fairfaxhouse.co.uk
e peterbrown@fairfaxhouse.co.uk

710 York

Jorvik

1 hr   All year

Discover what life was like over 1,000 years ago, see over 800 Viking items uncovered here, and journey through a reconstruction of actual Viking-age streets. Witness the skills of Viking craftsmen in a new interactive exhibition – Fearsome Craftsmen!

* Jorvik is the name given to York by Vikings in AD975
* Wheelchair users please ring 01904 543402

Location
A64 to York

Opening
Apr–Oct daily 10am–5pm
Nov–Mar daily 10am–4pm

Admission
Adult £7.20, Child £5.10, Concs £6.10

Contact
Jorvik, Coppergate, York YO1 9WT

t 01904 543403 / 643211
w jorvik-viking-centre.co.uk
e jorvik@yorkarchaeology.co.uk

711 York

Yorkshire Air Museum

3 hrs   All year

A fascinating museum authentically based on a Second World War Bomber Command station. The unique displays include the original control tower, air gunners collection, Barnes Wallis' prototype 'bouncing bomb' and an airborne forces display.

* See the only restored Halifax bomber
* Historical aircraft from earliest days of flight

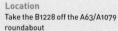 

Location
Take the B1228 off the A63/A1079 roundabout

Opening
Summer (Apr–Sep) daily 10am–5pm
Winter daily 10am–3.30pm

Admission
Adult £5, Child £3, Concs £4

Contact
Halifax Way, Elvington, York YO41 4AU

t 01904 608595
w yorkshireairmuseum.co.uk
e museum@yorkshireair
   museum.co.uk

712 York

National Railway Museum

3 hrs+   All year

The collection includes 103 locomotives and 177 items of rolling stock from the Rocket to the Eurostar. Permanent displays include Palaces on Wheels with pre-Victorian royal saloons and a Japanese Bullet Train.

* See 'Mallard' the world's fastest steam locomotive
* Literally millions of photographs and artefacts

Location
600 yards from railway station, signed from centre

Opening
Daily 10am–6pm closed Dec 24–26

Admission
Free except for special events

Contact
Leeman Road, YO26 4XJ

t 01904 621261
w nrm.org.uk
e nrm@nmsi.ac.uk

---

713 York

York Art Gallery

1 hr+   All year

See some of Europe's finest art with examples of oil and canvas, watercolours and ceramics. The gallery houses 600 years of British and European art, from the time of the Wars of the Roses right up to the present day.

* Outstanding collection of pioneer studio pottery
* Full programme of temporary exhibitions

Location
Opposite Tourist Information Centre, 3 mins walk from Minster

Opening
Daily 10am–5pm
Closed Dec 25/26 & Jan 1

Admission
Free

Contact
Exhibition Square, York YO1 7EW

t 01904 697979
w yorkartgallery.org.uk
e art.gallery@ymt.org.uk

---

714 York

York Castle Museum

1½ hr   All year

Experience life as a Victorian. Walk down cobbled streets and peer through windows of shops long gone. Take a journey through 400 years of life in Britain, from parlours to prisons, marriages to the mill house and see the toys that children used to treasure.

* Stumble into the underworld of the highwayman
* City at War exhibition

Location
City Centre

Opening
Daily 9.30am–5pm
Closed Dec 25/26, Jan 1

Admission
Adult £6, Child & Concs £3.50

Contact
Eye of York, York YO1 9RY

t 01904 650333
w york.trust.museum
e castle.museum@ymt.org.uk

715 York

York Dungeons

  1 hr All year

Deep in the heart of historic York, buried beneath its paving stones, lies the north of England's most chilling horror attraction. The York Dungeon brings more than 2,000 years of gruesomely authentic history vividly back to life.

* See how torture was part of everyday life until C19

Location
City centre

Opening
Oct–Mar daily 10.30am–4.30ppm
Apr–Sep daily 10am–5pm

Admission
Adult £8.95, 10–14 years £6.95, 5–9 years £4.95 under 5s free, Concs £7.95

Contact
The York Dungeon,
12 Clifford Street, York YO1 9RD

t 01904 632599
w thedungeons.com
e yorkdungeons@
merlinentertainments.biz

716 Barnsley

Elsecar Heritage Centre

 3 hrs All year

This award-winning history and craft centre is set in the attractive conservation village of Elsecar. Two beautiful antique centre buildings, a taste of railways past on the steam railway and historical insight in the living history centre.

* Set in former ironworks and colliery workshop
* Canal-side walks

Location
Exit M1 at junction 36 and follow signs

Opening
Daily 10am–5pm

Admission
Free, exhibitions may charge

Contact
Wath Road, Elsecar, Barnsley S74 8HJ

t 01226 740203
w barnsley.gov.uk
e elsecarheritagecentre@
barnsley.gov.uk

717 York

Yorkshire Museum & Gardens

  2 hrs All year

Walk in the footsteps of Romans and Vikings. See beasts turned to stone from a time when dinosaurs ruled the planet and a host of outstanding archaeological finds. The museum is set in 10 acres of botanical gardens.

* Ruins of St Mary's Abbey in grounds
* Preserved section of York's Roman fortress

Location
5–10 mins walk from railway station

Opening
Daily 10am–5pm

Admission
Adult £4, Concs £2.50

Contact
Museum Gardens, York YO1 7FR

t 01904 687687
w york.trust.museum
e yorkshire.museum@ymt.org.uk

718 Conisbrough

Conisbrough Castle

  2 hrs+ All year

The white, circular keep of this C12 castle is a spectacular structure made of magnesian limestone and is the oldest of its kind in England. Recently restored, with two new floors and a roof, it is a fine example of medieval architecture.

* Inspiration for Sir Walter Scott's classic novel *Ivanhoe*
* Closed for private functions some summer Saturdays

Location
NE of Conisbrough town centre on A630

Opening
Apr–Sep daily 10am–5pm
Oct–Mar daily 10am–4pm

Admission
Adult £3.75, Child £2.00, Concs £2.50

Contact
Castle Hill, Conisbrough DN12 3BU

t 01709 863329
w conisbroughcastle.org.uk
e info@conisbroughcastle.org.uk

719 Doncaster

Brodsworth Hall & Gardens

3 hrs Apr–Oct

One of England's most complete Victorian country houses, Brodsworth reflects the opulence of the 1860s with a stunning interior that belies the Italianate exterior. The work was commissioned by Charles Thelluson who inherited the Brodsworth estate in 1859.

* Gardens are classic examples of 1860s design
* Newly restored summer house

Location
5 miles NW of Doncaster off A635 or junction 37 off A1

Opening
House Apr–Sep Tue–Sun + Bank Hols 1pm–6pm.
Gardens Tue–Sun 12noon–6pm
Mon 11am–4pm

Admission
Adult £6, Child £3, Concs £4.50

Contact
Doncaster DN5 7XJ

t 01302 722598
w english-heritage.org.uk

720 Doncaster

Earth Centre

3 hrs+ All year

This amazing collection of attractions is centred around a mission to achieve a better understanding of sustainable development in everyday life. Attractions include indoor and outdoor exhibitions, unique 'eco' buildings, adventure playgrounds, gardens and wetlands.

* Built above two old collieries
* Recycling exhibition has attracted huge media attention

Location
From junction 36 of A1M follow signs along A630 and A6023

Opening
Mar 30–Sep 29 daily 10am–5pm
Sep 30–Mar 29 10am–3.30pm

Admission
Pricing by attractions used – see

website, £10 for access to all adventure activities, other prices vary

Contact
Denaby Main, Doncaster DN12 4EA

t 01709 513 933
w earthcentre.org.uk
e info@earthcentre.org.uk

721 Maltby

Roche Abbey

1 hr Apr–Oct

Founded in 1147, the fine early-Gothic transepts of this Cistercian monastery still survive to their original height. In the C18, Capability Brown transformed an already beautiful valley incorporating the ruins. Excavation has revealed the complete layout of the abbey.

* See web site for full programme of special events

Location
1½ miles S of Maltby off A634

Opening
Apr–Sep daily 10am–6pm
Oct 10am–5pm

Admission
Adult £2, Child £1, Concs £1.50

Contact
The Abbey Lodge, Maltby, nr Rotherham S66 8NW

t 01709 812739
w english-heritage.org.uk

722 Rotherham

Magna Science Adventure Centre

3 hrs+   All year

Set within a vast former steelworks, Magna is a new, hands-on visitor attraction that explores the powerful themes of earth, air, fire and water. Operate a real JCB, fire a water cannon or explode a rock face. Visit four pavilions, two shows and the outdoor adventure park.

* Feel the force of a tornado in the air pavilion
* Test your bravery as a virtual fireball races at you

Location
Just off M1, 1 mile along A6178 from Meadowhall shopping centre

Opening
Daily 10am–5pm

Admission
Adult £9, Child £7 & Concs £7

Contact
Sheffield Road, Templeborough, Rotherham S60 1DX

t 01709 720002
w visitmagna.co.uk
e info@magnatrust.co.uk

724 Sheffield

Millennium Galleries

2 hrs+   All year

With four individual galleries under one roof, there is something for everybody to enjoy. Explore treasures from the past, masterpieces from Britain's national collections and discover new creations by contemporary artists and makers.

* Material regularly borrowed from Tate and V&A
* Metalwork gallery

Location
City centre near the Winter Garden

Opening
Mon–Sat 10am–5pm
Sun 11am–5pm

Admission
Free, exhibitions may charge

Contact
Arundel Gate, Sheffield S1 2PP

t 0114 278 2600
w sheffieldgalleries.org.uk
e info@sheffieldgalleries.org.uk

723 Sheffield

The Graves Art Gallery

1 hr   All year

Displays the city's collections of C19 and C20 British and European Art. The collection encapsulates the story of the development of modern art, the main trends traced through works by many well-known artists including Picasso, Pierre Bonnard and Sir Stanley Spencer.

* Exciting programme of temporary exhibitions
* Restored to 1930s splendour in 2001

Location
City centre above Central Library

Opening
Mon–Sat 10am–5pm

Admission
Free

Contact
Surrey Street, Sheffield S1 1XZ

t 0114 278 2600
w sheffieldgalleries.org.uk
e info@sheffieldgalleries.org.uk

725 Bradford

Cartwright Hall

1 hr　　All year

Bradford's impressive art gallery was opened in 1904 with an important donation of Victorian and Edwardian works. The hall set in parkland offers exciting temporary exhibitions plus permanent art collections, including C20 British artists.

* Comprehensive educational programme
* Superb multicultural gallery

Location	Contact
Off the A650 Keighly Road, 1 mile from centre	Lister Park, Bradford BD9 4NS
Opening	t 01274 431212
Tue–Sat & Bank Hols 10am–5pm Sun 1–5pm	w bradford.gov.uk
	e cartwrighthall@bradford.gov.uk
Admission	
Free	

726 Bradford

Colour Museum

1 hr　　All year

Britain's only museum of colour. The Colour Museum is the place to come and find out about the weird and wonderful world of colour. Along with its interactive galleries and special exhibitions, the museum holds workshops on all aspects of colour.

* Situated in a former wool warehouse
* Workshops and educational programme (see website)

Location	Contact
City centre, near Metro Interchange	PO Box 244, Perkin House, 1 Providence Street, Bradford BD1 2PW
Opening	t 01274 390955
Tue–Sat 10am–4pm. Closed between Christmas and New Year	w sdc.org.uk/museum
	e museum@sdc.org.uk
Admission	
Adults £2, Child £1.50, Concs £1.50	

727 Bradford

Moorside Mill

3 hrs　　All year

Moorside Mills, an original spinning mill, is alive with magnificent machinery which once converted raw wool into worsted cloth. The mill yard rings to the sound of iron on stone as the shire horses pull a horse tram, or haul a horse-bus.

* Experience the sounds and smells of the engines
* Demonstrations of combing, spinning and weaving

Location	Contact
On the outer ring road, follow signs for the airport	Moorside Road, Eccleshill, Bradford BD2 3HP
Opening	t 01274 435900
Tue–Sat 10am–5pm, Sun & Bank Hols 12noon–5pm	w visitbradford.com
Admission	
Free	

728 Bradford

National Museum of Photography, Film & Television

2 hrs+　　All year

This is one of the most visited national museums outside London. It is located in Bradford in recognition of the city's historic contribution to the development of cinema and film-making in the UK. The museum's archive includes the first negative and the earliest television footage.

* First moving pictures – 1888 film of Leeds Bridge
* More than 3 million historical items

Location	Contact
City centre off Little Horton Lane	Bradford BD1 1NQ
Opening	t 0870 70 10 200
Tue–Sun 10am–6pm & Bank & Public Hols	w nmpft.org.uk
	e talk.nmpft@nmsi.ac.uk
Admission	
Free, except for cinemas	

729 Cleckheaton

Red House

1 hr+   All year

This house, which features in *Shirley*, was once the home to Charlotte Brontë's close friend, Mary Taylor. Beautifully furnished as a family home of the 1830s, there is also an exhibition detailing Charlotte's connections with the area and her local friendships.

* Listen in to Charlotte Brontë's correspondence
* Recreated 1830s garden

Location
Exit M62 at junction 26, follow A58 to Leeds then take A651

Opening
Mon–Fri 11am–5pm
Sat & Sun 12 noon–5pm

Admission
Free

Contact
Oxford Road, Gomersal BD19 4JP

t 01274 335100
w bronte-country.com/redhse.html

730 Hebden Bridge

Heptonstall Museum

1 hr   Easter–Oct

This museum is housed in a building which was once a school and a bank – remnants of both can still be seen. You can discover the interior of a weaver's cottage and displays of local industries such as clogmaking. See village life through the ages.

* Ideal starting point to explore this beautiful village
* Collection of local historical photography

Location
Signed from Heptonstall and Hebden Bridge

Opening
Easter-Oct Sat-Sun & Bank Hols
11am-4pm

Admission
Adult £2, Concs £1

Contact
Church Yard Bottom, Heptonstall, Hebden Bridge HX7 7PL

t 01422 843 738
w calderdale.gov.uk

731 Halifax

Bankfield Museum

1 hr   All year

Set within an Italianate mansion this former home of textile-mill owner Edward Ackroyd houses an impressive, internationally renowned collection of textiles. Specialising in contemporary craft with a diverse programme of exhibitions throughout the year.

* The Duke of Wellington Regiment permanent exhibit
* Family events, hands on craft and competitions

Location
On A647, 1 mile from Halifax town centre

Opening
Tue-Sat 10am-5pm, Sun 2-5pm
Bank Hols 10am-5pm

Admission
Free

Contact
Boothtown Road, Halifax HX3 6HG

t 01422 354 823
w calderdale.gov.uk
e bankfield_museum@
calderdale.gov.uk

732 Halifax

Shibden Hall

1 hr+   All year

Built in 1420, the hall was home to the Lister family for over 300 years. It contains furnishings from several different centuries. The barn houses a collection of horse drawn-vehicles and the folk museum is a reconstruction of an early C19 village.

* See coopers, wheelwrights, pharmacies, a Crispin Inn and an old ale brewery

Location
Signposted from Halifax and the M62

Opening
Mar-Nov Mon-Sat 10am-5pm
Sun 12 noon-5pm
Dec-Feb Mon-Sat 10am-4pm
Sun 12 noon-4pm

Admission
Adult £3.50, Child & Concs £2.50

Contact
Lister's Road, Halifax HX3 6XG

t 01422 352 246
w calderdale.gov.uk/tourism
e shibden.hall@calderdale.gov.uk

733 Keighley

Brontë Parsonage Museum

1 hr+   All year

The parsonage, built in 1778–79, was the lifelong home of the Brontë family opened as a museum in 1928 and contains the Brontës' own furniture and possessions, bringing the rooms to life as they would have been in the time of the Brontës.

* Examples of the world-famous little books
* Family clothes and furniture – including writing desks

Location
8 miles W of Bradford & 3 miles S of Keighley

Opening
Apr–Sep daily 10am–5.30pm
Oct–Mar 11am–5pm (closed Jan)

Admission
Adult £4.80, Child £1.50, Concs £3.50

Contact
Haworth, Keighley BD22 8DR

t 01535 642323
w bronte@bronte.org.uk

734 Keighley

Cliffe Castle Museum & Gallery

1 hr+   All year

Cliffe Castle was built between 1875 and 1882, as an elaborate mansion for textile mill-owner, Henry Isaac Butterfield. Set in an attractive hillside park, this museum specializes in natural history and geology and pottery, stained glass and fine furniture.

* Collection of toys and dolls
* See fossil of local 300-million-year-old giant newt

Location
On A629 N of town centre

Opening
Tue–Sat & Bank Hols 10am–5pm
Sun 12noon–5pm

Admission
Free

Contact
Spring Gardens Lane,
Keighley BD20 6LH

t 01535 618231
w bradford.gov.uk/
tourism/museums

735 Leeds

Harewood House & Bird Gardens

3–4 hr   Mar–Oct

This is one of the country's premier avian collections. Over 100 species of threatened and exotic birds are housed in sympathetic environments with the aim of promoting conservation and education. The Capability Brown gardens also provide many attractions.

* Boat trips across the lake
* Extensive collections of art and furniture in the house

Location
On A61, 7 miles from Leeds & Harrogate

Opening
Mar 17–Oct 31 daily 10am–5pm

Admission
All Attractions Adult £10, Child £5.50, Concs £8.25

Grounds £7.25, £4.50, £6.25

Contact
Harewood Estate, Harewood, Leeds LS17 9LQ

t 0113 218 1010
w harewood.org
e info@harewood.org

736 Leeds

Leeds City Art Gallery

2 hrs   All year

There is something for everyone at Leeds City Art Gallery from traditional prints, watercolours, paintings and sculptures to contemporary works made with plastic grapes and twintubs. Some of the most outstanding works of British art outside of London.

* Designated as a collection of national importance
* Features work by Turner, Rembrandt & Henry Moore

Location
City centre, next to central library

Opening
Mon–Sat 10am–5pm
Wed 10am–8pm, Sun 1–5pm
Closed on Bank Hols

Admission
Free

Contact
The Headrow, Leeds LS1 3AA

t 0113 247 8248
w leeds.gov.uk/gallery

737 Leeds

Royal Armouries Museum

4 hrs   All year

The Royal Armouries Museum in Leeds was opened in 1996 as the new home for the national collection of arms and armour. Five themed galleries cover war, tournament, self-defence, hunting and the arms and armour of the Orient.

* See Henry VIII's tournament armour
* Live action events and interactive technology

Location
S of Leeds city centre, near junction 4 of M621

Opening
Daily 10am–5pm

Admission
Free, on-site parking £3

Contact
Armouries Drive, Leeds LS10 1LT

t 08700 344344
w armouries.org.uk
e enquiries@armouries.org.uk

738 Leeds

Thackray Museum

3 hrs   All year

Established in a former workhouse building adjacent to St James's Hospital, the museum houses displays which show how people's lives have changed over the last 150 years as a result of improvements in public health, medicine and healthcare.

* Vast range of surgical instruments from C19 to today
* Unique collection of pharmacy ceramics

Location	Admission
Follow signs for St James's Hospital, museum is 100 yards past main entrance	Adult £4.90, Child £3.50, Concs £3.90 Parking £1
Opening	**Contact**
Daily 10am–5pm, last admission 3pm	Beckett Street, Leeds LS9 7LN
	t 0113 244 4343
	w thackraymuseum.org
	e info@thackraymuseum.org

739 Wakefield

National Coalmining Museum

3 hrs+   All year

Tours take visitors 460 feet (140 m) underground and trace mining techniques and conditions through the ages from the C19 when women and children worked underground, to how pit ponies were used before mechanical systems were implemented.

* Exhibition of modern mining methods
* Each guide is a former local miner

Location	Contact
On the A642 between Wakefield and Huddersfield	Caphouse Colliery, New Road, Overton, Wakefield WF4 4RH
Opening	t 01924 848806
Daily 10am–5pm	w ncm.org.uk
Closed Dec 24–26, & Jan 1	e info@ncm.org.uk
Admission	
Free	

740 Wakefield

Nostell Priory

2 hrs+   Mar-Oct

Nostell Priory takes its name from the priory dedicated to St Oswald founded here in the C12. It is most famous for its magnificent plasterwork interiors by the architects Robert Adam and James Paine and its superb collection of furniture by Thomas Chippendale.

* Art includes Pieter Brueghel & Angelica Kauffman
* Lakeside walks

Location
On the A638 5 miles SE of Wakefield towards Doncaster

Opening
Mar 27-Oct 31 Wed-Sun 1-5pm
Nov 6-Dec 19 Sat-Sun 12 noon-4.30pm

Admission
Adult £5, Child £2.50

Contact
Doncaster Road, Nostell,
Wakefield WF4 1QE

t 01924 863892
w nationaltrust.org.uk/nostellpriory
e nostellpriory@nationaltrust.org.uk

741 Wakefield

Wakefield Cathedral

½ hr+   All year

This site has been a place of worship since Anglo-Saxon times, but the current building of the Cathedral Church of All Saints dates from the C14. Along with the tallest spire in Yorkshire it boasts a fine collection of stained glass and wood carvings.

* The cathedral shop stocks books, music and souvenirs

Location
City centre

Opening
8am-5pm. Call for service times or visit our website.

Admission
Free, but contributions are welcome

Contact
Cathedral office, Northgate,
Wakefield WF1 1HG

t 01924 373923
w wakefield-cathedral.org.uk
e admin@wakefield-cathedral.org.uk

742 Wakefield

Yorkshire Sculpture Park

2 hrs+   All year

One of Europe's leading open-air gallerys showing modern and contemporary work by leading UK and international artists. A changing programme of exhibitions, displays and projects is held throughout 500 acres of C18 landscaped grounds.

* Three indoor galleries
* New underground gallery for summer 2004

Location
1 mile from M1 junction 38 on A637

Opening
Summer 10am-6pm
Winter 10am-5pm

Admission
Free, parking £2

Contact
West Bretton, Wakefield WF4 4LG

t 01924 830 302
w ysp.co.uk
e info@ysp.co.uk

Lake Windemere, Cumbria

North West

Cheshire Cumbria Greater Manchester
Lancashire Merseyside

GWYNEDD

666 662
660 Conwy
659 Colwyn Bay
658
Llandudno
Great Ormes Head
Blaenau Ffestiniog
Ffestiniog
Bala
Betws-y-coed
Bethesda
Llanfairfechan
Abergele
Rhyl
Prestatyn
Llanrwst
CONWY
DENBIGHSHIRE
Ruthin
Denbigh
St Asaph
Holywell
Mold
Flint
FLINTSHIRE
657
656
Llangollen
Ruabon
Oswestry
Ellesmere
Wem
667
Wrexham
WREXHAM
762
Whitchurch
763
Nantwich
Crewe
CHESHIRE
Winsford
Middlewich
Northwich
756
Frodsham
755
Chester
744-745
747
844
840-843
Birkenhead
867
847-864
Bootle
Crosby
Skelmersdale
Formby
865-866
Southport
823
Ormskirk
800-803
Blackpool
Kirkham
817 Fleetwood
Garstang
824-827
Lytham St Anne's
Preston
M55
Leyland
Standish
Wigan
830
814
Chorley
828
798-799
804-811
818
829
Blackburn
Rawtenstall
Todmorden
796-797 730
Burnley
Nelson
Colne
815
816
795
733
734
703-704
Skipton
Ilkley
Keighley
Bingley
Shipley
Yeadon
731-732 725-728
729 739
723-724
716
693
Harrogate
LEEDS
LEEDS & BRADFORD
BRADFORD
Brighouse
Halifax
Huddersfield
Battey
Rochdale
Middleton
Oldham
Bolton
Bury
Salford
MANCHESTER
831-839
760-761 Stockport
Glossop
Penistone
Stocksbridge
SHEFFIELD
Peak District
438
439
440
436
446
441
449
448
Matlock
Bakewell
Buxton
Whaley Bridge
750-754
Knutsford
Wilmslow
758
746
551
Congleton
Biddulph
Kidsgrove
550
Newcastle-under-Lyme
STOKE-ON-TRENT
556 561-562
557
566
Leek
Stone
Uttoxeter
Market Drayton
STAFFORDSHIRE
Ashbourne
Belper
Alfreton
Clay Cross
Dronfield
445
442-444
DERBY
Wirksworth
Burton upon
443
765
766
759
845-846
LIVERPOOL
Widnes
Runcorn
757
Warrington
764
743
Altrincham
748-749
Sale
M62
M57
M58
M56
M6
M60
M61
M62
M65
M66
M67
M621
M1
Kirkby
St Helens
Pennines
550/561
543
CWMBRAN
DENBIGH
Lanwrst

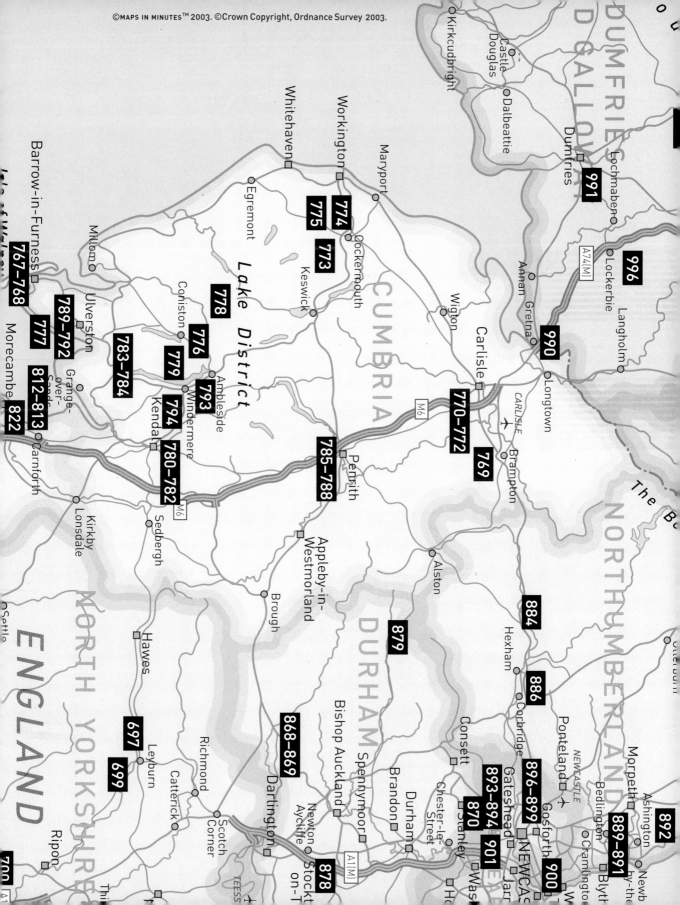

DUMFRIES
D GALLOWAY

Castle
Douglas
Kirkcudbright
Dalbeattie
Lochmaben
Dumfries
991

A74(M)
Lockerbie
Langholm
996

Workington
Whitehaven
Maryport
Cockermouth
Keswick
Egremont

Wigton
Annan
Gretna
990
Longtown
CARLISLE
Carlisle
770-772
769
Brampton

774
775
773
778
776
779
793

Lake District

CUMBRIA

M6

Penrith
785-788

Barrow-in-Furness
767-768
Millom
Ulverston
Coniston
Ambleside
Windermere
Kendal
789-792
777
783-784
794
780-782
812-813
822

Grange-over-Sand
Morecambe
Carnforth

M6

Kirkby
Lonsdale

Sedbergh
Hawes
697
699

Leyburn
Richmond
Catterick
Ripon
Settle

NORTH YORKSHIRE

ENGLAND

Appleby-in-Westmorland
Brough
Alston

DURHAM
879
Bishop Auckland
Spennymoor
Brandon
Durham
Newton Aycliffe
Darlington
868-869
878
A1(M)
Stockton-on-T

Hexham
884
Corbridge
886
Consett
Chester-le-Street
Stanley

NORTHUMBERLAND

The Bo

Ponteland
NEWCASTLE
Gateshead
896-899
893-894
870
901
NEWCAS
Gosforth
900
Jarr
Was

Morpeth
Ashington
Newb
Bedlington
Cramlington
Blyth
889-891
892

TEES

MANCHESTER

MERSEYSIDE

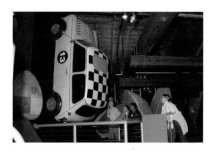

743   Altrincham

Dunham Massey

2 hrs   **Mar–Nov**

This early Georgian house was extensively renovated in the early C20. The result is one of Britain's most sumptuous Edwardian interiors, housing collections of C18 walnut furniture, paintings and Huguenot silver, as well as extensive servants' quarters.

* Plantsman's gardens with richly planted borders
* Orangery, Victorian bark house and Well house

Location	Contact
3 miles SW of Altrincham, M6 junction 19, M56 junction 7	Altrincham WA14 4SJ
Opening	t 0161 941 1025
Mar–Oct Sat–Wed 12noon–5pm	w national-trust.org.uk
Oct–Nov Sat–Wed 12noon–4pm	e dunhammassey@ntrust.org.uk
Admission	
Adult £5.80, Child £2.90	

744   Chester

Chester Cathedral

1 hr   **All year**

This is the most complete medieval monastic complex standing in the UK. Records show a church has existed on this site since the early C10, and the foundation of a Benedictine monastery in 1092. In 1541, it became the Cathedral Church of Christ and the Blessed Virgin Mary.

* Restoration in latter part of C19 by Sir Gilbert Scott
* Stunning stained glass, fabrics and sculptures

Location	Contact
Chester city centre	12 Abbey Square, Chester CH1 2HU
Opening	t 01244 324756
Mon–Sat 8am–6pm	w chestercathedral.com
Sun 12.30am–6pm	e fry@chestercathedral.com
Admission	
Free, donations welcome	

745   Chester

Grosvenor Museum

1 hr+   **All year**

This museum provides an introduction to the story of Chester from the Roman fortress of Deva, its people, army and buildings, to the present day. Visit a Roman graveyard with tombstones of the 20th Legion's soldiers and contemplate artists' views of the city's past.

* Explore natural history of Cheshire
* Georgian house with re-created period rooms

Location	Contact
Chester city centre	27 Grosvenor Street, Chester CH1 2DD
Opening	t 01244 402008
Mon–Sat 10.30am–5pm	w clasteric.gov.uk/heritage/ museum/home.html
Sun 1pm–4pm	e srogers@chestercc.gov.uk
Admission	
Free	

746 Congleton

Little Moreton Hall

2 hrs   Mar–Dec

This moated house, with its irregular half-timbered façades opening onto a cobbled courtyard, was originally built in the mid C15. The house was extended between 1570 and 1580 when the Long Gallery was added, giving the hall its curious top-heavy look.

* A warren of rooms, some no larger than cupboards
* *Moll Flanders* and *Lady Jane* were filmed here

Location
4 miles S of Congleton on A34, 10 mins from junctions 16 & 17 of M6

Opening
Mar–Oct Wed–Sun 11.30am–5pm
Nov–Dec Sat & Sun 11.30am–4pm

Admission
Adult £5, Child £2.50

Contact
Congleton CW12 4SD
t 01260 272018
w nationaltrust.org.uk
e littlemoretonhall@ntrust.org.uk

747 Ellesmere Port

Boat Museum

4 hrs+   All year

Board some of the boats from the world's largest floating collection of traditional canal craft. Discover how people lived in homes no larger than a hallway of a modern house. Tour the Georgian and Victorian buildings full of fascinating exhibitions.

* Visit the Pump House and Power Hall
* Experience domestic life in dock workers' cottages

Location
Junction 9 off the M53, signposted

Opening
Apr–Oct daily 10am–5pm
Nov–Mar Sat–Wed 11am–4pm

Admission
Adult £5.50, Child £3.70, Concs £4.30

Contact
South Pier Road, Ellesmere Port CH65 4FW
t 0151 355 5017
w boatmuseum.org.uk
e paul.taylor@thewaterwaystrust.org

748 Knutsford

Tabley House Collection

1 hr+   Apr–Oct

The house was designed by John Carr of York and completed in 1767. With its nine-bay, south-facing central block, flanked by pavilions and quadrant passages and splendid doric portico reached by curved stairs, Tabley is the only C18 Palladian country house in the region.

* First collection of English paintings ever made
* Furniture includes pieces by Gillow & Bullock

Location
2 miles W of Knutsford, on Northwich road

Opening
Apr–Oct Thu–Sun & Bank Hols 2pm–5pm

Admission
Adult £4, Child & Concs £1.50

Contact
Knutsford WA16 0HB
t 01565 750151
w tableyhouse.co.uk
e enquiries@tableyhouse.co.uk

749 Knutsford

Tatton Park

4 hrs+   Mar–Sep

An impresive estate with over 1,000 acres of stunning parkland with herds of red and fallow deer. Its major attractions include a neo-classical mansion, Tudor hall, working farm and award-winning gardens.

* Classic car show, fine food fairs & classical concerts
* Victorian kitchens and servants' quarters

Location
Signposted from junction 19 of M6, & junction 57 of M56

Opening
Mar–Sep Tue–Sun 12 noon–5pm
Times for individual attractions vary, please phone for details

Admission
Adult £5 Child £2

Contact
Knutsford WA16 6QN
t 01625 534 400
w tattonpark.org.uk
e tatton@cheshire.gov.uk

750 Macclesfield

Adlington Hall

4 hrs Jun–Aug

The present structure dates back to 1315 and incorporates Tudor and Elizabethan architecture. Key features are the black and white Tudor manor, the south front and west wing. The great hall is supported by two oak trees from the original hunting lodge.

* Tudor, Elizabethan and Georgian archecture
* Gardens include a rose garden and wilderness area

Location
Just off the A523, follow signposts

Opening
Jun–Aug Wed 2pm–5pm

Admission
Adult £5, Child £2

Contact
Adlington, Macclesfield SK10 4LF
t 01625 820875
w adlingtonhall.com
e enquiries@adlingtonhall.com

751 Macclesfield

Capesthorne Hall

2–4 hrs Apr–Oct

A turreted, red brick C18 Jacobean-style hall. Collections include fine art, marble sculptures, tapestries, Regency, Jacobean and rococco antiques and a treasured collection of Americana and children's toys.

* Guided tours by arrangement
* Grounds include a chapel, gardens and lakes

Location
Off A34 between Manchester & Stoke-on-Trent 3 miles S of Alderly Edge, Junction 6 of the M6

Opening
Apr–Oct Sun, Wed & Bank Hols
12noon–5pm

Admission
Adult £6.50, Child £3, Concs £5.50

Contact
Siddington, Macclesfield SK11 9JY
t 01625 861 221
w capesthorne.com
e info@capesthorne.com

752 Macclesfield

Gawsworth Hall

1 hr+ Apr–Oct

An ancient manor house which includes the Fitton-family chapel, licensed in 1365. The original Norman house was rebuilt in 1480 and remodelled in 1701. A famous duel took place in 1712 between Lord Mohun and the Duke of Hamilton in which both duellists were killed.

* S. Johnson, the last professional jester, lived here
* Open-air theatre season Jun–Aug

Location
On A536 between Macclesfield & Congleton

Opening
Apr–Oct Sun–Wed 2pm–5pm
Jun–Aug daily 2pm–5pm

Admission
Adult £5, Child £2.50

Contact
Church Lane, Macclesfield SK11 9RN
t 01260 223456
w gawsworthhall.com
e enquiries@gawsworthhall.com

753 Macclesfield

Jodrell Bank Science Centre & Arboretum

2 hrs+   Mar–Oct

This is the visitor centre for the Lovell radio telescope, the Jodrell Bank observatory and the astronomy research centre of the University of Manchester features exciting displays on astronomy, earth and space.

* The 35 -acre arboretum is a tree-lover's paradise
* Environmental discovery centre

Location
Between Holmes Chapel & Chelford, on A535, 8 miles W of Macclesfield

Opening
Mar–Oct 10.30am–5.30pm
The centre is under development so check for details

Admission
Adult £1 for 3-D theatre & £3 for car park

Contact
Lower Withington , Macclesfield SK11 9DL

t 01477 571339
w jb.man.ac.uk/scicen
e visitorcentre@jb.man.ac.uk

754 Macclesfield

Macclesfield Silk Museum

2 hrs   All year

This building was once the Macclesfield School of Art, built in 1877 to train designers for the silk industry. It now houses exhibitions exploring the properties of silk, design education, Macclesfield's diverse textile industries, workers' lives and historic machinery.

* Displays of costume & textiles
* Paradise Mill contains 26 jacquard handlooms

Location
Town centre

Opening
Mon–Sat 11am–5pm
Sun & Bank Hols 1pm–5pm

Admission
Adult £3.75, Concs £2.10

Contact
Roe Street, Macclesfield SK11 6UT

t 01625 613210
w silk-macclesfield.org
e silkmuseum@tiscali.co.uk

755 Neston

Ness Botanic Gardens

1 hr+   All year

When a Liverpool cotton merchant began to create a garden in 1898, he laid the foundations of one of the major botanic gardens in the UK. Now internationally renowned, the collection includes a beathtaking collection of rhododendrons and azaleas.

* Adopt a tree scheme
* Water, rose and herb gardens

Location
6 miles from exit M53, 5 miles from Western End M56, off A540 Chester Hoylake Road

Opening
Mar–Oct 9.30am–dusk
Nov–Feb 9.30am–4pm

Admission
Adult £4.70, Child free, Concs £4.30

Contact
Ness, Neston, South Wirral CH64 4AY

t 0151 353 0123
w merseyworld.com
e nessgdns@liv.ac.uk

756 Northwich

Arley Hall & Garden

2 hrs   Apr–Sep

This charming English garden features a double herbaceous border laid out in 1846, a pleached lime avenue, giant cylinders of Quercus Ilex, topiary and collections of roses, rhododendrons and azaleas. The hall reveals fine panelling and plasterwork.

* Voted one of the top 50 gardens in Europe
* Gardens include rose and fallen timber gardens

Location
Junction 19 or 20 of the M6, or junction 9 or 10 of the M56

Opening
Apr–Sep Tue–Sun & Bank Hols 11am–5pm

Admission
Adult £4.50, Child £2, Concs £3.90

Contact
Arley, Northwich CW9 6NA

t 01565 777353
w arleyhalland gardens.com
e enquiries@arleyhalland gardens. com

757 Runcorn

Norton Priory Museum

1 hr   Mar–Nov

This 38-acre site includes a museum, a magnificent 800-year-old vaulted storage range, an historic priory, remains excavated by archaelogists, and the unique St Christopher statue. The woodland gardens are the setting for a collection of contemporary sculpture.

* Walled garden won 4 North-West-in-Bloom awards
* BBC2's *Hidden Gardens* filmed here

Location
From junction 11 off M56. Turn for Warrington and follow signposts

Opening
Nov–Mar daily 12 noon–4pm
Apr–Oct Mon–Fri 12 noon–5pm
Sat & Sun 12 noon–6pm

Admission
Adult £4.25, Concs £2.95

Contact
Tudor Road, Manor Park, Runcorn WA7 1SX

t 01928 569895
w nortonpriory.org
e info@nortonpriory.org

---

759 Scholar Green

Rode Hall

2 hrs+   Apr–Sep

The house was constructed in two stages, the earlier two-storey wing and stable block around 1705 and the main building in 1752. The house contains examples of furniture by Gillow of Lancaster, a collection of portraits and an important collection of English porcelain.

* Rode stands in a Repton landscape
* Formal rose garden was designed by Nesfield in 1860

Location
5 miles SW of Congleton between A34 and A50

Opening
Apr–Sep Wed & Bank Hols 2pm–5pm

Admission
Adult £5, Concs £3.50

Contact
Scholar Green, Cheshire ST7 3QP

t 01270 873 237
w roddehall@scholargreen.fsnet.co.uk

---

758 Sandbach

Sandbach Crosses

½ hr   All year

Rare Saxon stone crosses, carved with animals and biblical scenes, stand in the cobbled market square of Sandbach. The crosses are believed to date from the C7. Close inspection reveals the ancient carvings.

* One of the most photographed sights in Cheshire
* Restored in 1816 after destruction by iconoclasts

Location
Market Square, Sandbach

Opening
Any reasonable time

Admission
Free

Contact
English Heritage, Canada House, 3 Chepstow St, Manchester M1 5FW

t 0161 242 1400
w english-heritage.org.uk
e northwest@english-heritage.org.uk

760 Stockport

Bramall Hall

2 hrs   All year

This is a grand black and white timber-framed building. The hall was built in the traditional local style with oak framework, joined using mortice and tenon joints and held in place with oak pegs. Wattle and daub or lath and plaster were used to fill the spaces in the timbers.

* Guided tours available on request
* Beautiful landscaped grounds

Location
Junction 1 or 27 of M60

Opening
Easter–Sep Mon–Sat 1pm–5pm
Sun & Bank Hols 11am–5pm
Oct–Jan Tue–Sat 1pm–4pm
Sun & Bank Hols 11am–4pm
Jan–Easter Sat 1pm–4pm
Sun 11am–4pm

Admission
Adult £3.95, Child & Concs £2.50

Contact
Bramall Park, Stockport
SK7 3NX

t 0161 485 3708
w stockport.gov.uk
e bramall.hall@stockport.gov.uk

761 Stockport

Lyme Park

2 hrs+   Apr–Nov

Originally a Tudor house, Lyme was transformed by the Venetian architect Leoni into an Italianate palace. Some of the Elizabethan interiors survive and contrast dramatically with later rooms. The state rooms are adorned with Mortlake tapestries.

* Featured in BBC's *Pride & Prejudice*
* Important collection of English clocks

Location
On A6, 6 miles S of the city centre, signposted

Opening
Park Apr–Oct 8am–8.30pm
House Apr–Oct Fri–Tue 11am–5pm
Gardens Apr–Oct Fri–Tue 1pm–5pm

Admission
House Adult £5.80 Child £2.90
Gardens £2.70, £1.40

Contact
Disley, Stockport SK12 2NX

t 01663 762023/766492
w nationaltrust.org.uk
e lymepark@nationaltrust.org.uk

762 Tarporley

Beeston Castle

1 hr+   All year

Standing majestically on sheer, rocky crags, Beeston has stunning views. Its history stretches back more than 4,000 years, to when it was a Bronze Age hill fort. The castle was built from 1226 and soon became a royal stronghold, only falling centuries later in the English Civil War.

* Exhibition outlines the history of this strategic site
* Panoramic views of the Cheshire Plain

Location
11 miles SE of Chester on a minor road off A49

Opening
Apr–Sep daily 10am–6pm
Oct daily 10am–4pm
Nov–Mar 10am–4pm

Admission
Adult £3.20, Child £1.60, Concs £2.40

Contact
Tarporley CW6 9TX

t 01829 260464
w english-heritage.org.uk

Cheshire

763 Tarporley

Hack Green Secret Nuclear Bunker

1 hr+   Jan–Nov

One of the nation's most secret defence sites, Hack Green has played a central role in the defence of Britain for almost 60 years. Through the blast doors visitors are transported into the chilling world of the Cold War and learn what living conditions were like.

* The sounds & smells of a civil defence HQ
* Labyrinth of fully-equipped rooms and corridors

Location
Off A530 Whitchurch road, outside Nantwich, 30 mins from Chester

Opening
Mar–Oct 10.30am–5.30pm
Nov & Jan–Feb 11am–4.30pm

Admission
Adult £5.30, Child £3.30, Concs £4.30

Contact
PO Box 127, Nantwich CW5 8AQ

t 01270 623353
w hackgreen.co.uk
e coldwar@hackgreen.co.uk

764 Warrington

Warrington Museum & Art Gallery

1 hr+   All year

This museum houses exhibitions on Warrington and the surrounding area, together with exhibitions by renowned artists. Exhibitions have included etchings by Picasso and fashions by Warrington designer, Ozzie Clark. There is also a new geology gallery with a fossil-handling section.

* Tempoary exhibition programme
* Education department for schools

Location
Town centre

Opening
Mon–Fri 10am–5.30pm
Sat 10am–5pm

Admission
Free

Contact
Bold Street, Warrington WA1 1JG

t 01925 442392
w warrington.gov.uk
e museum@warrington.gov.uk

765 Widnes

Catalyst Science Discovery Centre

3 hrs+   All year

This is the only science centre solely devoted to chemistry and how the products of chemistry are used in everyday life – from medicines to Meccano. This centre aims to inform visitors about chemistry and its role in our lives, past, present and future.

* Four interactive galleries with 100+ exhibits
* Panoramic views from the roof-top observatory

Location
Junction 12 of the M56 & junction 7 of the M52

Opening
Tue–Fri & Bank Hols 10am–5pm
Sat & Sun 11am–5pm

Admission
Adult £4.95, Child £3.50

Contact
Mersey Road, Widnes WA8 0DF

t 0151 420 1121
w catalyst.org.uk
e paul@catalyst.org.uk

766 Wirral

Port Sunlight Village & Heritage Centre

4 hrs+   All year

Picturesque C19 village founded by William Hesketh Lever for his soap factory workers and named after his famous Sunlight soap. The Heritage Centre explores the history of the village and community. The Lady Lever Art Gallery houses rich and varied collections.

* C18 furniture and Wedgwood china

Location
20 mins from Liverpool, Junction 5 off the M53 take the A41 to Birkenhead, follow signposts

Opening
Apr–Oct Mon–Fri 10am–4pm
Sat–Sun 10am–4pm
Nov–Mar Mon–Fri 10am–4pm
Sat–Sun 11am–4pm

Admission
Adult £1, Child 65p

Contact
95 Greendale Road, Port Sunlight, Wirral CH62 4XE

t 0151 644 6466
w portsunlightvillage.com

Cumbria

767 Barrow-in-Furness

The Dock Museum

3 hrs   Easter–Oct

A spectacular modern museum built over an original Victorian graving dock. Displays explore the history of Barrow-in-Furness and how it grew from a tiny C19 hamlet to become the biggest iron and steel centre in the world and a major shipbuilding force in just 40 years.

* Attractions include film shows & model ships
* Fine art gallery

Location
Follow signposts in Barrow

Opening
Summer Tue–Fri 10am–5pm
Sat & Sun 11am–5pm
Winter Weds–Fri 10am–5pm
Sat & Sun 11am–5pm

Admission
Free

Contact
North Road, Barrow-in-Furness
LA14 2PW

t 01229 894444
w dockmuseum@barrowbc.gov.uk
e dockmuseum.org.uk

768 Barrow-in-Furness

Furness Abbey

1 hr   All year

St Mary of Furness was founded in 1123 by Stephen, later king of England. It originally belonged to the small Order of Savigny but passed to the Cistercians in 1147, and became one of the richest monasteries in England, second only to Fountains Abbey in Yorkshire.

* A romantic building, often visited by Wordsworth
* Visitor centre with exhibition about the abbey

Location
½ mile NE of Barrow-in-Furness

Opening
Apr–Oct Wed–Sun 10am–6pm
Oct Wed–Sun 10am–5pm
Nov–Mar Wed–Sun 10am–4pm

Admission
Adult £3, Child £1.50, Concs £2.30

Contact
North West Region, Canada House,
3 Chepstow Street, Manchester M1 5FW

t 01229 823420
w english-heritage.org.uk
e northwest@english-heritage.org.uk

769 Brampton

Lanercost Priory

1 hr   Apr–Oct

Situated near the Scottish border in Cumbria are the impressive remains of this C12 Augustinian priory. It boasts a rich history, from the tranquillity of life as a monastic house to its involvement in the turbulent Anglo-Scottish wars of the C14 and eventual dissolution.

* Hadrian's Wall is close by
* West front is fine example of C12 English architecture

Location
Off minor road S of Lanercost, 2 miles
NE of Brampton

Opening
Apr–Oct daily 10am–6pm
Oct daily 10am–5pm

Admission
Adult £2.50, Child £1.50, Concs £2

Contact
Lanercost, Brampton CA8 2HQ

t 01697 73030
w english-heritage.org.uk
e northwest@english-heritage.org.uk

770 Carlisle

Carlisle Castle

1 hr   All year

This is a formidable border fortress with a long, rich and colourful history spanning over 900 years. Once commanding the western end of the Anglo-Scottish border, Carlisle Castle has witnessed, over the centuries, the conflict of countless sieges.

* Admission includes entrance to Roman exhibition
* See the legendary 'licking stones'

©English Heritage Photographic Library/Andrew Tryner

Location
City centre

Opening
Apr–Sep daily 9.30am–6pm
Oct daily 10am–5pm
Nov–Mar daily 10am–4pm

Admission
Adult £3.50, Child £1.80, Concs £2.70

Contact
Carlisle CA3 8UR

t 01228 591922
w english-heritage.org.uk
e northwest@english-heritage.org.uk

---

771 Carlisle

Carlisle Cathedral

2 hrs   All year

Founded in 1122 and battered by centuries of warfare, the cathedral retains many items of interest, perhaps most notably the east window with its fine tracery containing C14 stained glass. Other items include the magnificent C16 Brougham triptych and notable medieval painted panels.

* Beautifully painted ceiling in the choir
* Display of cathedral & diocesan silver in the treasury

Location
City centre

Opening
Mon–Sat 7.30am–6.15pm
Sun 7.30am–5pm

Admission
Free, donations welcome

Contact
The Abbey, Castle Street, Carlisle
CA3 8TZ

t 01228 535169
w carlislecathedral.org.uk
e office@carlislecathedral.org.uk

---

772 Carlisle

Tullie House

2 hrs   All year

Tullie House museum and art gallery offers a multi-faceted visitor experience, combining the features of an historic house with a modern museum. Tullie House has a superb collection of Roman artefacts. The displays include many hands-on exhibits that appeal to all ages.

* Underground space brings to life Carlisle's past
* Displays of key artworks by the Pre-Raphaelites

Location
Signed from junction 42, 43 & 44 of M6

Opening
Jul–Aug Mon–Sat 10am–5pm
Sun 11am–5pm
Nov–Mar Mon–Sat 10am–4pm
Sun 12noon–4pm
Apr–Jun & Sep–Oct Mon–Sat
10am–5pm, Sun 12noon–5pm

Admission
Adult £5.20, Child £2.60, Concs £3.60

Contact
Castle Street, Carlisle CA3 8TP

t 01228 534 781
w tulliehouse.co.uk
e enquiries@tullie-house.co.uk

773 Cockermouth

Castlegate House Gallery

½ hr   All year

Located in a listed Georgian house, the gallery exhibits contemporary paintings, sculpture, ceramics, jewellery and glass. It specialises in the work of Northern English and Scottish artists, including Cumbrian painters Sheila Fell, Percy Kelly and June Redfern.

* Sculpture exhibition in walled secret garden
* Changing programme of exhibitions

WC

Location
Leave A66 at Cockermouth, follow signs, opposite Cockermouth Castle

Opening
Daily 10am–5pm, Thu closed, Sun 2pm–5pm

Admission
Free

Contact
Cockermouth CA13 9HA

t 01900 822149
w castlegatehouse.co.uk
e gallery@castlegatehouse.co.uk

---

774 Cockermouth

The Lakeland Sheep & Wool Centre

2 hrs   All year

This centre offers visitors the opportunity to meet Cumbria's most famous residents – 19 different breeds of sheep. Discover interesting facts about each breed and see the speed of the shearer at work and the great skills of the sheepdogs handling a flock.

* Show theatre holds up to 300 people
* Extensive retail outlet for woolen goods

Location
On A66 at A5086 roundabout, Egremount Road, Cockermouth

Opening
Daily 9.30–5pm
Sheepdog shows Sun–Thu, Mar–Nov
10.30, 12noon, 2pm & 3.30pm

Admission
Adult £4, Child £3 (for sheepdog show)

Contact
Egremount Road, Cockermouth
BA1 30 2X

t 01900 822673
w sheep-woolcentre.co.uk

---

775 Cockermouth

Wordsworth House

2 hrs   Apr–Oct

William Wordsworth was born here in 1770, moving out on his mother's death in 1778. There are seven rooms furnished in Regency style, with some personal effects of the poet. Explore the walled Georgian garden with terrace overlooking the River Derwent.

* Wordsworth Lake District video in the stables
* Limited disabled access

Location
Main street in Cockermouth

Opening
June–Nov 5 Mon–Sat 11am–4.30pm

Admission
Adult £4.50, Child £2.50

Contact
Cockermouth CA13 GRX

t 01900 824 805
w nationaltrust.org.uk
e rwordh@smtp.ntrust.org.uk

776 Coniston

Brantwood

3 hrs   All year

As the home of John Ruskin, Brantwood became a great literary and artistic centre. The house is filled with Ruskin's work as well as his original furniture, books and personal items. Brantwood's attraction is increased through its 250 acres of woodland and lakeside meadows.

* The gardens cover 30 acres
* A well-marked nature trail winds through the estate

Location
Eastern shore of Coniston Water
on B5285

Opening
Mid Mar–mid Nov daily 11am–5.30pm
Winter Wed–Sun 11am–4.30pm

Admission
Adult £5.50, Child £1

Contact
Coniston LA21 8AD

t 015394 41396
w brantwood.org.uk
e enquiries@brantwood.org.uk

---

777 Dalton-in-Furness

South Lakes' Wild Animal Park

2-3 hrs   All year

The Lake District's only zoological park is recognised as one of Europe's leading conservation zoos. The rolling 17 acres are home to the rarest animals on earth which are saved from almost certain extinction in the wild thanks to co-ordinated breeding programmes.

* Many animals have freedom to wander at will
* Home of the Sumatran Tiger Trust

Location
Follow signposts from junction 36
of M6

Opening
Summer 10am–5pm
Winter 10am–4.30pm

Admission
Adult £7.50, Child £5.50, Concs £5

Contact
South Lakes Wild Animal Park,
Dalton-in-Furness LA15 8JR

t 01229 466086
w wildanimalpark.co.uk
e office@wildanimalpark.co.uk

---

778 Grasmere

Dove Cottage & Wordsworth Museum

1 hr   All year

This was the home of William Wordsworth from December 1799 to May 1808, the years of his supreme work as a poet. The cottage remains very much as it was during this time. The garden was a passion for Wordsworth and he spent many hours developing his 'domestic slip of mountainside'.

* Museum includes original manuscripts and rare books
* Also shows period images of Grasmere

Location
S of Grasmere on A591
Kendal/Keswick

Opening
Daily 9.30am–5.30pm

Admission
Adult £5.80, Child £2.60, Concs £5.20

Contact
Grasmere LA22 9SH

t 01539 435544
w wordsworth.org.uk
e enquiries@wordsworth.org.uk

779 Hawkshead

Beatrix Potter Gallery

½ hr   Apr–Oct

This gallery houses annually-changing exhibitions of original sketches and watercolours painted by Beatrix Potter for her children's stories. This C17 building was once the office of Beatrix's husband, William Heelis.

* The interior remains substantially unaltered

Location
Town centre

Opening
Apr 3–Oct 31 Wed–Sun
10.30am–4.30pm

Admission
Adult £3, Child £1.50

Contact
Beatrix Potter Gallery,
Main Street, Hawkshead LA22 0NS

t 01539 436355
w 1001daysout.com
e beatrixpottergallery@
   nationaltrust.org.uk

780 Kendal

Kendal Museum

1 hr+   All year

Founded in 1796, Kendal Museum houses one of the country's oldest collections of local archaeology, history, geology, an international natural history collection and lakeland flora and fauna from prehistory to the C20.

* A wildlife garden simulates local habitats
* Changing programme of temporary exhibitions

Location
10 mins from junction 36 of M6

Opening
Apr–Oct Mon–Sat 10.30am–5pm
Feb, Mar, Nov & Dec Mon–Sat
10.30am–4pm

Admission
Adult £2.50, Child free

Contact
Station Road, Kendal LA9 6BT

t 01539 721374
w kendalmuseum.org.uk
e info@kendalmuseum.org.uk

781 Kendal

Levens Hall

2 hrs   Apr–Oct

This world-famous C17 topiary garden was designed by Guillaume Beaumont who also laid out the gardens at Hampton Court. The original designs have remained largely unchanged for 300 years. The house has many beautiful Elizabethan rooms with many notable paintings.

* Dining room has embossed leather wall coverings
* Sundays and Bank Holidays ride on traction engines

Location
5 miles S of Kendal on A6

Opening
Mid Apr–mid Oct Sun–Thu 12noon
–5pm, Garden opens at 10am

Admission
Adult £7.50, Child £3.70

Contact
Kendal LA8 0PD

t 015395 60321
w levenshall.co.uk
e email@levenshall.fsnet.co.uk

782 Kendal

Museum of Lakeland Life

1 hr   Feb–Dec

In 1973 the museum was the first winner of the coveted Museum-of-the-Year award. The permanent collections include displays linked to the Arts and Crafts movement, *Swallows and Amazons* author Arthur Ransome, and the Victorian period.

* Temporary displays largely from costume collection
* Opposite the Abbot Hall Art Gallery

Location
Next to Albert Hall Gallery,
junction 36 M6

Opening
Apr–Oct Mon–Sat 10.30am–5pm
Jan 20–Mar, Nov & Dec
Mon–Sat 10.30am–4pm

Admission
Adult £2.75, Child £1.40

Contact
Kendal LA9 5AL

t 01539 722464
w lakelandmuseum.org.uk
e ws@lakelandmuseum.org.uk

783 Newby Bridge

Aquarium of the Lakes

1 hr All Year

Discover the fascinating wildlife in and alongside the lakes in over 30 displays. A dramatic mountain-top waterfall marks the start of the journey, leading down a moorland stream. Next you will see the otters before moving on to see nocturnal life on the riverbank.

* Also fish from the estuary and local shores
* At southern end of Windemere with panoramic views

Location
15 mins from junction 36 of M6, take A590 to Newby Bridge follow signs

Opening
Apr–Oct daily 9am–6pm
Nov–Mar 9am–5pm

Admission
Adult £5.95, Child £3.75, Concs £4.95

Contact
Aquarium of the Lakes,
Newby Bridge LA12 8AS

t 01539 530153
w aquariumofthelakes.co.uk
e aquariumofthelakes@reallive.co.uk

784 Newby Bridge

Scott Park Bobbin Mill

1 hr Apr–Oct

This gem of the industrial revolution has remained largely unchanged since it was built by John Harrison in 1835. Stott Park created the wooden bobbins vital to the spinning and weaving industries of Lancashire.

* Mill worked continuously until 1971
* Steam days' Tue, Wed & Thu show engines working

Location
2 miles N of Newby Bridge, off A590

Opening
Apr–Oct daily 10am–6pm
Oct daily 10am–5pm

Admission
Adult £3.50, Child £1.80, Concs £2.70

Contact
Finsthwaite, nr Newby Bridge,
Ulverston LA12 8AX

t 01539 531087
w english-heritage.org.uk
e northwest@english-heritage.org.uk

785 Penrith

Beckstones Art Gallery

1 hr All year

This specialist art gallery houses original work by up to 40 of the nation's top artists. There are over 300 paintings representing a variety of media and a wide range of subject matter.

* idyllically situated in small hamlet of Greystoke Ghyll

Location
Signposted off A66 3 miles W of Penrith

Opening
Mar–Oct daily 10.30am–5.30pm
Nov 10am–5pm, Dec–Feb Fri, Sat
& Sun 10.30am–4pm

Admission
Free

Contact
Greystoke Ghyll, Penrith CA11 0UQ

t 017684 83601
w beckstonesartgallery.co.uk
e enquiries@beckstonesartgallery.
   co.uk

©English Heritage Photographic Library/Steve Cole

786 Penrith

Acorn Bank Garden & Watermill

2 hrs   Mar–Nov

Ancient oaks and the high enclosing walls keep out the extremes of the Cumbrian climate, resulting in a spectacular display of shrubs, roses and herbaceous borders. Sheltered orchards contain a variety of traditional fruit trees. The watermill is under restoration.

* Famed herb garden has huge collection of plants
* Watermill remains open to public during restoration

Location	Contact
N of Temple Sowerby, 6 miles E of Penrith on A66	Temple Sowerby, nr Penrith CA10 1SP
Opening	t 01768 361893
Mar 27–Oct 31 Wed–Mon 10am–5pm	w nationaltrust.org.uk
Admission	e acornbank@nationaltrust.org.uk
Adult £2.60, Child £1.30	

787 Penrith

Brougham Castle

1 hr   Apr–Oct

Brougham Castle was built in 1092 on the site of a Roman fort, by William Rufus. The original castle was destroyed in 1172 and rebuilt by Henry II. His tower survives but later buildings were destroyed by fire in 1521. A stone-curtain wall was added around 1300.

* Once home to Lady Anne Clifford
* Introductory exhibition includes Roman carved stone

Location	Contact
½ mile SE of Penrith off A66	North West Region, Canada House, 3 Chepstow Street, Manchester M1 5FW
Opening	t 01768 862488
Apr–Sep daily 10am–6pm	w english-heritage.org.uk
Oct daily 10am–5pm	e northwest@english-heritage.org.uk
Admission	
Adult £2.50, Child £1.50, Concs £2	

788 Penrith

Dalemain Historic House & Gardens

2 hrs   Mar–Oct

A medieval, Tudor and early Georgian house that has been home to the Hasell family since 1679. The Tudor legacy is a series of winding passageway, unexpected rooms and oak panelling. A good example of the Georgian period is the breathtaking Chinese room.

* C15 medieval hall
* The Estate includes many famous valleys and fells

Location	Admission
On A592 Penrith to Ullswater road	Adult £5.50, Child £3.30
Opening	**Contact**
Mar 28–Aug	Penrith CA11 0HB
Gardens Sun–Thur 10.30am–5pm	t 01768 486450
House Sun–Thur 11am–4pm	w dalemain.com
Sep–Oct 21	e admin@dalemain.com
Gardens Sun–Thur 10.30–4pm	
House Sun–Thur 11am–3pm	

789 Ulverston

Conishead Priory & Buddhist Temple

1 hr   All year

A stunning example of early Victorian gothic architecture. It is dominated by two 100-foot (30m) octagonal towers. Special features include decorative ceilings and a vaulted great hall with fine stained glass. The Kadampa Temple was established at the priory in 1977.

* Anyone welcome to visit the temple
* Prayers for world peace every Sunday morning

Location	Contact
A5087, 2 miles S of Ulverston	Priory Road, Ulverston LA12 9QQ
Opening	t 01229 584029
Apr 26–Oct Sat & Sun & Bank Hols 2–5pm, Winter temple only Sat–Sun 10am–4pm	w manjushri.org.uk
	e info@manjushri.org.uk
Admission	
Free	

790 Ulverston

Gleaston Water Mill

1 hr   All year

This imposing watermill has been part of the local land-scape for over 400 years. Located close to the ruins of Gleaston Castle, the present building dates from 1774. Visitors can see the 18 foot (5½ m) waterwheel and machinery operating most days.

* Last major rebuild in 1700s

Location
Follow signs from A5087 Ulverston to Barrow-in-Furness road

Opening
Tue–Sun & Bank Hols 10.30am–5pm

Admission
Adult £2.50 Child £1.50

Contact
Gleaston, nr Ulverston LA12 0QH

t 01229 869244
w watermill.co.uk

791 Ulverston

Holker Hall, Gardens & Lakeland Motor Museum

3 hrs   Mar–Oct

Only a short distance from the sea, Holker Hall is situated on the magnificent wooded slopes of the Cartmel Peninsula. The house exhibits all the grandeur and prosperity of the late-Victorian era and is set in immaculate gardens.

* Home to Lakeland Motor Museum
* The Campbell Legend Bluebird exhibition

Location
Follow signs from A590 from Barrow or M6 junction 36

Opening
Mar 28–Oct 31 Mon–Fri & Sun 10am–4.30pm

Admission
Adult £9.25, Child £5.50

Contact
Cark-in-Cartmel, Cumbria LA 11 7PL

t 015395 58328
w holker-hall.co.uk
e publicopening@holker.co.uk

792 Ulverston

Laurel & Hardy Museum

1 hr   Feb–Dec

Visit the only museum in the world devoted to Laurel & Hardy in Ulverston, the town where Stan was born on 16 June 1890. Everything you want to know about them is here. The collection includes letters, photographs, personal items and furniture.

* Small cinema shows films & documentaries all day

Location
Town centre

Opening
Feb–Dec daily 10am–4.30pm

Admission
Adult £2.50, Child £1.50, Concs £1.50

Contact
4C Upper Brook Street, Ulverston LA12 7BH

t 01229 582292
w laurel-and-hardy-museum.co.uk

793 Windermere

Lake District National Park

4 hrs All year

Enjoy some of England's dramatic mountain and lake scenery in the largest of the country's national parks. Get a better understanding of the area at the visitor centre at Brockhole on Lake Windemere.

* Exhibition & displays & gardens down to the lake
* Always check weather before walking

Location
Visitor centre on A591 between Windermere & Ambleside

Opening
Visitor Centre Mar 23–Nov 3 daily 10am–5pm
Garden & Grounds all year

Admission
Free, £3 for parking half day

Contact
The Lake District Visitor Centre, Brockhole, Windermere LA23 1LJ
t 015394 46601
w lake-district.gov.uk

794 Windermere

Windermere Lake Cruises

3 hrs All year

Steamers and launches sail daily between Ambleside, Bowness and Lakeside with main season connections for the Lakeside & Haverthwaite Steam Railway, Wray Castle and the Lake District National Park (Brockhole). Daily sailings to the aquarium and the World of Beatrix Potter.

* 24 hour 'Freedom' tickets for unlimited travel
* Other links to lakes attractions–see website

Location
Leave the M6 at junction 36, follow the A590 to the lakeside or the A591 to Bowness (Windermere) & Ambleside

Opening
All year daily during daylight hours

Admission
Adult £5, Child £2.50

Contact
Lakeside, Newby Bridge, Ulverston LA12 8AS
t 01539 531188
w windemere-lakecruises.co.uk
e w.lakes@virgin.net

795 Accrington

Haworth Art Gallery

2 hrs All year

This Edwardian house, set in parkland houses the finest public collection of Tiffany art glass outside America. There is also an excellent collection of oil paintings from the C19.

* Regularly changing exhibitions

Location
Leave M65 at junction 7, M61 junction 9, M6 junction 29

Opening
Wed–Fri 2pm–5pm
Sat & Sun 12 noon–4.30pm

Admission
Free

Contact
Haworth Park, Manchester Road, Accrington BB5 2JS
t 01254 233782
w hyndburnbc.gov.uk

796 Burnley

Queen Street Mill

1 hr   Mar–Nov

A unique survivor of the textile industry, Queen Street Mill represents the last commercial steam-powered textile mill in Europe. The mill closed in 1982 but is preserved as a museum which recreates the days when steam ran the world.

* Smell the oil, hear the hiss & breathe the atmosphere
* 300 Lancashire looms

Location
Brier Cliff Road, Harle Syke

Opening
Mar & Nov Tue–Thu 12noon–4pm
Apr & Oct Tue–Fri 12noon–5pm
May–Sep Tue–Sat 12noon–5pm

Admission
Adult £2.50, Child free, Concs £1.25

Contact
Harle Syke, Burnley BB10 2HX

t 01282 412555
w lancashire.gov.uk
e info@1001daysout.com

---

797 Burnley

Gawthorpe Hall

2 hrs   Apr–Nov

An Elizabethan gem, Gawthorpe resembles the great Hardwick Hall and is probably by the same architect, Robert Smythson. In the mid-C19 Sir Charles Barry was commissioned to restore the house. Charlotte Brontë was a frequent visitor.

* There are many notable paintings & C17–C19 furniture
* Unparalleled collection of British C19–C20 needlework

Location
On E outskirts of Padiham, N of A671

Opening
Apr–Nov Tue–Thu Sat & Sun 1pm–5pm

Admission
Adult £3, Child free, Concs £1.50

Contact
Padiham, Burnley BB12 8UA

t 01282 771004
w nationaltrust.org.uk
e gawthorpehall@ntrust.org.uk

---

798 Blackburn

Blackburn Museum & Art Gallery

2 hrs   All year

The musuem is housed in an Arts and Crafts style building which opened in 1872 as a museum and a library. Highlights include the Hart Collection of over 10,000 rare coins, 500 books and illuminated manuscripts, and a superb collection of Victorian oils and watercolours.

* The Lewis Collection of over 1,000 Japanese prints
* The award-winning South Asian gallery

Location
Town centre

Opening
Tue–Sat 10am–4.45pm

Admission
Free

Contact
Museum Street, Blackburn BB1 7AJ

t 01254 667130
e paul.flintoff@blackburn.gov.uk

---

799 Blackburn

Whalley Abbey Gatehouse

1 hr   All year

Situated beside the River Calder, this is the outer gatehouse of the nearby Cistercian abbey. There was originally a chapel on the first floor. The adjacent parish church has further remains including three pre-Norman Conquest cross shafts. The nearby abbey has an exhibition centre.

* Vast display of remains

Location
In Whalley, 6 miles NE of Blackburn on minor road off A59

Opening
Any reasonable time

Admission
Free

Contact
Whalley, Clitheroe BB7 9SS

t 01793 414910
w english-heritage.org.uk

800 Blackpool

Blackpool Illuminations

2 hrs   Aug–Nov

Experience Blackpool's annual spectacular event. Six miles of lights electrify this well-loved resort's promenade as the world-famous illuminations shine out every night for 66 nights. Enjoy a grandstand seat aboard a cleverly disguised tram.

* View the giant clifftop tableaux
* 1879 electric arc lamps bathe promenade in light

Location
Central Promenade

Opening
End Aug–Nov

Admission
Free

Contact
Blackpool Tourism, 1 Clifton Street FY1 1LY

t 01253 478222
w www.blackpooltourism.com
e tourism@blackpool.gov.uk

801 Blackpool

Blackpool Lifeboat Station & Visitor Centre

1 hr   Mar–Nov

This lifeboat station accommodates an Atlantic 75 B-class and 2 D-class lifeboats, launching vehicles and ancillary equipment. The visitor centre incorporates current and historic displays and sea-safety information. There is an accessible public viewing area.

* This station was established by the Institution in 1864
* 1897 Nelson's flagship *Foudroyant* wrecked in gale

Location
Central Promenade

Opening
Easter–Nov 10am–4pm

Admission
Free

Contact
Central Promenade, Blackpool FY1 5YA

t 01253 620424/290816
w rnli.org.uk
e khorrocks@rnli.org.uk

802 Blackpool

Blackpool Tower

5 hrs+   Apr–Nov

Inside the tower visitors will find a circus and a world-famous ballroom. Explore the Charlie Cairoli exhibition, Under Sea World, the Hornpipe Gallery, Tower Top ride and the Walk of Faith.

* Contact venue for Kings of Swing & Memphis Belles
* Replica of Eiffel Tower in Paris

Location
M55 for Blackpool, follow signposts

Opening
Apr–May 10am–6pm
May–Nov 10am–11pm

Admission
Tower & Circus
Adult £11.50, Child £7.50, Concs £8

Contact
Leisure Parcs Ltd, Blackpool FY1 4BJ

t 01253 622242 /01253 29 20 29
w blackpooltower.co.uk
e website@leisure-parcs.co.uk

Lancashire

803 Blackpool

The UFO & Alien Connection

1 hr+   All year

This exhibition features six videos which show the latest footage of UFO sightings. There are themed displays of outsized beings from all over the universe. Walk in a flying saucer and experience an extensive advanced spiritual section and a meditation pyramid.

* Meditation pyramid
* World's most extensive collection of aliens

Location
Central promenade

Opening
Daily from 10am

Admission
Adult £4.50, Child £3

Contact
Blackpool FY1 5AA

t 01253 297522
w peoplesplanet.faceweb.com

804 Bolton

Animal World & Butterfly House

1 hr   All year

Animal World provides a living environment for a variety of animals and birds, from farm animals to chipmunks and from wildfowl to tropical birds. Butterfly House features free-flying butterflies and moths in a tropical environment, as well as insects, spiders and reptiles.

* Collection of tropical plants

Location
Bolton A58 to Moss Bank Way

Opening
Apr–Sep Daily 10am–4.30pm
Oct–Mar Sat–Thu 10am–3.30pm
Fri 10am–2.30pm

Admission
Free

Contact
Moss Bank Park, Moss Bank Way,
Bolton BL1 6NQ

t 01204 334050
w bolton.gov.uk
e animal.world@bolton.gov.uk

805 Bolton

Barrow Bridge Village

1 hr   All year

This model village, created during the Industrial Revolution, features cottages, bridges over a small stream, and 63 steps, built to help workers climb the hill to work. The village was once the home of two six-storey mills that used to employ 1,000 workers.

Location
N of the town centre

Opening
Any reasonable time

Admission
Free

Contact
Barrow Bridge Road, off Moss Bank
Way, Bolton

t 01204 333333 / 334321 (tourist info)
w visitbolton.com

806 Bolton

Bolton Aquarium

2 hrs   All year

Fish from all over the world are displayed here. Visitors can view the behaviour of freshwater species at close quarters. A new addition is a species of fish from Australia, the closest relatives of which were last present in the area over 200 million years ago.

* Collection of piranha fish
* Predatory Blue-head knifefish from Venezuela

Location
Town centre

Opening
Mon–Sat 10am–5pm
Closed Sun & Bank Hols

Admission
Free

Contact
Le Mans Crescent, Bolton BL1 1SE

t 01204 332 211
w boltonmuseums.org.uk
e aquarium@bolton.gov.uk

807 Bolton

Bolton Museum & Art Gallery

2 hrs   All year

This building houses an impressive collection of fine and decorative art dating from C18 to C20, including watercolours and drawings, a prominent collection of modern British art prints, and C20 sculpture and contemporary ceramics.

* Varied programme of events and exhibitions
* Ancient Egyptian sculpture 'The Princess'

Location
Town centre

Opening
Mon–Sat 10am–5pm
Closed Sun & Bank Hols

Admission
Free

Contact
Le Mans Crescent, Bolton BL1 1SE

t 01204 332 211
w boltonmuseums.org.uk
e museums@bolton.gov.uk

808 Bolton

Bolton Wanderers Football Club

2 hrs   All year

Look behind the scenes at the Reebok Stadium, home of Bolton Wanderers. Begin at the interactive museum where the history of the club is brought to life. Visit the players' dressing and warm-up rooms, the officials' changing rooms and the manager's dug-out.

Location
Junction 6 off the M61

Opening
Mon–Fri 9am–5pm
Sat 9am–4pm Sun 11am–4pm

Admission
Adult £2.50, Child & Concs £1.50

Contact
Burnden Way, Bolton BL6 6JW

t 01204 673670
w bwfc.premiumtv.co.uk
e sparker@bwfc.co.uk

809 Bolton

Hall i' th' Wood Museum

1 hr   Apr–Nov

This half-timbered hall, built in C15, was owned by wealthy yeomen and merchants. After 1697 it was rented out to various tenants. During this period a young Samuel Crompton lived here with his parents. He invented the spinning mule, which revolutionised the cotton industry.

* In 1902, Lord Leverhulme gave the hall to the people of Bolton
* Discover life in Tudor & Stuart times

Location
Town centre

Opening
Apr–Nov Wed–Sun & Bank Hols
11am–5pm

Admission
Adult £2, Child & Concs £1

Contact
Green Way, Bolton BL1 8UA

t 01204 332370
w boltonmuseums.org.uk
e info@1001daysout.com

Lancashire

810 Bolton

Smithills Hall

1 hr   Apr-Oct

This is one of the earliest examples of a Lancashire manor house, which has recently had additional rooms restored to their full splendour. The house has been developed by generations of owners and mirrors changes in fashion and living conditions from the late C14 to C19.

* Fine linenfold panelling and Stuart furniture
* Stained glass windows in the chapel

Location
Follow the M62 for Bolton

Opening
Apr–Sep Tue–Sat 11am–5pm
Sun 2pm–5pm
Oct Mar Tue & Sat 1pm–5pm,
Sun 2pm–5pm

Admission
Adult £3, Child & Concs £1.75

Contact
Smithills Dean Road, Bolton BL1 7NP

t 01204 332377
w smithills.org
e officesmithills.org

811 Bolton

Turton Tower

2 hrs   All year

This distinctive English country house on the edge of the West Pennine Moors was built by the Orrell family. The house was lavishly furnished and extended in the Tudor and early Stuart periods. After falling into decline during the Georgian era, the house was rescued by the Kay family.

* Collection of decorative woodwork & paintings
* Victorian follies, a Victorian tennis court

Location
A66 and A676, follow the signposts

Opening
Apr–Sep Mon–Thu 11am–5pm
Sat & Sun 1pm–5pm
Mar & Oct Mon–Wed 1pm–5pm
Sat & Sun 1pm–4pm
Nov & Feb Sat & Sun 1pm–4pm

Admission
Adult £3.50, Child free, Concs £1.50

Contact
Turton, Bolton BL7 0HG

t 01204 852203
w lancashire.gov.uk
e turtontower.lcc@btinternet.com

812 Carnforth

Leighton Hall

2 hrs   May–Sep

Leighton Hall is the home of the famous furniture-making Gillow dynasty. Explore the past of this ancient, Lancashire family, wander through the grounds and pretty gardens and witness displays from trained birds of prey.

* C19 walled garden, landscaped parkland & woodland
* Entertaining guides reveal the family's history

Location
Junction 35A M6, North Canthorp

Opening
May–Sep Tue–Fri & Sun 2pm–5pm

Admission
Adult £5, Child £3.50, Concs £4.50

Contact
Carnforth LA5 9ST

t 01524 734 474
w leightonhall.co.uk
e leightonhall@yahoo.co.uk

813 Carnforth

Warton Old Rectory

1 hr   All year

The Old Rectory was built in the early C14 and was the home of the de Thweng family who were patrons of the church. Courts of Justice were held here and the remains include impressive gable walls, windows and a huge stone fireplace.

* Grade I listed building & ancient monument
* Visit also St Oswald's Church, Warton

Location
At Warton, 1 mile N of Carnforth on minor road off A6

Opening
Apr–Sep daily 10am–6pm, Oct daily 10am–5pm, Nov–Mar daily 10am–4pm

Admission
Free

Contact
North West Region, Canada House, 3 Chepstow Street, Manchester M1 5FW

t 0161 242 1400
w english-heritage.org.uk
e northwest@english-heritage. org.uk

814 Chorley

Astley Hall Museum & Art Gallery

1 hr   All year

This hall dates back to Elizabethan times but changes have been made over the centuries. The collections range from C18 creamware and glass to the first Rugby League Cup and the contents of a clog-maker's workshop.

* Programme of special exhibitions, events & activities
* Textile collection includes civic robes and militaria

Location
W of Chorley town centre off A581 Chorley-Southport road

Opening
Apr–Oct Tue–Sun & Bank Hols 12noon–5pm
Nov–Mar Sat & Sun 12noon–4pm

Admission
Adult £2.95, Child & Concs £1.95

Contact
Astley Park, Chorley PR7 1NP

t 01257 515555
w astleyhall.co.uk
e astleyhall@lineone.net

815 Clitheroe

Clitheroe Castle Museum

½ hr   Feb–Dec

Set on a prominent limestone mound close to the ruined Norman keep of Clitheroe Castle, this museum houses collections of local history and geology. Displays cover the history of the Ribble Valley, the Hacking ferryboat, witchcraft, local birds and roadside geology.

* There is a reconstructed lead mine & a clogger's shop
* Edwardian kitchen

Location
Castle Hill

Opening
Easter–Oct daily 11am–4.30pm
Mar–Apr Sat–Wed 11am–4pm
Feb, Nov & Dec Sat & Sun 11am–4pm

Admission
Adult £1.70, Child 50p, Concs 80p

Contact
Castle Hill, Clitheroe BB7 1BA

t 01200 424635/01200 425566 (Tourist Information)
w ribblevalley.gov.uk
e museum@ribblevalley.gov.uk

816 Colne

British In India Museum

All year
1 hr

The museum was opened in 1972 and contains a fascinating collection of material, including model soldiers, dinramas, postage stamps, picture postcards, paintings and military uniforms.

* Museum opened in 1972
* Shows British and Indian military artefacts

Location
A56-A6068 between Burnley and Keighley

Opening
Wed & Sat 2pm–5pm

Admission
Adult £3, Child 50p

Contact
Newtown Street, Colne BB8 0JJ

t 01282 613129

Lancashire

817 Fleetwood

Fleetwood Museum

1 hr   All year

Built in 1838 and occupying the old Customs House designed by architect Decimus Burton, this fascinating museum brings the story of Fleetwood and the surrounding coast to life. Trace the story of Fleetwood, its cargo trade and famous fishing industry.

* Discover a fisherman's life & the harsh working conditions
* *Harriet* the last surviving northwest fishing smack

Location
M55 signposted Fleetwood follow the A585

Opening
Mon–Sat 10am–4pm
Sun 1pm–4pm

Admission
Adult £2, Child free, Concs £1

Contact
Queen's Terrace, Fleetwood FY7 6BT
t 01253 876621
w bringing historyalivi.co.uk

818 Horwich

Horwich Heritage Centre

1 hr   All year

This centre aims to preserve and present the rich history and heritage of Horwich, by featuring specific aspects of Horwich life over the centuries, using videos, displays, artefacts and exhibits. There is a guest speaker on the second Tuesday of every month.

* Exhibition of local historic works
* Full range of publications on Horwich available

Location
Junction 6 M61 and A673

Opening
Wed 2pm–4pm Sat 10am–12 noon
2nd Tue every month 7.30pm–9pm

Admission
Free

Contact
Longworth Road, Horwich BL6 7BG
t 01204 847797
w horich.herritage.co.uk
e info@1001daysout.com

819 Lancaster

Judges' Lodgings

1 hr   All year

This is Lancaster's oldest townhouse, home to Thomas Cavell, keeper of the castle during Lancashire's witch trials of 1612. Later used as a residence for judges visiting Lancaster Castle, it is now a museum displaying a wealth of furniture, porcelain, silver and paintings.

* Collection of Gillow furniture in period rooms
* Collection of dolls, toys & games from C18 to today

Location
Nr the train station, on the cobbled roads just down from the castle

Opening
Easter–Jun & Oct Mon–Fri 1pm–4pm
Sat & Sun 12noon–4pm
Jul–Sep Mon–Fri 10am–4pm
Sat & Sun 12noon–4pm

Admission
Adult £2, Child free, Concs £1

Contact
Church Street, Lancaster LA1 1YS
t 01524 32808
w lancashire.gov.uk
e judgeslodgings@mus.lancsscc.gov.uk

820 Lancaster

Lancaster Canal & Lune Aqueduct

1 hr+   All year

Built to carry trade between Kendal and Preston, the canal is a haven for wildlife. The towpath stretches over 55 miles and is ideal for countryside walks. The Lune Aqueduct was designed by Rennie and is 664 feet long and 51 feet high (202 x 15m).

* Railway once passed under one of its arches
* Built in 1797

Location
Lancaster, off Kanton Road, Junction 34 M6

Opening
Any reasonable time

Admission
Free

Contact
British Waterways, Lancaster LA2 0LQ
t 01524 751888
w waterscape.com

Lancaster Maritime Museum

2 hrs   All year

Lancaster Maritime Museum occupies two historic buildings on St. George's Quay, the main C18 harbour. The former Customs House of 1764, designed by Richard Gillow, contains displays on the history of the port of Lancaster and the local fishing industry.

* Lancaster Canal & Morecambe Bay ecology displays
* Vessels, *Sir William Priestley* & *Coronation Rose*

Location
St George's Quay

Opening
Easter–Oct 11am–5pm
Nov–Easter 12.30pm–4pm

Admission
Adult £2, Child £1, Concs £1

Contact
St George's Quay, Lancaster LA1 1RB
t 01524 64637
w lancaster.gov.uk /
   nettingthebay.org.uk
e awhite@lancaster.gov.uk

Eric Morecambe Stage & Statue

1 hr   All year

Unveiled by the Queen in 1999, the larger than life-sized statue depicts Eric Morecambe in a characteristic pose with a pair of binoculars around his neck (he was a keen ornithologist). The statue is set against the backdrop of Morecambe Bay and the Lake District hills.

* People queue to have their photograph taken here

Location
Leave M6 at junction. 34 or 35 & follow signs for Morecambe & statue is located on central promenade area

Opening
Any reasonable time

Admission
Free

Contact
Central Promenade, Morecambe
or the Tourist Information Centre
t 01524 582808
w visitmorecambe.co .uk

Rufford Old Hall

2 hrs+   Apr–Oct

This is a fine C16 building, famed for its Great Hall which has an intricately carved 'moveable' wooden screen and hammerbeam roof. It is rumoured that Shakespeare performed in this hall for the owner, Sir Thomas Hesketh.

* Fine collections of C16-C17 oak furniture
* Arms, armour and tapestries

Location
7 miles N of Ormskirk in village of Rufford on E side of A59

Opening
Apr 3–Oct 27 Sat–Wed 1pm–5pm
Check opening hours due to ongoing conservation work

Admission
Adult £4.50, Child £2

Contact
Rufford, Ormskirk L40 1SG
t 01704 821254
w nationaltrust.org.uk
e ruffordoldhall@ntrust.org.uk

Lancashire

824 Preston

British Commercial Vehicle Museum

2 hrs   Apr–Oct

This is one of Britain's most important heritage collections. It contains a unique line-up of historic commercial vehicles and buses representing a century of truck and bus building. It is located in the heart of Leyland.

* Sound and light Second World War theme
* Pope mobile

Location	Contact
M6 Junction 28, follow the signposts	King Street, Leyland, Preston PR25 2LE
Opening	t 01772 451011
Apr 1–Oct 31, call for times	w commercialvehiclemuseum.co.uk
Admission	
Adult £4 Child £2	

825 Preston

Harris Museum & Art Gallery

2 hrs   All year

Discover the best of Preston's heritage in a beautiful Grade I listed building. The Harris has large collections of paintings, sculpture, textiles, costume, glass and ceramics, as well as the Story of Preston gallery which brings the history of the town to life.

* Exciting programme of exhibitions
* National reputation for contemporary art shows

Location	Contact
City centre	Market Square, Preston PR1 2PP
Opening	t 01772 258 248
Mon–Sat 10am–5pm	w 1001daysout.com
Sun 11am–4pm	e harris.museum@preston.gov.uk
Admission	
Free	

826 Preston

Museum of Lancashire

2 hrs   All year

Located in the Old Sessions' House, which was built in 1825, this museum traces the history of the county and its people, from the Middle Ages through to recent times. It houses a collection of military objects and memorabilia, from three Lancashire regiments.

* Colourful uniforms & splendid swords are displayed
* Reconstruction of a First World War trench

Location	Contact
On the A6, Stanley Street, Preston	Stanley Street, Preston PR1 4YP
Opening	t 01772 264075
Mon–Wed, Fri & Sat 10.30am–5pm	w lancashire.gov.uk
Admission	e icc/museums.gov.uk
Adult £2, Child free, Concs £1	

827 Preston

National Football Museum

2 hrs   All year

Travel on a journey through football's history. Learn how the game was invented, how it has developed over the last 150 years, and what the future will hold for both the players and the supporters. Discover the individuals and teams who have helped to shape the game we know today.

* First black player to debut in English football in 1880s
* Women's team which attracted a 53,000 crowd in 1921

Location
2 miles from junction 31, 31A or 32 on M6, signposted

Opening
Tue–Sat 10am–5pm, Sun 11am–5pm

Admission
Free

Contact
Sir Tom Finney Way, Deepdale, Preston PR1 6RU
t 01772 908403 / 442
w nationalfootballmuseum.com
e enquiries@nationalfootball
    museum.com

828 Rossendale

Helmshore Textile Museums

2 hrs   All year

Experience two original textile mills, a waterwheel and textile machines from the Industrial Revolution. At Whitaker's Mill, a C19 cotton-spinning mill, visitors can see working spinning mules.

* Watch live demonstrations by skilled workers
* Activities' programme includes talks & workshops

Location
Holcome Road

Opening
Mon–Fri 12 noon–4pm
Sat & Sun 12 noon–5pm

Admission
Adult £3, Child free, Concs £1.50

Contact
Holcombe Road, Helmshore, Rossendale BB4 4NP
t 01706 226459
w museumoflancs.org.uk
e helmshoremuseum@
    museumoflancs.org.uk

829 Rivington

Lever Park

3 hrs+   All year

Set within the West Pennine moors, this park has facilities for fishing and walking as well as an arboretum, a pinetum, refreshments and toilets. Other interesting features include the remains of Lord Leverhulme's gardens and two cruck barns.

* Ruined replica of Liverpool Castle & Rivington Pike
* Reservoir

Location
Rivington Lane, Horwich

Opening
Wed–Sun & Bank Hols 10.30am–5pm

Admission
Free

Contact
Great House Information Centre, Rivington Lane, Horwich BL6 7SB
t 01204 691549

830 Wigan

Haigh Country Park

5 hrs+   All year

This park includes an art and craft gallery with exhibitions of pottery, embroidery and paintings. The model village features a railway, helipad, pub and castle. The walled garden originally supplied the hall with fruit and vegetables and now provides a peaceful retreat.

* Ranger guided walks around the park
* Miniature railway

Location
Nr B5238 and B5239

Opening
Dawn to dusk
Visitor Centre Mon–Sun 9am–5pm

Admission
Free

Contact
Haigh, Wigan WN2 1PE
t 01942 832895
w haighhall.net
e hhgen@wict.org

Manchester

The Chinese Arts Centre

2 hrs   All year

This new building offers changing contemporary arts' exhibitions, workshops, education programmes and information about Chinese art and culture, with a particular emphasis on supporting Sino-British artistic expression.

* The center has a state of the art education suite
* Traditional Chinese tea rooms

Location
Market Buildings, Thomas Street

Opening
Mon–Sat 10am–6pm
Sun–Bank Hols 11am–5pm

Admission
Free

Contact
Thomas Street, Manchester M4 1 EU

t 0161 832 7271
w chinese-arts-center.org
e info@chinese-arts-center.org

Manchester

Gallery of Costume

1 hr   All year

Housed in Platt Hall, an C18 textile merchant's house, this is one of the largest collections of clothing and fashion accessories in Britain. The collection contains clothes worn by men, women and children from the C18 to the present day.

* Many of the clothes represent high fashion of the day
* Fashions of Manchester's South Asian communities

Location
In Platt Fields Park, Wilmslow Road in South Manchester

Opening
Last Sat of every month 10am–5pm,
Open by appointment only Tue–Fri
10am–12noon & 1pm–5pm

Admission
Free

Contact
Platt Hall, Rusholme,
Manchester M14 5LL

t 0161 224 5217
w manchestergalleries.org.uk

Manchester

Heaton Hall

2 hrs   Apr–Sep

Heaton Hall is a magnificent C18 neo-classical country house set in 650 acres of rolling parkland. The hall is Grade I listed and its interiors have been beautifully restored to reflect late C18/C19 century life at Heaton.

* 1772 architect James Wyatt re-modelled the house
* One of the finest neo-classical houses in the country

Location
In the middle of Heaton Park off Middleton Road in East Manchester

Opening
Apr–Sep, Thu–Sun & Bank Hols
10am–12noon & 1pm–5pm
Call for Easter details

Admission
Free

Contact
Heaton Park, Prestwich,
Manchester M25 5SW

t 0161 2358888
w manchestergalleries.org

Manchester

Imperial War Museum North

1 hr+   All year

The museum, situated on the banks of the Manchester Ship Canal, offers people of all ages thought-provoking displays and direct access to the museum's collections. It offers insights into the enormous impact of war on the C20 and C21.

Location
M60 junction 9, follow the signs to the quays

Opening
Daily 10am–6pm

Admission
Free

Contact
Traford Wharf Road, The Quays,
Traford Park M17 ITZ

t 01618364000
w iwm.org.uk
e info@iwm.org.uk

835 Manchester

Manchester Art Gallery

4 hrs+   All year

This gallery houses one of the world's finest collections of art, displayed in spectacular surroundings. There are fun interactive displays and special exhibitions to enjoy. The contemporary Indian art and craft exhibition celebrates the culture of one this fascinating sub-continent.

* Collection spans six centuries of fine & decorative art
* Exceptional for C19 British oil & watercolour paintings

Location
City centre

Opening
Tue–Sun 10am–5pm
Closed Mon except Bank Hols

Admission
Free

Contact
Mosley Street, Manchester M2 3JL

t 0161 235 8888
w manchestergalleries.org

836 Manchester

The Manchester Museum

1 hr   All year

This museum, with its four floors of displays and exhibitions in 15 galleries, houses collections from all over the world. Visit the famous Egyptology galleries, the new science for life gallery and the zoology gallery which contains mammals, birds and live animals.

* Ethnology collections from South America
* Collections of fossils and minerals

Location
In Oxford Road to the south of the city centre

Opening
Mon–Sat 10am–5pm
Sun & Bank Hols 11am–4pm

Admission
Free, exhibitions may charge

Contact
The University of Manchester, Oxford Road, Manchester M13 9PL

t 0161 275 2634
w museum.man.ac.uk
e michael.rooney@man.ac.uk

837 Manchester

The Museum of Science & Industry

4 hrs+   All year

Situated in the oldest-surviving passenger railway buildings in the world, the museum tells the story of the history, science and industry of Manchester – the world's first industrial city. Stimulate the senses in Xperiment, an interactive science gallery.

* Demonstrators operate thunderous cotton machinery
* See the Avro Shackleton plane in the air & space hall

Location
On Liverpool Road in Castlefield, signposted from the city centre

Opening
Daily 10am–5pm

Admission
Free, exhibitions may charge

Contact
Liverpool Road, Castlefield, Manchester M3 4FP

t 0161 832 2244
w msim.org.uk
e marketing@msim.org.uk

Manchester

Merseyside

838 Manchester

Urbis

2 hrs   All year

This museum is set in a shimmering, high-rise, glass building. State-of-the-art interactive displays and exhibits lead visitors through an inspirational journey exploring life in different cities of the world, including Manchester, Los Angeles, São Paulo, Singapore and Paris.

* A visit begins with a sky glide in the glass elevator
* Combination of audio, visual & sensory environments

Location
City centre

Opening
10am–6pm

Admission
Adult £5, Child & Concs £3.50

Contact
Cathedral Gardens,
Manchester M4 3BG

t 0161 605 8200
w urbis.org.uk
e info@urbis.org.uk

839 Manchester

The Whitworth Art Gallery

1 hr   All year

This gallery houses an impressive range of watercolours, prints, drawings, modern art and sculpture, as well as the largest collection of textiles and wallpapers outside London. The Whitworth uses its collections to create changing exhibitions exploring different themes.

* A programme of innovative touring exhibitions
* Specialist centre for works on paper and textiles

Location
Oxford Road to the S of Manchester city centre and to the S of the University of Manchester campus

Opening
Mon–Sat 10am–5pm, Sun 2pm–5pm
Sat afternoon free eye-opener tour at 2pm

Admission
Free

Contact
The University of Manchester,
Oxford Road, Manchester M15 6ER

t 0161 275 7450
w whitworth.man.ac.uk
e whitworth@man.ac.uk

840 Birkenhead

Birkenhead Priory & St Mary's Tower

1 hr   All year

This Benedictine monastery, established in 1150 is the oldest building on Merseyside. Much of the original building remains and other parts have been restored to their former stature. Visit St Mary's Church (1822), climb the tower and experience panoramic views.

* Views of Birkenhead, Oxton Ridge, Bidston and Wirral
* Concerts on Sundays in August

Location
M53 onto the A41, follow signposts to Birkenhead

Opening
Easter–Oct Tue–Sun 1pm–5pm
Nov–Easter Tue–Sun 12 noon–4pm

Admission
Free

Contact
Priory Street, Birkenhead CH41 5JH

t 0151 666 1249
w wirral.gov.uk
e comments@wirral.gov.uk

841 Birkenhead

Birkenhead Tramway

1 hr   All year

Birkenhead is the home of the first street tramway in Europe. Take the tramway from Woodside visitor centre to the Old Colonial pub at the Taylor Street terminus. From there visit the heritage centre, which houses a collection of restored and part-restored local buses and trams.

* Open-topped 1901 Birkenhead tram 20
* Day-to-day service operated by two Hong Kong trams

Location
Signposted to Taylor Street from the Woodside ferry terminal

Opening
Apr–Oct Sat–Sun 1pm–5pm
Nov–Mar Sat–Sun 12 noon–4pm

Admission
Adult £1, Child 50p

Contact
Woodside ferry terminal

t 0151 647 6780

842 Birkenhead

Historic Warships

3 hrs   Feb–Dec

This is the largest collection of C20 fighting vessels in the UK. The collection includes the submarine *Onyx* and the anti submarine frigate HMS *Plymouth*. On the quayside explore the Bofors Gun and the LCVP which is ex HMS *Intrepid*.

* U534, the last U-boat to leave Germany in the Second World War
* LCT 7074, last surviving LCT of D-Day landings

Location
Leave M53 at junction 1, follow signs to All Docks. Signposted from there

Opening
Apr–Sep 10am–5pm
Oct–Mar 10am–4pm

Admission
Adult £6, Child £4, Concs £5

Contact
East Float, Dock Road, Birkenhead CH41 1DJ

t 0151 650 1573
w warships.freeserve.co.uk

843 Birkenhead

Williamson Art Gallery & Museum

1 hr   All year

This purpose-built gallery houses the majority of Birkenhead's collection of artistic masterpieces. On display are Victorian oil paintings, English watercolours, Liverpool porcelain, Della Robbia pottery. Collections feature local history, ship models and decorative arts.

* Part of the Merseyside embroidery trail
* Varied programme of temporary exhibitions

Location
Slatey Road

Opening
Tue–Sun & Bank Hols 10am–5pm

Admission
Free

Contact
Slatey Road, Birkenhead CH 43 4UE

t 0151 652 4177
w williamsonartgallery@wirrial.gov.uk

844 Ellesmere Port

Blue Planet Aquarium

2 hrs   All year

The aquarium features one of the world's largest underwater viewing tunnels. Visitors can get up close to huge sharks, graceful rays and hundreds of other fish. Exhibits encompass Scottish Highlands, the mighty Amazon, the depths of Lake Malawi and mangroves.

* A shark-inhabited Caribbean reef
* Touchpools with anemones, and costal rays

Location
Nr junction 10 of M53, adjacent to Cheshire Oaks designer outlet village

Opening
Apr–Nov Mon–Fri 10am–5pm
Sat & Sun 10am–6pm
Nov–Mar Mon–Fri 10am–5pm
Sat & Sun 11am–5pm

Admission
Adult £8.95, Child £6.50, Concs £6.95

Contact
Cheshire Oaks, Ellesmere Port CH65 9LF

t 0151 357 8800
w blueplanetaquarium.com
e info@blueplanetaquarium.com

845 Knowsley

National Wildflower Centre

2 hrs   Apr–Sep

The National Wildflower Centre is set in a Victorian park within 35 acres of parkland. It has an innovative visitor centre where visitors can learn about wildflowers. It places an emphasis on creative conservation and putting wildflowers back into Britain.

* Seasonal wildflower demonstration ares
* A working garden nursery

Location
Situated in Knowsley's Court Hey Park, off junction 5 of M62

Opening
Apr–Sep 10am–5pm

Admission
Adult £3, Child free, Concs £1.50

Contact
Court Hey Park, Knowsley L16 3NA

t 0151 737 1819 / 0151 7228292
w nwc.org.uk
e info@nwc.org.uk

846 Knowsley

Prescot Museum

1 hr   All year

This museum is located in a Georgian townhouse, which was once the site of the local cockerel-fighting pit. Exhibits reflect local history, in particular the clock- and watch-making tradition. On display are local longcase clocks, tools and a reconstruction of a C18 clockmaker's home.

* Displays of pottery manufacture and cable making
* Varied programme of exhibitions

Location
Signposted from the A56

Opening
Tue–Sat 10am–5pm
Sun 2pm–5pm

Admission
Free

Contact
34 Church Street, Prescot, Knowsley
L34 3LA

t 0151 430 7787
w knowsley.gov.uk
e knowsley.gov.ukleisure/museum

847 Liverpool

Aintree Racecourse & Visitor Centre

2 hrs   All year

A visit to Aintree Racecourse includes the museum, picture gallery and race of champions. Explore the weighing room, stables, parade ring, Red Rum's grave and statue. A virtual reality ride and tour of the racecourse are also available.

Location
3 miles from Liverpool city centre, well signposted

Opening
Group visits only, phone for details

Admission
Adult £7, Child & Concs £4

Contact
Ormskirk Road, Aintree, Liverpool
L9 5AS

t 0151 522 2921
w aintree.co.uk

848 Liverpool

Albert Dock

4 hrs+   All year

The Albert Dock is an architectural triumph. Opened in 1846, it became a treasure house of precious cargoes from all over the world. Today, redevelopment has transformed it into a busy and cosmopolitan centre as well as a top heritage attraction.

* Converted C19 warehouse buildings
* Visit albertdock.com for a web-cam view of the attraction

Location
Situated on Liverpool's waterfront adjacent to the Pier Head

Opening
Any reasonable time

Admission
Free

Contact
The Colonnades, Albert Dock,
Liverpool L3 4AE

t 0151 708 7334
w albertdock.com
e enquiries@albertdock.com

849 Liverpool

Cains Brewery

1 hr+   All year

Cains has always been renowned for producing award-winning cask ales. Incorporating the Brewery Tap, now one of Liverpool's drinking landmarks, Robert Cains' original mersey brewery stands today as a fine example of Victorian brewhouse architecture.

* Tours include buffet & 2 pints in the Brewery Tap pub

Location
In West Parliament Street, near Albert Dock

Opening
Mon–Thu, closes at 6.30pm

Admission
Advance booking essential

Contact
Stanhope Street, Liverpool L8 5XJ

t 0151 7098734
w gew@cainsbeer.com
e brewerytour@cainsbeers.com

850 Liverpool

Beatles Story

2 hrs · All year

The fascinating story of the Beatles is told in 18 separate sections, including a street in Hamburg, a replica of the Cavern Club complete with basement smells, a psychedelic scene, a walk-through yellow submarine in an underwater setting, music and rare film footage.

* Includes street scenes & Beatlemania
* The Cavern Club, the music & the instruments

Location
Follow signposts to Albert Dock

Opening
Daily 10am–6pm

Admission
Adult £8.45, Child £4.95, Concs £5.45

Contact
Albert Dock, Britannia Vaults, Liverpool L3 4AA

t 0151 709 1963
w beatlesstory.com

851 Liverpool

The Cavern Club

4 hrs+ · All year

Visit the most famous club in the world and learn all there is to know about the Cavern Club, from its early days as a jazz club in the cellar of a fruit warehouse, to the live music venue of today. This is a carbon copy of the original club where the Beatles found fame.

* Paul McCartney played his last gig of the century here
* Wall of Fame

Location
City Centre

Opening
Mon–Wed 12 noon–6pm
Thu 12 noon–2am
Fri–Sat 12 noon–2.45am
Sun 12 noon–12.30am

Admission
Adult £4

Contact
Mathew Street, Liverpool L2 6RE

t 0151 236 1965
w cavern-liverpool.co.uk
e office@thecavernliverpool.com

852 Liverpool

Conservation Centre

1 hr · All year

This Conservation Centre is housed in the former Midland Railway goods depot which was built in the 1870s. The centre cares for all of the National Museums' Liverpool collections. There are over a million objects, ranging from tiny natural history specimens to space rockets.

* Conservation science section
* Many world-famous masterpieces are cared for

Location
Nr Queen's Square bus station

Opening
Mon–Sat 10am–5pm
Sun 12 noon–5pm

Admission
Free

Contact
Whitechapel, Liverpool L1 6HZ

t 0151 478 4999
w conservationcentre.org.uk
e conservation@liverpoolmuseums.org.uk

853 Liverpool

Customs & Excise National Museum

2 hrs   All year

This museum tells the story of smuggling and contraband from the 1700s to the present day. The collection includes a display of tools of the trade, prints, paintings and photographs relating to the work of the Department of Customs and Excise.

* Collection of Department of Customs & Excise
* Discover how far people will go to avoid paying duty

Location	Contact
Follow signposts to Albert Dock	Albert Dock, Liverpool L3 4AQ
Opening	t 0151 478 4499
Daily 10am-5pm	w customsandexcisemuseum.org.uk
Admission	e info@1001daysout.com
Free	

854 Liverpool

Everton Football Club

2 hrs   All year

A tour of Goodison Park will include a behind-the-scenes look at what it's like to play for the Toffees. Walk down the tunnel and imagine the roar of 40,000 fans, explore the dressing room and see where the players relax after a game.

Location	Contact
3 miles N of Liverpool city centre	Goodison Park, Liverpool L4 4EL
Opening	t 0151 3302277
Daily, except on match days	w evertonfc.com
Admission	e boxoffice@evertonfc.com
Adult £6.50, Child & Concs £4.50	
Pre-booking essential	

855 Liverpool

Fingerprints of Elvis

1 hr   All year

Elvis Presley's enormous influence on the emergence of the Beatles and the whole Merseybeat scene is legendary. The legend of the King lives on through a number of his personal items, including a set of fingerprints, his Harley Davidson and stage costumes.

* Extraordinary jewellery & army insignia
* Audio tour by David Stanley – Elvis' stepbrother

Location	Contact
Follow the M62, then the brown signposts to Albert Dock	19 The Colonnades, Albert Dock, Liverpool L3 4AA
Opening	t 0151 709 1790
Daily 10am-6pm	w fingerprintsofelvis.com
Admission	
Adult £7.95, Child £4.95, Concs £5.45	

Liverpool Cathedral

2 hrs   All year

This is the largest Anglican cathedral in Britain and one of the great buildings of the C20. The massive tower stands over the city and the cathedral boasts the highest gothic arches, the largest organ and the heaviest ring of bells. The cathedral hosts exhibitions, concerts and recitals.

* Designed by Sir Giles Gilbert Scott
* The grand organ has 9765 pipes

Location
City centre

Opening
8am-6pm (subject to services)

Admission
Free, donations welcome

Contact
St James' Mount, Liverpool L1 7AZ

t 0151 709 6271
w liverpoolcathedral.org.uk
e info@liverpoolcathedral.org.uk

Liverpool Football Club

1 hr   All year

A tour of Anfield includes a walk down the players' tunnel and the opportunity to touch the famous sign that proclaims 'This is Anfield'. Experience the dressing room where the manager delivers his team talks. The museum is packed with things to do, see and listen to.

* Film takes visitors through a day in the life of the club
* Hillsborough memorial tribute to 96 fans who died in 1989

Location
3 miles from city centre, 4 miles from M62 & 7 miles from end of M57 & M58

Opening
Daily 10am-5pm
(closes 1 hour before kick off)

Admission
Adult £5, Child £3

Contact
Anfield Road, Liverpool L4 0TH

t 0151 260 6677
w liverpoolfc.tv
e events@liverpoolfc.tv

Liverpool Museum

2 hrs   All year

This is the largest of the National Museums of Liverpool venues. The fascinating and varied collections cover archaeology, ethnology and the natural and physical sciences. Special attractions include the award-winning natural history centre and the planetarium.

* Exhibition galleries include Egypt & the Near East
* Space & time gallery

Location
Opposite entrance to Birkenhead tunnel,5 mins walk fromTourist information Centre in Queen's Square

Opening
Mon-Sat 10am-5pm
Sun 12 noon-5pm

Admission
Free

Contact
William Brown Street, Liverpool L3 8EN

t 0151 478 4399
w liverpoolmuseum.org.uk
e themuseum@liverpoolmuseums. org.uk

Mathew Street Gallery

1 hr   All year

Specialising in the art of John Lennon, this gallery has more than 50 limited edition prints on display. The gallery has John Lennon drawings, Beatles' photography, artwork by Klaus Voorman and photography by Astrid Kirchherr.

* Prints are numbered and signed by Yoko Ono lennon

Location
Situated above the Beatles shop, yards from the Cavern Club

Opening
Mon-Sat 10am-5 pm Sun 11am-4pm

Admission
Free

Contact
31 Mathew Street, Liverpool L2 6RE

t 0151 236 0009
w lennonart.co.uk
e mathewstreetgallery@lennonart. co.uk

860 Liverpool

Mendips & 20 Forthlin Road

2 hrs   All year

This is a joint tour of Mendips, the childhood home of John Lennon, and Forthlin Road, the home of the McCartney family, where the Beatles met, rehearsed and wrote many of their earliest songs. Displays include contemporary photographs and Beatles' memorabilia.

* Audio tour features Sir Paul McCartney
* Evocative photographs of life at 20 Forthlin Road

Location
Tours leave from Albert Dock in central Liverpool, or Speke Hall

Opening
Tours depart 10.30am & 11.20am from Albert Dock & 1.50pm & 3.55pm from Speke Hall

Admission
Adult £10, Child free

Contact
20 Forthlin Road, Allerton, Liverpool L24 1YP

t 0151 708 8574/0151 427 7231
w spekehall.org.uk
e spekehall@nationaltrust.org.uk

861 Liverpool

Sefton Park Palm House

1 hr   All year

Sefton Park Palm House is a Grade II listed Victorian glasshouse, it is an octagonal three-tiered structure, showcasing the Liverpool botanical collection which was brought to the city from all over the world during its maritime history.

* One of the largest municipal collections in the country
* Four sculptures by Leon-Joseph Chavailiaur

Location
M62 onto the A5058 toward Queen's Drive & Alliton Road

Opening
Nov–Mar 10.30am–4pm
Apr–Oct 10.30am–5pm
Restricted opening during events

Admission
Free

Contact
Sefton Park, Liverpool L17 1AP

t 0151 726 2415
w palmhouse.org.uk
e info@palmhouse.org.uk

Speke Hall, Garden & Estate

2 hrs — Mar–Dec

Behind the black-and-white half-timbered façade of this hall are interiors which represent many centuries. The Great Hall and priests' holes evoke Tudor times, while the oak parlour and smaller rooms show the Victorian desire for privacy and comfort.

* Fine Jacobean plasterwork & carved furniture
* A fully-equipped Victorian kitchen and servants' hall

Location
8 miles SE of central Liverpool, next to Liverpool airport, signposted

Opening
Mar–Oct Wed–Sun 1pm–5.30pm
Oct–Dec Sat & Sun 1pm–4.30pm

Admission
Adult £6, Child £3.50

Contact
The Walk, Speke, Liverpool L24 1XD

t 0151 427 7231
w spekehall.org.uk
e spekehall@nationaltrust.org.uk

Tate Liverpool

2 hrs — All year

Tate Liverpool houses two main types of exhibits – art selected from the Tate Collection, and special exhibitions of contemporary art. Over 80 different presentations featuring work by more than 300 artists, have taken place since the gallery opened.

* Photography, printmaking, painting & sculpture
* Video, performance & installation

Location
Walking distance from Liverpool Lime Street station, signposted from city centre

Opening
Tue–Sun 10am–5.50pm

Admission
Tate Collection **Free**

Exhibition Adult £4, Child & Concs £3

Contact
The Colonnades, Albert Dock, Liverpool L3 4BB

t 0151 702 7400
w tate.org.uk/liverpool
e liverpoolinfo@tate.org.uk

The Walker

1 hr — All year

The Walker holds one of the finest collections of fine and decorative art in Europe. The gallery has recently undergone a major £4.3m refurbishment programme. These improvements include special exhibition galleries which display important touring shows.

* Refurbishment of the C17 European galleries
* New craft & design gallery of decorative arts

Location
Opposite entrance to Birkenhead tunnel, 5 mins from Tourist Infromation Centre

Opening
Mon–Sat 10am–5pm
Sun 12noon–5pm

Admission
Free

Contact
William Brown Street, Liverpool L3 8EL

t 0151 478 4199
w thewalker.org.uk
e thewalker@liverpoolmuseums.org.uk

865 Southport

Atkinson Art Gallery

½ hr   All year

This gallery houses C17–C20 British art, including works by Lely, Cotman, Ford Madox Brown, Sickert and Ginner, as well as The Death of General Wolfe by Benjamin West. It also holds a large collection of British watercolours, etchings and engravings.

* Ceramics, oriental arts & crafts & sculpture
* Monthly spotlights on paintings or sculpture with talks

Location
Situated between the library & arts centre nr junction with Eastbank Street

Opening
Mon–Wed & Fri 10am–5pm
Thu & Sat 10am–1pm

Admission
Free

Contact
Lord Street, Southport PR8 1DH

t 01704 533133
w seftonarts.co.uk
e atkinson.gallery@leisure.sefton.
   gov.uk

866 Southport

Formby Squirrel Reserve

2 hrs   All year

This nature reserve is home to one of Britain's last thriving colonies of red squirrels. These squirrels can be seen in the pine trees and the shoreline attracts waders such as oyster-catchers and sanderlings. As well as the beautiful beach there are miles of walks across the sand dunes.

Location
15 miles N of Liverpool, 2 miles W of Formby, 2 miles off A565 & 6 miles S of Southport

Opening
All year, dawn to dusk

Admission
Adult £2.80

Contact
Blundell Avenue, Formby L37 1PH

t 01704 878 591
w nationaltrust.org.uk
e formby@nationaltrust.org.uk

867 Wirral

Hilbre Island

2 hrs   All year

The three tidal islands lying at the mouth of the Dee Estuary, Little Eye, Middle Eye and Hilbre, are designated a local nature reserve. The islands are cut off from the mainland by the tide for up to four hours out of every twelve, so check the tide times before travelling.

* Overwintering site for wildfowl & waders
* Hilbre island bird observatory

Location
Access is by foot, 2 miles from West Kirby

Opening
Check tide times before setting out
www.ukho.gov.uk/tideprediction.cfm

Admission
Free

Contact
West Kirby, Wirral

t 0151 648 4371/3884
w wirral.gov.uk/er

Angel of the North, Gateshead, Tyne & Wear

North East

Durham Northumberland Tyne & Wear

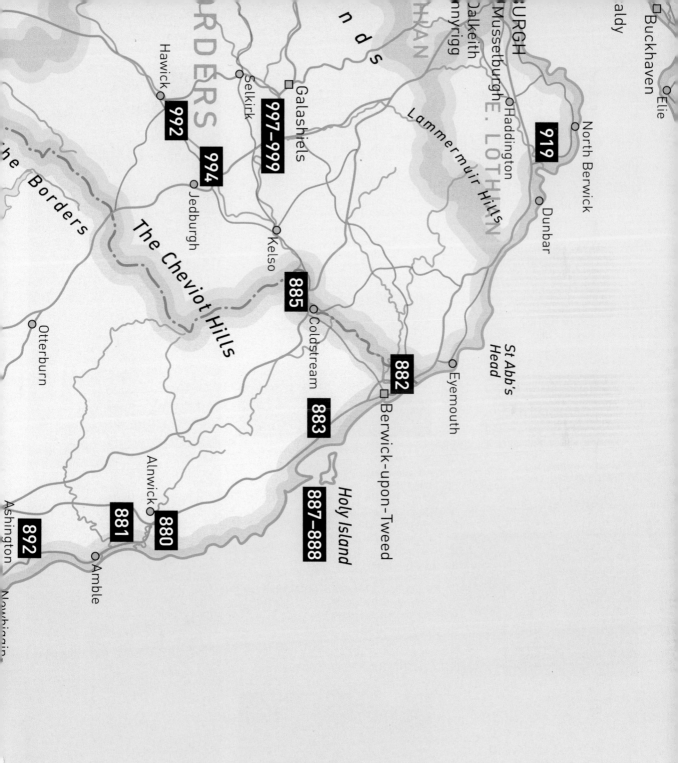

Buckhaven

aldy

Elie

URGH

Mussetburgh

Dalkeith

nnyrigg

E. LOTHIAN

Haddington

919

North Berwick

Dunbar

n d s

Lammermuir Hills

ORDERS

Hawick

Selkirk

992

Galashiels

997–999

994

Jedburgh

Kelso

The Borders

The Cheviot Hills

Otterburn

885

Coldstream

St Abb's Head

882

Eyemouth

883

Berwick-upon-Tweed

Alnwick

881

880

887–888

Holy Island

Ashington

892

Amble

Newbiggin

868 Barnard Castle

Bowes Museum

3 hrs   All year

Founded by local businessman, John Bowes, and his French wife, Josephine, this magnificent museum, which opened in 1892, houses one of Britain's finest collections of paintings, ceramics, furniture and textiles. Special outdoor events and family fun days.

* Set in 23 acres of parkland, with parterre garden
* Outstanding temporary art exhibition programme

Location
Just off A66, 20 mins from Scotch Corner (A1)

Opening
Daily 11am–5pm
Closed Dec 25/26 & Jan 1

Admission
Adult £6, Child free, Concs £5

Contact
Barnard Castle DL12 8NP

t 01833 690606
w bowesmuseum.org.uk
e info@bowesmuseum.org.uk

869 Barnard Castle

Rokeby Park

1 hr+   All year

A palladian-style country house which was the setting for Sir Walter Scott's ballad 'Rokeby'. Contains a unique collection of C18 needlepainting pictures, period furniture and an interesting print room.

Location
N of A66 between A1(M) and Bowes

Opening
May Bank Holiday then each Mon & Tue until 1st Tue in Sep, 2–5pm

Admission
Adult £5, Child £2

Contact
Rokeby,
Barnard Castle DL12 9RZ

t 01833 637334
w durham.gov.uk

870 Beamish

Beamish, The North of England Open Air Museum

4 hrs+   Apr–Oct

Beamish is a unique living, working experience of life as it was in the north of England in both the early C18 and C19. It shows how the region was transformed in that time from its thinly populated rural roots to being the home to heavy industrialisation.

* Costumed guides explain each attraction
* Former European Museum of the Year

Location
Follow signs from junction 63 of A1M

Opening
Apr–Oct Tue–Thu & Sat–Mon 10am–5pm
Nov–Apr 10am–4pm (closed Dec 13–Jan 3)

Admission
Adult £12, Child £7, Concs £10

Contact
Beamish DH9 0RG

t 0191 370 4000
w beamish.org.uk
e museum@beamish.org.uk

871 · Darlington

Darlington Railway Centre & Museum

2 hrs   All year

Celebrating nearly 180 years of railway history in the town and the North East of England in general. Of greatest significance is Stephenson's Rocket which hauled the inaugural multi-carriage train on the Stockton and Darlington Railway.

* Including an 1840s Darlington-built locomotive
* The museum is in the 1842 railway station

Location
1 mile from town centre on A167

Opening
Daily 10am–5pm
Closed Dec 25/26 & Jan 1

Admission
Adult £2.20, Child £1.10, Concs £1.50

Contact
North Road Station, Darlington DL3 6ST
t 01325 460532
w drcm.org.uk
e museum@darlington.gov.uk

872 · Darlington

Raby Castle

3 hrs+   Daily

Built in the C14, Raby Castle is one of the largest and most impressive of English medieval castles, with towers, turrets, embattled walls, interiors and artworks from the medieval, Regency and Victorian periods. Walled gardens combine ancient and modern features.

* Great kitchen little altered in 600 years
* Paintings by Reynolds and other masters

Location
1 mile N of Staindrop on A688

Opening
Easter Sat–Wed 11am–5.30pm
May & Sep Wed–Sun 11am–5.30pm
Jun–Aug Sun–Fri 11am–5.30pm

Admission
Adult £7, Child £3, Concs £6

Contact
PO Box 50, Staindrop, Darlington DL2 3AH
t 01833 660 202
w rabycastle.com
e admin@rabycastle.com

873 · Durham

Crook Hall Gardens

1 hr+   Easter–Sep

On the banks of the River Wear with views of Durham cathedral and castle, Crook Hall is a Grade I medieval manor house with C13 hall. There are a variety of beautiful gardens including ancient and modern planting schemes and a newly planted maze.

* Fruit trees wreathed in rambling roses
* 'A tapestry of colourful blooms', Alan Titchmarsh

Location
Short walk from Durham's Millburngate shopping centre, opposite the Gala theatre

Opening
Easter, Bank Hols & Sun in May & Sep. Jun–Aug Sun–Fri 1pm–5pm

Admission
Adult £4, Concs £3.50

Contact
Frankland Lane, Sidegate, Durham DH1 5SZ
t 0191 384 8028
w crookhallgardens.co.uk
e info@crookhallgardens.co.uk

874 · Durham

Durham Light Infantry & Durham Art Gallery

3 hrs   All year

Tells the story of the Durham Light Infantry from 1758 to 1968. The displays focus on the experience of war, using letter & diary extracts, plus the actual voices of DLI Second World War soldiers. Upstairs, Durham Art Gallery hosts a wide range of exhibitions and events.

* Exhibition of Durham home front during WW2
* Reopened in 2000 after major redevelopment

Location
½ mile NW of Durham city centre, off A691 near railway station

Opening
Apr–Oct 10am–5pm
Nov–Mar 10am–4pm

Admission
Adult £2.50, Concs £1.25

Contact
Aykley Heads, Durham DH1 5TU
t 0191 384 2214
w durham.gov.uk/dli
e dli@durham.gov.uk

875 Durham

Old Fulling Mill Museum of Archaeology

1 hr   All year

Discover Durham city's ancient hidden past and learn about the curious carved rings in prehistoric stones, the life and times of Anglo-Saxons and Vikings who lived in Durham and see the work carried out for the cathedral's clergy by the town's medieval craftsmen.

* Hands–on activities
* Views of the cathedral and riverbank walks

Location
Banks of the river, under the cathedral

Opening
Apr–Oct daily 11am–4pm
Nov–Mar Fri–Mon 11.30–3.30pm

Admission
Adult £1, Concs 50p

Contact
The Banks, Durham DH1 3EB

t 0191 334 1823
w dur.ac.uk/fulling.mill
e fulling.mill@dur.ac.uk

877 Hartlepool

HMS *Trincomalee* – Hartlepool Quay

1 hr   All year

Built for the Admiralty in Bombay in 1817, HMS *Trincomalee* is the oldest ship afloat in the UK. An award-winning restoration provides a unique opportunity to experience the atmosphere of a classic British frigate from the time of Nelson's navy.

* Excellent disabled access to most decks
* One of several attractions around Historic Quay

Location
Follow signs for Hartlepool Historic Quay

Opening
Apr–Oct 10.30am–5pm
Nov–Mar 10.30am–4pm

Admission
Adult £4.25, Child £3.25, Concs £3.25

Contact
HMS Trincomalee Trust, Jackson Dock, Hartlepool TS24 0SQ

t 01429 223193
w hms–trincomalee.co.uk
e office@trincomalee.co.uk

876 Durham

Oriental Museum

1 hr   All year

The only museum of its kind in the UK, entirely devoted to art and archaeology from cultures throughout the Orient. The collections range from prehistoric Egypt and China to the work of living artists. The museum is part of Durham university.

* Used as resource by researchers around the world
* Students of higher education enter for free

Location
S side of Durham, signposted from A177

Opening
Mon–Fri 10am–5pm
Sat & Sun 12noon–5pm

Admission
Adult £1.50, Concs 75p

Contact
Elvet Hill, off South Road, Durham DH1 3TH

t 0191 334 5694
w dur.ac.uk/oriental.museum
e oriental.museum@durham.ac.uk

Durham   Northumberland

878 Stockton-on-Tees

Castlegate Quay – HM Bark *Endeavour*

1 hr   All year

The North-East's premier watersports centre funded by £1.6m of Sport England Lottery funding is home to HM Bark *Endeavour*, a full-size replica of the ship Captain Cook used in his first voyage of discovery to Australia. Guides on hand to provide insight into life at sea.

* Part of the regeneration of the quayside
* Next to Castlegate Quay Watersports' Centre

Location
Next to Millennium Bridge

Opening
Apr–Oct Mon–Wed 11am–4pm

Admission
Adult £3, Child £2

Contact
Castlegate Quay Heritage Project, Watersports' Centre, Moat Street, Stockton-on-Tees TS18 3AZ

t 01642 676844
w castlegatequay.co.uk
e enquiries@castlegatequay.co.uk

879 Upper Weardale

Killhope Lead Mining Museum

4 hrs   Apr–Oct

This fully-restored lead mine to explores the lives of Victorian mining families. Guided tours take visitors along the original tunnels (wellingtons, hard-hat and cap lamp provided). Woodland walk gives access to further reminders of lead mining.

* Warm clothes required even during summer
* Red squirrels can be observed in woodland

Location
Off A689 between Stanhope & Alston

Opening
Apr–Sep daily 10.30am–5pm
Oct weekends only + autumn
half–term daily 10.30am–5pm

Admission
Adult £5, Child £2.50
No under 4s are allowed in the mine

Contact
The North of England Lead Mining Museum, nr Cowshill, Upper Weardale DL13 1AR

t 01388 537505
w durham.gov.uk/killhope
e killhope@durham.gov.uk

880 Alnwick

Alnwick Castle

1 hr+   Apr–Oct

Foreboding medieval castle known as the Windsor of the North. Stunning state rooms, fine furniture and paintings by Canaletto, Van Dyck and Titian. Filming location for *Harry Potter*. Castle overlooks Capability Brown landscape. Peaceful walks with superb views.

* Home to Percy family for 700 years
* Museum of Royal Northumberland Fusiliers

Location
Outskirts of Alnwick, 35 miles N of Newcastle upon Tyne, 1 mile from A1

Opening
Apr–Oct daily 11am–5pm

Admission
Adult £7.50, Child (under 16) free, Concs £6.50

Contact
Alnwick NE66 1NQ

t 01665 510777
w alnwickcastle.com
e enquiries@alnwickcastle.com

881 Amble

Warkworth Castle

1 hr+   All year

The magnificent eight-towered keep stands high on a hill overlooking the River Croquet. Home to the Percy family who at times wielded more power in the north than the King. Most famous was Harry Hotspur (Sir Henry Percy) immortalised in Shakespeare's *Henry IV*.

* Opening scenes of *Henry IV* were set in Warkworth
* Duke's rooms first opened in 2003

Location
8 miles S of Alnwick, on A1068

Opening
Apr–Sep daily 10am–6pm, Oct daily 10am–5pm, Nov–Mar 10am–4pm

Admission
Adult £3, Child £1.50, Concs £2.30

Contact
Nr Amble,
Morpeth NE65 0VJ

t 01665 711423
w english–heritage.org.uk

882 Berwick–upon–Tweed

Berwick Barracks, Museum & Art Gallery

2 hrs   All year

One of the earliest purpose-built barracks in the country now houses three museums including By Beat of Drum, chronicling the history of the British Army, the Berwick Borough Art Gallery and the King's Own Scottish Borderers' Regimental Museum.

* Walk on ramparts affords great views of River Tweed

Location
Off Church Street in centre of town

Opening
Easter–Sep 10am–6pm, Oct 5pm
Nov–Mar Wed–Sun 10am–4pm

Admission
Adult £3, Child £1.50, Concs £2.30

Contact
The Parade,
Berwick–upon–Tweed PD15 1DF

t 01289 304493
w english–heritage.org.uk

883 Bamburgh

Bamburgh Castle

2 hrs   Mar–Oct

Probably one of the finest castles in England. Perched on a basalt outcrop on the very edge of the North Sea. Restored in 1750 and again extensively by C19 industrialist, Lord Armstrong. Tour includes magnificent King's Hall, Cross Hall, receptions rooms and armoury.

* Still home to the Armstrong family
* Exhibits include fine furniture, tapestries and arms

Location
20 miles S of Berwick–upon–Tweed by the B1342

Opening
Mar 13–Oct 31 daily 11am–5pm

Admission
Adult £5, Child £2, Concs £4

Contact
Bamburgh NE69 7DF

t 01668 214 515
w bamburghcastle.com
e bamburghcastle@aol.com

884 Carlisle–Newcastle

Hadrian's Wall

1 hr+   All year

One of the most important monuments built by the Romans in Britain. It is the best-known frontier in the entire Roman Empire and is designated a World Heritage site. Various attractions along the wall include Roman forts and several museums.

* Museum brings Roman history to life
* 84 mile coast-to-coast walk along wall now open

Location
A69 between Newcastle & Carlisle runs parallel to Hadrian's Wall (approximately 2–5 miles S)

Opening
Times vary, phone for details

Admission
Prices vary, phone for details

Contact
Hadrian's Wall Tourism Partnership, 14b Gilesgate, Hexham NE46 3NJ

t 01434 322002
w hadrians-wall.org
e info@hadrians-wall.org

885 Chillingham

Chillingham Castle

1 hr+   May–Sep

This remarkable castle with alarming dungeons and torture chamber has been in the family of the Earls Grey and their relations since the C13. See active restoration of complex masonry, metalwork and ornamental plaster in a wide diversity of rooms and styles.

* Beautiful grounds with commanding views
* Formal gardens and woodland walks open to public

Location
Signposted from the A1 & A697

Opening
May–Sep Sun–Fri 12 noon–5pm
Oct–Apr by appointment

Admission
Adult £6, Child £2.50, Concs £5.50 under 5s 70p

Contact
Chillingham NE66 5NJ

t 01668 215 359
w chillingham-castle.com
e enquiries@chillingham-castle.com

886 Hexham

Cherryburn

1 hr   Mar–Oct

This C19 farmhouse was the birthplace of Thomas Bewick who pioneered wood-engraving. Bewick was an outstanding artist and naturalist and used this passion to produce beautiful engravings of wildlife. The cottage contains an exhibition of his life and works.

* Demonstrations of wood-engraving and printing
* Stunning views of valley of the River Tyne from garden

Location
A695 to Mickley Square, follow signs, 11 miles from Hexham

Opening
Mar 29–Oct 31 Mon, Thu–Sun
1pm–5.30pm

Admission
Adult £3.20, Child £1.60

Contact
Station Bank, Mickley, nr Stocksfield NE43 7DD

t 01661 843276
w nationaltrust.org.uk

887 Holy Island–Lindisfarne

Lindisfarne Castle

½ hr   Mar–Nov

Perched on top of a rocky crag and accessible over a causeway at low tide only. Originally a Tudor fort, it was converted into a private house in 1903 by the young Edwin Lutyens. The small rooms are full of intimate decoration and design.

* Charming walled garden planned by Gertrude Jekyll
* Check crossing times before making long journey

Location
Holy Island, 6 miles E of A1, across causeway

Opening
Feb 14–Feb 22, Mar 20–Oct 31 Tue–Sun and Bank Hols. Times vary depending upon tides, usually 10.30am–3pm or 12noon–4pm

Admission
Adult £5, Child £2.50

Contact
Holy Island, Berwick-upon-Tweed TD15 2SH

t 01289 389244
w nationaltrust.org.uk

©National Trust Photographic Library/Joe Cornish

©English Heritage Photographic Library/Paul Highnam

888 Holy Island–Lindisfarne

Lindisfarne Priory

1 hr+   All year

A holy site since being founded by St Aidan in AD 635, Lindisfarne remains a place of pilgrimage today. Lindisfarne Priory was the site of one of the most important early centres of Christianity in Anglo-Saxon England. Check tides before visiting.

* Anglo-Saxon carvings in museum
* Refurbished museum new for 2004

Location
Holy Island, 6 miles E of A1, across causeway

Opening
Apr–Sep daily 10am–6pm, Oct daily 10am–5pm. Nov–Mar daily 10am–4pm. Subject to tides.

Admission
Adult £3, Child £1.50, Concs £2.30

Contact
Holy Island, Berwick-upon-Tweed TD15 2RX

t 01289 389200
w english-heritage,org.uk

889 Morpeth

Belsay Hall, Castle & Gardens

3 hrs   All year

A dramatic, well-preserved medieval towerhouse, to which a Jacobean manor house was added in 1614. Belsay Hall (1807), designed by Sir Charles in Greek Revival style after the Temple of Theseus in Athens, has great architectural importance within Europe.

* Two acres of rhododendrons at best May & June
* Formal terraces and winter garden, original planting

Location	Admission
In Belsay, 14 miles NW of Newcastle on A696	Adult £4.50, Child £2.30, Concs £3.40
Opening	**Contact**
Apr–Sep daily 10am–6pm, Oct daily 10am–5pm, Nov–Mar daily 10am–4pm	Belsay NE20 0DX t 01661 881636 w english–heritage.org.uk

890 Morpeth

Wallington

3 hrs   Easter–Sep

Wallington House will reopen in 2004 after extensive renovation. The Wallington estate was laid out in the C18 by Sir Walter Blackett. The original formality underlies the natural landscape in which walks offer a variety of lawns, shrubberies, lakeand and woodland.

* Long walks encompass wooded valleys & moorland
* Buildings, sculpture and water features

Location	Admission
12 miles W of Morpeth on B6343	Adult £7, Child £3.50
Opening	**Contact**
House Easter–Sep Wed–Mon 1pm–5pm *Grounds* Easter–Sep daily 10am–7pm Oct 10am–6pm, Nov–Mar daily 10–4pm	Cambo, Morpeth NE61 4AR t 01670 773600 w nationaltrust.org.uk e wallington@nationaltrust.org.uk

©National Trust Photographic Library/Charlie Waite

891 Morpeth

Cragside House

3 hrs+   Apr–Sep

The first house in the world to use hydro electricity to power a revolutionary new lighting and internal telephone system. The brainchild of industrialist William Armstrong, the technology amazed contemporaries. Surrounded by beautiful gardens.

* Used to impress important armament customers
* 3 acre rock garden, fruit house and Italian garden

Location	Admission
1 mile N of Rothbury on B6341	Adult £8, Child £4
Opening	**Contact**
House Apr–Sep 1–5.30pm Oct 4.30	Rothbury,
Estate Apr–Oct 10.30am–7pm	Morpeth NE65 7PX
Closed Mon ex Bank Hols	
Nov–Dec 11am–4pm closed Mon & Tue	t 01669 620333
	w nationaltrust.org.uk
	e cragside@nationaltrust.org.uk

892 Rothbury

Brinkburn Priory

1 hr   Apr–Oct

Founded in 1135 as a house for the Augustinian canons, the church is the only complete surviving building of the monastery. In the summer season a number of choral events can be attended at this practicing church.

* Adjacent manor house has open ground floor
* Lovely setting beside River Coquet

Location	Contact
4½ miles SE of Rothbury off B6344	Longframlinton, Morpeth NE65 8AR
Opening	
Apr–Sep daily 10am–6pm, Oct 5pm	t 01665 570628
	w english-heritage.org.uk
Admission	
Adult £2, Child £1, Concs £1.50	

©English Heritage Photographic Library/Keith Buck

893 Gateshead

BALTIC

  1 hr+ All year

A major new international centre for contemporary art, situated on the south bank of the River Tyne. Housed in a 1950s' grain warehouse (part of the former Baltic Flour Mills), BALTIC is a site for the production, presentation and experience of contemporary art.

* Constantly changing programme of exhibitions
* Displays of artists in residence

Location
Gateshead Quayside, 10 mins walk from town centre

Opening
Mon, Tue, Wed, Fri & Sat 10am–7pm
Thu 10am–10pm, Sun 10am–5pm

Admission
Free

Contact
South Shore Road, Gateshead NE8 3BA

t 0191 4781810
w balticmill.com
e info@balticmill.com

894 Gateshead

Shipley Art Gallery

  1 hr All year

Home to a collection of over 700 pieces by the country's leading craft makers, including ceramics, glass, metalwork, jewellery, textiles and furniture. There is a temporary programme of exhibitions and a wide range events and activities.

* Constantly changing temporary exhibits
* Annual selling exhibition at Christmas

Location
Just off A167 to Newcastle, opposite the Springfield Hotel

Opening
Mon–Sat 10am–5pm, Sun 2–5pm

Admission
Free

Contact
Prince Consort Road,
Gateshead NE8 4JB

t 0191 4771495
w twmuseums.org.uk/shipley
e shipley@twmuseums.org.uk

895 Jarrow

Bede's World & St Paul's Church

  3 hrs All year

The extraordinary life of the Venerable Bede (AD 673–735) created a rich legacy that is celebrated today at Bede's World, where Bede lived and worked 1300 years ago. Stunning new museum building and site of Anglo-Saxon monastery of St Paul and medieval monastic ruins.

* Herb garden based on Anglo-Saxon & medieval plants
* Anglo-Saxon demo farm, complete with animals

Location
Near S end of Tyne tunnel, off A185

Opening
Apr–Oct Mon–Sat 10am–5.30pm
Sun 12 noon–5.30, Nov–Mar 4.30pm.
Church closed during services

Admission
Adult £4.50, Child £2.50, Concs £3

Contact
Church Bank NE32 3DY

t 0191 4892106
w bedesworld.co.uk
e visitorinfo@bedesworld.co.uk

896 Newcastle upon Tyne

Discovery Museum

2 hrs   All year

Discovery is the region's biggest free museum and the gateway to fun and facts about life on Tyneside. Explore Newcastle's past from Roman times to the present day, Tyneside's inventions that changed the world, a fun approach to science, and take a walk through fashion.

* See Roman, Norman and medieval Newcastle
* Fascinating model of the original Tyne Bridge

Location
Short walk from Newcastle Central Station

Opening
Mon–Sat 10am–5pm Sun 2pm–5pm

Admission
Free

Contact
Blandford Square,
Newcastle upon Tyne NE1 4JA

t 0191 232 6789
w twmuseums.org.uk
e discovery@twmuseums.org.uk

897 Newcastle upon Tyne

Hancock Museum

2 hrs+   All year

For more than 100 years this museum has provided visitors with an insight into the animal kingdom and the powerful forces of nature. From the dinosaurs to living animals, the Hancock is home to creatures past and present and even the odd Egyptian mummy.

* Live reptiles, snakes and and insects
* Always housing a blockbuster exhibition

Location
City centre nr Haymarket

Opening
All year Mon–Sat 10am–5pm, Sun 2–5pm

Admission
Prices vary please phone for details

Contact
Barras Bridge,
Newcastle upon Tyne NE2 4PT

t 0191 222 6765
w twmuseums.org.uk/hancock
e hancock.museum@ncl.ac.uk

898 Newcastle upon Tyne

Laing Art Gallery

1 hr   All year

Partially closed until April 2004, the new galleries and facilities will open with the third National Gallery touring exhibition entitled Making Faces, which features masterpieces by world-famous artists such as Rembrandt, Goya, Hogarth, Opie, Renoir and Warhol.

* Display of work by local engraver Thomas Bewick
* Refurbishment open from April 2004

Location
Signed from Newcastle city centre, 5 mins walk from Monument metro

Opening
Mon–Sat 10am–5pm, Sun 2–5pm

Admission
Free

Contact
New Bridge Street,
Newcastle upon Tyne NE1 8AG

t 0191 232 7734
w twmuseums.org.uk/laing
e laing@twmuseums.org.uk

899 Newcastle upon Tyne

Life Science Centre

 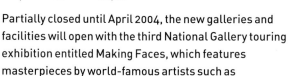

2 hrs+   All year

Discover amazing facts about life and learn to understand how DNA spells out instructions for every species. Explore where life comes from and how it works. Meet your 4-billion-year-old family, find out what makes you unique and test your brainpower.

* Open air ice rink in winter, carries a separate charge
* Enjoy the thrill of the motion simulator

Location
Near Central Station

Opening
Mon–Sat 10am–6pm, Sun 11am–6pm
Closed Dec 25, Jan 1

Admission
Adult £6.95, Child £4.50, Concs £5.50

Contact
Times Square,
Newcastle upon Tyne NE1 4EP

t 0191 243 8223 / 243 8210
w lifesciencecentre.org.uk
e bookings@life.org.uk

900 North Shields

Stephenson Railway Museum

1 hr   May–Sep

Re-live the glorious days of the steam railway at the Stephenson Railway Museum. The museum is home to George Stephenson's Billy, a forerunner to the world-famous Rocket, and many other engines from the age of steam. Rides on a steam train can be taken.

 * See the story of coal and electricity's impact on lives

Location
Well signposted from junction of A19/A1058

Opening
May–Sep Tue–Thu 11am–3pm
Sat, Sun & Bank Hols 11am–4pm

Admission
Free

Contact
Middle Engine Lane,
North Shields NE29 8DX

t 0191 2 007 146
w twmuseums.org.uk/stephenson
e stephenson@twmuseums.org.uk

902 South Shields

Arbeia Roman Fort & Museum

1 hr   All year

Four miles east of the end of Hadrian's Wall at South Shields, Arbeia Roman Fort guarded the entrance to the River Tyne. Built around AD 160, the stone fort played an essential role in the mighty frontier system. See reconstructions of original buildings.

* Excavated remains give insight into Roman life
* Time Quest activity for budding archaeologists

Location
10 mins signposted walk from South Shields metro

Opening
Easter–Oct Mon–Sat 10am–5.30pm
Sun 1–5pm
Oct–Easter Mon–Sat 10am–4pm

Admission
Free

Contact
Baring Street, South Shields NE33 2BB

t 0191 4 561 369
w twmuseums.org.uk
e arbeia@twmuseums.org.uk

901 Rowlands Gill

Gibside

3 hrs   All year

One of the north's finest landscapes, much of which is a SSSI, a forest garden currently under restoration and embracing many miles of riverside and forest walks. There are several outstanding buildings, including a Palladian chapel and the Column of Liberty-Lyons.

* Former home of Queen Mother's family
* Several buildings still under restoration

Location
6 miles SW of Gateshead on B6314

Opening
Grounds Mar–Oct Tue–Sun & bank hols 10am–5pm
Nov–Feb 10am–3.30pm
Chapel Apr–Oct Tue–Sun 11am–5pm

Admission
Adult £3.50, Child £2

Contact
Nr Rowlands Gill,
Burnopfield NE16 6BG

t 01207 541 820
w nationaltrust.org.uk
e gibside@nationaltrust.org.uk

903 South Shields

South Shields Museum & Art Gallery

2 hrs   All year

The complex reopens in spring 2004 after a £1m transformation. See local history, stunning paintings from the museum's collection (many shown for the first time) and a gallery dedicated to the local author, Catherine Cookson.

* Regular seasonal displays
* Hands–on and interactive activities

Location	Contact
South Shields town centre	Ocean Road, South Shields NE33 2JA
Opening	t 01914 568 740
Apr–Sep Mon–Sat 10am–5.30pm	w twmuseums.org.uk/southshields
Sun 1pm–5pm	e southshields@twmuseums.org.uk
Oct–Mar Mon–Sat 10am–5pm	
Admission	
Free	

904 Sunderland

National Glass Centre

1hr+   All year

Based in an innovative new building and set on the north bank of the River Wear, the National Glass Centre is dedicated to promoting glass in all its uses – in design and technology and as a vehicle for artistic expression.

* Home of International Institute for research in glass

Location	Contact
Signposted from all major roads	Liberty Way, Sunderland SR6 0GL
Opening	t 0191 515 5555
Daily 10am–5pm	w nationalglasscentre.co.uk
Closed Dec 25, Jan 1	e infor@nationalglasscentre.co.uk
Admission	
Adult £5, Child £3, Concs £3	

905 Sunderland

Souter Lighthouse

1 hr+   Apr–Nov

When it first shone its light in 1871, Souter was the most advanced lighthouse in the world, and the first purpose-built lighthouse to utilise electricity. Explore the compass room, Victorian keeper's cottage, engine room, the huge optic and enjoy the stunning views.

* When operational, light could be seen from 19 miles
* See the engine room and cramped living quarters

Location	Contact
2½ miles S of South Shields on A183	Coast Road, Whitburn, Sunderland SR6 7NH
Opening	
Feb 14–Feb 29 daily 11am–5pm	t 0191 529 3161
Mar 27–Oct 31 Sat–Thu 11am–5pm	w nationaltrust.org.uk
Admission	e souter@nationaltrust.org.uk
Adult £3.50, Child £2	

907 Washington

Washington Old Hall

2 hrs   Apr–Oct

From 1183 this house was the home of George Washington's direct ancestors, who took their surname from the village of Washington. The manor remained in the family until 1613. Mementoes of the American connection and the War of Independence are on display.

* Fine collection of contemporary blue and white delft
* Jacobean-style garden and brand new nuttery

Location	Contact
5 miles W of Sunderland, well signposted	The Avenue, District 4, Washington Village NE38 7LE
Opening	t 0191 416 6879
House Mar 28–Oct 31, Sun–Wed 11am–5pm. Open Good Friday	
Admission	
Adult £3.50, Child £1.50	

906 Sunderland

Sunderland Museum & Winter Gardens

4 hrs   All year

Hands-on exhibits and interactive displays tell the story of Sunderland from its prehistoric past through to the present day. The art gallery features paintings by L.S.Lowry alongside Victorian masterpieces. The winter gardens contain over 1,500 flowers and plants.

* Good disabled facilities
* Many educational exhibits

Location	Contact
City centre on Burdon Road	Burdon Road, Sunderland SR1 1PP
Opening	t 0191 553 2323
Mon–Sat 10am–5pm, Sun 2pm–5pm	w twmuseums.org.uk/sunderland
Admission	e sunderland@twmuseums.org.uk
Free	

908 Washington

Wildfowl & Wetlands Trust Washington

3 hrs   All year

Ideally placed to provide a stopover and wintering habitat for migratory waterbirds after their passage over the North Sea, this recreated wetland provides large flocks of curlew and redshank with a safe place to roost and herons with a place to breed.

* Nuthatch sited in 2003 for the first time in 10 years
* See waders, kingfishers, snipe and shovelers

Location	Contact
E of Washington, 4 miles from A1(M)	Pattinson, Washington NE38 8LE
Opening	t 0191 416 5454
Summer daily 9.30am–5pm	w wwt.org.uk
Winter daily 9.30am–4pm	e info.washington@wwt.org.uk
Closed Dec 25	
Admission	
Adult £5.50, Child £3.50, Concs £4.50	

Castle Stalker, Strathclyde

Scotland

Central Scotland Grampian
Highlands and Islands Southern Scotland

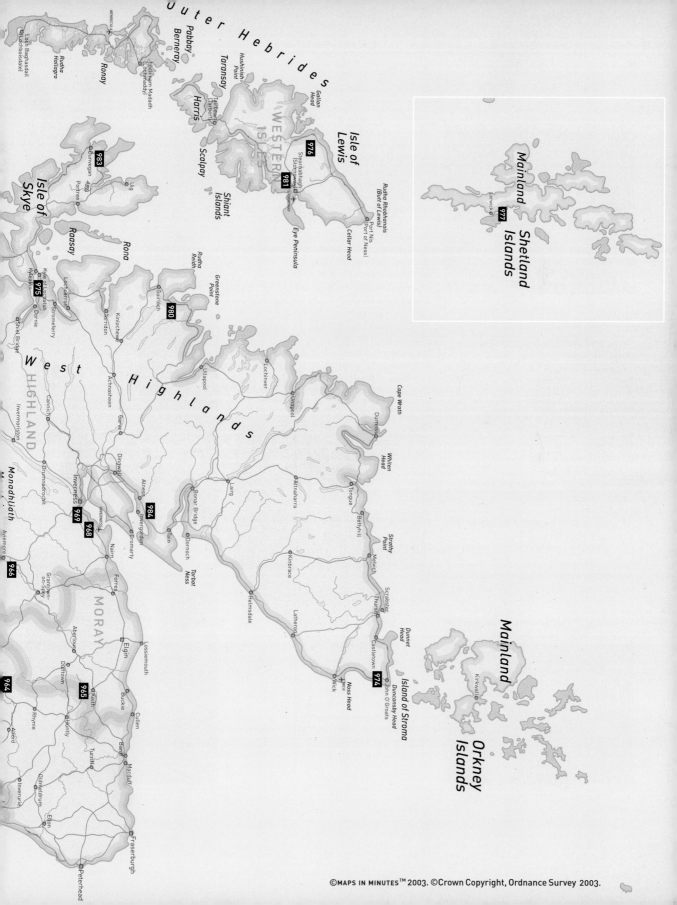

Outer Hebrides

Loch Baghasdail
[Lochboisdale]

Rudha Hallagro

Ronay

Eabh nam Madadh
[Lochmaddy]

Pabbay
Berneray

Taransay

Harris

Scalpay

Hushinish
Point

Gallan
Head

WESTERN ISLES

Isle of
Lewis

Steornabhagh
[Stornoway]

976

981

Jarrbeart
[Tarbert]

Shiant
Islands

Rudha Rhabhanais
[Butt of Lewis]

Port Nis
Port of Ness]

Celiar Head

Eye Peninsula

Isle of
Skye

983

Dunvegan

Portree

Raasay

Rona

Uig

Rudha
Reidh

Greenstone
Point

Gairloch

980

Mainland

Shetland
Islands

Lerwick

977

Kyle of Lochalsh

Kyleakin

Lochcarron

Stromeferry

Dornie

Shiel Bridge

Applecross

Kinlochewe

Achnasheen

Garve

Ullapool

Lochinver

Cape Wrath

Durness

Whiten
Head

W e s t

H i g h l a n d s

HIGHLAND

Invermoriston

Drumnadrochit

Cannich

Dingwall

969

968

INVERNESS

Inverness

Nairn

Forres

Cromarty

Alness

Invergordon

984

Bonar Bridge

Tain

Dornoch

Tarbat
Ness

Lairg

Altnaharra

Tongue

Bettyhill

Strathy
Point

Melvich

Kinbrace

Helmsdale

Latheron

Thurso

Scrabster

Dunnet
Head

Castletown

974

John O'Groats

Duncansby Head

Island of Stroma

Mainland

Kirkwall

Orkney
Islands

Monadhliath

Aviemore

966

MORAY

Grantown-
on-Spey

Aberlour

Dufftown

Elgin

Lossiemouth

Buckie

Cullen

Banff

Macduff

964

965

Keith

Rhynie

Huntly

Turriff

Alford

Oldmeldrum

Inverurie

Ellon

Fraserburgh

Peterhead

Latheron

Wick

Noss Head

©MAPS IN MINUTES™ 2003. ©Crown Copyright, Ordnance Survey 2003.

©The National Trust for Scotland

©The Royal Yacht Britannia

© The National Trust for Scotland

© The National Trust for Scotland

909 Anstruther

Scottish Fisheries Museum

1 hr+   All year

The Scottish Fisheries Museum tells the story of Scottish fishing and its people from the earliest times to the present day. There are many fine paintings and photographs on display, as well as a variety of real and models boats, fishing gear and other accoutrements.

* Overlooks a beautiful harbour
* Regular calendar of events and exhibitions

Location	Contact
Exit M90 junction 3, take A92	St Ayles, Harbourhead, Anstruther Fife KY10 3AB
Opening	
Mon–Sat 10am–5.30pm	t 01333 310628
Sun 11am–5pm	w scottish-fisheries-museum.org
Admission	e info@scottish-fisheries-museum. org
Adult £4.50, Child free, Concs £3.50	

910 Arbroath

Arbroath Abbey

2 hrs+   All year

This was the site of the signing of the Declaration of Arbroath in 1320, when Scotland's nobles affirmed their allegiance to Robert the Bruce as their king. The recent addition of a visitor centre has reinforced its reputation as one of Scotland's most important historical places.

* Audio-visual facilities
* Displays on abbey life

Location	Contact
On A92, in town centre	Arbroath, Angus DD11 1EG
Opening	t 01241 878756
Apr–Sep daily 9.30am–6.30pm	w historic-scotland.gov.uk
Oct–Mar daily 9.30am to 4.30pm	e hs.explorer@scotland.gsi.gov.uk
Admission	
Adult £3, Child £1, Concs £2.30	

911 Cupar

Hill of Tarvit Mansion House & Garden

2 hrs   Apr–Oct

A fascinating mansion house, built in 1906, reflects the period 1870–1920, when Scotland was the industrial workshop of the world. The house is a showcase for Flemish tapestries, Chinese porcelain and bronzes, French and English furniture and paintings by many eminent artists.

* Edwardian-style interior
* Set in beautiful gardens

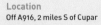

Location	Contact
Off A916, 2 miles S of Cupar	Cupar, Fife KY15 5PB
Opening	t 01334 653 127
Apr–Sep daily 1–5pm	w nts.org.uk
Oct Sat–Sun 1–5pm	e hilloftarvit@nts.org.uk
Admission	
Adult £5 Child & Concs £3.75	

912 Crieff

Auchingarrich Wildlife Centre

2 hrs+   Mar–Nov

This award-winning centre features the Highland Cattle Centre, where you can see these majestic beasts, stroke them and feed them. Other animals include wallabies, raccoons, otters, chipmunks, porcupines and Scotland's largest collection of waterfowl, ornamental and game birds.

* Over 150 species of animals and birds
* Hatchings every day from Easter to October

Location
On B827, 2 miles N of Comrie

Opening
Mar–Nov daily 10am–dusk

Admission
Adult £4.75, Child & Concs £3.75

Contact
Glascorrie Road, Crieff, Perthshire PH6 2JS

t 01764 679469
e auchingarrich@wilton.sol.co.uk

913 Crieff

Drummond Castle Gardens

1 hr   May–Oct

Drummond Castle Gardens are thought to be Scotland's most important formal gardens and are certainly among the finest in Europe. The magnificent Italianate parterre was first laid in C17 by John Drummond and renewed in the 1950s.

* Charles I's sundial
* Gardens featured in the film *Rob Roy*

Location
Off A822, 2 miles S of Crieff

Opening
May–Oct daily 2–6pm
Also open Easter

Admission
Adults £3.50, Child £1.50, Concs £2.50

Contact
Muthill, nr Crieff, Perthshire PH5 2AA

t 01764 681257
w drummondcastlegardens.co.uk
e info@drummondcastle.sol.co.uk

914 Crieff

The Famous Grouse Experience at Glenturret Distillery

1 hr+   All year

Scotlands only five-star, Bafta award-winning interactive whisky attraction is fun for young and old alike. Crack some ice, splash in the water and do a jigsaw puzzle with your feet or fly over the wonderous beauty of Scotland on the back of a grouse.

* New style audio-visual presentation
* New on-site restaurant

Location
Off A85, 1 mile from Crieff

Opening
Daily 9am–6pm

Admission
Adult £5.95, Child £3, Concs £4.95

Contact
Glenturret Distillery, The Hosh, Crieff, Perthshire PH7 4HA

t 01764 656565
w famousgrouse.com
e enquiries@famousgrouse.com

915 Crieff

Stuart Crystal Factory Shop

½ hr   All year

Come and see the wonderful craft of crystal at the Stuart Crystal Factory Shop. A large display of Stuart Crystal, Waterford Crystal and Wedgwood China, with factory seconds. There is also a crystal engraving service for that personalised special gift or memento.

* Souvenir gift shop
* Chip repair serice

Location
Signposted from town centre

Opening
Jun–Sep daily 10am–6pm
Oct–May Mon–Sat 10am–5pm
Sun 11am–5pm

Admission
Free

Contact
Muthill Road, Crieff, Perthshire PH7 4HQ

t 01764 654 004

916 Dunfermline

Knockhill Racing Circuit

3 hrs   All year

Scotland's national motorsport centre features major international and national motorsport events for both cars and bikes. It's also a major venue for corporate entertainment, as visitors can drive race and rally cars, go off-road on a 4x4 course and do many other activities.

* Hands-on driving experiences
* Relaxing hospitality at race events

Location
Signposted from M90 junction 4

Opening
Daily 8am–6pm

Admission
Prices vary depending on the event, telephone for details

Contact
Dunfermline, Fife KY12 9TF

t 01383 723337
w knockhill.com
e enquiries@knockhill.co.uk

917 Dunfermline

Dunfermline Abbey & Palace

1 hr   All year

The elegant ruins of Dunfermline Abbey are what is left of a great Benedictine abbey founded by Queen Margaret in the C11. Robert the Bruce was buried in the choir and the royal palace next door, also partially ruined, was the birthplace of Charles I.

* Substantial parts of the abbey buildings remain
* Next to the ruin of the royal palace

Location
Off M90, in town centre

Opening
Apr–Sep daily 9.30am–6.30pm
Oct–Mar Mon–Thu Sat
9.30am–4.30pm Sun 2–4.30pm

Admission
Adult £2.20, Child 75p, Concs £1.60

Contact
St. Margaret Street, Dunfermline,
Fife KY12 7PE

t 01383 739 026
w historic-scotland.gov.uk

918 Dundee

Discovery Point

1 hr+   All year

Climb aboard Captain Scott's royal research ship, *Discovery*, which was originally built in Dundee to sail to the Antarctic and is now berthed on the River Tay and open to visitors. The ship represents the city's shipbuilders' greatest achievement.

* State-of-the-art multimedia exhibitions
* All weather, multi-award-winning attraction

Location
City centre, opposite train station

Opening
Apr–Oct Mon–Sat 10am–6pm
Sun 11am–6pm
Nov–Mar Mon–Sat 10am–5pm
Sun 11am–5pm

Admission
Adult £6.25, Child £3.85, Concs £4.70

Contact
Discovery Quay, Dundee DD1 4XA

t 01382 201245
w rrsdiscovery.co.uk
e info@dundeeheritage.co.uk

919 East Fortune

Museum of Flight

2 hrs+   All year

Discover the story of man's ambition to take to the skies. Two massive hangars, part of a Second World War airfield, are packed with aeroplanes, rockets, models and memorabilia – from a 100-year-old hang glider to the Blue Streak rocket, and from a Spitfire to the massive Lightning.

* Regular calendar of events
* Site of take-off for first east-west Atlantic flight

Location
Off A1, 20m E of Edinburgh

Opening
Summer daily 10am–5pm,
Winter daily 11am–4pm

Admission
Adults £3, Child free, Concs £1.50

Contact
East Fortune Airfield, East Lothian
EH39 5LF

t 01620 880308
w nms.ac.uk/flight/

---

920 Edinburgh

Edinburgh Castle

1 hr+   All year

A majestic landmark that dominates the city's skyline, Edinburgh Castle is the most visited of Scotland's historic buildings. Perched on an extinct volcano and offering stunning views, this fortress is a powerful national symbol and part of Edinburgh's World Heritage site.

* Guided and audio tours
* The Scottish Crown Jewels and the Stone of Destiny

Location
At top of Royal Mile

Opening
Apr–Oct daily 9.30am–6pm
Nov–Mar daily 9.30am–5pm

Admission
Adult £8.50, Child £2, Concs £6.25

Contact
Castle Hill, Edinburgh EH1 2NG

t 0131 2259846
w historic-scotland.gov.uk

---

921 Edinburgh

Edinburgh Zoo

4 hrs   All year

This is Scotland's most popular wildlife attraction, with over a thousand animals, including meerkats, pygmy hippos, tigers, giraffes and blue poison arrow frogs. Set in beautiful parkland, the zoo has the world's biggest penguin pool, which is home to Europe's largest colony of penguins.

* African Plains Experience, Magic Forest, hilltop safari
  tour and maze

Location
10 mins from city centre

Opening
Apr–Sep daily 9am–6pm
Oct Mar daily 9am–5pm
Nov–Feb daily 9am–4.30pm

Admission
Adult £8, Child £5, Concs £5.50

Contact
134 Corstorphine Road, Edinburgh
EH12 6TS

t 0131 3349171
w edinburghzoo.org.uk
e info@edinburghzoo.org.uk

* NB an adult (over 17) must accompany
children under 14 at all times

---

922 Edinburgh

Museum of Childhood

1 hr   All year

Five galleries of childhood memorabilia including toys, games and displays relating to the health, education, clothing and upbringing of children past and present.

* Describes itself as 'noisiest museum in the world'
* Wonderful collection of historic toys, dolls and games

Location
On Royal Mile

Opening
Oct–Jun Mon–Sat 10am–5pm
Jul–Aug Mon–Sat 10am–5pm
Sun 12 noon–5pm

Admission
Free

Contact
42 High Street, Edinburgh EH1 1TG

t 0131 529 4142
w cac.org.uk
e admin@museumofchildhood.
   fsnet.co.uk

923 Edinburgh

Museum of Scotland

2 hrs+   All year

This museum presents, for the first time, the history of Scotland – its land, its people and their achievements – through the rich national collections. The stunning series of galleries takes you from Scotland's geological beginnings through time right up to C20.

* Over 10,000 artefacts
* Same site as Royal Museum

Location	Contact
Off A7 South Bridge, in city centre	Chambers Street, Edinburgh EH1 1JF
Opening	t 0131 2474422
Mon–Sat 10am–5pm Tue 10am–8pm	w nms.ac.uk
Sun 12noon–5pm	e info@nms.ac.uk
Admission	
Free	

924 Edinburgh

National Gallery of Scotland

½ – 2 hrs   All year

The gallery is home to Scotland's greatest collection of European paintings and sculpture, ranging from the Renaissance to Post-Impressionism. One of Edinburgh's major attractions, it is also one of the finest galleries of its size in the world.

* Includes masterpieces by Van Dyck and Tiepolo
* Comprehensive collection of Scottish paintings

Location	Contact
Off Princes Street	The Mound, Edinburgh EH2 2EL
Opening	t 0131 6246200
Mon–Wed Fri–Sun 10am–5pm	w nationalgalleries.org
Thu 10am–7pm	e enquiries@nationalgalleries.org
Admission	
Free, charges for some exhibitions	

925 Edinburgh

Our Dynamic Earth

1 hr+   All year

Take a fantastic journey of discovery. Travel back in time to witness the Big Bang from the deck of a space ship, then forward through the history of our planet. You'll be shaken by earthquakes, dive deep beneath the ocean, feel the chill of polar ice and even get caught in a tropical rainstorm.

* Find out if there's a monster in Loch Ness
* Live 4,500 million years in a day

Location	Admission
At the foot of Arthur's Seat, adjacent to the new Scottish Parliament	Adult £8.95, Child & Concs £5.45
	Contact
Opening	112 Holyrood Road, Edinburgh EH8 8AS
Mar–Aug daily 10am–6pm	t 0131 5507800
Sep–Oct 10am–5pm	w dynamicearth.co.uk
Nov–Mar Wed–Sun 10am–5pm	e enquiries@dynamicearth.co.uk

926 Edinburgh

Palace of Holyroodhouse

1 hr   All year

Originally founded in 1128 as a monastery, the Palace of Holyroodhouse in Edinburgh is the Queen's official residence in Scotland, and is no stranger to royalty, as Mary Queen of Scots, among others, lived here. In fact the palace has many associations with Scottish history.

* New Queen's gallery
* One of the finest art collections in the world

Location	Contact
At bottom of Royal Mile	Edinburgh EH8 8DX
Opening	t 0131 5565100
Nov–Mar daily 9.30am–4.30pm	w royal.gov.uk
Apr–Oct daily 9.30am–6pm	e information@royalcollection.org.uk
Admission	
Adult £7.50, Child £4 Concs £3	
By timed ticket slots	

927 Edinburgh

Royal Botanic Garden Edinburgh

2 hrs   All year

Founded in the C17 as a 'physic garden', growing medicinal plants, the Royal Botanic is now acknowledged as one of the finest gardens in the world, It's a place to rest and relax, away from the city's hustle and bustle, and is home to unusual and beautiful plants.

* Guided and themed tours
* Rock / peat / woodland gardens, chinese plants

Location
Off A902, 1 mile N of city centre

Opening
Apr–Sep daily 10am–7pm
Mar Oct daily 10am–6pm
Nov–Feb daily 10am–4pm

Admission
Free

Contact
20A Inverleith Row, Edinburgh EH3 5LR

t 0131 5527171
w rbge.org.uk
e info@rbge.org.uk

---

929 Edinburgh

Scotch Whisky Heritage Centre

1 hr   All year

This unique, interactive attraction brings 300 years of Scotch whisky history to life. It gives visitors the opportunity to discover how whisky is made and allows them to experience the sights, sounds and smells of the whisky business.

* Meet the resident ghost
* Whisky tasting tours (separate ticket required)

Location
On Royal Mile, nr castle

Opening
May–Sep daily 9.30am–6.30pm
Oct–Apr daily 10am–5pm

Admission
Adult £7.50, Child £3.95, Concs £5.50

Contact
354 Castle Hill, Royal Mile, Edinburgh EH1 2NE

t 0131 2200441
w whisky-heritage.co.uk
e info@whisky-heritage.co.uk

---

928 Edinburgh

St Giles' Cathedral

½ hr+   All year

This is the High Kirk of Edinburgh and it has been at the heart of the city's spiritual life for at least 900 years. A living church with an active congregation, it also welcomes visitors who come to experience the unique atmosphere of continuing worship and ages-old history.

* The mother church of Presbyterianism
* One of the most historic buildings in Scotland

Location
On Royal Mile

Opening
May–Sep Mon–Fri 9am–7pm
Sat 9am–5pm Sun 1–5pm
Oct–Apr Mon–Sat 9am–5pm
Sun 1–5pm

Admission
Free

Contact
High Street, Edinburgh EH1 1RE

t 0131 2259442
w stgiles.net
e info@stgiles.net

©Saul Gardiner

930 Glamis by Forfar

Glamis Castle

2 hrs+   Mar–Oct

Glamis Castle has a long and colourful history. It has a legendary association, at least according to Shakespeare, with the C11 Macbeth and has a place in C20 history as the childhood home of HM The Queen Mother.

* Rich variety of furnishings, tapestries and art
* Extensive estate and formal gardens

Location	Contact
On A94, between Aberdeen & Perth	The Castle Administrator, Estates Office, Glamis by Forfar, Angus DD8 1RJ
Opening Mar–Oct daily 10.30am–5.30pm	
Admission Adult £6.80, Child £3.70, Concs £5.50	t 01307 840393 w glamis-castle.co.uk e enquiries@glamis-castle.co.uk

931 Glasgow

Burrell Collection

½ hr+   All year

When Sir William Burrell gifted his collection of over 9,000 works of art to Glasgow, the city acquired one of its greatest collections. He had been an art collector since his teens and the collection is made up of a vast array of works of all periods, from all over the world.

* Medieval art, tapestries, alabasters and stained glass
* Paintings by Degas and Cézanne

Location	Contact
5 miles S of Glasgow	Pollok Country Park, 2060 Pollokshaws Road, Glasgow G43 1AT
Opening Mon–Thu Sat 10am–5pm Fri–Sun 11am–5pm	t 0141 2872550 w glasgowmuseums.com
Admission Free	e cls.glasgow.gov.uk

932 Glasgow

Gallery of Modern Art

½ hr   All year

GoMA is the second most visited contemporary art gallery outside London, offering a thought-provoking programme of temporary exhibitions and workshops. The focus of the gallery is on contemporary social issues, often featuring groups marginalised in today's society.

* Includes work by Bridget Riley and Scottish artist
  John Bellany

Location	Contact
In city centre, off Buchanan Street, close to central station	Queen Street, Glasgow G1 3AH
Opening Mon–Tue 10am–5pm Thu 10am–8pm Fri & Sun 11am–5pm Sat 10am–5pm	t 0141 2291996 w glasgowmuseums.com
Admission Free	

933 Glasgow

The Mackintosh House

½ hr   All year

This is a reconstruction of the principal interiors from the Glasgow home of the Scottish architect and designer Charles Rennie Mackintosh (1868–1928) and the artist Margaret Macdonald Mackintosh (1864–1933).

* Contains all the original furniture
* Decorated as closely as possible to the original house

Location
In Hillhead, 2 miles from city centre, opposite university

Opening
Mon–Sat 9.30am–12.30pm 1.30–5pm

Admission
Free

Contact
Hunterian Art Gallery, University of Glasgow, 82 Hillhead Street, Glasgow G12 8QQ
t 0141 330 5431
w hunterian.gla.ac.uk
e hunter@museum.gla.ac.uk

934 Glasgow

Museum of Piping

½ hr   All year

Nothing makes a Scotsman feel more patriotic than the sound of a pipe band. This is the sound of Scotland, a haunting melody or a noise fit to lift the soul. At the Museum of Piping you can witness hundreds of years of Scottish heritage, played right before your eyes and ears.

* An outstanding collection of piping artefacts
* Study the history and origins of bagpiping

Location
In city centre, in pedestrian area

Opening
Jun–Aug Mon–Sat 9.30am–4.30pm
Sun 10am–4pm
Sep–May Mon–Sat 9.30am–4.30pm

Admission
Free

Contact
30-34 McPhater Street, Cowcaddens, Glasgow G4 0HW
t 0141 353 0220
w thepipingcentre.co.uk
e reception@thepipingcentre.co.uk

935 Glasgow

Museum of Transport

2 hrs   All year

The museum uses its collections of vehicles and models to tell the story of transport by land and sea – with a unique Glasgow flavour. Here you'll find the oldest surviving pedal cycle and the finest collection in the world of Scottish-built cars.

* World famous makes such as Argyll and Albion
* Fully restored Spitfire on display

Location
In the West End, opposite Kelvingrove Art Gallery and Museum

Opening
Mon–Thu Sat 10am–5pm,
Fri & Sun 11am–5pm

Admission
Free

Contact
Kelvin Hall, 1 Bunhouse Road, Glasgow G3 8DP
t 0141 287 2720
w glasgowmuseums.com

936 Glasgow

Necropolis

1 hr+   All year

The Necropolis stands on a hill to the east of Glasgow Cathedral, just a short walk across the Bridge of Sighs. The monument to John Knox, which was erected in 1825, dominates the hill. This Victorian cemetery was modeled on Père-Lachaise in Paris.

* Glasgow's great architects are represented, including Thomson, Wilson, Baird, Bryce, and Hamilton

Location
nr Glasgow Cathedral

Opening
Daily 8am–4.30pm

Admission
Free

Contact
Cemeteries and Crematoria, 1st Floor, 20 Trongate, Glasgow G1 5ES
t 0141 287 3961

937 Glasgow

People's Palace

2 hrs+   All year

The People's Palace is Glasgow's social history museum and tells the story of the people and city of Glasgow from 1760 to the present. There are paintings, prints and photographs displayed alongside a wealth of historic artefacts, film and computer interactives.

* Discover how a family lived in a typical single end Glasgow tenement

Location	Admission
Short walk from city centre	Free
Opening	Contact
Mon–Thu Sat 10am–5pm	Glasgow Green, Glasgow G40 1AT
Fri & Sun 11am–5pm	t 0141 5540223
	w glasgowmuseums.com

938 Glasgow

Scottish Football Museum

2 hrs+   All year

The world's first national football museum is housed at Hampden Park, the oldest continuously used international ground in the world. It is owned by Queen's Park FC, the oldest association team in Scotland (founded 1867) and one with an unrivalled history and a collection to match.

* The world's most impressive collection of football memorabilia, covering 140 years of football history

Location	Admission
Junction 1 off M77, onto B768 (Titwood Road), right onto B766 (Battlefield Road), then Kings Park Road, left into Kinghorn Drive	Adult £5, Child & Concs £2.50
	Contact
	Hampden Park, Glasgow G42 9BA
Opening	t 0141 616 6139
Mon–Sat 10am–5pm Sun 11am–5pm	w scottishfootballmuseum.org.uk
	e info@scottishfootballmuseum.org.uk

939 Glasgow

Tall Ship in Glasgow Harbour

1 hr+   All year

Explore the tall ship *Glenlee*, one of only five Clyde-built sailing ships that remain afloat. Built in 1896, she operated as a long haul cargo vessel before being bought by the Spanish Navy as a training ship. She has circumnavigated the globe four times and passed Cape Horn on 15 occasions.

* New exhibition tells the *Glenlee* story
* Visitor centre

Location	Admission
Off M8 junction 19, follow brown thistle signs	Adult £4.50, Child & Concs £3.25 (one child free with each paying adult)
Opening	Contact
Mar–Nov daily 10am–5pm	100 Stobe Cross Road, Glasgow G3 8QQ
Dec–Feb daily 11am–4pm	t 0141 2222513
	w thetallship.com
	e info@thetallship.com

940 Glasgow

Tenement House

1 hr   Mar–Oct

Glasgow, more than any other Scottish city, is associated with tenements. This first floor flat is a typical late Victorian example from 1892, consisting of four rooms and retaining most of its original features, such as its bed recesses, kitchen range, coal bunker and bathroom.

* Exhibition about tenement life and a fascinating time capsule of the first half of C20

Location	Contact
Garnethill area, nr Glasgow School of Art	145 Buccleuch Street, Garnethill, Glasgow G3 6QN
Opening	t 0141 3330183
Mar–Oct 1–5pm	w nts.org.uk
Admission	e tenementhouse@nts.org.uk
Adult £3.50, Child & Concs £2.60	

941 Hamilton

John Hastie Museum

1 hr   Apr–Sep

Sitting on the edge of picturesque Strathaven Park, this local museum dates back to the 1920s. The displays focus on the life of the area, including its agriculture and weaving heritage and the community which bred fervent Covenanters in the 1600s and a radical revolt in the 1800s.

* The unique Strathaven toffee
* A jar of pickled snakes collected by John Hastie himself

Location
A726 from East Kilbride, M74 and A71 Kilmarnock to Strathaven road

Opening
Apr–Sep daily 12.30–4.30pm

Admission
Free

Contact
Threestanes Road, Strathaven, Lanarkshire ML10 6DX

t 01357 521257

942 Kinross

Loch Leven Castle

2 hrs   Apr–Oct

The dramatic ruins of this castle stand on an island in Loch Leven. This late C14 or early C15 tower is infamous as the place where Mary Queen of Scots was imprisoned in 1567. She escaped the following year, but her ghost is alleged to haunt the castle to this day.

* The Loch is an imortant RSPB site

Location
Accessible by boat from Scottish Angling Academy in Kinross, signposted from A922

Opening
Apr–Sep daily 9.30am–5.15pm
Oct Mon Wed–Thu Sat–Sun 9.30am–3.15pm

Admission
Adult £3.50, Child £1.20, Concs £2.50

Contact
Kinross, Perthshire KY13 7AR

t 07778 040483
w historic-scotland.gov.uk

943 Kirriemuir

Barrie's Birthplace

½ hr   All year

J.M. Barrie, the creator of the eternal magic of *Peter Pan*, was born here in 1860. The upper floor is furnished as it was when Barrie lived there. The adjacent house, number 11, houses an exhibition about Barrie's literary and theatrical works.

* Audio programme
* Near Kirriemuir camera obscura

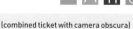   

Location
A901/A926 in Kirriemuir, 6 miles NW of Forfar

Opening
Jul–Aug daily 12noon–5pm
Sep–Jun Fri–Tue 12noon–5pm

Admission
Adult £5, Child free, Concs £3.75

(combined ticket with camera obscura)

Contact
9 Brechin Road, Kirriemuir, Angus DD8 4BX

t 01575 572 646
w nts.org.uk/barrie.html
e barriesbirthplace@nts.org.uk

©The National Trust for Scotland

944 Lanark

New Lanark World Heritage Village

2 hrs+   All year

The cotton mills of New Lanark were founded over 200 years ago and the village soon became famous because of the work of mill-owner Robert Owen, who provided a decent life for the villagers. Today, New Lanark has been restored and visitors can explore this fascinating village.

* Award-winning visitor centre
* Unesco World Heritage site

Location
Off M74 junction 13, signposted off all routes

Opening
Daily 11am–5pm

Admission
Adult £5.95, Child & Concs £3.95

Contact
New Lanark Mills, South Lanarkshire ML11 9DB

t 01555 661345
w newlanark.org
e trust@newlanark.org

945 Laurencekirk

Fettercairn Distillery

1 hr   May–Sep

On the north west side of the village of Fettercairn, set beautifully against the hills beyond, lies the whitewashed Fettercairn Distillery. It dates back to 1824, though much of what you see today is from a later rebuilding, and is one of the oldest licensed distilleries in Scotland.

* Free tasting
* Set in a glorious village with spectacular views

Location
Off A94, 5 miles inland

Opening
May–Sep Mon–Sat 10am–4pm

Admission
Free

Contact
Laurencekirk, Kincardineshire AB30 1YE

t 01561 340205

946 Leith

The Royal Yacht *Britannia*

1 hr+   All year

Now permanently moored in Edinburgh's historic port of Leith, the *Britannia* experience begins in the new visitor centre, located in Ocean Terminal, Edinburgh's stylish new waterfront shopping and leisure development. Then step onboard for a self-led audio tour of five decks.

* See royal apartments and crews' quarters
* Children's audio tour

Location
At Leith Docks, signposted from city outskirts

Opening
Apr–Sep daily 9.30am–4.30pm
Oct–Mar daily 10am–3.30pm

Admission
Adult £8.50, Child £4.50, Concs £6.50

Contact
Ocean Drive, Leith, Edinburgh EH6 6JJ

t 0131 5555566
w royalyachtbritannia.co.uk
e enquiries@tryb.co.uk

©The Royal Yacht Britannia

947 Linlithgow

Linlithgow Palace

1 hr   All year

This magnificent ruin of a great royal palace is set in its own park, beside Linlithgow Loch. It was a favoured home of the Stewart kings and queens, from James I (1406–37) onward, and building work from the eras of James I, III, IV, V and VI can be seen, including the great hall and chapel.

* Birthplace of James V and Mary Queen of Scots
* Special events throughout the year

Location On A803 / M9, in town centre	**Contact** Kirkgate, Linlithgow, West Lothian EH49 7AL	
Opening Apr–Sep daily 9.30am–6.30pm Oct–Mar Mon–Sat 9.30am–4.30pm Sun 2pm–4.30pm	t 01506 842896 w historic-scotland.gov.uk	
Admission Adult £3, Child £1, Concs £2.30		

948 Loch Tay

Scottish Crannog Centre

1 hr   Apr–Nov

Crannogs are a type of ancient loch dwelling found throughout Scotland and Ireland. The Scottish Crannog Centre features an authentic replica of an early Iron Age crannog, based on the underwater excavations of the 2,500-year-old Oakbank Crannog.

* Shore based exhibition with audio-visual presentation
* Tour the real thing

Location Croft-na-Caber just S of Kenmore	**Contact** Croft-na-Caber, Kenmore, Loch Tay, Perthshire PH15 2HW	
Opening Apr–Oct daily 10am–5.30pm Nov 10am–4pm	t 01887 830 583 w crannog.co.uk e info@crannog.co.uk	
Admission Adult £4.25, Child £3, Concs £3.85		

949 Newtongrange

Scottish Mining Museum

2 hrs   All year

This museum is based at one of the finest surviving examples of a Victorian colliery in Europe, the Lady Victoria Colliery at Newtongrange. A fully accessible, three-storey visitors centre allows everyone to experience the atmosphere and noise of a working pit.

* Two major exhibitions: The Story of Coal and A Race Apart
* Audio tour with 'magic helmets'

Location On A7, 9 miles S of Edinburgh	**Contact** Lady Victoria Colliery, Newtongrange, Midlothian EH22 4QN	
Opening Feb–Oct daily 10am–5pm Nov–Jan daily 10am–4pm	t 0131 6637519 w scottishminingmuseum.com e visitorservices@ scottishminingmuseum.com	
Admission Adult £4.75 ,Child & Concs £3.30		

950 North Queensferry

Deep Sea World

2 hrs+   All year

Explore the undersea world at the triple award-winning National Aquarium of Scotland. Situated on the banks of the Firth of Forth, below the Forth Railway Bridge, this spectacular attraction is perfect day out for the whole family.

* Also known as Scotland's shark capital

Location 1 mile from M90 on N side of Forth Road Bridge	**Admission** Adult £7.95, Child £5.75, Concs £6.50
Opening Apr–Oct daily 10am–6pm Nov–Mar Mon–Fri 11am–5pm Sat–Sun 10am–6pm	**Contact** North Queensferry, Fife KY11 1JR t 01383 411411 w deepseaworld.com e info@deepseaworld.com

951 Paisley

Coats Observatory

1 hr+   All year

The Coats Observatory is a little gem of a building, gifted by Thomas Coats, designed by John Honeyman and opened in 1883. In addition to astronomical equipment, meteorological readings are taken daily and continuous seismic recording is carried out.

* Displays relating to astronomy and astronautics,
  meteorology and seismology

WC

Location	Contact
Off M8 at junction 29	49 Oakshaw Street West, Paisley, Refrewshire PA1 2DE
Opening	
Tue–Sat 10am–5pm Sun 2pm–5pm	t 0141 889 3151 / 2013
Telescopes Oct–Mar Tue & Thu 7pm–9pm	w renfrewshire.gov.uk
	e museums.els@renfrewshire.gov.uk
Admission	
Free	

952 Paisley

Scottish Wool Centre

1 hr+   All year

Daily demonstrations of spinning and weaving plus, in the small in-house theatre see six border collies demonstrating obedience and agility and being put through their paces on a small assault course. There are also birds of prey displays during the summer months.

* Spin your own wool
* Fun for all the family

Location	Admission
Off Main Street in Aberfoyle	Centre free, charges for animal show
Opening	**Contact**
Apr–Oct daily 9.30am–5.30pm	Main Street, Aberfoyle, Stirling, Stirlingshire FK8 3UQ
Oct–Dec daily 10am–5pm	
Jan–Mar daily 10am–4.30pm	t 01877 382850

953 Perth

Scone Palace

1 hr+   Apr–Oct

In a spectacular setting above the River Tay, Scone Palace has been the seat of parliaments and the crowning place of kings. It has housed the Stone of Destiny and been immortalised in Shakespeare's *Macbeth*, and is regarded by many as the heart of Scottish history.

* One of the finest private collections of furniture in Britain
* Beautiful gardens, including Moot Hill

Location	Contact
Signposted from M90/A9, between Edinburgh & the Highlands	The Administrator, Scone Palace, Perth, Perthshire PH2 6BD
Opening	t 01738 552300
Apr–Oct daily 9.30am–5.30pm	w scone-palace.co.uk
	e visits@scone-palace.co.uk
Admission	
Adult £6.75, Child £3.80, Concs £5.70	

954 Pitlochry

Killiecrankie Visitor Centre

½ hr+   Apr–Oct

In 1689, the Pass of Killiecrankie echoed with the sounds of battle, when a Jacobite army defeated the government forces. The spectacular gorge is tranquil now and a fine example of mixed deciduous woodland. The visitor centre exhibits battle, natural history and ranger services.

* Site of special scientific interest
* Visitors can watch birds nesting via a remote camera

Location	Contact
On B8079, 3 miles N of Pitlochry	nr Pitlochry, Tayside PH16 5LG
Opening	t 01796 473233
Jul–Aug daily 9.30am–6pm	w nts.org.uk
Apr–Jun Sep–Oct daily 10am–5.30pm	
Admission	
Free, £2 charge for car park	

955 Pitlochry

Blair Castle

1 hr+   All year

Over 700 years of Scottish history await the visitor to Blair Castle. See displays of beautiful furniture, fine paintings, arms and armour, china, costumes, lace and embroidery, masonic regalia and Jacobite relics – all of which provides a colourful picture of Scottish life from the C16 to today.

* Spectacular setting in the Strath of Garry
* Guided tours available for parties of over 12

Location
At Blair Atholl, N of Pitlochry

Opening
Apr–Oct daily 9.30am–4.30pm
Nov–Mar Tue 9.30am–12.30pm

Admission
Adult £6.50, Child £4.20, Concs £5.70

Contact
Blair Atholl, Pitlochry,
Perthshire PH18 5TL

t 01796 481207
w blair-castle.co.uk
e office@blair-castle.co.uk

956 St Andrews

British Golf Museum

½ hr+   All year

Using a range of exciting, interactive displays, this museum tells the story of British golf, from its origins in the Middle Ages to the present day. The players, tournaments and equipment which make golf the game it now is are explored in detail.

* Regular calendar of events
* Guided walks on the Old Course (summer only)

Location
Signposted from town centre

Opening
May–Oct daily 9.30am–5.30pm
Winter times vary

Admission
Adult £4, Child £2, Concs £3

Contact
Bruce Embankment, St Andrews,
Fife KY16 9AB

t 01334 460046
w britishgolfmuseum.co.uk
e alisonwood@randagc.org

957 St Andrews

Scotland's Secret Bunker

1 hr+   Apr–Oct

Discover the twilight world of the government's Cold War headquarters. Hidden for over 40 years beneath a Scottish farmhouse, a tunnel leads to Scotland's Secret Bunker – 24,000 square feet of secret accommodation on two levels, 100 feet underground.

* Built in complete secrecy in 1950s
* Imagine life after a nuclear holocaust

Location
On B940, between St Andrews & Anstruther

Opening
Apr–Oct daily 10am–6pm

Admission
Adult £7.20, Child £4.50, Concs £5.95

Contact
Crown Buildings, Troywood,
nr St Andrews, Fife KY16 8QH

t 01333 310301
w secretbunker.co.uk
e mod@secretbunker.co.uk

958 Stirling

Stirling Castle

1 hr+   All year

Without doubt one of the grandest of all Scottish castles, both in its situation on a rocky outcrop and in its architecture. The Great Hall and the gatehouse of James IV, the marvellous palace of James V, the Chapel Royal and the artillery fortifications are all of outstanding interest.

* Audio-visual presentation
* Regimental Museum of the Highlanders

Location
Off M9, in old town

Opening
Apr–Sep daily 9.30am–6pm
Oct–Mar daily 9.30am–5pm

Admission
Adult £7.50, Child £2, Concs £5.50

Contact
Esplanade, Stirling,
Stirlingshire FK8 1EJ

t 01786 450000
w historic-scotland.gov.uk

959 Stirling

Argyll's Lodging

½ hr   All year

A superb mansion built around an earlier core in about 1630 and further extended by the Earl of Argyll in the 1670s. It is the most impressive town house of its period in Scotland. The principal rooms are now restored to their 1680 state.

* Beautiful furniture and furnishings
* Magnificent restoration

Location
Near town centre

Opening
Apr–Oct daily 9.30am–6pm
Nov–Mar daily 9.30am–5pm

Admission
Adult £3.30, Child £1.20, Concs £2.50

Contact
Castle Wynd, Stirling,
Stirlingshire FK8 1EG

t 01786 431319
w historic-scotland.gov.uk

960 Stirling

Wallace Monument

1 hr   All year

This is a chance to renew your acquaintance with Scotland's national hero and the Hollywood legend, Sir William Wallace, popularly known as Braveheart, at the spectacular 220 foot (67m) National Wallace Monument, completed in 1869.

* See the mighty two-handed broadsword
* Visit the Hall of Heroes

Location
Off M9 junction 10, 1 mile NE of Stirling town centre

Opening
Mar–May Oct daily 10am–5pm
Jun daily 10am–6pm
Jul–Aug daily 9.30am–6.30pm
Sep daily 9.30am–5pm
Nov–Feb daily 10.30am–4pm

Admission
Adult £5, Child & Concs £3.25

Contact
Abbey Craig, Stirling, Stirlingshire FK9 5LF

t 01786 472140
w scottish.heartlands.org
e nwm@aillst.ossian.net

961 Stirling

Bannockburn Heritage Centre

½ hr+   All year

Located at one of the most important historical sites in Scotland, this centre offers great insights into the Battle of Bannockburn, Robert the Bruce and William Wallace. Learn about the legendary battle in which Bruce and his army defeated Edward II of England.

* Wars of independence exhibition
* Audio-visual presentation of the famous battle

Location
Off M80/M9 junction 9, 2 miles S of Stirling

Opening
Feb–Mar Nov–Dec daily 10.30am–4pm
Apr–Oct 10am–5.30pm

Admission
Adult £3.50, Child & Concs £2.60

Contact
Glasgow Road, Whins of Milton,
Stirling, Stirlingshire FK7 0LJ

t 01786 812664
w nts.org.uk

Grampian

Aberdeen Maritime Museum

1 hr+   All year

This museum tells the story of Aberdeen's long relationship with the sea. It houses a unique collection, covering ship-building, fast sailing ships, fishing and port history, and is the only place in the UK where you can see displays on the North Sea oil industry.

* Incorporates Provost Ross's House, built in 1593
* Offers a spectacular viewpoint over the busy harbour

Location
On the harbour

Opening
Daily Mon-Sat 10am–5pm
Sun 12 noon–3pm

Admission
Free

Contact
Shiprow, Aberdeen AB11 5BY

t 01224 337700
w aberdeencity.gov.uk
e info@aagm.co.uk

Balmoral Castle & Estate

1 hr+   Apr–Jul

The Queen's favourite home is still a working estate. A visit provides a marvellous insight into royal heritage and the life of a large estate, that provides employment and housing, as well as working to conserve and regenerate the natural environment.

* Access to the grounds, gardens, exhibitions, shops, tearoom and ballroom

Location
Off A93, between Ballater & Braemar

Opening
Apr–July daily 10am–5pm

Admission
Adult £5, Child £1, Concs £4

Contact
Estates Office, Balmoral Estates,
Ballater, Aberdeenshire AB35 5TB

t 013397 42534
w balmoralcastle.com
e info@balmoralcastle.com

Glenfiddich Distillery

2 hrs   All year

Visit the home of the only Highland single malt Scotch whisky that is distilled, matured and bottled at its distillery. Whisky has flowed from the stills at this site since 1887. Tours of the distillery begin at the visitor centre.

* Distillery tours and shop
* Calendar of special events

Location
On A941, ½ mile N of Dufftown

Opening
Easter–mid Oct
Mon-Sat 9.30am–4.30pm
Sun 12noon–4.30pm
Mid Oct–Easter Mon–Fri
9.30am–4.30pm

Admission
Free

Contact
Dufftown, Banffshire AB55 4DH

t 01340 820373
w glenfiddich.com

Scottish Tartans Museums

1 hr+   Apr–Oct

This charming museum has over 1,000 artefacts including the famous Mauchlinware on display. There are over 700 Tartans on display in the Tartan Section including clan, family, military, district, corporate and commercial in a selection of modern designs.

* See a portrait of John Brown, commissioned by Queen Victoria
* A facsimile of the Falkirk Tartan – the oldest tartan ever found

Location
Keith town centre

Opening
Apr–Oct, Mon–Fri 11.00am–3.00pm,
Sat 11.00am–4.00pm

Admission
Adult £2.50, Child £1.50, Concs £2.00

Contact
138 Mid Street, Keith, Bamfshire
AB55 5BJ

t 01542 888419
w kiethcommunity.co.uk

966 Aviemore

Cairngorm Reindeer Centre

½ hr   Feb–Dec

See Britain's only reindeer herd roaming free in the Cairngorm mountains. These extremely tame and friendly animals are a joy to all who come and meet them. There are currently around 50 animals in this herd and, under supervision, visitors can feed and stroke them.

* Guided tours on the hills
* Wall displays tell visitors more about reindeer

Location
6 miles E of Aviemore

Opening
Feb–Apr Nov–Dec daily 11am
May–Oct daily 11am & 2.30pm

Admission
Adult £6, Child & Concs £3

Contact
Glenmore, Aviemore,
Invernesshire PH22 1QU

t 01479 861228
w reindeer-company.demon.co.uk
e info@reindeer-company.demon.co.uk

967 Balmaha

Loch Lomond National Nature Reserve

3 hrs   All year

Inchailloch, one of the most accessible of Loch Lomond's 38 islands, has a long association with Christianity. Cloaked in oak woodland, with a wealth of bird life and flora, there are several woodland trails giving fantastic views of the loch.

* Wonderful picnic site
* Remains of a C13 parish church

Location
Inchailloch is reached by ferry from the Balmaha boatyard.

Opening
Daily, wardens present Apr–Sep

Admission
Free

Contact
Loch Lomond & Trossochs National Park, Balmaha Visitor Centre

t 01360 444177

968 Culloden Moor

Culloden Battlefield

1 hr+   Feb–Dec

No name in Scottish history evokes more emotion than Culloden, the bleak moor where, in 1746, Bonnie Prince Charlie's hopes were crushed and the Jacobite Rising was put down. The prince's forces were greatly outnumbered, but nevertheless went into battle with legendary courage.

* Permanent exhibition of weapons used in the battle
* Audio-visual programme

Location
On B9006, 5 miles E of Inverness

Opening
Apr–Oct daily 9am–6pm
Nov–Dec Feb–Mar daily 11am–4pm

Admission
Adult £5, Child & Concs £3.75

Contact
The National Trust for Scotland,
Culloden Moor, Inverness IV1 2ED

t 01463 790607
w nts.org.uk/culloden

969 Drumnadrochit

Loch Ness Monster Exhibition Centre

1 hr+   Jul–May

Through photographs, descriptions and film footage, this exhibition presents the evidence about the existence of the Loch Ness Monster. It also highlights the efforts of various search expeditions, by both individuals and respected institutions, such as Operation Deepscan.

* Travel round the loch, view places and meet locals
* Exhibition cinema in eight different languages

Location
On A82, W of Inverness

Opening
Jul–Sep daily 9am–9pm
Oct–May daily 9am–5pm

Admission
Adult £4.75, Child £3.25, Concs £3.75

Contact
Drumnadrochit, Invernesshire
IV63 6TU

t 01456 450342
w lochness-centre.com
e donald@lochness-centre.com

970 Fort William

Vertical Descents

3 hrs+   Apr–Oct

Located at Inchree Falls, this is Scotland's first and longest canyoning descent. Canyoning involves a combination of abseiling, swimming and sliding through water flumes, plus jumping into giant rock pools, as you make your way downstream.

* No previous experience necessary
* All necessary clothing and equipment provided

Location
Off A82, 7 miles south of Fort William

Opening
Apr–mid–Oct

Admission
£30 per person (half-day canyoning)
£35 per person (half-day funyaking)

Contact
Inchree Falls, Inchree, Onich
nr Fort William PH33 6SE

t 01855 821593
w activities-scotland.com
e verticaldescents@yahoo.com

971 Fort William

The Jacobite Steam Train

6 hrs   Jun–Oct

Described as one of the great railway journeys of the world, the Jacobite Steam Train leaves Fort William and travels on an 84-mile round trip. It passes Ben Nevis, then crosses the Glenfinnan Viaduct used in the *Harry Potter* films and finally arrives by the Atlantic Ocean in Mallaig.

* Leaves Fort William at 10.20am and returns at 4pm
* 1½ hour stopover in Mallaig

Location
Fort William station, in town centre

Opening
Jun 14–Jul 24 Mon–Fri
Jul 25–Aug 29 Sun–Fri
Aug 30–Oct 8 Mon–Fri

Admission
Return Tickets Adult £25, Child £14.50
First Class Adult £38, Child £19

Contact
West Coast Railway Company, Warton
Road, Carnforth, Lancashire LA5 9HX

t 01463 239026
w steamtrain.info

972 Glencoe

Glencoe Visitor Centre

1 hr · All year

Some of the finest climbing and walking country in the Highlands is to be found within this area of dramatic landscapes and historical fact and legend. The infamous massacre of 1692 took place throughout the glen, one of the main locations being near the new visitor centre.

* Video about the massacre
* Display on the history of mountaineering in the glen

Location
On A82, between Glasgow & Fort William

Opening
Mar daily 10am–4pm
Apr–Aug daily 9.30am–5.30pm
Sep–Oct daily 10am–5pm
Nov–Feb Fri–Mon 10am–4pm

Admission
Adult £4.50, Child & Concs £2.95

Contact
Ballachulish, Argyll PH39 4HX

t 01855 811307
w nts.org.uk
e sborland@nts.org.uk

973 Inverary

Inverary Castle

1 hr · Apr–Oct

Also known as the 'Fairy Tale Castle', it's easy to see why this is one of Scotland's hidden treasures. Originally the home of the Campbell clan, the castle now boasts a selection of magnificent rooms through which the visitor can trace its history.

* History of the clan Campbell
* Remains the home of the Duke of Argyll

Location
On A83, on shores of Loch Fyne

Opening
Jun–Sep Mon–Sat 10am–5.45pm
Sun 1–5.45pm,
Apr–May Oct Mon–Thu Sat 10am–1pm
2–5.45pm Sun 1–5.45pm

Admission
Adult £5.90, Child £3.90, Concs £4.90

Contact
The Factor, Argyll Estates Office, Inverary, Argyll PA32 8XE

t 01499 302203
w inverary-castle.com
e enquiries@inveraray-castle.com

974 John o' Groats

The Last House in Scotland Museum

½ hr+ · All year

Visitors to the Last House in Scotland can enjoy a pictorial history of the area and see some of the wonderful artifacts of bygone times that have been loaned to the museum by local residents of John O'Groats.

* Postcards stamped with the official 'Last House' stamp

Location
17 miles N of Wick

Opening
Jun–Sep daily 8am–8pm
Oct–May daily 9am–5pm

Admission
Free

Contact
John O' Groats KW1 4YR

t 01955 611250

975 Kyle of Lochalsh

Eilean Donan Castle

1 hr   Mar–Nov

Eilean Donan is located on a small island near Dornie, Rossshire. In a superbly romantic setting amid silent, tree-clad hills, it possesses a rare and dream-like quality, but, in reality, is a fortress of solid stone and formidable defences. The Isle of Skye can be seen across the water.

* Visitor centre
* The most photographed castle in Scotland

Location	Admission
On A87, 8 miles from Kyle of Lochalsh	Adult £4.50, Child & Concs £3.40
Opening	**Contact**
Easter–Oct daily 10am–6pm	Dornie, Kyle of Lochalsh IV40 8DX
Mar–Easter Nov daily 10am–5.30pm	t 01599 555202
	w eileandonancastle.com
	e info@donan.f9.co.uk

976 Lewis

Calanais Standing Stones

1 hr   All year

This is a fascinating, cross-shaped setting of 50 standing stones. The site dates to c. 3000 BC and the configuration is unique in Scotland (and special in Great Britain). The audio- visual presentation in the visitor centre tells their story.

* Visitor centre
* Story of the Stones exhibition

Location	Admission
Off A859, 12 miles W of Stornoway	*Exhibition* Adult £1.75, Child £75p, Concs £1.25
Opening	
Site daily	**Contact**
Visitor centre Apr–Sep Mon–Sat	Visitor Centre, Calanais, Isle of Lewis,
10am–6pm Oct–Mar Mon–Sat	Western Isles HS2 9DY
10am–4pm	t 01851 621422
	w historic-scotland.gov.uk

977 Lerwick

Up-Helly-Aa Exhibition

½ hr   May–Sep

A traditional Viking fire festival is celebrated in Lerwick every January. The dazzling Up-Helly-Aa ceremony sees a procession of a thousand flaming torches and then a replica longship is set alight. Visitors can view Up-Helly-Aa regalia at an exhibition in Lerwick.

* Learn about the dazzling fire festival
* A beautiful full-size, wooden Viking longship

Location	Admission
Signposted from central Lerwick	Adult £2.50, Child & Concs £1
Opening	**Contact**
May–Sep Tue 2–4pm 5–7pm	St Sunniva Street, Lerwick, Shetland
Fri 5–7pm Sat 2–4pm	Islands

978 Newtonmore

Walzing Waters

1 hr+   All year

An elaborate light, water and music show, which takes place in the safety and comfort of a modern, indoor theatre. Visitors are overwhelmed by thousands of dazzling patterns, cast on moving water, synchronized with music in spectacular fashion.

* 45-minute show, on the hour, every hour

Location	Admission
Middle of main street	Adult £4, Child £2, Concs £3.50
Opening	**Contact**
Mid Jan–mid Dec daily 9.30–5pm	Balavil Brae, Newtonmore,
	Invernessshire PH20 1DR
	t 01540 673752

979 Oban

McCaig's Tower

1 hr — All year

Undoubtably Oban's most outstanding feature, McCaig's Tower was built in 1897 by local banker John Stuart McCaig to provide work for local stonemasons and a lasting monument to his family. The steep climb from the town centre is well worth the effort.

* Breathtaking views over Oban Bay to the Atlantic islands
* Peaceful gardens inside the tower

Location	Contact
Short, steep walk from town centre	Oban Tourist Information Centre, Argyll Square, Oban, Argyll
Opening	t 01631 563122
Daily	w oban.org.uk
Admission	e info@oban.org.uk
Free	

980 Poolewe

Inverewe Gardens

2 hrs+ — All year

This astonishing garden is impressively set on a peninsula on the shore of Loch Ewe. The warm currents of the North Atlantic Drift or Gulf Stream help nurture an oasis of colour and fertility and enable exotic plants from many countries to flourish on a latitude more northerly than Moscow.

* Marked footpaths
* Visitor centre

Location	Admission
In Wester Ross, on the NW coast, 1 mile from Polewe, N of Gairloch	Adult £7, Child & Concs £5.25
Opening	**Contact**
Mar–Oct daily 9.30am–9pm or sunset if earlier	Poolewe, Rosshire IV22 2LG
Nov–Feb 9.30am–4pm	t 01445 781200
	w nts.org.uk
	e Inverewe@nts.org.uk

981 Stornoway

The Black House Museum

½ hr+ — All year

The site includes a traditional Lewis thatched crofter's cottage, or black house, with byre and stackyard, complete with a peat fire burning in the central hearth. There is also a restored 1920s white house and a visitor centre with fascinating information about Herbridean life.

* Green Gold Tourism award-winner
* 5 star Scottish Tourism Award

Location	Admission
Off A858	Adult £3, Child £1, Concs £2.30
Opening	**Contact**
Apr–Sep Mon-Sat 9.30am–6pm	Arnol Isle of Lewis PA86 9DB
Oct–Mar 9.30am–4pm	t 01851 710395
	w historic-scotland.gov.uk

982 Spean Bridge

Monster Activities

2 hrs — All year

From its base in the Scottish Highlands, this sports centre offers outdoor activities of all kinds, including the country's most exciting whitewater rafting. Not only does it offer instruction, hire, courses and short breaks, it also guarantees fun for the whole family.

* All kinds of outdoor activities on land and water
* All necessary equipment available

Location	Contact
On A82, between Fort William & Inverness	Great Glen Water Park, South Laggan, Spean Bridge, Invernessshire PH34 4AE
Opening	
Daily 9.30am–5.30pm	t 01809 501340
Admission	w monsteractivities.com
Depends onactivity–phone for details	e info@monsteractivities.com

983 Skye

Dunvegan Castle

2 hrs   All year

The north of Scotland's oldest inhabited castle is also Skye's most famous landmark, having been the seat and home of the MacLeod chiefs for 800 years. Dunvegan Castle is a fortress stronghold in an idyllic lochside setting, surrounded by dramatic scenery.

* Many fine oil paintings and great clan treasures
* Picturesque woodland garden

Location
1 mile N of Dunvegan

Opening
Mar–Oct daily 10am–5.30pm
Nov–Feb daily 11am–4pm

Admission
Summer, Adult £6.50, Child £3.50,
Concs £5.50

Winter, Adult £4, Child £2.50,
Concs £3.50

Contact
Isle of Skye IV55 8WF

t 01470 521206
w dunvegancastle.com

984 Tain

Glenmorangie Distillery Centre

1 hr   All year

Tour the distillery in the company of one of the guides, who will explain the whisky-making process from beginning to end and introduce you to the Sixteen Men of Tain who make it, before a visit to the tasting room to sample the results of their industry and skill.

* Located in the Glen of Tranquility
* Regular distillery tours

Location
On A9, 1 hour N of Inverness

Opening
Shop Mon–Fri 9am–5pm
July–Aug Mon–Fri 9am–5pm
Sat 10am–4pm Sun 12 noon–4pm
Tours daily 10.30am 11.30am 2.30pm
3.30pm (prebooking advisable)

Admission
Adults £2 (redeemable)

Contact
Tain, Rosshire IV19 1PZ

t 01862 892477
w glenmorangie.com
e visitors@glenmorangieplc.co.uk

985 Taynuilt

Inverawe Smokehouse

1 hr   All year

Inverawe Smokehouse produces delicious, high-quality Scottish smoked salmon, made using the traditional smoking process. Other products from the Smokehouse include kippers and eels, and visitors can see the smokery in action.

* Fly and trout fishing waters
* Holiday cottages for rent

Location
Signposted from A85, between
Glasgow & Oban

Opening
Daily 8.30am–5.30pm

Admission
Free

Contact
Taynuilt, Argyll PA35 1HU

t 01866 822777
w inverawe.co.uk
e info@inverawe.co.uk

986 Mull

Hebridean Whale & Dolphin Trust

½ hr   All year

On land and sea. Mull has a greater variety and abundance of wildlife than any other Hebridean island. Go to the HWDT visitor centre in Tobermory for information on whale and dolphin watching trips, as well as a whole range of other wildlife 'safaris'.

* Huge variety of Scottish wildlife in its natural habitat
* Land and sea 'safaris'

Location
To reach Mull, take ferry from Oban to Craignure, Trust is opposite clock tower in Tobermoray

Opening
Apr–Oct daily 10am–5.30pm
Nov–Mar daily 11am–5pm

Admission
Free

Contact
28 Main Street, Tobermory,
Isle of Mull, Argyll PA75 6NU

t 01688 302620
w hwdt.org
e hwdt@sol.co.uk

987 Alloway

Burns National Heritage Park

2 hrs   All year

Now fully restored to its original state, Burns' cottage forms the heart of this attraction, offering a unique encounter with Scotland's most exceptional man. Set among the delightful scenery of historic Alloway, this is an unmatched opportunity to experience Scotland's national poet.

* Unique authentic locations and artefacts
* The world's most important Robert Burns collection

Location
On A719, south of Ayr

Opening
Apr–Oct daily 9.30am–5.30pm
Nov–Mar daily 10am–5pm

Admission
Adult £5, Child & Concs £2.50

Contact
Murdoch's Lone, Alloway, Ayr KA7 4PQ

t 01292 443700
w burnsheritagepark.com
e info@burnsheritagepark.com

988 Ayr

Dunaskin Heritage Centre

4 hrs+   Apr–Oct

Set in a 110-acre site amid the picturesque scenery of the Doon Valley, this museum was originally an ironworks, built around 1850, and today it tells the story of the ironworks, coal mining and brickworks at Dunaskin through the eyes of the people who lived and worked there.

* Audio tours
* Guided tours

Location
Off A713, between Ayr & Castle Douglas / Dumfries

Opening
Apr–Oct daily 10am–5pm

Admission
Adult £4.50, Child £2.50, Concs £3.75

Contact
Dalmellington Road, Waterside, Waterside by Patna, Ayrshire KA6 7JF

t 01292 531144
w dunaskin.co.uk
e dunaskin@btconnect.com

989 Ayr

The Electric Brae

½ hr   All year

This is a hill with a difference. While the views are spectacular, try placing a round object, like a ball, on the ground. What direction do you think it will roll? Due to an optical illusion the ball will roll upwards; let off the hand brake for a second and the car will move uphill!

Location
A719 9 miles S of Ayr, 2 miles S of Dunure, 1 mile N of the A719–B7023 junction, NW edge of the hamlet of Knoweside

Opening
Any reasonable time

Admission
Free

Contact
t 01292 678100
w ayrshire-arran.com

990 Dumfries

Gretna Green World Famous Blacksmith's Shop

1 hr+   All year

Runaway marriages began in 1753, when it became illegal to marry under 21. However, in Scotland it was, and still is, possible to marry at 16. Gretna Green is the first village across the border that many 'elopers' came to and the Blacksmith's Shop was the centre of the marriage trade.

* Old coach collection
* Juicy stories of romance, intrigue and scandal

Location
On A74, just N of the border

Opening
Apr–Sep daily 9am–7pm
Oct–Mar daily 9am–5pm

Admission
Exhibition Adult £2.50, Child £2

Contact
Gretna Green Group Ltd,
Headless Cross, Gretna Green,
Dumfriesshire DG16 5EA

t 01461 338441
w gretnagreen.com
e info@gretnagreen.com

991 Dumfries

Dumfries Museum & Camera Obscura

1 hr   Mar–Oct

A treasure house of the history of south west Scotland, the museum is centred on the C18 windmill tower that stands above the town. On the top floor, there is a camera obscura and on the tabletop screen visitors can see panoramic views of Dumfries and the surrounding countryside.

* Prehistoric reptile footprints
* Tools and weapons from the area's oldest people

Location
In town centre

Opening
Apr–Sep Mon–Sat 10am–5pm
Sun 2–5pm
Oct & Mar Tue–Sat 10am–1pm
2pm–5pm

Admission
Museum Free

Camera Obscura Adult £1.50,
Child &Concs 75p

Contact
Rotchell Road, Dumfries DG2 7SW

t 01387 253374
w dumfal.gov.uk/museums
e dumfriesmuseum2dumfal.gov.uk

992 Hawick

Drumlanrig's Tower

1 hr   All year

The Black Tower of Drumlanrig is an imposing landmark in the Scottish Borders town of Hawick. The tower has borne silent witness to the savage cross-border warfare and bitter inter-family feuding which marked the town's turbulent past.

* Exhibitions tells the story of the house
* Display of watercolours by the artist Tom Scott

Location
Hawick High Street

Opening
Jul–Aug Mon–Sat 10am–6pm
Sun 1–5pm
Apr–Jun & Sep–Oct Mon–Sat
10am–5pm Sun 1–5pm
Winter times vary, phone for details

Admission
Adult £2.50, Child free

Contact
1 Towerknowe, Hawick TD9 9EN

t 01450 373457

993 Isle of Arran

King's Cave

2 hrs   All year

This is said to be the legendary spot where Robert the Bruce, dejected and battle weary, was inspired by the tenacity of a small spider as it painstakingly spun its web. He went on to win many battles following this episode. On the cave wall are rare writings by Picts.

Location
Off A841, nr Blackwaterfoot, Isle of
Arran, access by coastal path only

Opening
Daily

Admission
Free

Contact
Blackwaterfoot, Isle of Arran

w showcaves.com

994 Jedburgh

Mary Queen of Scots Visitor Centre

½ hr   Mar–Nov

Situated in a garden of pear trees, this house was visited by Mary in October 1566. Today the house is a popular museum and visitor centre. The compelling drama of her life, with its tragic climax, is told in a series of rooms within this ancient house.

* Tapestries, oil paintings, furniture, arms and armour
* Collection of Mary's possessions

Location	Admission
Off Jedburgh High Street	Adult £3, Child free, Concs £2
Opening	**Contact**
Mar–Nov Mon–Sat 10am–4.30pm	Queen Street, Jedburgh, Borders
Sun 11am–4.30pm	TD8 6EN
	t 01835 863331

995 Largs

The Viking Experience

1 hr   Feb–Nov

This multimedia journey recounts the saga of the Vikings in Scotland, from their invasion to defeat at the battle of Largs in 1263. Meet the Gods and Valkyries in Valhalla, come face to face with Odin, the Viking god of war, and walk with him into the Viking world of 700 years ago.

* Shows begin regularly
* Viking myths and legends

Location	Admission
On the Largs seafront	Adult £4, Child & Concs £3
Opening	**Contact**
Apr–Sep daily 10.30am–5.30pm	Vikingar, Greenock Road,
Oct & Mar daily 10.30am–3.30pm	Largs, Ayrshire KA30 8QL
Nov & Feb Sat 12.30pm–3.30pm	t 01475 689777
Sun 10.30am–3.30pm	w vikingar.co.uk
	e info@vikingar.co.uk

996 Lockerbie

Carlyle's Birthplace

½ hr   May–Sep

The Arched House, in which Thomas Carlyle was born in 1795, was built by his father and uncle in 1791. Carlyle was a great writer and historian and one of the most powerful influences on C19 British thought. The house is now furnished to reflect Victorian domestic life.

* Collection of portraits
* Carlyle's belongings

Location	Contact
Off M74, on A74, in Ecclefechan,	The Arched House, Ecclefechan,
5½ miles SE of Lockerbie	Lockerbie, Dumfries & Galloway
	DG11 3DG
Opening	
May–Sep Thu–Mon 1pm–5pm	t 01576 300666
	w nts.org.uk
Admission	
Adult £2.50, Child & Concs £1.90	

997 Melrose

Abbotsford

1 hr+   Mar–Oct

Abbotsford is the house built and lived in by Sir Walter Scott, the C19 novelist and author of timeless classics such as *Waverley*, *Rob Roy* and *Ivanhoe*. Situated on the banks of the River Tweed, the house contains an impressive collection of relics, weapons and armour.

* Rob Roy's gun and Montrose's sword
* Extensive grounds and walled garden

Location	Contact
On A6091, 2 miles from Melrose	Melrose, Borders TD6 9BQ
Opening	t 01896 752043
Mar 15–Oct 31 Mon–Sat 9.30am–5pm	w melrose.bordernet.co.uk/
Sun 2–5pm	abbotsford
Admission	e abbotsford@melrose.bordernet.
Adult £4.50, Child £2.75	co.uk

998 Melrose

Melrose Abbey

½ hr   All year

Arguably the finest of Scotland's border abbeys, Melrose is a magnificent ruin on a grand scale with lavishly decorated masonry. It is thought to be the burial place of Robert the Bruce's heart, marked with a commemorative carved stone plaque within the grounds.

* Large collection of objects found during excavation
* Audio tours

Location
Off A7 / A68, in Melrose

Opening
Apr–Sep daily 9.30am–6.30pm
Oct–Mar Mon–Sat 9.30am–4.30pm
Sun 2–4.30pm

Admission
Adult £3.50, Child £1.20, Concs £2.50

Contact
Abbey Street, Melrose,
Roxburghshire TD6 9LG

t 01896 822562
w historic-scotland.gov.uk

999 Melrose

Trimontium Roman Fort

4 hrs   All year

The most important Roman military complex between Hadrian's Wall and the Antonine Wall guarded and secured the crossing of the Tweed at Newstead in C1 and C2 AD. Excavations have revealed much of what was going on there.

* Three Hills Roman heritage centre exhibition
* Viewing platforms and information boards

Location
1 mile E of Melrose, in Newstead

Opening
Walks Apr 1–Oct 31 Thu 1.30–5pm
Jun–Jul Tue & Thu 1.30–5pm
Exhibition Apr 1–Oct 31
10.30am–4.30pm
Nov 1–Mar 31 on request

Admission
Site free
Walks Adult £3, Child & Concs £2.50
Exhibition Adult £1.50, Child & Concs £1

Contact

t 01896 822651
w trimontium.net

1000 Newton Stewart

Galloway Red Deer Range

2 hrs   Jun–Sep

This attraction has a viewpoint near the road from which these beautiful red deer can be observed in their natural habitat. Visitors to the range can also walk among the deer, photograph them and even touch them, under supervision.

* Guided tours in summer
* See and hear roaring stags during the rutting season

Location
On A712, 3 miles SW of
Clatteringshaws Loch

Opening
End of Jun–mid Sep Tue & Thu
11am–2pm Sun 11am–2.30pm

Admission
Adult £3, Child £1, Concs £2

Contact
Red Deer Range Car Park,
nr Clatteringshaws, Newton Stewart,
Dumfries & Galloway DG7 3SQ

t 01671 402420
w forestry.gov.uk/
     gallowayforestpark
e galloway@forestry.gsi.gov.uk

1001 Sanquhar

Sanquhar Tolbooth Museum

1 hr   Apr–Sep

Find out about Sanquhar knitting, the mines and miners of Sanquhar and Kirkconnel, the history and customs of the Royal Burgh of Sanquhar, three centuries of local literature, what life was like in Sanquhar jail and the earliest inhabitants of the area, both native and Roman.

* Housed in a fine C18 tolbooth
* Community life in times past

Location
In town centre

Opening
Apr–Sep Tue–Sat 10am–1pm 2–5pm
Sun 2–5pm

Admission
Free

Contact
High Street, Sanquhar, Dumfries
J∆ & Galloway DG46BN

t 01659 50186
w dumfriesmuseum.demon.co.uk
e dumfriesmuseum@dumgal.gov.uk

Index

Acknowledgements & Picture Credits

The Publishers would like to acknowledge the important contribution the British Tourist Authority made to this publication through the use of images from its website, *www.britainonview.com*

The publishers would like to thank The National Trust, The National Trust for Scotland and English Heritage who kindly supplied photographs for use with their entries.

The publishers would also like to thank all contributors who provided information, and particularly all those who kindly supplied photographs.

Compiled, edited and designed by designsection. Compiled by Sallie Ferrier, Julian Flanders and Millie Ferrier. Edited by Julian Flanders, Dara O'Hare and Lisa Hughes. Design and layout by Lyn Davies and Carole McDonald. Special thanks to Liz Kingett, Shane Grimsley, Jesse Jenkins and Patrick Timms.